D1591744

Training the Right Stuff

THE AIRCRAFT THAT PRODUCED AMERICA'S JET PILOTS

Mark A. Frankel and Tommy H. Thomason

with Illustrations by Jack Morris

Schiffer Publishing Ltd
4880 Lower Valley Road • Atglen, PA 19310

On the front cover: Ed Gillespie, former Chief Test Pilot for North American Aviation, performs a post restoration test flight on a T-2B Buckeye owned by Wiley Sanders of Troy AL. The photograph was taken by Brian Silcox from the tail gunner's turret of a B-25 also owned by Sanders. "Ed was a fascinating person with a long history at North American," recalls Silcox. "We were amply impressed with his skills in the airplane during the photo missions. At one point, he joined up on the tail of the B-25 out of a barrel roll and stopped in perfect position on the tail gunner's view port."

Library of Congress Control Number: 2016935992

Book and Cover design by RoS
Type set in Bitstream Vera Sans/Minion Pro
ISBN: 978-0-7643-5030-6
Printed in the United States of America

Published by Schiffer Publishing, Ltd.
4880 Lower Valley Road
Atglen, PA 19310
Phone: (610) 593-1777; Fax: (610) 593-2002
E-mail: Info@schifferbooks.com
Web: www.schifferbooks.com

For our complete selection of fine books on this and related subjects, please visit our website at www.schifferbooks.com. You may also write for a free catalog.

Schiffer Publishing's titles are available at special discounts for bulk purchases for sales promotions or premiums. Special editions, including personalized covers, corporate imprints, and excerpts, can be created in large quantities for special needs. For more information, contact the publisher.

We are always looking for people to write books on new and related subjects. If you have an idea for a book, please contact us at proposals@schifferbooks.com.

Dedication

To Colonel Clarence S. Parker, USAF, retired: 3550th Pilot Training Wing
Commander, 1968 to 1971
To CAPT Edward A. Gillespie, USNR Retired: Chief Test Pilot, North
American Aviation

Epigraph

The trainer business is a fickle one. Everyone needs them, though nobody wants to spend the money. Procurement decisions are delayed as scarce budgets are diverted to sexier projects. There is rarely a quick return on investment, taxing the patience of even the most steadfast chief financial officer.

— Andy Nativi, *Aviation Week & Space Technology*, April 23, 2007

Contents

Foreword

DOING IT THE AIR FORCE WAY
by Jerry Singleton

In July 1962, I was on Highway 90, just east of Del Rio, Texas on my way to Laughlin AFB to become a jet pilot—hopefully a jet fighter pilot—when I saw a silver dot in the sky about ten miles ahead. Wow! I pulled over and stopped for about fifteen minutes, filled with anticipation.

By that time, the USAF had changed pilot training to be an all-jet curriculum. Gone were prop-driven trainers, replaced by the Cessna T-37A followed by the Lockheed T-33A or Northrop T-38A. I was happy with that, having drilled around the skies in a Cessna 150 for 36½ hours while in advanced Air Force ROTC.

That flight time was the result of course selection for my freshman year at the University of Tulsa. One decision was to take either Physical Education or ROTC. Not knowing what to do, I asked my dad for advice. He answered my question by asking one, "Do you want to be a private with an M-1 in a foxhole, or maybe get to fly?" It took a microsecond for me to make that decision.

I was thrilled that USAF pilot training was now all jet-powered aircraft. Flying "bug smashers" around at 100 miles per hour did not compare with the thrill of strapping into a jet airplane. The T-37 "Tweet" or "Tweety Bird" was perfect for young and inexperienced aspiring pilots. It was docile in its entire flight envelope except for spins. The aero engineers at Cessna (particularly the stability and control guys) deserve a real sincere pat on the back.

Some first impressions: when taxiing you felt like you were on the world's fastest tricycle, so low to the ground you thought you would stub a toe if your feet fell off the rudder pedals. Also, the shriek of the J-69 engine was something you could not escape on the flight line. Closing the canopy helped, but in the summer that was out of the question—no air conditioning.

Initial solo was fun and inspiring. I did it! Wow—just me and my Tweety Bird. You thought yourself invincible until your instructor brought you back to earth with "Well, you survived!" followed by a detailed evaluation of your pattern positioning, landings, and radio calls. It could have been worse: one of my Class 64A classmates had a stuck microphone on his initial solo. He transmitted his verbalization of his internal thoughts including "oh s___," etc. to the world as he made two touch and goes and a full stop. The first thing I did on my initial solo after raising the gear/flaps was make a blind call or two without depressing the microphone button to see if I got a reply—no stuck-mike performance for this kid.

Spinning the T-37B was an exciting experience. Climb to 20,000 feet, throttle to idle to slow down, full-back stick, jam the rudder left or right, and you are off on the wildest ride any amusement park can provide. Entry and the spin itself were okay but exiting the spin was jarring. Full opposite rudder and then violently jamming the stick full forward—literally banging it against the forward stop—resulted in a large pitch-down moment on the aircraft, throwing you up against your shoulder harness. The next step was quickly pulling the stick back to neutral, causing you to momentarily float in a zero-g environment. Then, almost vertical with the nose down, you slowly raised it as the air speed increased to recover back to level flight. What a ride! Do I have to do this again? After surviving and conquering this maneuver we all thought we were superman, able to leap tall buildings and fly to the moon, so to speak.

After six months of the T-37, we were "promoted" to the T-33A. Now we were flying a real jet fighter. You needed a ladder to get in the cockpit! The next thing you noticed was the instructor was behind you out of sight: he couldn't slap your helmet or hit you with his clipboard now. The biggest challenge of this old beast was controlling it on the ground: no nose wheel steering. Taking the T-Bird out of its parking spot was more difficult than either takeoff or landing. The most embarrassing moment for any student pilot was to cock the nose wheel and have to have a crew chief rescue you. Either that, or you had to use enough throttle to "un-cock" the nose wheel, thereby blowing everything behind you (chocks, fire bottles, crew chiefs, etc.) off the ramp.

The T-33A was easy to fly and very forgiving. It even had an ADF radio in the cockpit, which was great for listening to rock and roll while flying (only when solo, of course). One preflight task was to open the fuel cap on each wing tank to ensure they had been fully fueled. On a hot day at Del Rio there was not a student to be found who didn't get his flight gloves (and maybe flight suit) soaked with JP-4 when he popped the fuel cap, where upon "old faithful" would douse him. You then had to complete your sortie smelling like a fuel dump.

As students we did not spin the T-bird. Recovery was uncertain, we were told: you could end up in a "tumble" while attempting recovery. After the T-37 spin experience, I do not think anyone was disappointed. I did spin them many times later at the USAF Test Pilot School and it was not a difficult recovery—most of the time!

My class was envious of the students at the two USAF pilot training bases that had converted to the T-38A Talon. We did not get a Mach 1.0 pin like them. I kept trying to convince myself it did not matter—but it did. I wanted to fly a fighter in Tactical Air Command (F-100 or F-105) but only the T-38 grads got a TAC assignment. The T-33 classes were assigned to Air Defense Command so when I graduated after thirteen grueling months, I went to a Combat Crew Training Site for the F-102A.

After a twenty-year flying career totaling 5,500 hours in twelve different fighter/trainers, the only aircraft I flew for more than 1,000 hours was the T-33. But it was still a jet!

Jerry Singleton, Lt.Col. USAF (*Ret.*)
Texas, 2014

Foreword
DOING IT THE NAVY WAY
by Jack Woodul

I began Naval Air Training in Pensacola in March 1963. But, as a World War Two child, brought up in the airplane-rich environment of what is now called Dallas-Ft. Worth, I had been spooling up for it most of my life. Indeed, the chainlink fence of my backyard faced the Yellow Perils that buzzed around from NAS Grand Prairie and sometimes ended up, nose down, in my neighborhood. I always knew I would fly, but it was a little booklet in my third grade library, back in New Mexico, named "Wings of Gold," that made the Navy irresistible. That booklet kept reappearing all during my schooling, along with movies like *Task Force*, which kept me pointed.

My high school biology teacher had been a Navy fighter pilot in WWII and I had a little extra money to rent a Piper Super Cub. He taught me to fly, not for money, but for some little, black, twisted Italian cigars I would bring him on occasion. He would occasionally digress, take the airplane, and simulate strafing rabbits. When I could fly by myself, of course, so did I, along with playing crop duster pilot. Not being a rich kid, this only lasted about twenty-two hours.

But going to university meant Navy ROTC and the Navy smiled upon me and bought me my Private License my last semester. I flew something called a Shinn 2150, which was a low-wing miniature of the T-34 "Teeny Weeny" I would fly in Navy primary training. It was wonderful and I knew that I could at least fly an airplane.

But Preflight training in Pensacola taught me right quickly that you had better really want to fly if you wanted to hack the program. They asked you to look to your left, then look to your right, and two out of the three of you would be gone before the end of the process. Of course, we all thought "Those poor guys!"

My class was all officers, and they were a mixed bunch of some very shiny Marines, fresh from Quantico training; ROTC types like myself; and a couple of giants from the Air Force Academy who had taken Marine commissions. We soon learned that: 1) academics were part of the grade that, along with flight training grades during primary at Saufley Field, would determine our subsequent training paths; and 2) there were very few jet slots, so most of us would get something with a propeller or rotor on it. Of course, we all wanted to hear that whine at 20,000 feet and determined it would be the other guys that heard the pocketa-pocketa or wup-wup!

As it worked out, I got to hear both the pocketa-pocketa of round engines and that turbine whine. I went through an abbreviated Primary Training Syllabus in the T-34 and did well enough in the pecking order, only to find that there were *no* Navy jet slots for my class. Rat's fannies, thought I, but T-28's, here I come. Maybe I can sneak into Spads.

I loved the great, clattering radial engines and pretended I was in my Hellcat, searching for the illusive meatball in the sun. When I finally got to carrier qualifying on the Lexington, hanging on the prop at eighty knots, the canopy open to the noise, wind, hot engine smells, and the salt of the ocean, I was close to being that kid in the Wings of Gold pamphlet.

And the icing on my cake is that I had orders for jets in the Advanced Training Command!

My introduction to jets included learning how to get my G-suit laced up and the pleasures of the oxygen mask. The Grumman Iron Works TF-9J's and AF-9J's earned the company reputation by getting plonked around by students. Like all Navy training, it was like drinking out of a fire hose, but I must have swallowed enough without drowning, because I carrier qualified again; then, finished up my training in another Grumman product, the slick-looking, supersonic F-11 Tiger. I got the supersonic thing out of the way on my first hop, and got to shoot guns at a towed banner target. Best of all, most of the time was spent in what the Navy called "Air Combat Maneuvering," but everybody else called it "Dogfighting" or "Hassling," and it was some fun. At the end, I got a pair of Navy Gold Wings to go with my brown Ensign bars, and I was temporarily a very big kid, indeed.

That lasted about as long as it took me to report to VA-43, the A-4 Skyhawk RAG, or Replacement Air Group, to begin my training in that tiny attack airplane. Instead of a "Puke," I was now a "Firp," which was a Fleet Replacement Pilot. At the end of this familiarization, weapons training, and carrier qualification for both day and night, I would report to my fleet squadron as an "FNG, which usually meant something other than "Funny New Guy," starting the learning process all over again. But, as a reminder that nothing was ever locked in concrete, three Firps from the class in front of me did not complete their night CARQUAL's, and their golden wings got surgically removed.

But the payoff of finally reporting to a fleet squadron was that I was finally a big kid, Funny New Guy or not. No instructor to chunk kneeboards and scream or threaten to send you to waterlogged coastal freighters. Naval Aviators may eat their young, but it's FUN. Besides, usually you can eat back.

I truly loved it. When my squadron set sail to Viet Nam for my first cruise, I very proudly noted that I had 500 hours of flight time! My grizzled old Executive Officer, who had rows of gongs from WW2 and Korea snorted just loudly enough in disdain for me to remember I was among some Very Elder Gods.

"Ace of the Base" was still out there in the misty future, I felt sure. This "Seeing the Elephant" thing was why I came, and why Naval Aviation training put me on this big iron boat.

It was certainly pretty to think so.

Jack D. Woodul, Cdr. USN (*Ret.*)
New Mexico, 2014

Acknowledgments

The concept for this book was entirely Mike Machat's, the renowned aviation artist, author, and historian. Even the title, *Training The Right Stuff: The Aircraft That Produced America's Jet Pilots,* was his idea. He is also responsible in large part for us becoming authors in the first place. The overarching acknowledgment, therefore, is to Michael.

When writing aviation history we always strive to use primary documents but also the personal recollections of individuals involved, adding nuance and putting a human face on important events. We were exceptionally fortunate to find people like Wayne Fox, an instructor pilot at Whiting Field, who was present for the introduction of the Beechcraft T-34B as the SNJ was being phased out. He had a hand in evaluating the new primary trainer and developing a training syllabus for it. Wayne was also one of the first instructors to fly the Temco TT-1 Pinto during the Navy's all-jet experiment. Harry Clements started as a young aerodynamicist at Cessna in 1952 just as the T-37 was being developed. Harry had no military aircraft engineering experience but he became a key player in designing one of the most important military trainers of all time. Captain Tracy Rhodes spent much of his Air Force career as a T-37 instructor approximately twenty-five years after Harry Clements helped design it. His account of teaching spin recovery in a jet that occasionally exhibited unpredictable spin behavior is exceptional. The same is true of Lacey Collier's reflections on the Temco TT-1 Pinto's limited fuel supply, Walt Fink's stories and insights on the mysteries of mastering the Link instrument simulator, and Tom Kalfas's experience as an instructor when he learned an unexpected life lesson from an overconfident student. Ed Gillespie, who became Chief Test Pilot at North American, generously shared his flight test experience on the Navy T2J (T-2) program. John Jennista, whose first job at Beechcraft in the late 1960s was to sell the Navy on a new trainer, described the prolonged procurement process for the T-34C Turbo Mentor, that involved many dead ends but resulted in an outstanding trainer. Doug Barbier's T-38 tales are deserving of a separate book; Doug's gift for describing life at Mach 1 with a student who is flying with Mach 0.5 skills is illuminating. Steve Brandt, Darold Cummings, and John Sandford provided a more nuanced view of the ill-fated NGT program based on their first-hand knowledge.

Museums, archives, and libraries were the source of many of the photographs and documents relevant to our story. Rick Leisenring Jr., the Curator of the Curtiss Museum, Hammondsport, NY was a wonderful resource for the material on Glenn Curtiss and his contributions to early training aircraft—in particular the iconic JN-4 Jenny. Beth Kilmarx at The Binghamton Universities Library provided rare photographs of Edwin Link and his flight simulator. Joe Gordon at the Naval History and Heritage Command was very generous with his time and staff allowing us to duplicate countless documents and photographs. Larry Feliu and the rest of the volunteers at the Northrop Grumman History Center maintain that group's reputation for preserving and disseminating material from Grumman's many years of developing and producing airplanes. The volunteers at the Emil Buehler Naval Aviation Museum Library at Pensacola, led by Historian and Artifact Collection Manager Hill Goodspeed, are unequalled in responsiveness. Archie DiFante, Archivist at the Air Force Historical Research Agency, spent hours retrieving and duplicating Air Command Training Histories relating to the T-37 and T-38 programs. The same is true of Jeannine Geiger at the Air Force Test Center Library who allowed Tony Accurso unfettered access to the Center's historic files. Josh Stoff, curator of the Cradle of Aviation Museum provided many images of Fairchild Republic's final project, the T-46.

Many of our images were taken from private collections; some have never been published before. Gerald Baltzer, Doug Barbier, John Bennett, T.J. (Jeff) Brown, Tony Buttler, Capt.Rich Dann (USNR), Robert F. Dorr, Paul Minert, Jack Morris, Mark Nankivil, Terry Panopalis, Don Spering, and Bill Spidle were extremely generous in that regard. Of special note are the contributions of CDR Doug Siegfried (USNR) of the Tailhook Association. He not only found photographs on specific topics for us but also shared his unpublished manuscript, *Cleared to Solo*, on the history of Naval Aviation flight training. Tony Chong and Craig Kaston provided numerous Northrop drawings and documents revealing the engineering and business considerations that led to the enormously successful T-38 as well as other photos and material on US Navy trainer programs.

The spectacular photographs of civilian-owned trainers, used in chapter eleven, were provided by Sal Calvagna, Dennis Price, Mark Houpt, Scott McClain, Kevin Clark, Greg Morehead, Eric Van Gilder, Henning Henningsen, Robert McGregor, the Charlie Nelson Estate, Tom Passalaqua and Ryan Harris. The cover photograph was taken by Brian Silcox.

Finally, the color profiles in Appendix II are the work of Col. Jack Morris, USAF (Ret). Jack is a recognized authority on the color and markings of Cold War American aircraft and his renderings illustrate the ever-changing appearance of post-WWII trainers.

Introduction

By the end of World War II, the Army Air Forces (AAF) had trained more than 190,000 pilots and the Navy, almost 65,000. With the cessation of hostilities, there were far more pilots than needed and an equivalent surplus of obsolescent training airplanes. It was easy for defense planners to think that there was little need in the near future for more pilots or production—much less development—of new trainers.

Post-war austerity forced the US training commands to not only utilize their existing trainers but also revamp their programs to reduce cost. For example, both services retired their slow, fixed-gear primary trainer biplanes in favor of using their existing, bigger and more complicated, advanced trainers for primary training as well. (The change had been justified by a direct comparison of the two different approaches conducted with representative student classes through the full syllabus.) While it was the best use of the resources available at the time, it was akin to providing driver education in a dump truck.

The newly formed Air Force led the way to a total revamp of the training fleet necessary as a result of a new training challenge, the jet airplane. A jet's performance, endurance, handling qualities, operational characteristics, engine operation, and flight limitations were both notably and subtly different from existing propeller-driven fighters. The horrendous accident rate of the its first operational jet fighter, the Lockheed P-80 Shooting Star, demanded a new approach to both the training of new pilots and the transition of existing pilots from being pulled by a prop to being propelled by a jet.

The first step was the introduction of a two-seat jet trainer, the T-33. It was followed by the T-28, intended to replace the existing primary/basic trainer, the T-6 Texan. The most notable difference was the substitution of the tricycle landing gear for the Texan's "conventional" landing gear arrangement that featured a tail wheel. The tricycle gear was rapidly becoming standard on new airplanes and moreover, made landing easier to learn and much less prone to damaging excursions off the runway.

Although the use of a big, powerful trainer for initial flight instruction had previously been deemed the best use of resources after the war, it was counterintuitive. As a result, the Air Force introduced a new primary trainer, the T-34 Mentor. Like the T-28, it also incorporated a tricycle landing gear but was much less expensive to operate and somewhat less challenging to learn to fly.

Each of the new Air Force trainers played an important role in producing a jet fighting force by reducing the required flying hours and improving flight safety, while giving students experience in airplanes that behaved like the front line fighters that they would be expected to operate in squadron service.

The Navy also recognized the need to field new primary and advanced trainers after World War II but had to cancel the resulting programs before production began due to budget reductions. As a result, the admirals eventually elected to procure the same suite of trainers that the Air Force had developed, albeit with some modifications. Not only that, but they continued to employ them long after the Air Force moved on after less than ten years to an all-new and all-jet training fleet.

By the late 1950s, the Air Force had decided that there was little reason for its student pilots to spend any time learning to fly propeller-driven airplanes when most would spend their flying careers in the cockpit of jets. As a result, they implemented an all-jet training program, beginning with the relatively simple Cessna T-37 followed closely by the supersonic Northrop T-38. This seemingly disparate duo proved to be so suited to the Air Force fighter pilot training requirement that it has sufficed for fifty years—and counting in the case of the T-38.

The Navy accomplished a brief evaluation of a primary jet trainer as the Air Force was transitioning to all-jet training. It elected to stay with propeller-driven airplanes for the early phases of pilot training.

After primary training, Navy student pilots were directed into different tracks, flying different advanced trainers. The T-33s used to train those destined to fly jets were subsequently replaced about the time that the Air Force instituted all-jet training by a new carrier-capable jet trainers, very briefly by the Lockheed T2V and then for decades by the North American T2J (T-2). The obsolescent single-seat, carrier-based fighters that had been used for the final phases of Navy/Marine Corps training prior to the students receiving wings were eventually replaced with two-seat jet trainers for that purpose.

Up through 1992, all Air Force pilot candidates were trained in the same program. Students who would eventually be selected to fly transports, tankers, or helicopters moved on from the T-37 to the T-38 to earn their wings along with those who would subsequently fly fighters and bombers. The Air Force now follows a track program similar to the Navy's, with transport-type trainers substituted for the T-38 for those pilots selected to fly aircraft other than fighters or bombers.

While the Air Force simply upgraded its T-37s and T-38s, the Navy eventually phased in new production trainers. The T-34s and T-28s were eventually retired in favor of the T-34C, an extensively modified Mentor powered by a turboprop engine. The aging T-2s and TA-4Js were both replaced by a new jet trainer, the McDonnell-Douglas T-45. The Air Force had intended to replace the T-37 with a new jet trainer, the Fairchild Republic T-46, but it was subsequently canceled in a messy denouement of budget priorities and contractor problems.

After having basically utilized the same training airplanes up through the late 1950s, the Air Force and Navy diverged into completely independent programs with very different trainers, despite periodic attempts by the Department of Defense and Congress to combine them or at least utilize the same type of airplane for some requirements. However, budget circumstances conspired at the end of the 1990s to force the services back to a common primary/basic trainer with the same popular name, Texan, as the one that they both used throughout World War II for a few years thereafter. It replaced both the Air Force's T-37 and the Navy's T-34C.

There will be another change to the training fleet in the next ten years or so because the Air Force is in the process of replacing its venerable T-38. This promises to be a very interesting chapter in the history of US trainer development but one that we have to leave the writing of to others.

While not intended to be an encyclopedia of trainers, this book is a detailed examination of the aircraft that produced America's jet fighter pilots. We have chosen an airplane-centric approach as the best way to describe the history of Air Force and Navy training programs for jet fighter pilots over the past seventy years. For one thing, the number of changes in organization, syllabi, squadron designations and assignments, training bases, use of simulators, etc. defies straightforward exposition. As a result, the reader who spent twelve months or so in flight training at some point may think (sometimes rightly) that our contributors or we are in error in describing some details of his experience. However, the difference may not be error as much as illustrating the changes that occurred before or after his time as a student in the training command.

We have also focused to an extent on the basics of flight instruction as well as the specification and development effort required to provide airplanes to the training commands that allow flight instructors to safely teach them. One ongoing thread that you will note concerns spins, familiarity with (and avoidance of when unintended) them being an essential part of military flight training. A common problem in trainer development—especially primary trainers—has been difficulty with achieving acceptable spin propensity and recovery. Aircraft designers and NACA/NASA have striven to perfect their prediction and test of spin characteristics, respectively. Yet two programs, the T-34C and the T-37, both of which ultimately became well-regarded trainers, were nearly canceled because of unpredictable spin characteristics. A relatively minor change to the T-28 to add a tail hook resulted in unsatisfactory spin recovery when wing stores were carried. On the other hand, the T2J was predicted by NACA to require different spin recovery techniques depending on the airplane's configuration; it proved in spin demonstrations to be not only well behaved but that one set of control positions was adequate for recovery in all the configurations.

In writing this account we have researched the files of the National Archives, the Naval History and Heritage Command, the Air Force Museum, the Museum of Naval Aviation, the Smithsonian Air and Space Museum, the Air Force and Naval Training Commands, and the archives of several manufacturers, but the most important sources by far were the student pilots, instructor pilots, engineers, and maintainers who were there.

Mark A. Frankel
Gladwyne, Pennsylvania

Tommy H. Thomason
Mystic, Connecticut
April 2015

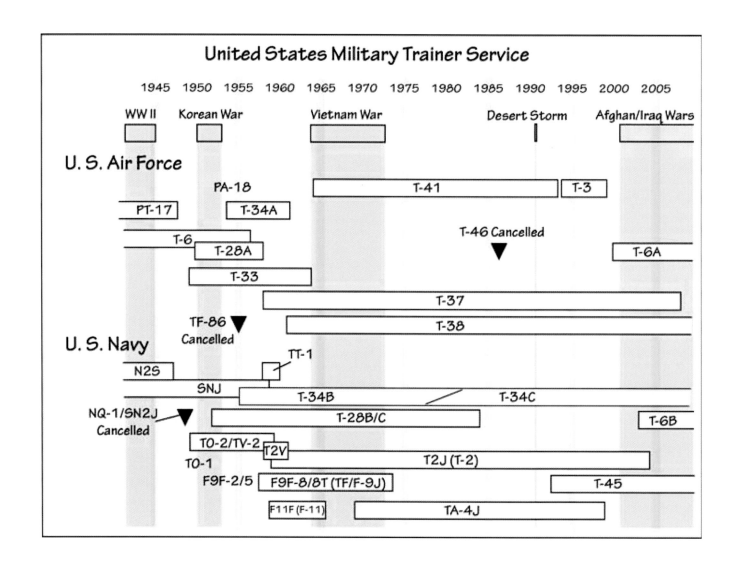

Chapter One
FLIGHT TRAINING BEFORE JETS

Simply put, the objective of military flight training has always been the creation of competent aviators in the shortest possible time with the least possible expense. Equipment and techniques have changed over the years, but the fundamental objective for producing pilots has not. The French model of pilot training from World War I is still the basis for modern pilot production. It consists of three distinct training phases: primary, basic (or intermediate), and advanced. Occasionally, these phases have been blurred by budget, equipment, and manpower limitations, but to this day, the building-block nature of flight training remains intact. The primary, or *ab initio*, phase screens students for the necessary aptitude to become a military pilot. Fear of flying, airsickness, poor judgment, and lack of coordination are grounds for elimination. This stage typically has a high failure rate and is often flown with low-powered, simple aircraft producing a student who has soloed. The next phase includes aerobatics, night flying, formation flying, cross-country navigation, and instrument flight. This phase was usually flown in higher-powered, more complex aircraft. It is here that a student's

mission specialty, such as fighter versus attack or transport versus special mission, is determined. The final phase, advanced, precedes a student's receiving his wings. The syllabus repeats much of the prior phase, and is usually flown in even higher-performance aircraft, and may include tactical weapons training. At the end of it the student, now a fully proficient pilot, is ready for assignment to front-line service.

The three-phase structure of military flight training is not the only element that has endured since the earliest days of military flying. Concern for safety has always been present. The risky business of creating an aviator led to airplanes designed specifically for that requirement. Trainer aircraft acquired dual controls and good visibility for both the student and instructor. They were relatively easy to fly, but not so easy that the instructor would have difficulty assessing the student's aptitude. They were durable to absorb a student's heavy-handed control inputs and landing mistakes. Above all, they were reliable to provide maximum availability and preclude in-flight emergencies that could overwhelm a student.

One of the most successful trainers of all times, the Curtiss Aeroplane and Motor Company Jenny. This JN-6 model was photographed on August 17, 1918 at Hammondsport New York. The Jenny became the principal trainer for the Allied Powers during World War I and served in the US inventory until 1927. Over 4,000 examples were built. *Glenn H. Curtiss Museum*

A. Early Military Flight Training 1909–1919

The first military flight instructor in the United States was Wilbur Wright, who was thrust into that role in 1909 when the United States government bought its first airplane—a Wright Model B. It was the only acceptable competitor for the Army contract, meeting or even exceeding all criteria by flying ten miles on its distance test, staying aloft for one hour, twelve minutes, and forty seconds on its endurance test, and reaching a maximum speed of 47.431 miles per hour on its speed test. The contract required the successful bidder to provide flight instruction for two Army officers, so it fell to Wilbur Wright to instruct Lts. Frank Purdy Lahm and Frederic E. Humphreys in the safe operation of the Army's first airplane.[1]

The training was unstructured and based largely on Wilbur's intuition. Wright would sit alongside Lahm or Humphreys in flight (the Wright Model B was capable of carrying two people) teaching a sense of proper steering and balance. Straight flight, gentle turns, and safe returns to the ground—with emphasis on the dangerous effects of wind—made up the core of Wright's curriculum. The training was complete within a month and both officers were considered qualified aviators capable of carrying passengers.

Congress was slow to appreciate the importance of military aviation, and it wasn't until 1911 that the first appropriation for Army aeronautical purposes was passed. The amount was $125,000 allowing the Army to order five new airplanes, three from the Wrights and two from Curtiss Aeroplane Company. With the orders for new airplanes came the responsibility for more flight instruction. The Wright brothers began to formalize their training, which was now conducted at the Wright factory in Dayton Ohio.

Air Force historian Rebecca Hancock Cameron writes: "More systematically than had been possible previously, at the factory the Army officers learned about the construction, maintenance, and assembly of the motor and the airframe. Next came ground training—aeronautical theory and the techniques of flight—followed by flight instruction. From that sequential approach arose the system of flight training that the Air Service and its successors—the Air Corps and the Army Air Forces—would employ thereafter."[2]

Before taking to the air with an instructor, trainees became familiar with the airplane's roll control by practicing in a primitive simulator. It consisted of a Wright B airframe, less tail assembly, mounted on a cradle so it could be rolled left and right by an electric motor. The motor was controlled by the stick that twisted the wings to differentially change lift and cause the Flyer to roll and therefore turn—or be restored to level flight if upset by a gust.

Use of this first ground-based simulator was important because of the Wright's idiosyncratic approach to roll control in the two-seat Flyer: both pilots used the same stick between their seats rather than being provided with individual ones as they were for pitch control. What's worse, the common stick wasn't moved left for a roll to the left, it was pushed forward instead; a right roll was accomplished by pulling it back. This stick was also connected to the rudder to yaw the airplane in the direction of the roll (the wing warped to create more lift would also create drag but in the opposite direction to the turn desired) but there was a small separate lever on top of it to adjust the amount of rudder input. Unlike the roll control stick, however, the independent rudder control moved laterally, e.g. left for more left rudder. Pitch was controlled by a stick on the outboard side of each seat, which meant that the pilot in the left seat controlled pitch with his left hand and roll control with his right; the one in the right seat controlled pitch with his right hand and roll control with his left. (A foot pedal provided throttle control.) As a result, Wright pilots were either "right-handed" (flew from the left seat) or "left-handed" (flew from the right seat). Orville was a right-handed pilot so all his students became left-handed pilots. (He made one near-disastrous flight in the right seat and vowed to never try that again.)

The Curtiss Aeroplane Company was a fierce competitor of the Wright Brothers, and in many ways it was more innovative and attentive to its customer's needs. Its founder, Glenn H. Curtiss, was not only a brilliant self-taught engineer; he was an astute businessman who realized that there were only two markets for his airplanes, exhibition flights and government sales. He further realized that the Wrights' success with the Army meant that he had to concentrate on the Navy. Curtiss set up a flight school on North Island near San Diego, California. Unlike the Wrights' training operations in the east, the Curtiss North Island flying school provided near perfect flying weather the entire year. As an enticement to sell airplanes to the government, Curtiss offered to provide free flying lessons to selected officers. The Navy sent one officer, Lt. Theodore "Spuds" Ellyson, while the Army enrolled three: 1st Lt. Paul Beck, 2nd Lt. G.E.M. Kelly, and 2nd Lt. John C. Walker Jr., in the first Curtiss class on January 19, 1911.[3] A Curtiss Type D single-seat pusher biplane, nicknamed the "Lizzie" was used for training at North Island. It had a control system quite different from the Wright machine: a "steering" wheel was moved forward and aft for pitch control and turned for yaw control; for roll control, a shoulder harness actuated moveable control surfaces known as ailerons. The Curtiss control system was considered more natural than the counterintuitive Wright system.

The Wright Military Flyer at Fort Meyers, Virginia July 27, 1909 during Army trials. Orville Wright is piloting the aircraft that became the first airplane purchased by the US government. *Smithsonian National Air and Space Museum*

The Wright Military Flyer on launch rail during the Army trials in 1909. The structure behind it was used to drop a weight that accelerated the Flyer to takeoff speed. *Smithsonian National Air and Space Museum*

A Wright Model B Military Flyer attached to the First Aero Squadron, Texas City, Texas, in 1910. This aircraft used wheeled landing gear rather that the skid employed on earlier Wright aircraft. It was capable of carrying an instructor and a student. *NARA*

Nevertheless, Curtiss flight training was deemed less effective than Wright instruction because the student was required to fly solo in the single-seat Curtiss D from the outset. This made ground training lengthier and prevented the student from experiencing wind and other weather-related conditions at the side of an experienced instructor. In response to this shortcoming Curtiss built a two-seat, dual-control training aircraft in 1912. It became apparent that Wright-trained airmen were incapable of flying Curtiss airplanes and vice versa—the need for control standardization was essential.

The Army's affection for the Curtiss control system grew, and in 1914 a board of Army officers issued a report that resulted in the phasing out of the Wright airplanes altogether. This made Curtiss the primary supplier of military training aircraft. In 1915, Curtiss refined his control system further by using a foot bar to control the rudder and the wheel to control the ailerons, thus eliminating the need for a shoulder harness. This "Dep" control system, named after its inventor Armand Deperdussin, became the standard for all American airplanes. About that same time the Army became concerned with the pusher-engine configuration that was common to both Wright and Curtiss airplanes. In the event of a crash the rear-mounted engine was likely to be thrown forward onto the pilot, which resulted in several fatalities. In 1914, The Army condemned this feature and specified tractor-mounted engines for all future purchases. The Navy also had concerns about the pusher configuration. Pusher airplanes displayed a nasty post-stall dive, making recovery difficult. LCDR Henry C. Mustin, the officer in charge of the aviation school at Pensacola, engaged in a bitter confrontation with his superiors over the safety of pushers. Ultimately, Mustin convinced the Chief of Naval Operations to ground all pushers and replace them with tractor aircraft.

It so happened that Glenn Curtiss had visited the Sopwith factory in England a year earlier, and was highly impressed with their advanced tractor designs. He hired Sopwith designer, B. Douglas Thomas to design a tandem two-seat tractor trainer. Thomas's first attempt was designated the Model J, a promising but underpowered airplane, which was followed by the improved Model N. But the real breakthrough occurred when the best features of both designs were combined in the Model JN, which became

The Curtiss Model D in flight at North Island, San Diego, California, where Glen Curtiss established a flight training school. Curtiss offered free flying lessons to select military officers to stimulate sales of his aircraft to the government. The surfaces between the upper and lower wings were used for roll control and became known as ailerons. Curtiss' technique for roll control became the basis for a prolonged legal battle with the Wright brothers. *Glen H. Curtiss Museum*

Lt. "Spuds" Ellyson, the first Naval Aviator, at the controls of a Curtiss Model D at North Island. *Tailhook Collection via Cdr. Doug Siegfried*

The Curtiss Model D was nicknamed "Lizzie" and used a control system more intuitive than the Wright Flyer. However it carried only one occupant that made training more difficult. *Tailhook Collection via Cdr. Doug Siegfried*

the iconic Jenny trainer.[4] The Navy employed a single pontoon version of the Jenny called the N-9. It was the Navy's first truly satisfactory training plane and represented nearly half of its training fleet during WWI.[5]

During this time aviators began to wrestle with the mysteries of stability and control. In the earliest days of aviation, the tailspin was believed to result in near certain death. The airplane appeared to literally fall out of the sky, spinning around like a top with the nose well down below the horizon.

Early airplanes were particularly susceptible to the so-called tailspin because they were underpowered, reducing the margin above stall speed. Novice aviators also tended to turn the airplane with the rudder like a boat, rather than banking into the turn, particularly if they were near the ground.

What was happening was that the airplane was being slowed and also turned about its vertical axis rather than rolling into a turn. As a result, the wing(s) on the inside of the turn would be at a higher angle of attack and stall first. Stalling, i.e. reaching the angle of attack at which lift began to decrease rather than continuing to increase, also significantly increased the drag of that wing, causing the rate of yaw in its direction to quickly increase and that wing to suddenly drop, further increasing its angle of attack and drag. Uncorrected, the result was a descending rotation in the direction of the more stalled wing.

The entry into the tailspin was abrupt and disconcerting. What was worse, the pilot's attempt to stop the roll and the nose-down pitch actually had the opposite effect, causing the stalled wing to be at an even higher angle of attack. In other words, the pilot's attempt to stop the roll and nosedive by pulling the stick and to the side would likely result in the airplane momentarily rolling upside down and the nose falling well below the horizon.

Once in a fully developed spin with the nose pointed toward the ground and altitude decreasing rapidly, the pilot would naturally continue to pull back on the stick as hard as possible to bring the nose up, which was unfortunately the opposite of what was needed to regain control.

The first Curtiss tractor aircraft flying at North Island after pusher aircraft were grounded by the Army in 1914. It retained the tricycle landing gear arrangement. *Glen H. Curtiss Museum*

The Curtiss Model J designed by B. Douglas Thomas was a dramatic advance in training aircraft, however it was underpowered. In only three years Curtiss trainers had evolved from crude single occupant pushers to more modern two-place tractor designs. *Glenn H. Curtiss Museum*

Various pilots are credited with discovering how to recover from a spin. The almost certainly apocryphal version concerned an early aviator who found himself in a spin at altitude. He elected to shorten the unpleasantness of watching the ground come up to kill him and pushed the stick forward. As a result, he "broke" the spin and converted from it into a nosedive, from which recovery to level flight was straightforward.

A spin recovery was reportedly accomplished by Avro Aircraft test pilot Fred Raynham in September 1911; however, he lost control while flying in a cloud without instruments and probably got into a spiral dive instead. Another frequently cited first was Parke's dive, named for Lt. Wilfred Parke, Royal Navy. However, his detailed description of the incident, published less than a week later in the August 31, 1912, issue of the British magazine *Flight*, was clearly that of a spiral dive and not a spin. Although similar in appearance from both the pilot and ground observers viewpoints, the airspeed in a spiral dive is high and increasing whereas in a spin, it is low and unchanging. The response is also quite different: for a spiral dive, roll to wings level and pull out; for a spin, nose-down elevator (usually combined with opposite rudder) and wait for the transition from the spin into a dive, then pull out.

American stunt pilot Lincoln Beachey may or may not have been demonstrating a true spin entry and recovery at his airshows by 1912. It's possible that he was simply doing a spiral dive. In any event, he is widely credited with creating a name, tailspin, for the maneuver.

Among the more likely candidates for first developing the technique for recovering from the tailspin are Wilbur Wright himself according to Grover C. Loening, an early aviator and airplane designer. In the June 1, 1959 issue of *The Atlantic*, he wrote:

At Dayton, in 1913, we witnessed a vital moment in airplane operation. This was when Orville Wright, so discouraged by the accidents that were happening to his exhibition fliers and to a whole series of Army fliers (Hazelhurst, Love, Kelly, and others), was determined to test out what was happening.

Before long he himself came back from a test flight smiling instead of grim, because he had discovered what a "spin" is and how to get out of it: namely, by pushing forward on the controls; and why so many aviators had been killed: namely, by pulling back on the controls at the wrong time.

Sopwith test pilot Harry Hawker independently discovered how to recover from a spin in June 1914 in England. He had crashed as a result of an accidental spin off the top of a loop but survived unhurt because the airplane landed in a tree. Undeterred by his nearly fatal experience, he took off the next day and developed the counter-intuitive recovery technique.

In December 1915, US Army 2nd Lt. Byron Quimby Jones reportedly demonstrated a spin recovery. He was assigned to the predecessor of the Army Air Corps, the Aviation Section of the Signal Corps, in San Diego at North Field. Nevertheless, Grover Loening's book, *Military Aeroplanes: An Explanatory Consideration of their Characteristics, Performances, Construction, Maintenance and Operation, for the Use of Aviators* published in 1916 makes no mention of spins.

The promulgation of understanding spin was rapid, however. By the time the US entered the World War in 1917, demonstration of a spin and recovery was required of military student pilots. Entering a spin (at altitude) was even used as an escape maneuver in combat since following, much less shooting at, an airplane in a spin was problematic.

An early JN model which represented a major breakthrough combining excellent flight characteristics with adequate power. This JN-4D is taking off with an instructor and student from the Curtiss factory. The JN series would become the standard for training aircraft in WWI and would serve until late in the 1920s. *Glen H. Curtiss Museum*

A navalized version of the JN-4, the N-9C, floating on its pontoons. Because the pontoons compromised directional stability in flight, additional vertical area was added to the upper wings. *Glen H. Curtiss Museum*

In the 1918 edition of Loening's *Military Aeroplanes*, he provides an excellent annotated diagram of the "nose spin" (which he notes is also called the tailspin and in French, *la vrille*). His description of the spin recovery is "Put all controls at neutral. Hold them there! Push stick forward until the wind begins to whistle a bit, then pull the stick back gently and carry on." For some reason he did not recommend rudder against the spin before "the wind begins to whistle a bit."

While deaths from tailspins continued (those that resulted from a skidding turn during an approach to landing generally did not occur at a high enough altitude for recovery), the incidence was dramatically reduced with the emphasis being placed on spin recovery in flight training.

Trainers were therefore required to have good stall-warning characteristics and to spin only when provoked, with spin recovery to quickly follow the proper application of the controls. NACA devoted considerable effort to understanding the aerodynamics of the spin with an eye to predicting spin characteristics and recommended recovery techniques for a new airplane as well as developing spin-resistant designs. (One unfortunate axiom, however, was that an airplane that was difficult to force into a spin was often equally reluctant, if not more so, to recover from one when it was achieved.)

In the process, NACA also created a series of spin-test vertical wind tunnels at Langley that were used to evaluate the spin characteristics and recovery techniques of specific airplane designs. This was accomplished using scale models. These were relatively large (three-foot wing span maximum initially) but relatively fragile since they had to be scaled for dynamic similarity, including mass distribution, while still having positionable controls as well as the means for changing their position to effect spin recovery during the test.

As it happened, however, the results from spin-tunnel testing of models did not always accurately predict the spin and recovery characteristics of the full-scale airplane. In at least one case, the airplane demonstrated far more benign spin results than predicted and in some, test pilots had to spend an inordinate amount of spin-test time to establish a configuration that approached the behavior that the model had predicted.

At the outset of World War I in August 1914, several trends were apparent. Airplane development had advanced rapidly in Europe, while it was stagnant in the United States. The American military regarded the airplane as a mere reconnaissance or scouting tool with no offensive value, while European air arms developed ground attack and aerial combat capability. Furthermore, the Wright brothers' role in military aviation was diminishing while the influence of Glenn Curtiss was rising. By 1914, Curtiss was recognized as a world leader in the design and construction of flying boats, and his JN trainer had gained a reputation as a serviceable plane that could produce scores of pilots for service at the front.

The United States was not yet involved in the hostilities, but its nascent aircraft industry was about to be overwhelmed. The sudden demand for airplanes in Europe exceeded the combatants' production capacity, so England, Russia, and a number of smaller countries turned to the United States. The Curtiss Aeroplane Company was the principal beneficiary of these orders, forcing that company to increase plant capacity rapidly. The onslaught of demand for airplanes proved to be both a blessing and a curse for Curtiss, causing the company to expand explosively. Orders for the new JN trainer and H-4 flying boats required Curtiss to relocate headquarters from rural Hammondsport, New York, to the more industrial Buffalo, New York. Plant capacity was expanded twice, and additional production was licensed to a Canadian subsidiary in Toronto.

When the United States finally entered the War in 1917, it was woefully ill prepared. The Army had only fifty-six trained pilots and approximately 300 airplanes, none of which was suitable for combat. The Navy had forty-eight pilots with fifty-four airplanes, nearly all trainers.[6] Suddenly, the importance of military aviation dawned on American policy makers who vowed to build an air arm that would darken the skies over Germany. Congress authorized a massive spending program of $640 million, the largest single appropriation ever passed at that time. This allowed the Army to order 12,000 combat planes and 5,000 training planes. The Navy was allocated funds to order 1,700 aircraft. Curtiss received orders for 1,400 JN-4 trainers in addition to the commitments it already had from England, Russia, and Spain. Curtiss also received orders for 2,000 French-designed Spad XIII fighters that were to be built under license for use by the US Army. The volume was far beyond Curtiss's production and managerial capacity, so he turned to a noted expert from the automotive industry, John North Willys, president of the Willys-Overland Company. However, even Willys was incapable of managing the chaos that ensued from the flood of orders. The Army, which had little experience in acquiring war planes, issued conflicting specifications for the engines and machine guns that were to be installed in the Spads, forcing Curtiss engineers to recalculate and redesign the aircraft several times. Suddenly, the entire order was canceled for fear that the Spads would be obsolete by the time they reached the front. A British airplane, the Bristol Fighter, was substituted for the canceled Spads, but the Army insisted on installing a heavier American-designed Liberty engine in place of the British Rolls-Royce. The increased engine weight made the Curtiss-built Bristol unsafe—three examples crashed during testing. Again, the contract was canceled and by the end of the war the American aviation industry failed to deliver the ambitious number of fighters that it had promised to its allies in Europe. There was a general impression of failure, and the post-war government report on aviation production concluded that much of the $640 million appropriation had been wasted.[7] Nevertheless, Curtiss emerged as the country's leading airplane manufacturer with nine plants, 18,000 workers, and an exceptionally gifted staff of engineers. Furthermore Curtiss's success with training aircraft was remarkable. The Jenny had become the principal trainer for much of the world. More than 4,000 JNs were delivered by Curtiss and nearly 2,000 built under license by six other firms. The Jenny made standardized flight instruction possible and pilots were able to master their initial training in six to eight weeks with approximately ten hours of dual instruction, twenty-four hours of solo and sixteen hours of cross-country navigation. The Jenny represented a higher-powered, more stoutly constructed machine that allowed precision in teaching and permitted flight instruction to become organized into phases—which would come to be called primary, basic, and advanced.[8]

By the time the United States entered WWI, the Curtiss Aeroplane Company was one of the largest aircraft manufacturers in the world. In addition to orders for thousands of JN-4 trainers, Curtiss was awarded orders for tactical aircraft such as this Spad XIII. *Glen H. Curtiss Museum*

B. Flight Training between the Wars 1919–1941

Nearly all of the tactical aircraft flown by Americans during World War I were of European manufacture, leaving the United States with an air arm of domestically built deHavilland DH-4 and Curtiss JN-4 training planes after the armistice.

But what might have been a satisfying postwar sufficiency of equipment became a liability, as stores of soon outdated and decrepit aircraft and engines had to be used until wartime stocks were depleted. Successive models of the DH-4, for example, remained in the active inventory through 1931. Moreover, specialized aircraft still remained to be designed and built.[9]

The Army recognized the dangers of an obsolete, non-tactical aircraft fleet. Four years after the war, a committee of officers headed by Maj. Gen. William Lassiter determined that the American Air Service was using deteriorating war-built aircraft, 80 percent of which were obsolescent training machines or were otherwise unsuitable for combat. New aircraft were slow to be developed as the Army and Navy rapidly demobilized and the government entered a period of austerity. Making matters worse was a new system of competitive bidding imposed by Congress in response to the wartime $640 million production fiasco. Under this system, a manufacturer's proprietary right to a new design was not recognized. Designs became the property of the military, and production contracts were often awarded to manufacturers who had incurred none of the design costs. The system was ruinous to many companies and post-war military aircraft development nearly came to a halt in the United States. Yet, aeronautical advances were plentiful in the civilian market. Airframes became more refined and engines became more powerful. Metal replaced wood in structures and monoplanes replaced biplanes in configuration. Variable-pitch propellers, retractable landing gear, and fully enclosed cockpits began to appear on high-performance airplanes. But the military was slow to enjoy incorporate these new advances because of post-war austerity.

In this environment, training aircraft evolved at an even slower pace than tactical planes. It became apparent to the Army and Navy in the early 1920s that their JN-4 Jennies and pontoon-equipped N-9s were outdated. But these trainers remained in service until late in the decade (the Navy retired the N-9 in 1926, and the Army ceased training in the Jenny one year later). Finally, in the late 1920s, a steel-tube-framed Consolidated PT-1 replaced the Army's aging wooden Jenny and the Navy purchased a modified version designated the Consolidated NY.[10] But

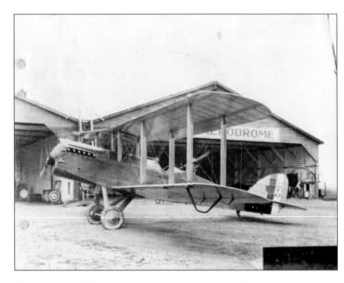

The deHavilland DH-4 was one of several airplanes built under license by Curtiss. At the end of the war large numbers of DH-4s remained in the Army's inventory and were used for both training and tactical purposes. *Glen H. Curtiss Museum*

intermediate or basic training was still flown with the World War I deHavilland DH-4 until 1931 (the DH-4 was regarded obsolete for combat purposes even during the war). In addition to equipment obsolescence, the problem of budgetary restrictions limited flying hours, making the training mission even more difficult. In 1930, the Chief of the Air Corps, Maj. Gen. J.E. Fechet, cautioned his staff of the

> urgent need for action … to assure that all airplane pilots continue adequate flying practice. Analysis of aircraft accidents indicates that a number of pilots exhibit a serious lapse in piloting ability, and many pilots have, over periods of years, failed to perform the minimum amount of flying necessary to handle airplanes with reasonable safety under all conditions … The cumulative effects of such neglect are becoming increasingly serious … The infrequent flier is the most dangerous pilot.[11]

As of May 1, 1932, the Air Corps owned only 251 primary trainers, which had to be long-lived because of constant hard use.[12] The Consolidated PT-3, a radial-engined descendent of the PT-1, emerged as a successful trainer, and a further refinement, the PT-11, was regarded as the standard Air Corps trainer by 1933. However, several developments were about to occur that would have a profound effect on trainer aircraft.

In 1933, the Navy, looking to replace its aging fleet of Consolidated NY trainers, directed the Naval Aircraft Factory (a design and manufacturing facility wholly-owned and operated by the Navy at the Philadelphia Navy Yard, Pennsylvania) to design and build an experimental training

PT-1   PT-3

The Consolidated Aircraft Corporation of Buffalo, New York produced the PT-1, a primary trainer constructed on a steel tube frame which represented a significant advance over the wooden frame JN-4 Jenny. A total of 171 were built. The Consolidated PT-3A, an improved version of the PT-1 used a 220 hp R-790 engine that gave it a top speed of 102 mph. 120 PT-3As were produced. *NARA*

airplane. The Bureau of Aeronautics reasoned that the Naval Aircraft Factory (NAF) could develop a primary trainer specifically tailored to the needs of the Navy while optimizing ruggedness, ease of maintenance, and flying stability. Furthermore, the Navy was sitting on a large stockpile of Wright J-5 Whirlwind 9 engines (the same engine that had powered Lindbergh's Spirit of St. Louis) that had become obsolete. Using these engines in a new trainer seemed particularly attractive during the Great Depression. The airplane that emerged did not look very different from the Consolidated NYs it replaced, but the structure was far more robust. It featured a bolted steel tubular frame with removable side panels for inspection and maintenance. The wings and tail were metal framed and fabric covered. The initial article, designated XN3N-1,[13] made its maiden flight at Mustin Field adjacent to the Naval Aircraft Factory on 23 August 1935. It displayed some tail heaviness and difficulty with spin recovery, which required moving the engine forward to relocate the center of gravity, and an increase of the tail area, but the Navy ordered eighty-five examples into production in April 1936, twenty-five as conventional wheeled-land planes and sixty as single-pontoon float planes. The NAF trainer ultimately received an updated Wright J-6 Whirlwind engine along with several airframe improvements under the new designation N3N-3. A total of 997 N3Ns were built by the NAF and remained in primary training service throughout WWII. A few were used in the midshipmen's curriculum at the United States Naval Academy as late as 1961.

Parallel to the government-funded N3N program, another primary trainer was being developed with private funds by a small Kansas manufacturer, the Stearman Aircraft Corporation. The initial Stearman effort, called the Model 6, was built in response to a 1932 Navy specification, but it failed to generate any orders. A follow-on, the Model 70, was built in 1934 to meet an Air Corps specification. It was an attractive airplane with cantilevered

The PT-11 was the most refined of Consolidated primary trainer series. Early examples had a top speed of 118 mph with 200 hp engines. A 300 horsepower example had performance beyond that necessary for primary training and was redesignated BT-7 (a basic trainer). The Navy version of the Consolidated PT-11 was designated N4Y-1. It was ordered in small numbers. It shared the same performance as the Army PT-11. *Tailhook Collection via Cdr. Doug Siegfried*

The N3N-1 built by the Naval Aircraft Factory at the Philadelphia Navy Yard became a landmark in trainer development. It featured a very robust steel structure and ease of maintenance. A total of 179 N3N-1s were built, and the majority of N3N-1s were ordered as single-pontoon floatplanes. This N3N-1 at Pensacola is coming on the step as it accelerates for takeoff. *Tailhook Collection via Cdr. Doug Siegfried*

A detailed side view of the N3N-3 showing the improved landing gear, and the exposed engine. Early N3N-1s were delivered with a cowl ring but these were removed in service and eliminated altogether on N3N-3s. *NARA*

landing gear and a remarkably durable structure capable of +12g and -9g. Powered with a nine-cylinder, 210-hp Lycoming R-680 engine, the Model 70 had a top speed of 125 mph and endurance of four hours. The first flight occurred on January 1, 1934. Stearman's test pilot, David "Deed" Levy, reported that it flew well, exhibited no bad habits, and would make an excellent trainer. Confident of the new airplane, Levy ferried the Model 70 to Wright Field, Dayton, Ohio, where it was evaluated by Army test pilots against other trainers. The Stearman was selected as winner of the competition, but the Army lacked current funding to order it. Fortunately, a Navy representative, LT Laxton, observed the competition and was highly impressed by the Stearman. He arranged for it to be flown to Naval Air Station Anacostia near Washington, DC where Lt.Cdr. Gerald Bogan, chief of flight test, agreed with Laxton's assessment. Brogan sent the Model 70 to the Navy's training headquarters at Pensacola, Florida, and again it was enthusiastically received. The Navy placed an order for forty-one Stearmans, but required that they be delivered with Wright J5 engines from the Navy's inventory. The designation NS-1 was assigned to the trainer and the first example was delivered in December 1934.

Army orders were slow to materialize, but in July 1935 the Air Corps ordered twenty examples (plus enough spares to build six additional airframes) assigning the designation PT-13 to the Stearman. The first was delivered in June 1936 and the following year ninety-two additional units were ordered. Ultimately, the PT-13 evolved into the PT-17 Kaydet and over 10,000 examples were produced. Like the Curtiss JN-4 Jenny two decades earlier, the Stearman series became iconic primary training aircraft with a remarkably long service life.

Other primary airplanes were developed in the 1930s but none was as successful as the Stearman. Fairchild produced a small trainer in 1937 that was unusual for its time. Army policy favored biplanes for primary training, but the Fairchild design (company designation M-62) was a low-wing monoplane with substantial dihedral for lateral stability. The wing was cantilevered with no external bracing and skinned with plywood. The wide-tread landing gear used oleo shock absorbers for benign ground handling, and it was powered with a tightly cowled six-cylinder Ranger in-line engine. The Fairchild design was very streamlined for a primary trainer; its monoplane configuration eliminated drag associated with a second wing and its attendant struts and flying wires. The in-line engine reduced the frontal area associated with typical radial-engined biplanes. As a result, the Fairchild M-62 offered remarkable performance—135 mph top speed, with a 48 mph stall speed.[14] The Army assigned the

Three early Stearman NS-1s in formation. These were part of the first sixty-one Stearman trainers delivered to the Navy in 1935-36. Stearmans would evolve into the most important primary trainers of the WWII era. *Tailhook Collection via Cdr. Doug Siegfried*

The Navy N2S-5 was identical to the Army PT-13D. These aircraft were so interchangeable that some received the Navy designations but Army serial numbers. This all silver N2S-5 was photographed at Patuxent River in 1943. *Tailhook Collection via Cdr. Doug Siegfried*

Left: an early PT-13 photographed on May 5, 1936 prior to the official delivery to the Army. This was one of the first twenty PT-13s ordered by the Army in July 1935. It was powered by a Lycoming R-680-5 engine.
Right: the most famous variant of the Stearman series was the PT-17. It was essentially a PT-13A airframe with a Continental engine. This example, photographed on May 6, 1940, was powered by a Continental R-670-5. The Army received 3,519 examples. *NARA*

As a sailor cranks the inertial starter on a Lycoming R-680-8 engine the student and his instructor prepare for a training sortie in a N2S-2. The red band on the aft fuselage identifies the primary training squadron of this Stearman based at NAS Corpus Christi. *Tailhook Collection via Cdr. Doug Siegfried*

designation PT-19 and ordered 270 units in 1940. Ultimately, the PT-19 would be ordered in large quantity, over 3,500 units, forcing Fairchild to license production to Aeronca, Howard, Fleet, and St. Louis Aircraft Corp. However, limited availability of the in-line Ranger engine caused Fairchild to adapt a radial Continental R-670 to the airframe that became the PT-23 (the radial engine reduced top speed by 5 mph even though it provided 45 additional hp). Another variant, the PT-26 with an enclosed cockpit, was produced for Canadian use. However, in a 1943 memo to the Joint Aircraft Committee, Brig. General Robert W. Harper noted:

> The PT-17 has proven to be a most satisfactory type and maintenance difficulties negligible compared to the Fairchild wooden types. The wood aircraft will not stand up in the hot dry climate where many of our schools are located, and much difficulty is being experienced with the PT-23 due to the vibration trouble.[15]

Another low-wing monoplane trainer of the era was developed by the Ryan Aeronautical Co., famous for its production of Charles Lindbergh's *Spirit of St. Louis*. In 1933, Ryan designed the ST, a low-wing monoplane with external wire bracing to the fuselage and the landing gear. The fuselage was metal skinned but the wing and tail were fabric covered. Initially intended for Ryan's civilian flight school, the Army purchased a single model ST-A to evaluate the feasibility of monoplanes for military training. Encouraged by initial trials, the Army ordered an additional fifty-five units to permit a more thorough evaluation between 1939 and 1940. Early examples received the designation of PT-16, while later models with enlarged cockpits and external stiffening received the designation of PT-20. But it became apparent that the elaborate wheel fairings were more trouble from a maintenance standpoint than they were worth in performance and the in-line Menasco engines were not reliable. The wheel fairings were soon removed and the Menasco engine was replaced by a Kinner R-440 radial. This variant received the designation PT-22 with production reaching 1,023 units, but production ended in 1942 shortly after the United States entered World War II.

The prototype XPT-23 photographed on April 11, 1941. The lack of Ranger in-line engines forced Fairchild to adapt a Continental R-670-5 radial to the PT-19 airframe. Drag from the radial engine diminished the top speed by 5 mph even though it produced 45 additional horsepower. *NARA*

A Fairchild PT-19 powered by a Ranger L-440-1 in-line engine. The PT-19 had a top speed similar to the Stearman even though its engine produced 45 less horsepower. *Tom Doll via Mark Nankivil Collection*

The Fairchild PT-26 was similar to the PT-19 with a canopy-enclosed cockpit. This variant was used for cold weather operations. Fairchild built 670 and exported them to Canada under the Lend-Lease program. *NARA*

The top view of a PT-20 in a sideslip showing its advanced features such as the streamlined cowling, all metal structure, and landing flaps. *NARA*

The Navy version of the Ryan was designated NR-1 seen here with a polished aluminum fuselage and yellow wings. *Tailhook Collection via Cdr. Doug Siegfried*

These civilian STAs were used to train military pilots at the Ryan operated flight school in San Diego in 1939. This was an early example of primary training by civilian contractors that produced large numbers of pilots quickly. Until 1939, all Army trainers had been biplanes, this was the first monoplane trainer. When Ryan produced the STA for the Air Corps it received the designation PT-20. *Author's Collection*

The PT-21 was a Kinner R-440-3 radial engine variant of the Ryan. The Army ordwered 100 of these trainers in 1941. *NARA*

The basic training phase used modified observation or primary trainers during the early interwar years. These aircraft were designated BT (for basic trainers) but they were little more than the simple airplanes used for primary instruction. The breakthrough in basic training aircraft was described by Rebecca Hancock Cameron:

In 1936, the Seversky Aircraft Company delivered the first true BT, the BT-8, the result of a design competition. It was a two-seat, low-wing monoplane powered with a 450-horsepower Pratt and Whitney Wasp Junior engine. The fuselage was monocoque; the wings were multispar, reinforced inside with corrugated sheets of metal. The BT-8 evidenced noteworthy advances in design and construction, but it quickly proved to be too fast and difficult for novices to fly. A series of accidents convinced the Air Corps to discontinue it in favor of the BT-9. This airplane too, contributed to the high fatality rate in air training, but it remained in use for several more years. An improved version, the XBT-12 was not tested and approved for purchase until 1941.[16]

In 1939, Vultee Aircraft of Nashville, Tennessee, using private funds, developed the Model 54. It was a docile, low-wing metal-skinned monoplane with fixed landing gear powered by a 450 hp. Pratt &Whitney R-985 engine. It flew at a top speed of 180 mph and had a 725-mile range. The Army recognized Vultee's design as a viable basic trainer and placed an order for 300, assigning the designation BT-13. This was the Army's largest basic trainer order up to that time; however, after 1941 substantially larger

The Seversky BT-8 at Randolph field in 1938. This was the first purpose-designed basic trainer. Prior examples were former tactical aircraft assigned training duties due to obsolescence. *Rich Dann Collection via Mark Nankivil*

As a result of trainer standardization many BT-13s received both Army and Navy markings. The Navy designation was SNV. *Rich Dann Collection via Mark Nankivil*

The Vultee BT-13 Valiant (nicknamed Vibrator) became the most important basic trainer of WWII. More than 6,400 examples were produced far outnumbering all other types in that category. *NARA*

The BT-13 was an excellent aerobatic aircraft but it suffered some structural failures that resulted in a restriction on violent maneuvers. Nevertheless it was regarded as a superb formation and instrument trainer. *Rich Dann Collection via Mark Nankivil*

This is a BT-15 that was powered by the Wright R-975-11 engine. It was identical to the Pratt & Whitney R-985-AN-1 powered BT-13 in all other respects. *Rich Dann Collection via Mark Nankivil*

contracts were issued. By the end of its production run in 1944 over 6400 BT-13s and BT-15s (a Wright R-975 powered variant) were delivered, far outnumbering all other basic training types. Vultee assigned the name Valiant to the design, but in service it earned the nickname of "Vibrator" due to its tendency to shake violently at stall speed, and because of its characteristic canopy vibration during aggressive maneuvers, it also displayed an irritating propeller vibration in high pitch. The syllabus for basic training during this period consisted of fifty-two hours of navigation, five hours of individual combat, five hours of elementary formation flying, twelve hours of instrument flight, twelve hours of night flying, ten hours of performance flying, and nine hours of radio communication.

Advanced flight training also suffered for lack of equipment during the interwar years. As late as 1936, the advanced school was using obsolete biplanes such as the Curtiss A-3B or Boeing P-12 that were hand-me-downs from tactical units. As the United States began to rearm in the late 1930s, the lack of suitable advanced trainers became acute. The Army was forced to abridge the four month advanced training course into three months with the 111-hour flight syllabus reduced to seventy-five hours. Specialized training in attack, bombardment, pursuit, or observation was shifted from the advanced phase to tactical units. It was not until 1940 that a purpose-built advanced trainer, the North American AT-6 Texan, entered the inventory. The AT-6, an all-metal (except for fabric-covered control surfaces) low-wing monoplane with retractable landing gear and a variable-pitch propeller, was developed from North American's first training aircraft, the BT-9. Designed in 1935, the BT-9 looked much like the AT-6 that it would evolve into, but it had fixed landing gear and a fabric covered fuselage (a later variant, the BT-14, employed a metal-skinned fuselage). These early North American trainers were built in small numbers, but their offspring, the AT-6, was about to become a very important trainer.

The BT-9 was North American Aviation's privately funded entry into training aircraft in 1935. It was evaluated at Wright Field and immediately generated an order for forty-two aircraft. Within a year it was regarded as the standard Army basic trainer and it would evolve into one of the most important trainers ever built, the AT-6. *Rich Dann Collection via Mark Nankivil*

The North American BT-14 built in 1940 was a modernized BT-9 with a metal covered fuselage. It served as an interim step between the BT-9 and the classic AT-6. *Rich Dann Collection via Mark Nankivil*

Originally designated BC-1 (basic combat) and later redesignated AT-6 (advanced trainer), it would become one of the most prolific trainers in history. This example still has a fabric fuselage but it employs the retractable landing gear, radio equipment, and navigation lights typical of the breed. *Rich Dann Collection via Mark Nankivil*

C. Flight Training during World War II 1941–1945

The United States had been preparing for an impending war since September 1, 1939, when Germany invaded Poland, but the pace of preparation could be described as leisurely. In the last six months of 1939, the Air Corps graduated only 982 men from flight training. In 1940, the total rose to 8,125 and grew to 27,531 in 1941.[17] When the Japanese attack on Pearl Harbor plunged the United States into war, pilot production was accelerated to a peak of 74,000 per year. In sum, the Army graduated 193,440 pilots between July 1, 1939, and August 31, 1945.[18] The Navy experienced similar growth, expanding from 6,206 pilots in 1940 to 60,747 at the end of the war.[19]

The war had a profound effect on the volume of training, the speed of training, the size of training bases, and the number of training aircraft produced, but it had little effect on the development of new trainer designs. War planners and industry executives gave little thought to developing new training aircraft during the war years. For the most part, the trainers from the 1930s taught the pilots of WWII how to fly combat aircraft of the 1940s.

As the United States prepared for war, the Army delegated primary training to select civilian flight schools. By December 7, 1941, forty-one schools were in operation. Flight instruction was provided by civilian instructors, with military check pilots giving evaluation rides at various points in the training. Check pilot duty was not desirable, as noted by Lt. John Frisbee:

> After mastering the AT-6 or the AT-9, and maybe getting a little time in the operational aircraft, going back to a sparsely instrumented primary trainer that might do 120 mph nose-down and with throttle firewalled was like repeating fifth grade at the age of sixteen.[20]

By May 1943, at the height of primary training, fifty-six civilian schools were in operation. The washout rate was intentionally highest during this phase (averaging 27.5%) when the financial investment in the student was at its lowest. The Navy also used civilian instructors, but assigned them to naval facilities. The partnership between the military and civilians worked well in producing the required number of pilots for the war effort. The Stearman series of primary trainers (PT-13, 17, 18, and 27 for the Air Corps; N2S-1 through 4 for the Navy) was the most prevalent type by far. However, some Air Corps students learned in the Fairchild PT-19, PT-23, PT-26; or the Ryan PT-20, PT-21, or PT-22. The Navy used small numbers of the Naval Aircraft Factory N3Ns, Ryan NR-1s, Timm N2T-1s, and Spartan NP-1s.

Basic training, being sandwiched between primary and advanced, suffered frequent changes in curriculum. There was a constant conflict between perfecting the elementary flight skills learned in primary and the development of new skills required for formation, instrument, and night flying. Early in WWII, the predominant basic trainer was the Vultee BT-13 or 15 Valiant (Navy designation SNV), which was regarded as an excellent formation trainer because of its weight and stability. But it had a tendency toward wingtip stalls, and it suffered several in-flight tail failures that restricted it from aerobatics and violent maneuvers. It was also prone to engine failures and had aggressive spin characteristics. Yet it was effective in teaching the techniques necessary to handle heavier, higher-powered machines. Toward the end of the war, AT-6s (and Navy SNJs) that were excess to advanced training requirements were released to basic training schools allowing intermediate students to hone their skills with a state-of-the-art airplane. The advanced phase became the point at which specialization was introduced. Those students assigned to a single-engine syllabus would become fighter pilots, and those assigned to a twin-engine syllabus would become bomber pilots. The need for bomber pilots made twin-engine slots three times as likely as single-engine slots, yet a disproportionate number of cadets opted for single-engine trainers hoping to become fighter pilots. By the time a pilot entered the advanced phase, it was assumed that he was competent and the relationship between student and instructor became less formal. Virtually all single-engine advanced training was flown with the AT-6, but the twin-engine pipeline offered no standard trainer. Some students were assigned to the Beechcraft AT-7, AT-10, or Cessna AT-17, and as the war progressed, tactical aircraft, such as the B-25 and B-17, were assigned to advanced training schools.

On December 7, 1941, no one could have predicted the enormously successful buildup of military flight training that would occur during the next four years. The recruiting, the screening, the facility expansion, the aircraft production, and the sheer motivation of the training community produced an unimaginable result. The training effort was so successfully managed that midway through the conflict the rate of pilot production had to be reduced. Since 1909, two fundamental lessons have been learned: 1) in emergencies it is enormously difficult to field a well-trained pilot force quickly; therefore, it is necessary to maintain a viable pool of experienced pilots at all times; 2) standards for pilot selection should never be compromised; only a certain type of person is best suited for aviation.

Rebecca Hancock Cameron's conclusion of *Training to Fly* summarizes these lessons and provides an eloquent definition of "The Right Stuff:"

> … Even when it was subject to enormous pressure to produce trained airmen quickly, and even when it had the money, the air arm never accepted all comers. It firmly believed that a certain type of man was best suited to aviation, and it could not afford to take the others. Not only did flying call for special physical acuity, but the inordinately high fatality rate in air training proved that the service had to select its people with particular care … the measure of a pilot could never be taken scientifically. Airmen knew who were the good pilots, just as the Wright brothers knew and taught their pupils to feel the wind and camber of the wings and the sound of the wires. That reliance on self, instincts, and personal experience to achieve technical mastery imbued an air force culture from its infancy. Despite the constant drive for standardization in air training, airmen believed in their hearts that they were engaged in an individualistic, improvisational enterprise for which only an exceptional few possessed the temperament, talent, and luck.[21]

Chapter One Endnotes

1. Rebecca Hancock Cameron, *Training to Fly: Military Flight Training, 1907–1945*. Air Force History and Museums Program, 1999. pp.7-8.

2. Ibid. p.31.

3. Cdr. Douglas Siegfried, USN (retired), "The Early Days and World War I, 1903 to 1919," *Cleared for Solo* (unpublished manuscript), p.3.

4. Louis R. Eltscher and Edward M. Young, Curtiss-Wright: *Greatness and Decline*. New York: Twayne Publishers, 1998, pp.14-15.

5. Siegfried, "The Early Days and World War I, 1903 to 1919," p.40.

6. Eltscher and Young, p.19.

7. Ibid. p.24.

8. Cameron, p.65.

9. Ibid. p.205.

10. F.G. Swanborough and Peter M. Bowers, *United States Military Aircraft since 1909*. London and New York: Putnam, 1963, pp.126-129, and 158-163.

11. Cameron, pp.250-251.

12. Ibid. p.253.

13. The designation XN3N-1 represents: experimental (X), trainer (N), of the third type (3), from the Naval Aircraft Factory (N), first model (- 1).

14. Alan Abel, *Fairchild's Golden Age*. Brawley, California: Wind Canyon Books, 2008), p.82.

15. Cameron, p.394.

16. Ibid. pp.254-255.

17. Ibid. pp.370-371.

18. Ibid. p.388.

19. Siegfried, *World War II, 1942 to 1945*, p.1.

20. John L. Frisbee, "The Cloud with the Mild Blue Lining," *Air Force Magazine* 64: no.7 (Jul 1981), p.88.

21. Cameron, p.560.

Chapter Two
NORTH AMERICAN T-28—THE FIRST MODERN TRAINER

The rapid drawdown of forces at the conclusion of World War II had a particularly significant impact on flight training. The Army Air Corps found itself with a large surplus of pilots and little demand for their services and therefore decided to suspend training temporarily. The surplus, however, dwindled rapidly as experienced pilots resigned from service, passed their effective combat age, or developed physical handicaps. Within a year, pilot training was restarted to avert a shortage. The Navy, faced with a similar surplus, did not suspend training; it did consolidate its training program into three centralized complexes—Pensacola, Florida; Corpus Christi, Texas; and Jacksonville, Florida—and accepted a limited number of students. The training aircraft inventory was so far in excess of either service's needs that thousands of airplanes were mothballed, sold at auction, or scrapped. Both services standardized their fleet to the Boeing Stearman PT=13/N2S Kaydet for primary training and the North American T-6/SNJ Texan for basic/intermediate training. Although they used the same airplanes and similar syllabi, the programs were completely independent and differed somewhat in detail.

The North American T-28 Trojan saw relatively limited service as an US Air Force trainer but became a mainstay of the US Navy training command. *US Air Force*

Although the Stearman biplane was used to train pilots well after the First World War and the T-6/SNJ Texan somewhat before second, they exemplified the difference in airplane technology utilized in the two wars. After World War II, both the Air Force and the Navy continued to use the relatively primitive Stearman for Primary Training for a short while. *US Navy*

The Stearman, with the designation PT for Primary Trainer in the Army Air Forces and N for trainer in the US Navy, introduced students to the fundamental principles of flight for more than a decade. *US Navy*

While both services continued to use leftover training aircraft that had been designed in the 1930s, a major transition was occurring in front-line aircraft. Jet airplanes had just been introduced into combat; propeller-driven fighters were clearly obsolete. Within a few years it became apparent that most pilots transitioning into jets needed more than just a cockpit checkout and assistance in starting one for the first time. In the meantime, they would have to make do with what they had.

To the casual observer, the Stearman wouldn't have been out of place in a movie involving World War I air combat against the Red Baron. It was a biplane with non-retractable landing gear, no takeoff/landing flaps, open cockpits, a fixed-pitch propeller, only the most basic of flying instruments, and an uncowled 220-hp engine that was started with a hand crank or even by pulling the propeller through by hand. The student sat in the rear cockpit because, for center-of-gravity reasons, that was where the pilot sat when flying solo. The instructor could talk to the student by means of a hose leading to the earpieces on the student's helmet; the student was not provided with any means of responding other than doing what he was told to do or shaking his head. It was slow, simple, sturdy, and only suitable for teaching fundamental flying skills. However, it provided a solid grounding for the next phase of training as well as an inexpensive means of washing out students unlikely to succeed as pilots.

The T-6/SNJ was much more modern in appearance than the Stearman although it was still essentially a prewar design. It was similar in size to World War II fighters, the major difference being much less horsepower. It had a constant-speed, variable-pitch propeller but lacked the engine supercharger of a fighter and its associated power management controls and workload. Nevertheless, its cruising speed was high enough to challenge a student's navigation skills and prepare him for operational fighters from that standpoint. Most importantly, although it was a major step up in performance and complexity from the Stearman, it was still relatively vice-less in handling qualities and stall and spin characteristics. As a result, it proved adequate to prepare neophyte fighter pilots for their first flight in the propeller-driven, single-seat fighters of the day. The flight situations that couldn't be demonstrated in a trainer, such as compressibility-induced buffet and control problems in a high-speed dive, could be dealt with in the classroom.

During the war the development of new trainers had been a low priority. The available engineering resources and funding were dedicated to tactical aircraft. The buildup of the training fleet was therefore accomplished with airplanes that had been designed before the War and

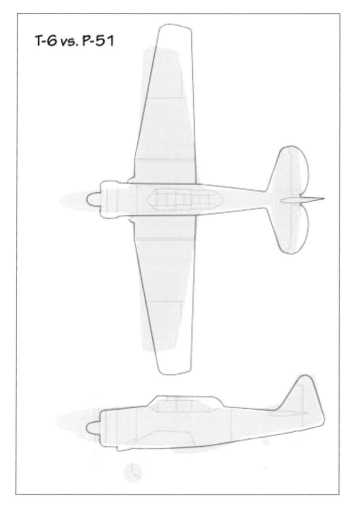

T-6 vs. P-51

The T-6 Texan was approximately as big as the P-51 Mustang that it was used to prepare students to fly. The notable difference, of course, was the greater installed horsepower and wing loading. The forward visibility in the Mustang when it was on the ground was also even worse than the Texan's. *T.H. Thomason*

A. Fairchild XNQ-1 Primary Trainer

In appearance, the XNQ-1 resembled a downsized SNJ with a single-piece "bubble" canopy: it was 1,600 pounds lighter with a much less powerful radial engine. The pilot and instructor sat in tandem. The conventional (meaning one with a tail wheel and not a nose wheel) landing gear was retractable. The fuselage and wings were metal skinned although the controls surfaces, like the SNJ and many other airplanes at the time, were fabric covered. Powered by a 295 hp Lycoming R-680-13 nine-cylinder radial engine turning a constant-speed propeller, its top speed in level flight was projected to be 170 mph and the rate of climb 1,000 feet per minute.

A mock-up inspection was held at the Fairchild plant in Hagerstown Maryland September 21–28, 1945. The first XNQ-1 flew on October 7, 1946, piloted by Richard Henson. Shortly after that milestone, Fairchild touted its features in an advertisement in the January 1947 issue of *Fortune* magazine:

> A new plane for "the line" at Naval training stations has flown its first tests—a primary trainer that looks and "feels" like the shipboard fighters some of the cadets will eventually fly.
>
> Sleek, clean-line, powerful, and with new safety features, this latest product of Fairchild design and engineering development is the XNQ-1. It embodies flight and safety characteristics never before attained in a plane of this type—characteristics that a farsighted Navy specified for the ideal training airplane.

minimally improved during it. And even though there was a surplus of trainers after the war, attrition at the hands of student pilots was high enough that eventually the time would come for the PT-13/N2S and T-6/SNJ fleet to be replaced.

The Navy made the first move in 1945 in accordance with its New Training Plan, which was to result in two new trainers, one for primary and the other for intermediate/advanced. The Request For Proposal (RFP) was released on April 26, 1945. Fairchild was selected to develop the primary trainer, which the Navy designated XNQ-1. The prototypes were assigned Bureau Numbers 75725 and 75726. North American won the competition for the intermediate/advanced trainer with its design NA-142 and received a contract in September 1945 for two XSN2J-1 prototypes and a static test article. The prototypes were assigned Bureau Numbers 121449 and 121450.[1]

The Fairchild's XNQ-1 was the result of the Navy's first attempt to replace the Stearman as its primary trainer. Postwar budget cuts resulted in only two flying prototypes and one static article being built. (The second prototype survives as civil registered N5726, see Chapter Eleven) *National Archives 395918*

Careful research and engineering skill mark the XNQ-1, as they mark all Fairchild products, with "the touch of tomorrow." These engineering skills won for Fairchild the XNQ-1 contract in a competition among the nation's topflight designers—a competition sponsored by the Navy's Bureau of Aeronautics.[2]

According to the advertisement, the Navy's specifications included a "Navy-developed safety cockpit" and the "Stability and control of carrier-based aircraft."

The safety cockpit requirement referred to a major configuration difference with the antiquated T-6/SNJ. The cockpit complied with the National Research Council's new standards including the placement of the basic flight instruments, the use of a wheel shape on the landing gear control handle and a flap shape on the flap control handle, and the location of radio controls on the right console.

The second XNQ-1 flew on February 10, 1947. The prototypes were subsequently delivered to the Navy in 1947 at Patuxent River for evaluation.

In July 1947, Fairchild Aircraft proposed a minimally modified XNQ-1 to the Navy. The major changes were a substitution of a nose landing gear for the traditional tail-wheel configured arrangement and a more powerful, horizontally opposed engine for the original radial. Fairchild stated that its M92-T was "designed to would meet the demand for a trainer which will prepare the student pilot for tricycle gear aircraft." The engine change provided better performance and improved student pilot visibility over the nose. In September, the Navy declined the opportunity to incorporate the improvements.

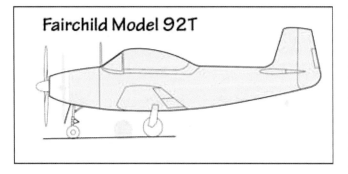

Fairchild proposed various improvements to the XNQ-1. One was a tricycle landing gear configuration. Unlike the Air Force however, the Navy strongly preferred the "conventional" landing gear arrangement with a tailwheel. *T.H. Thomason*

B. North American XSN2J Intermediate/Advanced Trainer

The XSN2J was very similar in appearance to the XNQ-1, with which it is occasionally confused. The SN2J, however, was larger and heavier, intended to be much more capable in the intermediate/advanced training role than even the SNJ. It was equipped with dive brakes on the upper surface of the wing and could drop bombs and fire rockets. There were also provisions for two .50 caliber machine guns, one in each wing, and an Mk 8 gun sight.

Because of its increased size and weight, the XSN2J required a more powerful engine, the Wright R-1820 Cyclone.

	T-6/SNJ	XSN2J
WING SPAN (FT.)	42	43
LENGTH (FT.)	29	34
GROSS WEIGHT (LBS.)	5282	9370
HORSEPOWER (TAKE OFF)	600	1,100
INTERNAL FUEL (GALLONS)	111	260
MAX LOAD FACTOR	5.3 @ 5,500 LBS.	7.5@ 8,626 LBS.
POWER TO WEIGHT (HP/LB.)	0.11	0.12

Carrier landing features and strength were incorporated in the original XSN2J design instead of just scabbing on a tailhook with a local reinforcement of the fuselage at its attach point and providing a rope to release it as had been done with the SNJ. It was also designed to be catapulted if desired, a feature that the SNJ did not have.

One innovative feature for instrument flight instruction was that the instructor in the rear seat was to have the ability to "upset" instruments in the student's cockpit to simulate emergencies.

The SN2J's first flight was accomplished on February 10, 1947 by North American test pilot George Welch. Like the XNQ-1, the prototypes were formerly evaluated by NATC at Patuxent River.

Unfortunately, neither the NQ-1 nor the SN2J-1 provided enough of a training benefit in light of the significant military budget reductions that were imposed by the Truman administration in 1948. In any event, replacing propeller-driven fighters and bombers with jets was a much higher priority than replacing trainers that were adequate to the task. The vast fleet of existing trainers would suffice for several years at the much lower level of pilot training that had resulted from the cessation of hostilities. The reduction in the operational fleet requirements also meant that there was a steady supply of obsolescent airplanes available for the advanced phase of flight training that led to the awarding of wings.

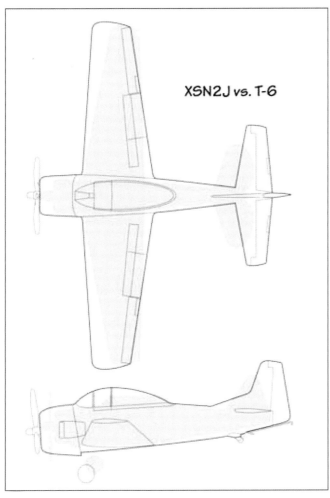

XSN2J vs. T-6

The North American SN2J was intended to replace the SNJ as the Navy's intermediate trainer and to be used for advanced training as well. It was significantly heavier than the SNJ with almost twice the horsepower. Due to budget cuts and the existence of higher priority airplane development programs, it did not go into production. *T.H. Thomason*

The SN2J was equipped to provide an introduction to carrier-based fighter-bomber airplanes. The XSN2J was designed for carrier operation unlike its predecessor, which had the tailhook added as an afterthought. It was also provided with dive brakes, a gun sight, and armament provisions for guns, rockets, and bombs for initial weapons delivery training. *US Navy*

Both the NQ-1 and SN2J-1 programs were therefore canceled. The SNJ would have to continue to suffice in the Navy for the time being, which turned out to be several years. Nevertheless, the XSN2J-1 program, while soon forgotten, would be the genesis for the first new primary/ basic trainer to be utilized by the Air Force and Navy training commands in more than a decade.

One of the training innovations to be introduced with the SN2J was the ability of the instructor to introduce simulated emergencies. The instructor in the back seat of the SN2J was provided with a control panel that could disable flight and engine instruments in the front cockpit. *US Navy*

Like the SNJ, the SN2J student and instructor sat in tandem, with the instructor in the rear seat. The instructor in the back seat of the SN2J sat under a bubble canopy with an excellent view aft, above, and to the sides. The view forward, particularly when landing due to the tail-wheel configuration, left a lot to be desired but it was typical for tail-wheel-configured airplanes at the time. *US Navy*

C. The Navy Makes Do; the Air Force Buys a New Trainer

The Navy simplified its training fleet in 1947 by eliminating the Stearman N2S for primary. To evaluate the feasibility of doing so, or at least reducing the number of flight hours required in the simpler airplane, the Navy evaluated two different programs in the training command. One training unit used the N2S for an initial twenty hours of flight time (the previous syllabus was seventy) before transitioning the students into the SNJ. Another unit began flight training in the SNJ with no prior experience in the lighter, simpler, slower biplane. The washout rate was the same, 40%, but even though the students' total flight time was less in the SNJ-only syllabus, they were considered better prepared for the follow-on flight training in more advanced airplanes.

Similarly, in October 1947, the Air Force[3] combined primary and basic training into one program, "Basic Pilot Training," using the T-6. Follow-on advanced training was separated into two tracks, single-engine (jets) and twin-engine.

Moreover the newly created Air Force released preliminary requirements for a new basic trainer in May 1947. Although the Navy was in the process of evaluating a very similar trainer, the SN2J, which met many of the Air Force requirements, the Air Force's emphasis on maintenance access, a tricycle landing gear configuration, and the differences between the Navy and Air Force's design specifications dictated a new design competition.

D. Tricycles Are Not Just for Kids

For its new trainer, the Air Force specified a landing gear with a nose wheel as opposed to a tail wheel. The tail-wheel arrangement had been so ubiquitous that for many years after the overall superiority of the nose-wheel configuration was apparent, it was still referred to as the "conventional" landing gear. Although a few very early airplanes had a nose wheel, the tail-wheel configuration became dominant because it was lighter in weight, had less drag in cruise flight if the landing gear was not retractable, and was more suitable for landing fields that were formerly pastures. However, an airplane with a tail wheel is more demanding to land, particularly in a crosswind. For one thing, if the touchdown occurs with more than a modest sink rate, the rebound imparted by the main landing gear, which is located ahead of the center of gravity, will result in an increased angle of attack, causing the airplane to bounce into the air, particularly if the landing speed is too high. Absent the addition of power and aft stick, the airplane

will then settle again for an even harder touchdown and higher bounce. If the pilot responds to the original bounce by shoving the stick forward when the nose came up, the second touchdown will be harder yet. A landing gear collapse and/or a ground loop is frequently the result of poor flare technique.

If the pilot touches down smoothly in a "tail dragger," the landing is still fraught with potential for error, again because of the location of the center of gravity behind the main landing gear. It is imperative that the pilot lands with no sideward drift and keeps the airplane rolling straight once on the runway. If the touchdown occurs when the airplane is drifting sideways or a swerve is allowed to develop, both generally caused by a crosswind, the result was all too often a ground loop, with the airplane swapping ends and often departing the runway in a cloud of dust and coming to rest, often with at least one collapsed main landing gear and broken wing.

The nose-wheel configuration almost completely eliminated the likelihood of these two undesirable landing outcomes. With the main landing gear aft of the center of gravity, a sink rate on touchdown caused the nose to drop, reducing lift, not rise, increasing it. A swerve was self-correcting. Moreover, the nose wheel was usually in contact with the runway quickly, providing positive steering—particularly for a crosswind takeoff or landing and at low speeds when the rudder wasn't as effective. The tail wheel would tend to skip, reducing directional control, unless the pilot held the stick hard back; when the tail wheel was on the runway, the visibility directly forward was usually limited if not nonexistent, increasing the degree of difficulty in keeping the airplane tracking straight down the runway, which was essential to avoiding a ground loop, not to mention going off the runway itself.

The nose-wheel arrangement wasn't foolproof, however, only idiot resistant. If a pilot approached too fast and/or flared too late so the nose wheel touched down first and fairly hard, the result would be the same as too much sink rate when landing a taildragger. The airplane would rebound back into the air momentarily and then, if the pilot didn't immediately add throttle and back stick, touch down again on the nose wheel, only harder. Nose gear collapse was likely, if not on the first or second "landing," then on the third.

Because of the degree of difficulty associated with flying tail-wheel equipped airplanes, which comprised most of the operational fleet at the time, there was some controversy about introducing a trainer with a nose-wheel arrangement that didn't prepare the student for them. However, most new designs (and all jets) would have nose wheels. Training incidents/accidents would be dramatically reduced by the use of an airplane with a nose wheel and

Tail Dragger Bounce on Touchdown Without Proper Power/Pitch Correction

Too Much Sink

Rebound Pitching Up

Momentary Lift Increase

Way Too Much Sink

Finally...

In a tail dragger, if the touchdown is at too high a sink rate, the result will be a significant pitch up and momentary increase in lift because the main-landing-gear rebound is ahead of the center of gravity. Unless the subsequent pitch down and loss of lift is counteracted by quick and appropriate application of power and pitch (the instinctive and totally inappropriate response to the nose coming up is forward stick) then the next arrival will either be an even bigger bounce or the collapse of the landing gear. *T.H. Thomason*

The lack of forward visibility when landing was not the only problem with tail draggers. Taxiing a tail dragger required frequent S-turns to ensure that the way forward was clear. *US Navy*

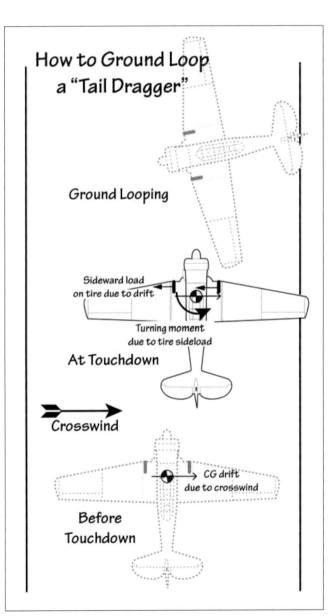

How to Ground Loop a "Tail Dragger"

Ground Looping

Sideward load on tire due to drift

Turning moment due to tire sideload

At Touchdown

Crosswind

CG drift due to crosswind

Before Touchdown

It didn't take much inattention on the part of a student pilot, particularly in a crosswind, to lose control on the landing rollout of a tail dragger and ground loop. *T.H. Thomason*

students would transition more quickly to solo. If a pilot were assigned to fly the dwindling number of airplanes with a tail wheel, only then would he need to learn its handling-quality eccentricities. Presumably an experienced pilot would also have less difficulty in picking up the nuances associated with tail-wheel landings when not burdened at the same time with learning to stay on a proper glide path for the touchdown point, timing the flare for a smooth touchdown, correcting for crosswind, etc.[4]

Even before World War II, the nose-wheel arrangement had begun to be favored by the Air Force beginning with multi-engine bombers like the Douglas B-19, Consolidated B-24, North American B-25, and Martin B-26; it provided better directional control in the event of an engine failure on the takeoff roll or a single-engine landing. The nose landing gear arrangement had almost immediately become standard on jet aircraft since they lacked the "prop wash" to help raise the tail for acceleration to takeoff speed.

E. The Air Force Trainer Competition and Selection

In 1948, the Air Force issued a Request For Proposal for its new trainer. In the process, it simplified its designation practice for trainers, eliminating the use of P for Primary, B for Basic, and A for Advanced as prefixes. The numbering for new trainers was to begin with twenty-eight since the highest number reached in the P/B/A series was the PT-27. (The AT-6 was now the T-6.) Fourteen companies submitted a total of 28 designs. The two finalists in the competition were North American and Douglas.[5] Their winning proposals were designated XT-28 and XT-30 respectively.[6] Both were powered by the 800-horsepower Wright R-1300 radial engine.

In its proposal that became the XT-28, North American placed particular emphasis on maintainability in addition to meeting all the other specific requirements. Easily opened doors were provided for access to system components. The engine accessory components mounted on the rear of the engine were accessed through the nose wheel well and an access door in the firewall that was reached with an integral ladder. The engine cowling was quick opening and self-supporting.

In order to meet the performance requirement with an 800-horsepower engine compared to the 1,100-horsepower engine in the XSN2J, North American engineers changed to new low-drag airfoils for the wing and empennage.

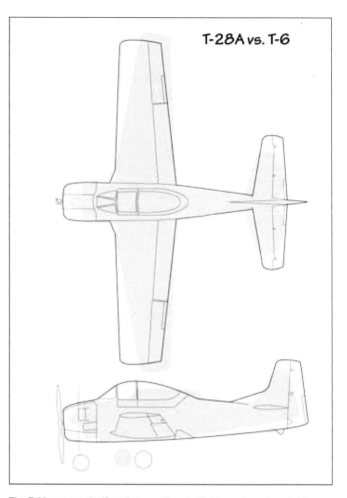

The T-28 was not significantly larger than the T-6 it was to replace but it was 50% heavier. The additional weight was not completely offset by greater horsepower. The Air Force emphasis on visibility was addressed by the tall canopy and higher seating position of the student and instructor. The more forward location of the engine and cockpit required a larger empennage. *T.H. Thomason*

The Air Force decided that its Texan trainer replacement would be configured with a nose landing gear instead of the traditional tail wheel arrangement. The large, minimally framed canopy was also now the norm for trainers rather than the multi-panel enclosure. This is an early artist's concept of North American's winning proposal, which the Air Force designated the T-28. *US Air Force*

As a result of all the redesign required to meet the Air Force's requirements, North American's proposal bore a definite resemblance to the SN2J but in fact only a handful of components were the same.[7]

The prospective XT-30 was an unusual configuration. Douglas engineers were driven in part by the Air Force requirement for good over-the-nose visibility and also, reportedly, the ease of replacing the reciprocating engine with a jet engine in the future. Its Wright R-1300 was therefore located behind the rear cockpit with an extension shaft driving the nose-mounted propeller and a cooling fan drawing air in from a nose-mounted inlet. The mid-fuselage arrangement had been proven on the Bell P-39 albeit with a liquid-cooled engine. (In the case of the P-39, the engine location was driven by the need to locate a 30 mm cannon in the nose.) Douglas claimed that there was no maintenance penalty associated with the submerged engine arrangement. There were, however, few examples of airplanes with engines buried in the fuselage and even fewer had been carried forward into production.

The Air Force evaluation favored the North American proposal for its maintainability features but expressed some concern about the airplane's rollout directional stability and turnover angle. A landing gear of a nose-wheel-configured airplane with a radial engine in its nose was forced to be relatively short coupled because of center-of-gravity considerations.[8] This reduced directional stability during rollout, particularly in crosswinds. Raising the cockpit to provide the requisite visibility over the nose resulted in a relatively high center of gravity. If a student pilot lost control on roll out and ran off the runway or landed hard on the nose wheel, the nose landing gear could fail. The result might be the airplane flipping over onto its back, a much more dire outcome than the usual result of a bad landing in the ground-loop-prone T-6/SNJ. Since this was to be an *ab initio* trainer that student pilots with little experience were expected to solo, both scenarios were distinct possibilities.

Because of its mid-fuselage-mounted engine, which allowed a slightly smaller-diameter propeller; less dihedral, which allowed the main landing gear to be farther apart; and forward cockpit location, the Douglas XT-30 had a lower turnover angle and greater directional stability on the ground. However, it also had a major potential shortcoming, overheating of the air-cooled engine during ground operation; this was all the more likely because Air Force training bases were located in the south and southwest regions of the United States.

After careful consideration of the respective potential drawbacks of the two finalists, the Air Force awarded North American a contract in May 1948 for T-28 prototypes.

However, the Air Force hedged its commitment to the North American design by also awarding a contract to Douglas for a Phase I (preliminary design and mockup) program. The statement of work included a demonstration of engine cooling during prolonged ground operations and high-power climbs using a powered test rig. In the event that the T-28 turnover-angle and ground-handling characteristics were determined to be unsatisfactory, little time would be lost in fielding a new trainer if the submerged engine installation proposed by Douglas proved to be acceptable.

The Air Force inspected the XT-30 mockup in late September 1948. To demonstrate the engine change, Douglas removed and reinstalled an actual engine in approximately twenty minutes with a crew of six mechanics using a small mobile hoist. The mockup committee agreed that the XT-30 would be no more difficult to maintain than a comparable aircraft with a conventionally mounted engine.[9]

The ground test rig consisted of a complete engine installation housed within the shape of the T-30 fuselage from the tip of the spinner to aft of the engine compartment. A total of twenty hours of ground run operation of the T-30 test rig was subsequently accomplished. The ground and climb cooling was determined to be satisfactory, as was engine accessibility.[10]

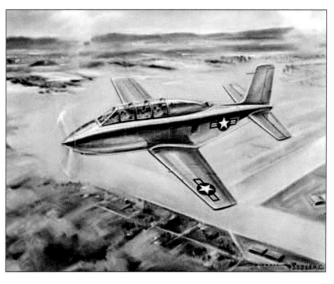

Douglas was the runner up in the Air Force's competition to replace the T-6 Texas. In order to place the cockpit forward for maximum visibility over the nose, Douglas chose to locate the big radial engine behind the rear seat, driving the nose-mounted propeller through an extension shaft. *US Air Force*

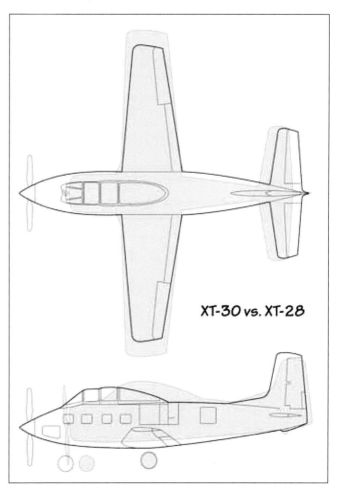

The unusual aft location of the engine allowed the XT-30's cockpits to be located well forward compared to the XT-28's. It also resulted in a lower center of gravity and a longer wheelbase, both beneficial for handling qualities during landing rollout, particularly with a stiff crosswind. *T.H. Thomason*

Although the Air Force provided North American with a contract for the XT-28, it also issued a contract to Douglas to build a mockup of its proposal, designated the XT-30, and a ground test rig of the unusual engine installation. Note the gun pod for armament training located under the left wing of the mockup. *US Air Force*

In addition to providing an evaluation of the acceptability of XT-30 engine cooling during a prolonged ground idle, the propeller blast from a Douglas B-26 was used to simulate a high-power climb, another critical engine-cooling condition. *US Air Force*

The Douglas XT-30 mockup included an actual Wright engine, which could be removed and replaced to demonstrate maintainability. *US Air Force*

It was all for naught, however, because the Air Force had decided in January 1949 to begin training students in one of the basic trainers then under consideration rather than the T-28. In a tech report it is stated: "Since the XT-28 will not be used as a basic trainer, it can be assumed that the theoretical difficulties in the ground handling characteristics, because of the landing gear geometry, can be counteracted by pilot technique and that material improvement in ground stability over the T-6 aircraft will be realized."[11] Since there was no longer justification for a backup trainer, the XT-30 program effort ended with the conclusion of its Phase I contract.[12]

The XT-28, 48-1371, first flew on September 24, 1949 at the Los Angeles International Airport, piloted by NAA test pilot Jean "Skip" Ziegler. An order for 266 T-28As followed with the popular name of Trojan.

The Air Force, perhaps concerned about the compatibility of a student pilot and 800 horsepower, evaluated a Navy XNQ-1 in 1947 as a candidate for a new primary[13] training airplane. As a result, it planned to order almost identical T-31s from Fairchild. As will be described in Chapter 3, that procurement was delayed and production never implemented. Due to the delay (and in consideration of the risk of problems in the development and production of the T-28) an upgrade to the T-6 fleet was initiated in 1949. Selected Texans were refurbished to the T-6G configuration. The airframes were completely stripped down and cleaned, the engines and propellers overhauled, and the avionics upgraded.

The XT-30 ground test rig consisted of a complete engine/drive train/propeller installation and a fuselage shape from the tip of the spinner to the rear of the engine compartment. The ground rig was remotely controlled from a blockhouse. *US Air Force*

The XT-28's first flight was accomplished on September 24, 1949. The prototype was equipped with an ejection seat since the development program would include relatively high-risk evaluations and demonstrations. The booms extending from each wingtip are equipped with flight-test instrumentation. *US Air Force*

Because of concerns about the timely delivery of T-28s to the training command, the Air Force elected to refurbish a number of T-6s, including upgraded avionics. One of the changes was to incorporate a steerable tail wheel similar to the arrangement on the P-51. The modified Texans were designated T-6G, readily identified by the large ADF antenna behind the canopy. *US Air Force*

From the front, the excellent view of the T-28 over the nose due to its nose landing gear arrangement is readily apparent. The width of the propeller blades compared to its diameter is indicative of the increased engine horsepower of the T-28 compared to the T-6. *T.H. Thomason*

F. T-28A Description

The nose wheel was not only a new feature for trainers, the T-28A's was steerable. (The T-6G's tail wheel was steerable to a limited degree, moving with the rudder when the stick was full aft.)

The nose-wheel configuration significantly improved the visibility forward when taxiing. The over-the-nose visibility requirement in flight was provided by a high seating position under a large canopy. The canopy segments over the front and rear seats were opened by hydraulic power. The canopy sill was relatively low; with the canopies open, much of the pilot's torso was exposed, an advantage for entry/exit and more importantly, for bailout. (During taxi with the canopy open, it has been likened to riding an elephant.)

The T-28 had a notably large amount of dihedral, the angle of the wing relative to the horizon when viewed from the front or rear. Eight degrees was often seen on flying model airplanes for stability but rarely incorporated on a piloted airplane. While an excessive amount of stability would not be appropriate for a fighter, the extra dihedral meant that the T-28 would be slow to diverge into a spiral dive if the student were distracted from flying the airplane for any reason.

There were significant features related to initial cost and maintainability. For example, the outer wing panels could be removed without disconnecting the aileron cable system. The horizontal stabilizers were identical. Two men could remove a horizontal stabilizer or the vertical fin in ten minutes. The left and right elevators and trim tabs were also interchangeable.

The trainer was almost as well equipped from a navigation and communication standpoint for cross-country instrument flight as any commercial airliner: VHF radio, four-leg range receiver, marker beacon receiver, radio compass, and instrument landing system.

The T-28A was heavier and somewhat bigger than the T-6 it replaced.

	T-6/SNJ	T-28A
Wing Span (ft.)	42	40
Length (ft.)	29	32
Gross Weight (lbs.)	5,282	7,812
Horsepower (Take Off)	600	800
Internal Fuel (gallons)	111	125
Limit Load Factor	5.3 @ 5,500 lbs	6.9 @7,550 lbs
Power to Weight (hp/lb.)	0.11	0.10

Although the power-to-weight ratio remained about the same as the T-6's, T-28A performance was noted for being anemic, particularly on takeoff. It may have had something to do with the sound difference. The T-6 propeller tips were moving at a fairly high speed that created a loud snarl in some flight conditions; the T-28A's Wright engine's distinctive aural signature was more of an ugly clatter.

The usual takeoff weight for early T-28As was about 6,900 lbs. The gross weight of later ones with the added fuel capacity was about 500 pounds heavier. The maximum takeoff weight that could be reached with the addition of external stores was 7,900 pounds.

The original T-28 design included a belly-mounted speed brake located on the belly of the fuselage between the main landing gear wheel wells and the baggage compartment. As one result of its XT-28A flight evaluation, the Air Force Training Command determined that a speed brake was not required. *US Air Force*

The first T-28s featured a turnover truss between the pilot and the instructor. In the event that a crash resulted in the airplane upside down, this protected them from injury. Part way through the production run, the T-28A turnover truss was eliminated and the canopy profile was lowered to reduce drag. *US Air Force*

G. T-28 Development and Qualification

The two XT-28As were equipped with speed brakes. These were deleted for production although provisions were retained according to the T-28 Flight Handbook.

The fuel capacity was increased by fifty-two gallons beginning with sn. 51-3463 via an additional tank in each wing outboard of the main tank. The rollover pylon (turnover truss bar per North American) that had been incorporated due to the potential for turnover proved to be unnecessary and was deleted. As a result, after evaluation on 49-1709, the canopy was lowered four inches effective with 51-3763. The windscreen angle was increased by 2.5 degrees. These changes improved the instructor's visibility forward and were a slight benefit to speed and range.

H. Armament Training

The T-28A also had provisions for armament training: pylons on the wings and a gun sight. It could be configured to carry a single .50 caliber machine gun in a pod under each wing. The pod contained 100 rounds of ammunition and the cartridges were retained in the pod. Alternatively, the pylons could be loaded with bombs, a practice-bomb container, or a three-tube rocket launcher. The first 600 or so T-28As were equipped with the A-1CM sighting system; 51-3663 and subsequent T-28As had the N-9-1 fixed sight that was more appropriate for dropping bombs.

I. T-28 Air Force Service

The first-production T-28As were delivered in April 1950. Production totaled 1,194 airplanes although not all were delivered to the US Air Force. Together with the T-6G, they initially provided all the Air Force flight training prior to the students' transition to the T-33 jet trainer. In November 1952, however, initial screening of student-pilot candidates once again began to be accomplished with civilian contractors in light civil airplanes like the Piper Cub.[14] This provided an early and relatively inexpensive means of weeding out those with a previously unrealized fear of flight, the poor souls prone to airsickness, the klutzes with little coordination, slow learners/thinkers, etc.

Some wags opined that the T-28's lack of power, particularly evident on takeoff, was intended to accustom the student pilot to the sluggish acceleration of the early jets that did not have afterburners. The Wright engine, in addition to sounding rough, did have to be handled with some care to prevent actual failure of a cylinder. Early problems with crankshaft failures were subsequently eliminated, however. Nevertheless, the engine was never popular; for one thing, it was difficult to tell the difference between it running normally and badly. Student pilots, particularly in formation flying and aerobatics, tended to treat the engine roughly. This shortened its life and occasionally justified the emphasis placed early in flight training on finding and utilizing a place to more or less safely land/crash the airplane after an engine failure.

The T-28 had provisions for mounting a .50-caliber gun pod (shown here) and weapons pylons on its wings for armament training. *US Air Force*

The Air Force reinstituted a screening program in the early 1950s, buying 242 PA-18 Piper Cubs with bucket seats to accommodate a parachute, a larger horizontal stabilizer, wings with no flaps, toe brakes instead of heel brakes, and a 108 hp engine. The CAA registration "N" numbers ended with T, so they were referred to as the Tango Cubs. *Mark Frankel Collection*

One of the military training requirements that had no commercial counterpart was formation flying. In order of degree of difficulty from highest to lowest, the requisite tasks to be mastered were joining up, changing lead or position, holding formation, and breaking up. *US Air Force*

The aircraft was pleasant to fly, with light control loads and an excellent roll rate. The incipient stall was clearly heralded by significant buffeting. Accidentally spinning a T-28 was unlikely; if forced to spin, it did not resist recovery. It was fully aerobatic except for "snap rolls," which were prohibited. The snap roll was initiated from level flight at a speed well above stall by jerking full back on the stick, resulting in an accelerated stall (i.e., at a speed above normal 1 g stall) and kicking a rudder. The result was a spin, in effect, but with the airplane traveling forward during the first turn rather than downward. The maneuver imposed fairly high loads on the T-28's aft fuselage, which was weakened by the large structural opening aft of the wing for a baggage compartment. A snap-roll entry that was overly enthusiastic would result in a permanent twist of the fuselage between the wing and the empennage, requiring a major structural repair or more likely, the early retirement of that airframe.

The T-28As had a short career in the Air Force as trainers, being replaced by jets in Primary beginning at Bainbridge Air Base, Georgia, in 1957. They last departed the training command in 1960. These were relatively new airplanes (the last-production T-28A for the Air Force had been delivered in 1953) so many soldiered in other roles and applications. For example, there were National Guard squadrons that had to give up their North American F-51 Mustangs due to service-life issues and were waiting for their runways to be lengthened for jets; these were issued T-28As to maintain a modicum of proficiency. The last of these assignments ended in 1959.

The T-28 had a large door on the bottom of the fuselage just aft of the wing. It provided access to a small cargo/baggage compartment, a convenience for cross-country flights. However, the structural cutout resulted in a restriction against snap rolls. *US Air Force*

The Navy evaluated two T-28As as a replacement for its aging SNJ Texans. This one, BuNo 137636, was subsequently modified with the T-28B's engine installation. *US Air Force*

As evidenced by these Barin Field SNJ's, Navy's Texans were long overdue for replacement, not having been through as extensive a modification and upgrade program as the Air Force's T-6s. *US Navy*

J. The Navy Comes on Board

Although there had been a big surplus of SNJs after the war, student pilots tend to be hard on airplanes. By 1952, the Navy really needed a replacement. It evaluated two T-28As as Bureau Numbers 137636 and 137637 in 1951, primarily for procurement as an advanced instrument trainer to replace the SNJs then being used. The Navy required a more powerful engine, however. North American redesigned the engine installation to accommodate one. North American test pilot "Bob" Hoover made the first flight of the prototype T-28B, modified from 137636, on April 6, 1953.[15]

In 1962, the Department of Defense-directed a service-wide common designation of aircraft. Although the change received a great deal of attention and gnashing of teeth, the Air Force and the Navy had agreed in principal in 1952 to use a common designation system, starting with trainers and progressing to transports, with the follow-on procurement by a service to use the designation originally given it by the other service. The Navy therefore gave its new trainer the designation T-28B rather than T2J as it would have been under its existing methodology.[16]

The production T-28B primarily differed from the Air Force T-28A in having a three-bladed propeller driven by the much more powerful Wright R-1820-86 engine in a notably larger cowling. Whereas the T-28A trundled aloft pulled by a maximum of 800 horses, the B leaped into the air behind 1,425. Although the B had a 20% higher gross weight 8,095 lbs, it was more than offset by a 78% increase in horsepower, resulting in a weight-to-horsepower ratio of 5.8. The engine was mounted with a down-thrust angle of five degrees, twice that of the T-28A, because of the higher thrust of the big Wright driving a three-bladed propeller.

The service ceiling increased by about 50%, a significant improvement provided in large part by the single-stage supercharger of the R-1820. The additional performance at altitude, however, required that the pilot manually shift to supercharging when climbing through approximately 13,500 feet for military power or 15,000 feet for normal rated power. This was accomplished—like shifting the manual transmission in an automobile—by first reducing the power with the throttle and rpm control, changing to the high blower setting, and then pushing the rpm and throttle back up to climb power. Mismanagement of the shift risked overboosting the engine, which shortened its life, as did forgetting to change back to the lower blower setting when descending through the critical altitude and then adding enough power to overboost the engine.

The first flight of the T-28B, modified from one of the Navy's two T-28As, was accomplished by North American test pilot Robert A. "Bob" Hoover, pictured here. *T.H. Thomason collection*

The T-28B's bigger engine required a bigger cowling and oil cooler installation. Early T-28Bs were delivered with the original T-28A nose wheel. A smaller nose wheel was subsequently substituted, possibly to provide for a more nose-down stance for the takeoff and landing rolls. *US Air Force*

The deleted T-28A speed brake installation was reinstated on the T-28B. Although unnecessary in a propeller-driven airplane that had a built-in speed brake, i.e. the propeller, it served to familiarize the student with the function of the speed brake that was a necessary feature on jet airplanes. It came with a flight-manual caution. When deployed, the speed brake caused a nose-up pitching moment that increased with speed. Even though North American incorporated a limiter valve in the speed-brake hydraulic system to keep it from opening fully at high speeds, a "large" forward stick movement was required above 250-knots indicated airspeed to counter the pitch up and avoid overstressing the airframe. As a result, "the speed brake should not be extended at the initiation of or during a high-speed pullout."

There were other minor changes. At the time, the Navy had yet to appreciate the benefit of nose-wheel steering (it was also believed to limit the ability to turn tightly, a drawback on a crowded aircraft carrier deck) so it was deleted, requiring the pilot to steer with the brakes at low speeds. The battery was moved further aft in the fuselage to help balance the heavier engine.

The T-28Bs were first delivered to Navy Advanced Instrument squadrons beginning in 1954. The 489 production T-28Bs also replaced the SNJs for all Basic training except for carrier qualification, which remained the province of the SNJ-5Cs. Almost all were built at the North American plant in Downey, California, with the last forty-nine or so produced in a Navy-owned plant in Columbus, Ohio, along with other North American airplanes being built for the Navy.

At one point, there were eleven Navy training squadrons operating T-28Bs, nine in the Pensacola, Florida, area and another two at Meridian, Mississippi. It served far longer in the Navy training command than in the Air Force's. Capt. William B. Nevius, USN (Ret.) was a flight instructor in T-28Bs with ATU-803 in 1955 when his daughter Colleen was born. The day he brought his wife and daughter home from the hospital, he had been flying BuNo 137648. Colleen attended Purdue University on the Naval ROTC program, which had just been opened up to women. Upon graduation in 1977, she was accepted for Naval Aviation training, which had just been made available to women. She soloed in 1978 in the same T-28 that her father had flown twenty-three years earlier.[17]

The Navy reinstated the T-28's belly-mounted speed brake for its training requirements. It was now perforated to reduce buffet when extended. *US Navy*

The Navy T-28s were originally painted overall orange-yellow like the SNJs. This is T-28B, BuNo 137724, fresh off the North American production line as the eighty-seventh built. It does not yet have the tail code applied of the training unit to which it was assigned. *US Navy*

In 1959, the T-28 paint scheme was changed to red and white; the tail codes had previously changed to one number and one letter to indicate the unit, in this case "2P" for VT-6. *US Navy*

VT-27, based at NAS Corpus Christi, Texas, was the last squadron to provide training in the T-28B. In 1979, the Basic training syllabus totaled about sixty-five hours. During this phase, the student was taught to fly, soloed, and received initial instruction on instrument, aerobatic, night, and formation flying. If selected for jets, the student then moved on NAS Kingsville or Beeville in Texas or NAS Meridian, Mississippi for intermediate training. VT-27's last training flight using the T-28 landed in early 1984. The Navy Training Command's last T-28B, BuNo 137796, was ferried to the Naval Support Facility at Anacostia, Virginia on March 14, 1984, for static display.

This ATU-800 T-28B flying over Corpus Christi was marked with light green bands on the fuselage and wings at the time to warn the pilots of other airplanes that it is being used for instrument training. The student is in the rear cockpit, covered by the "bag" so he has to fly solely by reference to his instruments. *US Navy via Doug Siegfried*

K. The Navy T-28 Goes Aboard

Landing on an aircraft carrier is one of the significant differentiators between Air Force and Navy pilot training. It is a very exacting maneuver, requiring precise low-speed control and glide-slope/lineup positioning. Even the moment to turn in from downwind onto final approach dictated precision because of the need to keep a close interval, but not too close, on the airplane ahead in the pattern so as to minimize the time the carrier has to spend on the course required to keep the wind aligned with the landing area.

The Navy used the SNJ for carrier-landing training by modifying it to add a tailhook and minimally beefing-up of the aft fuselage structure. *US Navy*

One of the most difficult tasks to master in aviation is landing aboard an aircraft, even more so before the introduction of the angled deck. Being low on approach risked crashing into the stern of the ship or striking the ramp; being high/low virtually guaranteed a trip into the steel cables that formed a barrier for the airplanes and personnel forward. The margin of error was small. *US Navy*

Before being allowed to land aboard a carrier, the student pilot spent several hours in Field Carrier Landing Practice. Here, the LSO is giving the student a wave-off signal to abort the approach and go around the pattern for another landing attempt. *US Navy*

The aiming point for landing on a carrier is moving in six ways: translating as surge, heave, and sway; and rotating in roll, pitch, and yaw; sometimes, all at the same time. Not to mention that the landing area is small, moving away, and there is turbulence behind it. Missing the touchdown area was fraught with peril: sinking too much just a bit short of the deck would result in the dreaded ramp strike or even crashing into the stern of the ship; touching down a little too long on a straight-deck carrier wasn't much better, because it meant being stopped by steel-cable barriers rather than the arresting wires.

Before the introduction of the angled deck, the technique used for landing on the carrier was virtually identical to that for landing on a short field: "dragging it in" at a speed just above stall with enough power to maintain level flight just above deck level, then "cutting" the power just before the beginning of the runway. Because of the low speed and height above deck, the airplane would immediately settle onto the landing area just forward of the ramp, maximizing

Trainer handling qualities were very important. Low speed handling qualities—particularly accurate control of pitch, roll, and yaw—just above stall, were especially important for carrier operations. Here, an SNJ-5C pilot has stalled and is about to crash into the water during carrier qualifications aboard *Monterey* (CVL-26) in August 1953. *US Navy*

the distance available for the airplane's tailhook to pick up one of series of arresting gear cables stretched across the deck before hitting the first barrier. The likelihood that the tailhook would not engage a cable had been reduced by development test involving an extensive test series of arrested landings of every carrier-based airplane, first ashore and then at sea. However, poor pilot technique or bad luck occasionally resulted in a hook skip, bounce, or delayed touchdown that resulted in the tailhook missing all the cables and a trip into the barriers. Training insured the inculcation of the right technique.

Most importantly, a Landing Signal Officer (LSO) was on hand to coach the pilot as to speed, altitude, and line-up prior to cutting the engine for landing. The LSO was positioned on the left side of the landing area. He would ultimately give one of two signals, the wave off or the cut, both of which were mandatory. Being waved off meant that the deck wasn't ready for a landing, the plane wasn't properly configured for landing (flaps, landing gear, or hook not down), or the pilot had no chance of correcting his position to one that was satisfactory for a cut, the signal to chop the power for landing. The pilot could choose to wave himself off and go around for another attempt. The cut was solely the responsibility of the LSO and not to be second-guessed or anticipated by the pilot.

The process was so exacting and critical that it was preceded by many hours of shore-based approaches and landings. Initial carrier landings were also so fraught with peril (and the lack of time for an instructor to correct an error at the cut) that the initial at-sea qualifications were accomplished solo with instructors observing from the safety of the deck.

During World War II, the trainer for carrier qualification was the SNJ-3/4/5C, with the C suffix indicating that it was equipped with a Navy-installed tail hook for carrier landings. It was sturdy and had the added advantage of not requiring the student to check out in a different, more powerful airplane for carrier qualification.

Even the fleet of carrier-capable SNJs was not going to last forever, particularly given the wear and tear of high-sink-rate touchdowns and high loads in the aft fuselage inevitable in arrested landings aboard an aircraft carrier. The logical replacement was the T-28. The first T-28C, was

modified from a T-28B for a first flight on September 19, 1955. (In this case, the C no longer stood for carrier-compatibility but was simply the next revision letter alphabetically.) The lower aft fuselage and rudder were notched to accommodate a tail hook, the landing gear modified for greater oleo stroke to absorb even harder touchdowns, and the propeller shortened to provide an additional five inches of ground clearance and hopefully avoid the pecking of the deck after an in-flight engagement. (The blades were slightly wider to maintain the solidity.) The changes resulted in a gross weight increase of about 250 lbs, which slightly reduced speed, rate of climb, service ceiling and range, but not by enough to compromise its training effectiveness.

T-28B, BuNo 138187, was modified with a tailhook for shore-based and at-sea carrier landing evaluation of the T-28C configuration. At-sea qualification was accomplished from *Tarawa*, CVS-40, in November 1955. *US Navy*

	T-28B	T-28C
EMPTY	6502	6778
BASIC	6556	6778
GROSS	8095	8247
MAXIMUM LOAD FACTOR	6.2 AT 8,038 LBS	6 AT 8,216 LBS
MAXIMUM SPEED (KTS.)	290	286
SERVICE CEILING (FT.)	35,600	34,300
SEA LEVEL RATE OF CLIMB (FPM)	3070	2830
RANGE (NM)	830	750

(All data from respective Standard Aircraft Characteristics Charts)

The Naval Air Test Center (NATC) accomplished at-sea carrier suitability testing of the T-28C (actually T-28B BuNo 138187 modified to the carrier configuration) in November 1955 aboard the *Essex*-class aircraft carrier *Tarawa* (CVS-40). Lt.Cdr. W.F. Tobin and Lt. Robert R. King accomplished fifty landings during the at-sea evaluation that had been preceded by the usual and extensive shore-based testing.

Introduction of the T-28C for carrier qualification was delayed until April 1957 when an *Essex*-class carrier with an angle-deck, *Antietam* (CVS-36), became available to replace the smaller, more challenging, straight-deck CVL.

At that point, the days of the SNJ in the Navy were numbered. The last training flight in one was completed on May 21, 1958. The last SNJ was retired from the Navy in February 1960.

North American produced 299 T-28Cs between 1955 and 1957. It was operated by four training squadrons in the Pensacola, Florida area: VT-2, 3, and 6 at NAS Whiting Field and VT-5 at Saufley Field.

The T-28Bs and C could be configured for armament training like the T-28A. An Mk 8 gun sight would be installed for armament training. Training provisions also included the use of a few T-28Bs incorporating a two-pod system for streaming a tow target, with the cable being carried in one pod and the banner in the other. Strakes on the T-28C cowling were required to be installed when underwing armament was carried. During qualification testing in late 1956, North American determined that the aft fuselage and rudder modification required for the tailhook resulted in unsatisfactory spin recovery characteristics. NACA was requested to conduct wind-tunnel spin tests. These established the strake configuration that provided satisfactory spin recovery with the gun pods installed.

Like the SNJ, the T-28C was not capable of being catapulted from the carrier. This pack of T-28Cs is positioned for deck-run takeoffs by students about to carrier qualify aboard *Antietam* (CVS-36) circa 1959. *US Navy*

The pilot of this T-28 has fully configured it for the upcoming carrier landing: hook, landing gear, and flaps down; speed brake extended; and canopy open for rapid exit in the unlikely event of a water landing. *US Navy*

The T-28Cs were used for other training requirements in addition to carrier takeoffs and landings. This one is armed with the machine gun pods for gunnery training. The spin-strakes just visible on the side of the cowl were required when the gun pod was installed. *US Navy*

L. The T-28: Filling One Square but Not Sufficient

The T-28 was the first really new trainer to reach the Air Force and Navy training commands in a decade and a significant improvement over the legacy T-6 trainers. However both services had now came to the conclusion that the T-28, a big and complex airplane, was not cost effective for *ab initio* students. A smaller, simpler, and cheaper airplane would be more appropriate in primary training for the purpose of identifying students who were likely to wash out before completing the training program.

The services had also been reequipping as rapidly as possible with jet fighters and bombers. While the T-28 was initially more than adequate for the basic/intermediate training phases, the training commands in both services were beginning to wonder whether too much "unlearning" was being required of new pilots who were moving on in advanced training to jets.

As a result, development and evaluation of new trainers to address both of these issues began to receive more attention and funding priority. The Air Force would again lead the way.

The Navy kept its T-28s in service for far longer than the Air Force did. Nevertheless, the time would eventually come for its retirement due to attrition, if nothing else. In this case, an engine failure might have ended this T-28C's service life. *US Navy*

Chapter Two Endnotes

1. The large difference in Bureau Numbers between the XNQ-1 and the SN2J-1 appears to be that the XNQ-1 was assigned two unused BuNos that had originally been planned for Sikorsky helicopters.

2. Fairchild advertisement, "Gleam in the Eye of a Navy Cadet," *Fortune* (1/1947): 35.

3. The Army Air Forces became the independent United States Air Force on 18 September 1947.

4. As it happened, the Air Force subsequently introduced a pilot-screening program that used light general aviation airplanes with tail wheels, providing an early introduction to the takeoff and landing nuances of that configuration.

5. Stanley Evans, "USAF Trainer Aircraft, *Flight*, December 22, 1949: 2032-2033.

6. The T-29 was a twin-engine transport built by Convair. The Air Force, and subsequently the Navy, used it as a flying classroom for navigator training.

7. According to Kevin Thompson in his book, *North American Aircraft, Volume 2, 1934–1999*, p.9, "The only usable parts of the XSN2J-1 were the canopy operating mechanism, the rudder pedal hangers and a few odds and ends."

8. On a twin-engine airplane with a nose landing gear, the heavy engines were located much farther aft relative to the center of gravity. As a result, its nose, and therefore the nose landing gear, could be extended well forward.

9. AMC Memorandum Report No. MCREOA-5-8 dated October 13, 1948, Mock-up Inspection of the XT-30 Airplane.

10. Douglas Reports No. Dev-279 and -245.

11. AF Technical Report No. 6161 dated September 1950, Final Douglas XT-30 Trainer Aircraft Phase I Report, R.C. Anderson, Major, USAF.

12. As it happened, the Air Force did not proceed with the procurement of a primary trainer in time to provide a lead-in to the T-28. However, the concerns about student pilots losing control on landing and winding upside down proved to be unwarranted.

13. At the time, the Air Force had combined the primary and basic training phases into one, basic.

14. Ann Krueger Hussey, *Air Force Flight Screening*, p.20.

15. Robert A. "Bob' Hoover was one of the students who almost washed out of Air Force flight screening due to airsickness; he conquered it and went on to get his wings, fly in combat, become a test pilot, and—most notably—one of the best demonstration pilots of all time.

16. The Navy had changed from the prefix N for trainer to T in 1953 and had already designated a final variant of the SNJ as the TJ. The Navy also designated snow-ski equipped C-130Bs it bought for use in Antarctica support as UV-1Ls but soon changed the designation to C-130BL to simplify communication with the Air Force supply system. Ironically, in the 1962 Department of Defense designation standardization, the C-130BL was redesignated LC-130F.

17. Howard Wheeler, Commander USN, "T-28 Spans the Generation Gap," *Naval Aviation News* (July 1982): 22-23. Colleen Nevius went on to become the first female aviator to graduate from the Naval Test Pilot School and retired as a Captain in 2001.

Chapter Three
BEECHCRAFT T-34—THE FIRST MODERN PRIMARY TRAINER

The Air Force T-28 was the first new US trainer produced in over a decade. Initially it was intended to serve both primary and basic training needs, but second thoughts emerged about using such a complex, high-powered airplane for inexperienced primary students and interest in a lighter airplane gained favor. The Navy had already come to that conclusion a few years earlier when it contracted for and evaluated a new design for its primary/basic training requirement; a production contract was not issued due to the federal budget austerity of the late 1940s. The Air Force chose to start fresh in 1947, but a series of halting decisions, aggressive contractor marketing, interservice disputes, and funding issues resulted in a procurement program that required two fly-off competitions, the use of eighteen aircraft,[1] and seven years to complete. Nevertheless it produced the highly successful T-34 Mentor—the first modern primary trainer.

The process began on April 26, 1945 with the publication of Navy trainer specification, (NAVAER SD-400). The only respondent was the Fairchild Engine and Airplane Corp, which offered a two-place tandem, all metal low-wing monoplane. The Navy awarded Fairchild a development contract for the XNQ-1 as described in chapter 2.[2] Realizing that funding for the new trainer was uncertain, the Navy attempted to interest the Army Air Force (AAF) in a joint contract. This would result in a sharing of development costs and lowering of unit costs. In May 1946 the Navy invited the AAF to examine the Fairchild trainer, but the offer was declined because their post-war training program was still in a tentative stage. In August, the AAF finally agreed to inspect the XNQ-1, however they determined that it did not meet their emerging Training Command requirements. In a last-ditch effort, the Navy invited the Army Air Force to attend the service acceptance trials of

the XNQ-1 at the Naval Air Test Center, Patuxent River, Maryland in May 1947. The new Fairchild trainer performed so impressively that the AAF reconsidered its position and began to evaluate the XNQ-1 for Air Reserve, Air National Guard, and national emergency needs. Four months after the Patuxent River trials the Army Air Force became the United States Air Force (USAF), a separate branch of the military with separate funding. With new budget resources, the Air Force requested funds for the procurement of 334 Fairchild NQs (since it was no longer experimental the X had been dropped; the Air Force subsequently changed the designation to T-31A). In the fall of 1948 the Secretary of the Air Force, Stuart Symington, presented a plan to the Secretary of Defense, James Forrestal, to make funds available for the first 100 T-31As. On January 6, 1949, President Truman approved the procurement funds, but they were never spent. Just as the T-31 contract was about to be negotiated the Air Force decided to examine a last-minute proposal from Walter Beech.[3]

The Fairchild XNQ-1 was initially the only response to the Navy's April 1945 trainer specification. From the outset it seemed certain that the XNQ-1 would go into production, but the government never awarded a contract. *Naval History and Heritage Command*

The second Fairchild XNQ-1, Bureau Number 75726, showing its retractable landing gear—a novel feature for a primary trainer at that time. *Naval History and Heritage Command*

In 1947, the Air Force became an independent branch of the service and planned to purchase the Fairchild trainer now designated T-31, but the contract was never awarded. *Naval History and Heritage Command*

A. Walter Beech Enters the Competition

Walter Beech had become a major force in the aviation industry by the end of WWII. He was a self-taught pioneer who founded two successful companies, built numerous landmark aircraft, and counted Charles Lindbergh and Amelia Earhart among his customers.

Beech had joined with two other aviation notables, Lloyd Stearman and Clyde Cessna, in 1925 to form the Travel Air Manufacturing Company. Cessna provided most of the $30,000 capital needed for the new venture and was named president. The company rented a small portion (less than 1,000 square feet) of the Kansas Planning Mill Co. factory in downtown Wichita. Their first airplane had no specific name, it was merely called the Travel Air, but it employed the steel tube frame that Beech and Stearman championed as the limitations of wooden framed airplanes became apparent. The Travel Air was more streamlined than other airplanes of the period and used several features that made it a remarkably efficient design. It could reach a maximum speed of nearly 100 miles per hour using the same ninety-hp OX-5 engine that powered the 75 mph World War I Jenny. It could lift almost its own weight in payload, and it could carry two passengers in comfort in its wide forward cockpit (a feature borrowed from the Laird Swallow). Balanced ailerons were used to relieve heavy pressures in the roll axis, and redundant steel cables were used to move the elevator providing full pitch control even if one cable failed. Pitch trim was available from the cockpit which gave the pilot enough authority to land the airplane.

From the outset Walter Beech was convinced the most effective way to sell airplanes was to win at air racing. During the mid-1920s the public was becoming increasingly air minded and air races were attracting huge audiences that loved the spectacle of new airplanes performing to their limits. Walter Beech's marketing strategy proved correct—most airplane customers based their purchase decisions on the outcome of these contests.

Beech, Stearman, and Cessna subsequently parted ways, each to head airplane companies in the Wichita area named for themselves, and each would also play a significant role in developing trainers for the US military during WWII.

Following World War II Walter Beech was quick to realize that a modern training fleet was essential to maintaining America's air might. The government, however, wasn't interested since the armistice left the military with thousands of training aircraft, little need to train new pilots, and little budget to spend on non-tactical aircraft.

Walter Beech in 1947 at the time he decided to use private funds to build a modern primary trainer based on his Bonanza design. *Beechcraft Heritage Museum via Robert Parmerter*

Yet this fleet of trainers had become obsolete; their large-radial engines consumed enormous amounts of fuel and their landing gear was prone to ground loops, which resulted in propeller strikes and airframe damage. Training costs had become unnecessarily high, but worse, the leftover Stearmans and Texans were not suited for preparing students to fly the new generation of airplanes entering front line service. After all, the new tactical aircraft had tricycle landing gear with modern cockpits and jet engines that handled nothing like the old radial-powered trainers.

The Model 35 Bonanza was an innovative post war design that flew for the first time on December 22, 1945. It was an immediate success and became the basis for Walter Beech's modern trainer proposal to the military, the Model D-45 Mentor. The Bonanza gained a reputation for durability and high performance with superb flying qualities. More than 1,500 examples of the Model 35 were built, this is the oldest airworthy example, serial D18 built in 1946. *Robert Burns Beechcraft Heritage Museum via Robert Parmerter*

In 1947 Beech decided to take an enormous risk and build three experimental trainer prototypes using his own funds. His ardent sales instinct assured him that the risk would pay off handsomely. Beech based the new trainer on his successful civilian Model 35 Bonanza using many of the same components. The Bonanza was a blend of proven features and radical new ones. The most radical was the Bonanza's empennage. Instead of conventional horizontal and vertical stabilizers mounted perpendicular to each other, the Model 35 had only two tail surfaces mounted at a thirty-degree angle to the fuselage, forming a distinctive "V tail." The control surfaces moved in unison to provide pitch authority and moved in opposition to provide yaw authority. This unique tail offered weight savings and drag reduction. The Bonanza used retractable tricycle landing gear, which made ground handling far more positive than conventional landing gear with a tail wheel arrangement. It could carry four in a modern cabin cruising at 180 miles per hour using only 165 horsepower.

The Bonanza's first flight took place in December 1945, and customer deliveries started in February 1947.

Relying on his proven marketing strategy, Beech staged a record setting event to make the public aware of the new airplane. In March 1949, William P. Olden flew a Bonanza (named the "Waikiki Beech") non-stop from Honolulu to Teterboro Airport in New Jersey- a distance of 5,273 miles. Olden consumed only 272.25 gallons of fuel with the 165 horsepower Continental engine. The Bonanza's speed and efficiency convinced Beech that it could be made into an ideal military trainer.

Beech committed substantial engineering talent, marketing resources and capital to develop the trainer, which became known as the Model D-45 Mentor. It was a sleek, all-metal, low-wing airframe with retractable tricycle landing gear. It used a two-place tandem cockpit enclosed by a large bubble canopy that gave the student and instructor ample 360-degree visibility. Its fuselage was slightly narrower than the Bonanza's and it used a conventional tail (though one example was proposed to use a "V" tail). The first two prototypes, N8591A and N8592A, were powered by 185-horsepower, six-cylinder, horizontally opposed Continental E-185-8 engines, while a 225-horsepower E-225-8 was installed in the third prototype, N8593A. The Mentor was designed with a more robust structure than the Bonanza and could withstand an impressive 10 positive and 4.5 negative Gs.

The D-45 made its first flight on December 2, 1948, flown by company test pilot Vern L. Carstens, who declared the flight a complete success. He commented: "I like its roomy cockpits, its excellent visibility from either seat. It's a very stable airplane: directionally, laterally, and longitudinally. It has the performance and characteristics to make it a good trainer."[3] One week later the Beechcraft Director of Military Sales, Lynn D. Richardson, sent a letter to the Air Force Procurement Division requesting an opportunity to demonstrate the new trainer. This was followed by a lengthy press release intended for a Sunday morning newspaper publication on December 12. The purpose of the press release was to make the general public aware of the Mentor's virtues and pressure the military into replacing their outmoded trainers. The press release pointed out six justifications for an Air Force order:

1. The Mentor was stronger than other trainers of the day.
2. The Mentor was ready for immediate delivery.
3. It was built largely of "non-strategic" materials, which would not divert critical assets from important tactical programs.
4. Beech estimated that it could deliver a complete unit for $20,000—about half the price of any other comparable trainer.
5. The Model 45 would be substantially more economical to operate than the BT-13 or AT-6, saving as much as 150,000 gallons of gasoline and $9,700 in engine maintenance costs per aircraft over a five year period.
6. Bonanza parts commonality provided the Mentor with a large inventory of spares plus a nationwide network of Beech service stations that could provide maintenance when the Mentor was away from its home base.[4]

Walter Beech's sales tactics bore fruit when Col. G. E. Schaetzel issued a memo questioning the unorthodox procurement process surrounding the Fairchild NQ/T-31 trainer. He argued that the Air Force had never published the specific military characteristics expected of their new trainer, and he pointed out, "the Beech Aircraft Corporation have, as a result of direct contact with personnel of the Training Command, modified their Bonanza aircraft so as to make it meet the expressed desires of the Training Command."[5] Col. Schaetzel suggested that a set of military characteristics be drafted, and that a fly-off competition be held between the Fairchild and Beechcraft airplanes. His position was supported by the Under Secretary of the Air Force who wrote a memo in favor of the Beech D-45, and proposed an evaluation within forty-five days.

The first Model D-45 Mentor prototype. Because it was based on the successful Model B-35 Bonanza it carried a high level of parts commonality with the Bonanza fleet, a fact that Beech used as a selling point to the military. Since the first three Mentors were factory owned they carried civilian registrations. *NARA*

One of the three D-45 prototypes over the Kansas countryside. It was clear from the outset that the Mentor had exceptional flying qualities. *Naval History and Heritage Command*

A Beechcraft official demonstrates the modern cockpit features of the prototype D-45 Mentor. Note that it had cowl flaps at this point. *NARA*

Fashion model Eloise Strewe stands on the wing of a Temco Swift. Like the Beechcraft Bonanza, the Swift became the basis for Temco's primary trainer. *Bill Kientz Collection*

The first TE-1A that was essentially a tandem-cockpit modification of the civilian Temco Swift. Robert McCulloch hoped to sell this to the newly independent Air Force as an inexpensive primary trainer. *Bill Kientz Collection*

The second TE-1A built for the trainer fly-off had an improved molded canopy and featured a larger engine. A third TE-1A was built but the Air Force rejected the Temco entry on the grounds that it was too light and deficient in performance. *Bill Kientz Collection*

B. The Temco Proposal

A third aircraft emerged for consideration on December 23, 1948, when Robert McCulloch, the President of the Texas Engineering and Manufacturing Company Inc. (Temco), sent a letter to the Air Material Command offering a new trainer based on the civilian Temco Swift. McCulloch stated that this airplane would be available for evaluation no later than January 15, 1949, and he quoted a production price of $12,000, far below Fairchild's $50,000 and Beechcraft's $20,000.

The Temco TE-1A was a hand-built modification of the civilian Temco Swift. It featured tandem seating and controls (the Swift used side-by-side seating), a new bubble canopy, and a larger rudder with a squared-off tip. Initially, the TE-1A retained the Swift's 125 hp Continental engine, but after initial flight tests, a 145 hp engine was substituted. The Air Force invited Temco to participate in the competition, and two additional Swifts were quickly modified to the TE-1A standard.[6] While the Temco was the least expensive of the three competitors, it was also the smallest, lightest, lowest powered, least durable, and lowest in performance.

C. The First Evaluation

On January 18, 1949, the Pentagon ordered the Air Material Command and the Training Command to conduct a fly-off competition of the three training aircraft. The Fairchild, Beechcraft, and Temco trainers were evaluated by each of the five divisions of the Air Material Command.[7] The Flight Test Division had six pilots fly each airplane, and its final report concluded:

It is the opinion of the pilots of this Division that the Beechcraft airplane has the most reasonable flying characteristics and has no peculiarities of flight that would require correction. The Fairchild airplane would be a close second from the pilot's viewpoint with the TEMCO a rather poor third. It is desired to point out, however, that it was very difficult to make a comparative evaluation between these three airplanes since they represent almost three entirely different classes of aircraft, and each has advantages peculiar to the particular airplane and powerplant configuration.[8]

But the other four divisions disagreed with the Flight Test Division and ranked Fairchild first, Beechcraft second, and Temco third. However the decision was reversed again by the senior members of the Evaluation Board, who met on February 23–24 and selected Beechcraft over Fairchild in a four to one vote. Yet, the matter was still not settled. The Commanding General of the Air Training Command, Gen. K.P. McNaughton, dissented from his Evaluation Board's recommendation on the following grounds:

a) The Fairchild is a handbook airplane whereas the Beechcraft is not.

b) The Fairchild has a proven engine; the Beechcraft has not.

c) The Fairchild airplane is considerably more rugged and will operate with less maintenance cost than the Beechcraft.

d) Students should be trained on the conventional-type landing gear until there are no conventional-type gear (airplanes) left in the Air Force.

e) The Fairchild aircraft can be converted to a tricycle gear without significant cost.

f) The relatively small differential in cost between the Fairchild and the Beechcraft should not be a deciding factor.

g) The Navy is not interested in the Beechcraft.

h) The Fairchild is a possible replacement for the T-28 in the event that airplane does not prove satisfactory.

i) The Beechcraft aircraft will not provide a normal progression to a more advanced type aircraft for those students who have received training under the Reserve Officers' Training Corps Act of 1949.

j) The Commanding General of the Air Training Command favors the Fairchild aircraft and recommends that it should be given consideration for purchase over the Beechcraft.[9]

On March 24, the Air Force issued a press release supporting Gen. McNaughton's position stating that the Fairchild T-31 had been selected and production of 100 examples would begin in the near future—but production was never authorized. A controversy arose when Beechcraft angrily alleged that Gen. McNaughton acted in collusion with retired Gen. W.W. Welsh, now employed by Fairchild. The matter was brought to the attention of Stuart Symington, Secretary of the Air Force, who had been outspoken against aircraft manufacturers hiring senior officers in sales positions. Historian Elliott Converse noted, "No evidence has been uncovered to indicate that the Air Force's initial selection of the Fairchild design had anything to do with the Welsh-McNaughton relationship. Similarly there is no proof that the Air Force decided not to product the Fairchild trainer as a result of Beech's allegation. Nevertheless, the incident illustrated how 'revolving door' connections

[military officers being hired by industry] might poison the acquisition atmosphere."[10] Further clouding the Air Force decision, a dispute arose with Fairchild over the procurement of government-furnished equipment for the T-31, and Fairchild management was in disarray from a recent proxy fight. The contract award was delayed and then budgetary disputes in Congress resulted in cancellation of T-31 production for fiscal 1949. On August 5, 1949, a decision was made to place the trainer procurement in abeyance and overhaul existing T-6s to meet the military's immediate requirements. Recognizing the stopgap nature of this decision, the Air Force earmarked funds for a second, more definitive evaluation of the new trainers.

Walter Beech, the master marketer, was undaunted by the Air Force's failure to award a contract. He redoubled his efforts to promote the D-45 Mentor. The three prototypes were sent on a tour of military bases and civilian air shows throughout the United States. The Mentor was showcased to huge public audiences at the Chicago National Air Fair on the Fourth of July weekend, 1949, and the Cleveland Air Races the following month. These demonstrations were flown by a twenty-two-year-old women's international aerobatic champion, Betty Skelton. It is reported that she put the Mentor through a stunning aerobatic display that dramatically emphasized its agility and durability.

This T-6G was an upgraded WWII vintage AT-6. On August 5, 1949, the primary trainer contract was placed in abeyance and available funds were allocated to upgrade existing AT-6 and SNJ airframes. The reworked airframes, designated T-6G or SNJ-7, received new canopies, increased fuel capacity, modernized avionics, improved tailwheels and hydraulic systems, and the instructor seat was raised for better visibility. *NARA*

During this period the Navy also evaluated Beech's D-45 at its training headquarters in Pensacola. The Navy's report was generally favorable, but concluded: "The aircraft was not visualized as one that should be in the training program except in a national emergency, but rather as an administrative plane or one for maintaining flight proficiency."[11]

Betty Skelton, the women's international aerobatic champion was the demonstration pilot at the National Air Fair. This photograph was taken of her when she flew the D-45 as a demonstration pilot for Walter Beech after the trainer competition failed to produce a contract. Betty Skelton inscribed this photograph to another noteworthy T-34 pilot, Julie Clark. *T-34 Association via Julie Clark*

Walter Beech displayed the Mentor at numerous Naval Air Stations during the marketing campaign. Lynn Richardson, director of military sales for Beechcraft (standing on the wing) shows the new D-45 Mentor to students and instructors at Corry Field, Pensacola Florida during its publicity tour. *NARA*

When the government deferred the primary trainer decision, Walter Beech mounted an aggressive marketing campaign. The three Mentors were flown by prominent pilots at major airshows around the country. The third Mentor, N8593A, is pictured here along with a ticket stub from the National Air Fair where it was displayed. *Dave Menard Collection*

For the second evaluation the Air Force purchased three new Mentors that featured improved engines and several airframe changes from the original Model D-45 prototypes. The Air Force designated these YT-34s. *Naval History and Heritage Command*

Temco dramatically redesigned the TE-1 for the new competition. The Air Force funded this second-generation Temco trainer and assigned the designation YT-35. Temco nicknamed the aircraft "Buckaroo." *Vought Heritage Foundation*

D. The Second Evaluation

The search for a new trainer continued in late 1949, when the Defense Department directed the Navy to join the Air Force in a new evaluation. This was to be a test of the airplanes in actual service use. Students from Randolph Air Force Base were selected to receive instruction in the Fairchild, Beechcraft, and Temco as well as a Canadian deHavilland Chipmunk DCH-1B and a British Boulton Paul Balliol T. Mk.2. The Air Force negotiated the purchase of three newly built examples of the most up-to-date models from Beechcraft and Temco and in March 1950 contracts were issued for three YT-34s and three YT-35s respectively. Fairchild's price for three new NQ/T-31s was considered prohibitive so it was decided to proceed with the two existing Fairchild trainers used in the first evaluation.[12]

Beechcraft installed 0-470-13 Continental engines (rated at 225 hp) along with improved exhaust systems, propellers, and cockpits in their YT-34s. Temco started from scratch with a substantial redesign of their entry. Only a small portion of the earlier TE-1A was retained in the new Phase II airplane that was given the factory designation TE-1B. The original Continental 145 hp powerplant was upgraded to a 165 hp Franklin with an Aeromatic propeller. The fuselage was narrowed to conform to the tandem-seating configuration, the nose was extended, and the deck was raised. The wing center section was redesigned to incorporate fillets and fairings, and a new landing gear was employed (still of the conventional tail wheel type). The outer wing panels were strengthened to withstand an ultimate load of 9 Gs, and squared wingtips were added. After flight testing, the stabilizer was modified by removing the upswept dihedral angle and relocating it higher to avoid disturbed air generated by the wing. The cowl was redesigned to provide more efficient downdraft cooling and drag reduction. Temco conferred the nickname "Buckaroo" to the new TE-1B.

The second evaluation was flown in the fall of 1950 with the Randolph Air Force Base students' progress being carefully monitored. But Walter Beech never lived to see the result of his efforts. On November 29, 1950, at a dinner party, he was stricken with a fatal heart attack. The Model D-45 Mentor was his last project.

At first Fairchild seemed to be the winner again. The December 11, 1950, issue of *Aviation Week* carried an article titled, "USAF Decides on Fairchild T-31," but still no production contract was issued. Inter-service disputes between the Air Force and Navy prevented a decision. The points of disagreement included: the landing gear (the Navy wanted conventional landing gear suitable for carrier training while the Air Force now favored tricycle landing gear); the Air Force wanted a six-cylinder flat-opposed engine while the Navy insisted on a radial engine; and both services were unsure of the wisdom of using the heavier Fairchild for inexperienced primary students.[13] The outbreak of the Korean War forced a halt to the trainer program once more, and the Training Commands continued flying refurbished T-6/SNJs.

The Air Force could not come to terms with Fairchild on building new aircraft for the second evaluation, so the original prototypes that were already government owned were prepared for the second evaluation. In this photograph the first prototype, 75725, was undergoing trials with a horizontally opposed Lycoming GSO-580 engine installed that produced 350 hp. But this was replaced with the original R-680-13 radial engine prior to the evaluation. *Lyle S. Mitchell Collection via Don Pellegreno*

The deHavilland DCH-1B Chipmunk was at the opposite end of the spectrum from the Balliol. It weighed a mere 1,425 pounds empty and was powered by a 145 hp de Havilland Gipsy Minor four-cylinder engine. Only the Temco YT-35 Buckaroo was lighter at 1,385 pounds (empty) and the Buckaroo was powered with a 165 hp engine. *Canada Science and Technology Museums Corporation*

The British Boulton Paul Balliol flies in formation with a North American T-28A. The Balliol was included in the evaluation to determine the value of side-by-side seating in a trainer. It was the heaviest (6,730 pounds empty) and highest powered (1,280 hp) of the five types evaluated. The T-28A was substantially lighter (5,111 pounds empty) and less powerful (800 hp) than the Balliol, yet both outweighed and overpowered all of the other aircraft considered in the second evaluation. *Tony Buttler Collection*

E. The Air Force Contract

When the second evaluation failed to produce a contract Fairchild chose to leave the trainer business and concentrate on their more lucrative C-119 transport contract. Temco's YT-35 was considered too light with too little performance and lacked the tricycle landing gear that the Air Force Training Command now desired. The Beechcraft YT-34 became the default choice and underwent continued flight testing at Edwards Air Force Base, California. The Air Force found the T-34's stamina remarkable. One test airplane performed a "round-the-clock" run flying twenty-three hours, twenty minutes continuously with only brief stops for refueling and crew change. The same airplane logged an incredible 434 hours of flight in slightly more than a month. During the test program, another YT-34 incurred serious damage when its wing struck a wire cable while in flight. The Mentor recovered from the impact and flew back to Edwards where the damage was inspected. The Air Force was impressed with the Mentor's durability and noted that most aircraft could not have survived that mishap.[14]

On March 5, 1953, the Department of Defense and Beech Aircraft Corporation issued a joint news release announcing a production order for the T-34A:

> The Beech-designed USAF T-34A primary trainer has been ordered into sustained and quantity production in the United States and Canada for the US Air Force. …
>
> The two-place trainer, according to US Air Force spokesmen, will replace the familiar T-6 "Texan" that, since the end of World War II, has been used as an interim primary trainer in lieu of a more suitable aircraft.[15]

The Air Force ordered 450 units—350 to be built by Beechcraft in Wichita Kansas, and 100 to be built under license by the Canadian Car and Foundry Company in Montreal, Canada.

The first-production Mentor was given Beechcraft serial number G-7 and was delivered to the Air Force in September 1953. The Air Force assigned serial number 52-7626, and designated it T-34A (the pre-production Y was removed from the designation). Before entering training service it was tested from September 16 to October 14, 1953, at the Beechcraft factory by Air Force test pilot, Capt. James R. Gannett, to determine compliance with Air Force specifications and verify manufacturer performance guarantees. The test program involved thirty-eight flights totaling 48:55 hours. Capt. Gannett concluded, "that the airplane can safely and efficiently perform its intended mission as a primary trainer. The airplane meets all performance guarantees and exhibits only minor stability and control deficiencies." The addition of a stall warning indicator and limitation of right rudder deflection (to improve aft center of gravity spin recovery) were the only two corrections recommended.[16]

Further testing continued at Eglin Air Force Base, Florida in December 1953 where three production T-34As were evaluated for instrument training, night flight training, and aerobatic training suitability. These Mentors were subjected to abusive conditions (continuous sod field operations) while maintenance procedures and technical publications were evaluated. The tests revealed that the engines malfunctioned during inverted flight—oil did not reach the propeller with sufficient pressure causing an over speed. Beechcraft developed a new oil tank to ensure lubrication of the propeller in any position. Also, a new nose gear up-lock was designed to insure proper release when the gear was lowered. In January, two Mentors were flown to Minneapolis for cold-weather tests. After overnight storage at fifteen degrees Fahrenheit, the engines were started repeatedly without difficulty. The Eglin test program was completed on February 14, 1954, with the conclusion that the T-34 was suitable for primary training. It was deemed safer and more economical than the T-6 that it would replace.

In May 1954, the Air Force, now assured of the Mentor's suitability, placed the new model in primary training service at Marana Air Force Base. This was followed by Spence in September 1954, Moore in January 1955, Bainbridge in March 1955, Malden in August 1955, and Hondo in November 1955. During this period the Air Force used civilian contractors to provide primary flight instruction. This practice had been used with great success during WWII since it allowed military pilots to concentrate on tactical missions; however, it had become controversial in the post-war years. Proponents argued that civilian instructors were less expensive than military instructors, while opponents insisted that it deprived student pilots of immersion in the military culture and harmed pilot retention.[17]

In service, the T-34A proved to be an outstanding primary trainer for the Air Force providing a safe, reliable, economical introduction to flying for thousands of students, but on occasion it could provide unexpected lessons. Charlie Pydych entered flight training as an ROTC candidate from Amherst College in January 1956. He was assigned to a primary training at Marana Air Force Base where he received his instruction from a civilian contractor named Dan Hitch, a former B-24 pilot in WWII. Hitch was a superb pilot and patient, supportive instructor who passed his skills on to his students, but nothing could prepare

The third production T-34A as it appeared shortly after delivery to the Air Force Test Center, Edwards AFB, California, in 1953, prior to entering training service. *Air Force Test Center History Office*

T-34A, 53-3334, as it entered Training Command service. The large US Air Force and buzz number left no room for the national insignia on the unpainted aluminum fuselage. *Dave Menard Collection*

Pydych for his first emergency which happened during a solo flight early in his T-34A training. Dan Hitch had been flying all day and he had one last sortie before heading home. To expedite the lesson Hitch, offered a reward to the first student in the air. Of course this meant that everyone rushed through their preflight inspections. Pydych was the first airborne but shortly after takeoff he noticed that the airspeed indicator was swinging from zero to maximum airspeed erratically. Unable to read his airspeed he tried tapping on the instrument glass to no avail. Hesitantly he declared his first emergency—a memorable event for a green pilot. Hitch was flying with another student in the area when he heard Pydych's "Mayday." He formed on Pydych's wing and said that he would follow him in the landing pattern calling out airspeeds until touch down. Pydych had no formation experience, but he felt confident with Hitch on his wing. The inexperienced and apprehensive Pydych overshot the first approach but executed a go-around and landed successfully on the second attempt. With fire trucks on both sides Pydych brought the T-34A to a full stop as Air Force personnel swarmed around the airplane. Fearful that he failed to remove the pitot cover during his hurried preflight inspection, Pydych had visions of being washed out. But to his great relief the inspection crew confirmed that cover had been removed before flight and that the assembly had been improperly installed after recent maintenance. Pydych received a high grade for handling the emergency and he completed his primary phase on August 4, 1956, with no further mishaps.[18]

In the late 1950s, the Training Command began to explore changes to the syllabus intended to shorten the overall training cycle. Since its introduction in 1954, primary students had been given forty hours in the T-34A,

An Air Force public relations photograph showing that the fifth-production T-34A was receiving careful scrutiny from Edwards Test Center personnel. *Air Force Test Center History Office*

then transitioned to the heavier, more complex T-28A. But in April 1958 some classes received only thirty hours in the T-34A, then transitioned to the T-37 jet. This change seemed to accelerate jet pilot production. By November 1960, less than seven years after the T-34A had entered service, the Air Force committed to an all-jet syllabus and ceased using propeller training aircraft. The T-34A inventory was declared surplus—some Mentors were transferred to the Forestry Service or Civil Air Patrol while others were given to Air Force Base flying clubs.

A later markings variation consisted of a smaller US Air Force with the buzz number underneath, but still no national insignia and the tail number is only four digits. *Beech Aircraft Corporation via Don Spering A.I.R. Collection*

By 1955, the T-34A was fully integrated into the Air Force primary training syllabus and large national insignias were painted on the fuselage. On some Mentors the buzz number appeared under the canopy. *Dave Menard Collection*

In the late 1950s, fluorescent paint was applied to the T-34A fleet to improve visibility in high-traffic environments. Notice the absence of nose gear doors that had been removed on some T-34As for maintenance reasons. *Tom Doll Collection via Mark Nankivil*

F. The Navy Contract

One of the reasons that the joint Air Force and Navy trainer evaluation of 1949–50 failed to produce a contract was the divergence between the services on landing gear. The Navy wanted a tail-wheeled airplane like much of its carrier-based fleet, while the Air Force favored tricycle landing gear—similar to its tactical jets. Gradually the Navy's thinking changed, and they too came to prefer tricycle gear. The inconclusive 1950 fly-off forced the Naval Air Training Command to continue using SNJs (the Navy equivalent of the T-6) that had been designed in 1939. Heavy, fuel thirsty, and prone to ground loops—the SNJ was expensive to operate, and its flight characteristics required a lot of un-learning when students progressed to jets. In July 1953 the Navy announced a new primary/basic trainer competition. Proposals were received from several manufacturers, but three aircraft were selected for the evaluation, the Beechcraft T-34, the Temco Plebe, and the Ryan Model 72 Navion. The T-34 was a default choice because of the Air Force contract. The Plebe, built in Temco's rapid prototype fashion of only seventy-five days, was a new development of the TE-1B Buckaroo. It featured tricycle landing gear and a Continental 225 hp engine. The Ryan Model 72 had been built in 1949 as a standard Navion but it was never sold, instead it was used by Ryan as a test bed for options and modifications planned for production aircraft. In preparation for the Navy competition the standard Navion wing and fuselage were reinforced to withstand +9/-4 Gs. Elliptical wingtip extensions were added for handling requirements (the standard Navion wing was deemed too stable for spin and aerobatic training). A castering nose wheel with differential braking was used for ground steering, the control yokes were replaced with military-style control sticks, a military instrument panel and throttle quadrant was installed, and the rear seats were removed.

These aircraft were evaluated from September to December 1953 at Corry Field, Pensacola Florida, where twelve students paired with four instructors flew under actual training conditions. The instructors rotated among the three aircraft, but the students were assigned to only one type. Data from the evaluation was submitted to RADM Apollo Soucek, Chief of the Navy's Bureau of Aeronautics.

On June 17, 1954, Beechcraft was awarded a contract.[19] The Navy required several changes from the Air Force T-34A standard, which resulted in a new designation, T-34B. The Navy specified a castering (non-steerable) nose wheel, adjustable rudder pedals, seats that adjusted only in the vertical, an additional degree of dihedral in the wings, an on-off fuel selector with both tanks feeding simultaneously, a spring system to increase elevator forces,

The Navy primary trainer evaluation of 1953 included three participants (front to rear): Temco Model 33 Plebe, Beechcraft Model D-45 Mentor, and Ryan Model 72 Navion. *NARA*

a twenty-eight-volt electrical system, a bulge in the battery compartment door to accommodate a larger battery, removal of the fairing under the rudder, and the installation of an arrowhead antenna on the rear fuselage.[20]

The first Air Force T-34A, 52-7626 (Beechcraft serial G-7), was bailed to Beechcraft for modification to the Navy's T-34B standard. The Air Force inspected the modified airplane to determine if any of the Navy's changes should be retrofitted to their A models. An evaluation was held at the Beechcraft plant on July 21-23, 1954 by Maj. R.M. Terry, Operations Officer, and Mr. E.E. Staugaard, Director of Material. The report, dated August, 4, 1954, identified several improvements:

The Ryan Navion Model 72 was selected to compete in the Navy's primary trainer evaluation. At the time of this photograph, September 1953, the prototype was fitted with a reinforced canopy. *NARA*

The standard Navion interior was modified to comply with military requirements. The control yoke was replaced by a stick, the rear seats were removed, and the instrument panel was modified to Navy standards. *Mark Cyrier Collection via Mark Nankivil*

During the evaluation, the original reinforced canopy was removed and replaced with a clear canopy for improved visibility. *Mark Cyrier Collection via Mark Nankivil*

The Temco Model 33 Plebe was developed from the TE-1B Buckaroo. Temco built this article in the amazingly short time of seventy-five days. It was Temco's first trainer with tricycle landing gear. *NARA*

a) The propeller was shortened from 88" to 84" providing more efficiency.

b) The fuel system used a simple "on- off" switch that fed from both wing tanks simultaneously to a 1-gallon sump tank that contained the boost pump. The boost pump was on whenever the fuel switch was on.

c) An improved fuel tank cap that was easier to get off and impossible to secure improperly.

d) The use of a single fuel gauge with a toggle switch to read the left or right tank.

e) Strengthened landing gear capable of withstanding a drop of 17.5 feet per second (T-34A landing gear could withstand a drop of 15 feet per second).

f) T-34B flaps were made of aluminum that was easier to repair and less prone to cracking than the T-34A flaps made of magnesium.

g) The T-34B canopy had a handle on both sides making it easier to open and less prone to jamming than the T-34A canopy.

h) The T-34B's rudder travel was increased to 30° while the T-34A was limited to 25°, it was felt that the increased rudder throw would be beneficial in aerobatic maneuvers and cross wind landings.

i) The dihedral angle of the T-34B wings was 7° while the T-34A was 6° providing better stability.

j) The dorsal fairing under the rudder was removed on the T-34B, which dampened a directional oscillation that the T-34A exhibited in rough air.

After studying the recommended modifications for a year, the Air Force chose not to modify their T-34As due to the expense of the improvements and the limited benefits they provided.

The Navy received its first T-34B (BuNo. 140667, Beech serial BG-1) on December 17, 1954. A total of 423 aircraft were built in two batches (the first 290 aircraft, BuNos 140667 to 140956 were followed by 133 aircraft 143984 to 144116). Unlike the Air Force, the Navy used only military pilots for primary flight instruction, and the training was conducted at only one base, Pensacola. By June 1955, the Basic Training Unit had developed a new syllabus under the direction of Lt. Cdr. E.C. Fry, Officer-in-Charge of syllabus evaluation. The first students to solo in the T-34B were ENS D.E. White of Los Angeles, California and L.S. Seigler of Hollywood, California, on August 4, 1955. The Navy proudly reported that these solo flights occurred in half the time that it would have taken in the SNJ. [21]

The first T-34B delivery occurred on December 17, 1954. Olive Beech, the president of Beechcraft is in the center of the officials assembled for the occasion. *T-34 Association*

The official ribbon cutting by Mrs. J.P. Monroe, wife of the Chief of Naval Air Basic Training, at Whiting Field on November 2, 1955. The Mentor had been in Training Command service since June 1955. *NARA*

As part of the first order for 290 aircraft this recently produced T-34B is on a contractor pre-delivery test flight. This Mentor has not received any squadron markings yet. *Naval History and Heritage Command*

A T-34B cruising along the Pensacola coastline in 1956. T-34Bs were delivered with polished aluminum canopy frames and spinners, but these were later painted for corrosion protection. NARA

The T-34 was regarded as an excellent spin trainer, entering and recovering from all spin modes reliably. *Naval History and Heritage Command*

Training maneuvers such as inverted spin recoveries often exposed the T-34B to abnormal loads. Here an aggressive pull-up (note the elevator deflection) wrinkles the wing skin. *Naval History and Heritage Command*

As part of the pre-flight syllabus students were required to become proficient with the cockpit layout and emergency procedures. These cockpit-familiarization trainers were not simulators; however they were accurate replicas of an airworthy cockpit, duplicating every instrument and switch. *Naval History and Heritage Command*

The Mentor was not designed for carrier operations; however this photograph shows a highly unusual T-34B takeoff from the deck of the *USS Lexington* (CVT-16). This T-34B was probably hoisted aboard in port and would have no difficulty with a free deck launch when the carrier was underway. *Naval History and Heritage Command*

Lt. Wayne H. Fox, USNR, an instructor at Whiting Field, recalled the transition from SNJs to the T-34Bs:

I was assigned to BSG, which is the Basic Standardization Group. We taught instructors how to be instructors and kept them standardized. There was not a lot of difference between the SNJ and the T-34 in the air, but the T-34 was easier in the area of ground handling and this made student advancement much faster. The SNJ had twice the horsepower but it was also bigger and heavier. The T-34 was more nimble which made it more maneuverable—it was the best aerobatic plane I ever flew. It was the only airplane that I could do an intentional inverted spin in. When I was a staff instructor at the Instructors School in Pensacola we had a rash of fatal accidents, not from the T-34 as much as other planes such as the T-28. The powers to be decided that each new instructor should be proficient with the inverted spin so they could recognize it and make a recovery if that was happening. Since the T-34 was the only plane capable of this maneuver it was delegated to us to teach every new instructor how to enter and recover from an inverted spin. This was the most vicious maneuver I have ever done and somewhat difficult to perform. We found that the vast majority of the new instructors, even very experienced pilots, were oblivious to what they had been in let alone do one and make a recovery. After that we just showed them one and hoped they would recognize it if they did encounter this spin. I also had the opportunity to put on a flight demonstration at an airshow in Pensacola where the Blue Angels also performed on the same day. This aircraft was a dream while doing aerobatics so I was able to stay within the boundaries of airfield while performing at low altitude. My final maneuver was to come out of an Immelmann and go into a two-turn spin. I had planned to force it into a spin early and do my first half turn horizontally before I went vertical. A cloud layer had moved in so I had to pull harder in the loop that killed off my speed so I was lower and slower than planned. I still kicked it into the spin and did the two full turns. I am sure the heaver air at low altitude helped me. My skipper said that when I came out of the Immelmann and chopped the throttle and went into the spin there was one big "OH!" from the crowd. I am sure they thought I had had it. The skipper said later that I stole the whole show. This of course was due to the fact that I could stay right in front of the crowd because of the superb T-34. [22]

In December 1956, primary training was moved from Whiting Field to Saufley Field within the Pensacola complex. Martin Zeller, a young NAVCAD, recalls his introduction to the Mentor at Saufley on March 4, 1957:

Training was all about procedures and learning to fly smoothly but with deliberate, precise control inputs. There was continuing emphasis on maintaining trim in all flight conditions. I became so proficient that I could fly a complete approach (although not recommended or taught) on trim tabs alone. This was also due to the great inherent stability of the T-34. The use of proper trim techniques would play an important part in our instrument training.

The most fun was the take-off and landing practice and shooting emergency power off landings to open fields. We didn't actually touch down at these fields but would power up after clearing the fence. In primary, we did not conduct carrier approaches, but it was important to touch down consistently on the numbers. [23]

Beechcraft delivered the 423rd and final T-34B on December 12, 1957. Maintenance costs were down, time to solo was down, the washout rate was down, and the accident rate was down. The Training Command was able to reduce primary training from twelve weeks to eight weeks and total flying time from seventy-four to thirty-eight hours.

T-34 students soloed in half the time and suffered half the accidents of SNJ students. Furthermore, the Mentor's reliability was remarkable. In 1957, the T-34 fleet accumulated 163,885 hours of flight time, and experienced the best safety record in the Training Command. Over a nine-year period one aircraft, BuNo 140737, logged more than 6,000 hours and 36,000 landings. Another Mentor recorded 17,904 stalls, 3,401 spins, and 4,604 loops during its service life.

An early production T-34B, BuNo. 140743 the 76th T-34B delivered, during engine start. The student, in the forward cockpit with his instructor in the aft is about to taxi to the active for a pre-solo training sortie. The ribbed flight helmets indicating that this photograph is circa 1954-55. *Naval History and Heritage Command*

The stability of the Mentor made it an exceptional formation platform. These formation sorties became a fundamental part of the primary training syllabus at Whiting and Saufley Fields. A student's inability to master formation flight was a common reason for washout. *NARA and Naval History and Heritage Command*

By now, the T-34B had completely replaced the SNJ in primary training, and the T-28B was replacing the SNJ in basic training as well. The SNJ's final training responsibility was carrier qualification, but in 1958 the new tailhook-equipped T-28C assumed that duty and the last SNJ, a relic of WWII flight training, was soon retired.

The Naval Air Training Command was well on its way to developing a program suitable for a modern jet force, however initial Air Force experience with the Cessna T-37 suggested that an all-jet flight syllabus might produce the better jet pilots in a shorter time. The Navy evaluated all-jet training in the late 1950s with fourteen Temco TT-1 Pintos but decided to abandon that approach and continued using propeller powered T-34Bs that had become a model of dependability. Not until the late 1970s was the T-34B replaced by a more modern turboprop derivative, the T-34C (see chapter 7). By the end of its busy service life, the Beechcraft T-34B Mentor had trained 36,077 Naval Aviators in the Navy's two primary training squadrons, VT-1 and VT-5. [24]

The T-34B displayed superb landing characteristics. The large-slotted flaps allowed slow approach speeds and the rugged landing gear handled cross winds and high rates of descent easily. While it was not standard procedure, some student pilots were able to land using only elevator trim. *Naval History and Heritage Command*

A formation of T-34Bs flies over a retiring SNJ at Whiting Field in 1957. SNJs had been in the Naval Training Command since the early 1940s. *NARA*

The SNJ-5, a relic of WWII, was used in various training roles alongside the T-34B and the T-28B until 1958. *NARA*

In later service many T-34Bs received painted canopy frames and spinners for corrosion control; the anti-glare panel was repainted flat black. *US Navy via Jay Sarver*

The last yellow T-34B, BuNo. 140920, nicknamed "Ole Yeller," receives honors from Cdr. H.E. Kendrick, Commanding Officer of VT-1 before being repainted in the new high visibility split scheme of Day-Glo red and white. This Mentor was delivered to Saufley Field in 1956 and had acquired 2,984 flight hours at the time of this photograph August 21, 1962. *Naval History and Heritage Command*

In the early 1960s, the orange-yellow scheme was replaced by a very bright fluorescent red-orange and Insignia white scheme for high visibility. The fluorescent paint was applied to nearly one half of the airframe and it became known as the "split scheme." *Don Spering A.I.R. Collection*

The Training Command's highest time T-34B, Bureau No.140737, this had accumulated more than 6,000 hours in nine years while logging over 36,000 landings. *Naval History and Heritage Command*

Since fluorescent paint faded very rapidly in the Florida sun and maintenance was expensive, the color scheme was revised with smaller fluorescent areas. By the late 1960s, fluorescent paint was replaced by a more durable International orange. *Tailhook Collection via Cdr. Doug Siegfried*

The VT-1 flight line at Saufley Field in 1964 showing a mixture of T-34B color schemes. Many aircraft are in the original orange-yellow scheme, while others have been repainted in the "split scheme." Tailhook Collection via Cdr. Doug Siegfried

In the 1970s, T-34Bs wore a scheme of International Orange on the cowl, fin, and outboard wing panels. This scheme would be passed on to the T-34C Turbo Mentor. Both Navy and Air Force maintainers found T-34 nose gear doors difficult to rig, and often removed them as an expedient. *Paul Minert Collection*

The Navy, like the Air Force, released several of their Mentors to the US Forestry Service and the Civil Air Patrol when they were beyond their useful military training life. This T-34B was used for fire spotting, missing aircraft searches, and other utility duties. No longer a military asset, it was assigned a civilian registration number, N101Z. Note the Navy AJ Savage in the background, a carrier-based nuclear bomber converted to "borate bomber." *Tom Doll Collection via Mark Nankivil*

Chapter Three Endnotes

1. The first evaluation used two Fairchild XNQ-1s, three Beechcraft Model D-45 Mentors, and three Temco TE-1A Swifts. The second evaluation used the two existing Fairchild XNQ-1s (re-designated T-31), three newly built Beechcraft D-45 Mentors (designated YT-34), three newly built Temco TE-1Bs (designated YT-35 Buckaroo), two DeHavilland Chipmunks, and two Boulton Paul Balliols.

2. For more on the XQN-1/T-31 see Kent Mitchell, "The Fairchild XQN-1/T-31 Trainer" *American Aviation Historical Society Journal*, Vol. 22, No. 1, Spring 1977 pp.48-55.

3. "The New Beechcraft 'Mentor' … An Initial Pilot trainer," The Beech Log, Nov.-Dec. 1948, p.3.

4. Beech Aircraft Corporation press release, December 11, 1948.

5. Don Pellegreno, "The T-31, T-34, and T-35 competition," *American Aviation Historical Society Journal*, Winter 1995, p.269.

6. Stanley G. Thomas, *The Globe/Temco Swift Story*. Destin, Florida: Aviation Publishing Inc., 1996, p.68.

7. The five divisions consisted of Propeller, Aeromedical, Equipment, Aircraft Laboratories, and Flight Test.

8. Pellegreno, p.273.

9. Ibid. p. 275.

10. Elliott V. Converse III, Rearming For The Cold War 1945–1960, (Washington, DC Historical Office of The Secretary of Defense, 2012) pp.294 -295.

11. CDR. Douglas Siegfried, USN (retired), "The Search For New Trainers," *Cleared For Solo*, (unpublished manuscript) p.46.

12. The Navy funded the two Fairchild XNQ-1s, BuNos 75725 and 75726, pursuant to the Bureau of Naval Aeronautics specification NAVAER SD-400 of 26 April 1945. These aircraft were bailed to the Air Force for the first evaluation and remained in Air Force possession throughout the second evaluation.

13. Ann Holtgren Pellegreno, "The Fairchild XNQ-1" *Sport Aviation*, April, 1993, p.31.

14. Frank Morris, "A Short History of the Beechcraft Mentor" www.philfarq.com/t-34/t-34_history.htm also published as "Salute the Mentor," *Air Classics* (undated), p. 11.

15. Department of Defense and Beech Aircraft Corporation Joint News Release, March 5, 1953, "New Beech Trainer Ordered by US Air Force."

16. A.F. Technical Report No. AFFTC 54-1, Phase II and IV Flight Tests On The T-34A Aircraft USAF No. 27626, James R. Gannett, Captain, USAF.

17. William A. Johansen, "Contract Versus Military Pilot Training in Today's Air Force," Air War College Research Report No. AN-AWC-88-144, May 1987.

18. Letter from Charles Pydych to Mark A. Frankel, April 8, 2014.

19. Beechcraft News Release, June 18, 1954, "U.S. NAVY CHOOSES T-34 AS NEW AIRCRAFT TRAINER."

20. Lou Drendel, *T-34 Mentor In Action*. Carrollton, Texas: Squadron/Signal Publications Inc., 1990, p.11.

21. Navy Press Release, August 4, 1955, "FIRST STUDENTS SOLO IN THE NEW T-34B "MENTOR."

22. E-mail correspondence from Wayne H. Fox to Mark A. Frankel, 10 October, 8 November, and November 10, 2012.

23. E-mail correspondence from Martin C. Zeller to Mark A. Frankel, December 4, 2012.

24. Siegfried, *New Trainers*, p.17.

Chapter Four
INITIAL TRANSITION TO JETS

A. Baby Steps, Bell Airacomet

The first US jet-propelled airplanes were single-seat fighters developed during World War II. The Bell Aircraft P-59A Airacomet, piloted by Bell's Robert Stanley, lifted off on October 1, 1942 during high-speed taxi tests. The official first flight was made the next day by Col. Lawrence Craigie, US Army. The Lockheed XP-80 Shooting Star first flew on January 8, 1944, piloted by Milo Burcham; the XP-80A, modified to accommodate a more powerful engine, was flown by Tony LeVier, on June 10, 1944. Woodward Burke was the pilot for the first flight of The US Navy's first jet airplane, the McDonnell FD-1 Phantom, on January 26, 1945.[1]

Maj.Gen. Henry H. (Hap) Arnold had witnessed tests of the first British jet airplane in May 1941. He returned to Washington with the goal of bringing the Army Air Forces into the jet age as soon as possible. General Electric was selected to produce the Whittle Power Jets Limited Model W.2B, a development of Britain's first jet engine. In September 1941, Bell Aircraft received a contract to create a single-seat fighter powered by two of those engines.

Due to the very urgent nature of the program, Bell designed the P-59A airframe to be well within the state-of-the art for 1941.[2] This low-risk approach together with the engine-technology transfer from Whittle to General

Electric resulted in a first flight little more than a year after Bell received the go-ahead for the program. However, given the unproven status of the engine, the Army was surprisingly ambitious with respect to its first jet airplane. The P-59A was not a demonstrator or engine test bed. It was intended from the first to be a combat aircraft and was therefore armed with a 37 mm cannon and three .50 caliber machine guns. Because of uncertainty about the actual thrust of the engine, it had a relatively large and thick wing to provide low-speed lift and a high service ceiling. This proved to be appropriate, as two of the first General Electric I-A engines produced a maximum of 2,500 lbs of thrust; the resulting thrust-to-weight ratio was only 0.2.

The P-51 Mustang, at a gross weight of 10,000 lbs, had a wing loading of 42.9 pounds per foot; takeoff distances were on the order of 1,200 feet. The bigger P-47 had a wing loading of 46.7 pounds per square foot and a takeoff distance about twice the Mustang's. With its big wing, the YP-59 had a wing loading of only 26 pounds per square foot with full internal fuel. As a result, the takeoff roll at sea level and 59 degrees Fahrenheit was only 1,080 feet, actually less than the P-51's. The distance to clear a 50-foot obstacle wasn't significantly greater. However, the P-59 handbook noted that every 18-degree Fahrenheit increase in temperature increased the takeoff distance by 12%. It was one of the first indications of the very different nature of jet airplanes compared to those powered by reciprocating engines.

Although it provided adequate takeoff and landing performance, the big wing doomed any chance the P-59 had of being used in combat. It contributed to shortcomings in speed, rate of climb, and range compared to the existing propeller-driven fighters. Even with an eventual increase in thrust to 1,400 lbs with the General Electric I-16 (subsequently designated J31), its top speed of 413 mph at 30,000 feet was inferior to that of the P-51 Mustang, P-47 Thunderbolt, and F4U Corsair. The rate of climb compared even less well and the range was downright pathetic, less than half that of existing fighters even at 40,000 feet, where it was three times better than at sea level.

Development problems with the engines and the airplane, e.g., directional stability, slowed flight test progress and it wasn't until late 1943 that the Army ordered 100 production Airacomets.

The first operational squadron was to be the 412th Fighter Group based at Muroc AAF, now Edwards Air Force Base. It consisted of three squadrons and received its first P-59s in early 1945. However, by then it was already evident that the Airacomet would not be replacing or even supplementing existing propeller-driven fighters in combat.

The Army had decided in late 1944 that the P-59 would only be utilized in a training role stateside and canceled production except for the first fifty that were already on contract and in work.

Although a disappointment in that regard, the Airacomet provided an early, if limited, introduction to the differences between a propeller-driven airplane and one that was jet propelled. One of the benefits was that it had two of the blowtorches. It was more likely that the budding jet pilot would bring it back after an engine failure, which happened fairly frequently.

For all practical purposes, the P-59A was a jet kiddy-car. It was very easy to taxi, takeoff, and land with its nose landing gear and widely separated main landing gear wheels. The only problem was getting it rolling with the low-thrust engines. Not being equipped with speed brakes, it was also very slow to decelerate for landing, another useful lesson for the neophyte jet pilot. The only system complexity, a welcome one, was the incorporation of a pressurized cockpit for more comfortable flight at the high altitudes where a jet preferred to cruise.[3]

The limited endurance and range was another feature with educational value. The P-59As had an internal fuel capacity of 290 gallons. (A sixty-six-gallon tank was added in each outer wing panel of the P-59Bs to increase the fuel by a sorely needed 132 gallons.) Since a climb to 30,000 feet required about ninety gallons of fuel, and at a maximum-range cruise there was a fuel burn of 240 gallons per hour, a P-59 wasn't going to be in the air for much more than an hour or so.

Engines are basically air pumps and jet engines are simpler air pumps than piston engines: jets turned fuel more or less directly into thrust; reciprocating engines turned fuel into power, which then turned a propeller to produce thrust. While simpler in concept, however, the jet engine was far more difficult to make a reality from a hardware standpoint.

The main impediment to the development of the jet engine was metallurgy. The propulsion cycle required a compressor at the front of the engine to be turned by a turbine spun by the very hot exhaust from the fuel burners. Gas-flow dynamics dictated that the turbine blades be small and thin. Keeping them from melting required innovations in material temperature tolerance that only became available in the early 1940s. Even then, the time between engine overhauls to replace the turbines was only tens of hours initially (about three hours total in the case of the first engines installed in the P-59).

From a pilot standpoint, it was quickly obvious that jets were different, beginning with starting and operating them. Only one control, the throttle, and a few instruments and switches were necessary to manage the jet engine. The

Except for its jet engine propulsion, the Bell P-59A was very conventional, unlike the twin-boom pusher-propeller P-59 design, the designation that was used to conceal its purpose. An exceptionally large wing was incorporated in anticipation of a shortfall in engine thrust from the still-experimental power plant. *US Army Air Forces photo*

Like Bell's P-39 Airacobra, the P-59A had a tricycle landing gear. Only two or three of the early jets had a tail wheel instead, which penalized their takeoff performance since there was no propeller blast to raise the tail for best acceleration during the takeoff roll. *US Army Air Forces photo*

The pilot of a high-performance propeller-driven airplane was provided with many levers and a few switches for powerplant control. From left to right in this picture of the F6F-5N throttle quadrant, they were cowl flaps, oil cooler shutter, propeller rpm, throttle, mixture (just inboard of the throttle), and supercharger. The ADI (anti-detonation injection) switch is just above the supercharger knob. Not shown is the ignition switch that selected one or both of the magnetos and the control for alternate air in the event of carburetor icing. *T.H. Thomason Collection*

pilot of an airplane powered by a supercharged engine generally required additional levers to manage the propeller rpm, mixture, cowl flaps, carburetor heat, alternate air, oil cooler and intercooler shutters, and the supercharger. Some of these required monitoring a dedicated instrument for that lever. There were also a few more switches required for the magnetos, oil dilution, ADI (Anti-Detonate Injection) pump, etc. Setting power was a two-step process involving the propeller and throttle controls while monitoring the tachometer and manifold pressure instruments (the other ones provided systems pressure or temperature status). In some Navy propeller-driven fighters, the supercharger setting required management when passing critical altitudes.[4] By contrast, the jet pilot set thrust using only the rpm and turbine temperature gages and monitored the oil pressure/ temperature gages for exceedances. In cold weather, he didn't have to pay much attention to turbine temperature.

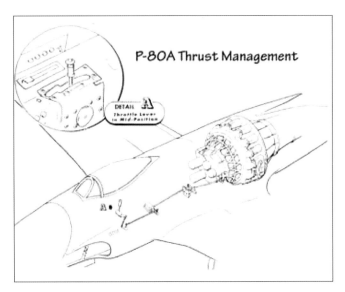

In contrast to the number of levers and switches required for management of a supercharged reciprocating engine, the jet pilot had only one, the throttle. Note that in this P-80 illustration, the throttle image is reversed in direction from the one showing the throttle's relationship to the engine. *T.H. Thomason Collection*

The left side of a propeller-driven fighter's cockpit was devoted to power plant levers and switches. A significant portion of the instrument panel was dedicated to engine instruments: Tachometer, Manifold Pressure, ADI Water Quantity Cylinder Head Temperature, Oil Pressure, Oil-In Temperature, and Fuel Pressure. *T. H. Thomason Collection*

Starting the jet engine was theoretically simpler than starting a big piston engine which required timely manipulation of the primer, ignition switch, mixture control, and throttle. The jet pilot only had the throttle to worry about. However, in the beginning, the engine start required a careful and knowledgeable touch. Before fuel flow regulation and limit features were added to the jet's fuel control, the pilot was directly opening and closing a fuel spigot. Too little fuel and the engine would not accelerate to idle speed and stagnate, possibly overtemping and certainly wearing down the battery; too much and an over temperature was assured. Only a few seconds over the maximum temperature limit required removal and repair/replacement of the turbine.

Jet engines did not need any significant warm up or checks before they were ready for full power and flight. This was a good thing because another aspect of the jet engine that had to be taken into account by the fledgling jet pilot was its extremely high fuel consumption at idle. The Vought F4U Corsair and F6U Pirate were about the same size, the former powered by a Pratt & Whitney R-2800 piston engine and the latter, a Westinghouse J34 jet engine. The R-2800 engine consumed only 180 pounds of fuel per hour at idle. The J34 consumed 1,140 lbs. of fuel per hour at idle, about the same fuel burn as the R-2800 required at maximum continuous power (at maximum continuous power the J34 was burning 1,600 lbs. of fuel per hour). Brevity between engine start and takeoff was necessary to maximize flight time.

The next lesson in the differences between flying a propeller-driven airplane and one pushed aloft by a blowtorch was that the full-throttle acceleration at low speeds of the jet airplane was disappointing, to say the least. The static thrust of the big propeller was much greater than that of the jet engine. The jet's takeoff roll could be agonizingly slow. The takeoff distance also increased notably with increasing ambient temperature, unlike that of a propeller-driven airplane. Wave off/go-around capability were similarly affected.

Another difference that "squirt" pilots had to learn was that jet thrust and power did not decrease with speed like propeller thrust and power did. As a result, the best rate of climb of a jet airplane was achieved at roughly the maximum air speed of a propeller-driven fighter, almost twice its climbing speed. Best angle of climb was also accomplished at a higher speed, adding to a jet pilot's obstacle clearance apprehension on takeoff.

A jet's best range was achieved at the angle of attack for best lift over drag at the highest altitude at which the engine could maintain 100% rpm. This mean cruising at 35,000 feet and even higher if the temperature there was below standard.[5] One trick to increase range was the idle-

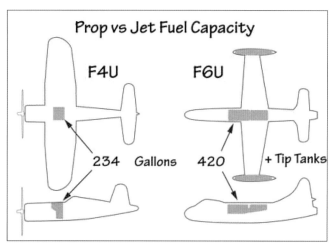

The Vought F4U and F6U carrier-based fighters were about the same size. Due to the thirst of the F6U's jet engine, compared to that of the F4U's reciprocating engine, the F6U had half (or less) of the F4U's endurance even though it had roughly twice the fuel capacity. Following first flight, most of the early jets were modified to increase fuel capacity by lengthening the fuselage and/or adding tip tanks. *Tommy H. Thomason*

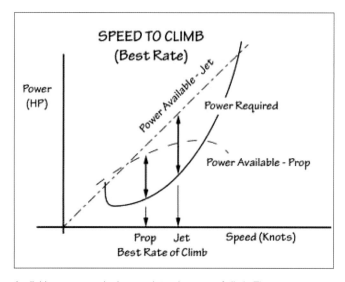

Available versus required power determines rate of climb. The power available from a propeller-driven engine dropped off with speed whereas the power available from a jet engine increased with speed. As a result, the jet pilot needed to accelerate to a much higher speed to achieve his best rate of climb than he did in a propeller-driven airplane. *Tommy H. Thomason*

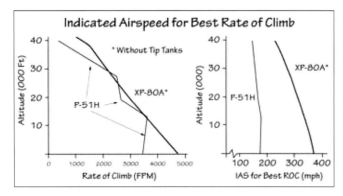

Indicated Airspeed for Best Rate of Climb

Performance test results in 1944 illustrated the dramatic difference in best rate of climb speed for the XP-80A versus the propeller-driven P-51H. The XP-80A's indicated airspeed for its best rate of climb without tip tanks at sea level was 370 mph, twice that of the P-51H. *Tommy H. Thomason*

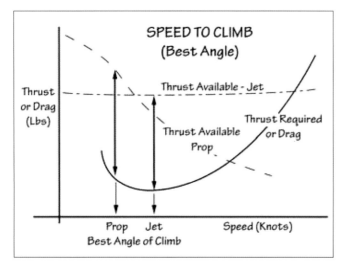

SPEED TO CLIMB
(Best Angle)

Thrust available versus drag determines angle of climb. Because of the jet's virtually constant thrust versus speed compared to the propeller's drop off in thrust with increasing speed, the best angle of climb was achieved at a notably higher speed in a jet airplane than one with a propeller. *Tommy H. Thomason*

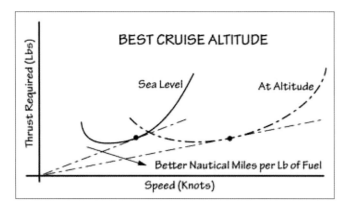

BEST CRUISE ALTITUDE

Maximum range, absent wind-aloft considerations, tends not to vary significantly with cruise altitude in a propeller-driven airplane. A jet airplane, on the other hand, achieves far better range when flown at altitude. *Tommy H. Thomason*

power descent, again at the speed for maximum lift over drag; to maximize range, a pilot could actually shut the engine down when starting the descent and restart it at a safe altitude.

Endurance was also better at altitude, unlike a reciprocating engine's, which consumed the least fuel at sea level. In fact, if an unexpected landing delay was encountered after a descent from cruise, the well-informed jet pilot would consider climbing back up to a higher altitude to loiter.

Care had to be taken at altitude with throttle movements, however, since there was initially minimal if any protection from compressor stall or flameouts. In particular, early jet engines were prone to flameout at altitude if the throttle were moved too abruptly in either direction; fortunately, damage to the engine was not likely and there was usually plenty of altitude to work with to get the engine going again.[6]

Jet engine power management was otherwise fairly straightforward, once the student learned that its thrust was disproportionate to rpm and not to let rpm get too low when the need for an increase in thrust might be imminent. For example, 70% rpm only resulted in about 30% of the thrust at full throttle and increasing rpm back to 100% from 70% would take several seconds.

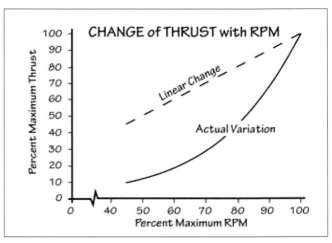

CHANGE of THRUST with RPM

Because some of the energy required by jet engine operation was devoted to turning the compressor, the thrust versus rpm was notably nonlinear. At idle, about 45% of maximum rpm, the thrust was only 10% of that at 100% of rpm. *Tommy H. Thomason*

Awareness of the nonlinear relationship of thrust and rpm was particularly important when returning to land. The jet airplane was also very slow to decelerate when the engine was pulled back to idle because of the lack of a big windmilling propeller to provide drag. If the pilot did pull the throttle all the way back to slow down quicker, he had better bring the rpm back up to something on the order of 85 or 90% well before the potential need to add thrust. (Speed brakes proved beneficial in this regard, the extra drag enabling the pilot to keep the engine rpm high while at approach speeds.)

Besides powerplant management, some differences when flying a jet airplane for the first time did not require caution and could be immediately appreciated. The most immediately obvious was that the cockpit was quieter since the engine was located well behind the pilot. The airframe did not buffet due to propeller blast on the airframe, canopy, or control surfaces at high power settings or vibrate due to resonance with engine operation because it was turning at such a high rpm. The jet's handling qualities were different in a good way because there was no propeller. On a propeller-driven fighter there were forces and moments resulting from propeller wash, torque, gyroscopic precession, and P (for propeller) factor. These were each induced by throttle or pitch control changes, requiring the pilot to make compensating rudder and/or control stick movements when making throttle or angle of attack changes. In many airplanes with powerful reciprocating engines, the vertical fin leading edge was angled left or had an asymmetric airfoil to provide built-in compensation for some power effects; however, that was only good for certain combinations of speed and power: in general, changes required control corrections.

The Navy utilized a few Airacomets as a single-seat jet trainer following a brief flight evaluation at NAS Patuxent River. Of the Navy's first 100 jet pilots, all but three made their first-jet propelled flight in a P-59. The last of the P-59s was still being used for jet familiarization at Patuxent in January 1948. *US Navy photo*

B. The Shooting Star

If the generals and the admirals had made a decision as to the value of the jet airplane based solely on the P-59, there would have been no more. Its only virtues compared to existing fighters were that it was quiet and smooth. Fortunately, it was recognized to be a baby step and development of other, more powerful jet engines was being funded. Moreover, in June 1943 the Army contracted with Lockheed to design and build the XP-80. It was to be powered by a single de Havilland Halford Goblin derated to 2,240 lbs. of thrust for durability.

One indication of the learning curve involved with jet engines was an incident during the XP-80's ground running prior to first flight. The inlet ducts proved inadequate for the suction of the jet engine and they collapsed. Serendipitously, the close inspection of the engine compressor that was required resulted in the detection of a forging flaw in a compressor vane that probably wouldn't have been detected otherwise and could have caused a catastrophic failure at the worst possible moment.[7]

Except for the long takeoff run (early US jet airplane testing was sensibly done on the huge dry lakebed in the Mojave desert in southern California that would become part of Edwards AFB), the XP-80 performance was very promising. It soon demonstrated a top speed of 500 mph. It was immediately evident that the XP-80, even with a slightly lower thrust to weight ratio than the P-59A's, had better performance and a faster rate of roll. The much smaller and thinner wing, more streamlined shape, and smooth finish helped.

Even before the XP-80 first flew, however, Lockheed proposed a derivative of it with the more powerful General Electric I-40 with 4,000 lbs of thrust. A few weeks after its first flight on January 8, 1944, the Army ordered two XP-80As with that engine by amending the original contract.

Lulu Bell, the first P-80, is pictured being prepared for its first flight on January 8, 1944 from the dry lakebed at Muroc, California. Kelly Johnson, in a dark overcoat and fedora, is walking past the nose. *US Army Air Forces photo*

The tail cone has been removed from this P-80's jet engine so the turbine that turns the compressor is visible. The multiple light-colored canisters are where the fuel (at this time, either gasoline or kerosene) is mixed with the high-pressure air coming from the compressor and burned. The turbine blades were already been subjected to temperatures very close to their melting point; the potential for damage by misuse of the throttle during engine starts was therefore high. *T.H. Thomason collection*

In less than a month after that, the Army ordered thirteen pre-production YP-80As and committed to 500 production P-80As. Amazingly, the first XP-80A first flight was accomplished on June 10, 1944, only five months after the XP-80's.

Even with the more powerful engine, the newly named Shooting Star still had a slightly lower thrust-to-weight ratio than the P-59A due to an increase in the size and empty weight. Combined with a wing loading of about sixty pounds per square foot, the impact on takeoff performance was horrific. The P-80's ground roll on takeoff was about 3,000 feet, almost three times that of a P-51 Mustang. To clear a fifty-foot obstacle required another 1,300 feet or so.

The slow acceleration and long roll on takeoff required patience on the part of the pilot to delay rotation and limit his initial pitch angle on takeoff. It was all too easy to initiate rotation too early as the airplane ate up runway on the takeoff roll. The result of raising the nose too high too soon might not even result in an initial liftoff; if it did, the increase in drag and climb out of ground effect quickly resulted in the airplane slowing and settling back to the runway. That substantially increased the takeoff distance and if the pilot had retracted the landing gear, precluded takeoff altogether.

Lockheed engineers' inexperience with jet-engine duct design continued to be evident. This time it was a phenomenon termed duct rumble, precipitated by a thick

Unlike the Bell P-59A, the Lockheed P-80 Shooting Star proved to be worthy of operational use as a front line fighter, albeit briefly and after a somewhat troubled development program. This picture was probably taken during a Lockheed production test pilot, since the pilot is clearly wearing a fedora and headphones, not the usual headgear of a USAF pilot. *US Air Force photo*

layer of low-energy air pulsing along the inboard side of the duct. Although the sound was disconcerting for the pilot, the real impact was the reduction of thrust due to the intake of low energy air into the compressor. That resulted in inlet modifications that removed the slow-moving layer of air present on the side of the fuselage in flight. Boundary layer control of inlet air was to become standard on jet airplanes with side inlets.

Another set of challenges also arose that had become evident in high-speed dives of propeller-driven airplane: Mach-number effects. In this case, the first unwelcome effect of transonic flight was aileron buzz that began at about Mach 0.8 and increased in intensity with speed. After tests of several solutions, the P-80 aileron buzz was finally eliminated by the use of very high tension on the aileron control cables to stiffen the aileron against the unsteady airflow.

With the additional thrust, the somewhat bigger XP-80A was even faster than the XP-80. Its development was not without tragedy resulting from the failures of its nascent jet engine. Milo Burcham was killed in October 1944 on the first production flight of a P-80 from Burbank when his engine flamed out after failure of its engine-driven fuel pump. In March 1945, Tony LeVier was on a routine test flight when the turbine wheel failed catastrophically, cutting off the aft fuselage; fortunately he was able to bail out. Dick Bong, America's leading ace, was killed in August 1945 when his engine fuel pump failed on takeoff. He hadn't switched on the electrically driven backup pump added after Burcham's fatal crash.

As previously noted, a critical difference for pilots between jets and propeller-driven airplanes was cruise planning. The best-range speed and altitude for even high-performance fighters with supercharged piston engines was low and slow compared to a jet, which needed to be flown almost as high as possible to go the farthest unless headwinds had to be taken into account. With two external tip-mounted 165-gallon tanks the F-80C, for example, had a range of a little over 1,000 nautical miles when climbed to and cruised at 35,000 feet. However, if it was allowed to drift upward to 41,500 feet from its initial service ceiling of 36,000 feet as its weight decreased, the so-called "climb cruise," the range increased to 1,200 nautical miles.

Flying high and fast placed somewhat more of a premium on instrument flight and radio-navigation proficiency than had been required of the fighter pilot of propeller-driven fighters. Knowledge of winds aloft at cruise altitudes rarely visited heretofore was important for cross-country planning. Even the letdown from cruise altitude required more planning, since it took time and was a significant factor in maximizing range.

There wasn't much that could be done about the jet's low endurance: pilots and mission planners had to be very aware of and take into account the high rate of fuel consumption and the need to maximize endurance by loitering at altitude. The Navy was particularly affected from a carrier deck-cycle standpoint because of the need to land the early jets only ninety minutes after takeoff. Destination weather forecasts became of even more interest than before since a jet pilot couldn't wait around for low ceilings and/or visibility to improve and wasn't able to fly very far to find better weather before his fuel was exhausted.

As a result, transition to jets was difficult for some fighter pilots. The situation wasn't improved by the fact that there were initially no two-seat jets. The transition from the T-6 Texan trainer to the P-51 Mustang or F8F Bearcat, all propeller-driven airplanes, was relatively straightforward. The transition from the propeller-driven fighters to jets was initially considered to be of a similar degree of difficulty. It was accomplished informally at the squadron level rather than formally at a training unit dedicated to the purpose. What's worse, many of the differences associated with safely and effectively operating jet airplanes were unknown to many of those piloting them.

It was soon apparent that a more formal introduction incorporating a two-seat jet trainer was necessary. Experienced pilots in particular were being sent out in jets without a proper checkout. One senior officer reportedly utilized a substantial portion of engine turbine life (which was very low initially) while sitting in the warm-up area running the engine at high rpm and doing the equivalent of power checks he was familiar with in propeller-driven airplanes.

In early 1945, the Army Air Forces began P-80 pilot transition training at Williams Army Air Field, Arizona.[8] A student would have had acquired 180 hours in the T-6 and then fifty hours in a P-51. Some pilots, of course, would have been much more experienced and were simply there for the jet familiarization.

Before then, the budding jet fighter pilot would have transitioned directly from the P-51 into the P-80A. It was soon apparent that this was not appropriate. The P-80A accident rate was twice that of any other fighter except the P-59A, the other Army Air Forces jet. Although many of the accidents were caused by the fragility of early jet engines, pilot error was a contributor if not the primary cause. Another was a lack of thorough indoctrination in the unique aspects of jet airplane aerodynamics.

The second Air Force jet fighter to be used operationally was the Republic P-84 Thunderjet. It first flew on February 28, 1946, but required a long gestation (and almost as long a takeoff roll). Like the F-80, it was primarily assigned to ground-attack missions during the Korean War. *USAF photo*

Although it proved to be of relatively limited value, there was an intermediate step between the first airplane an Air Force pilot trainee flew, the T-6 Texan, and the frontline fighter, the F-80 in the background. It was however, the P-51 Mustang, which provided little in the way of flight characteristics, handling qualities, and power management experience needed to safely fly a jet. *US Air Force photo*

Leon Gray Col., USAF (Ret.), remembers a flight in early 1946 when he took off in an F-80 from Washington, DC, with Robin Olds as a wingman:

We literally jumped off the ground and climbed at 270 miles per hour. It was cold and snowy, but we couldn't understand why we were getting better performance. At 92 percent of power we were going about 30 miles per hour faster than usual. As we flew up to West Point to buzz the cadets, and then on over to Mitchell Field, Robin and I discussed the situation. That's how we learned about air density. I told my guys that if they flew to Lowry or Kirtland, they should take off from those fields with less than full tanks. That's one reason why we had fewer accidents than the 1st Fighter Group. It took us a year to figure out the effect of air density. [9]

The accident rate continued to be prohibitive so beginning in 1947, the initial jet experience was gained through the operation of a fully functional P-80 mounted on a stand that allowed retraction of the landing gear and running the engine at full thrust. It became known as the Captivair. The instructor was located in an adjacent control house. He could simulate any flight condition or emergency on the cockpit instruments. About twenty-five hours were required in the Captivair before a first flight in the Shooting Star.

In response to an unacceptably high F-80 accident rate, the Air Force introduced the Captivair, which provided hands-on experience with power management and emergency procedures while firmly attached to the ground. An instructor in the adjacent blockhouse would subject the student to various failures during the simulated flight, which was accomplished with the engine running. *USAF photo via Craig Kaston*

C. The First US Navy Jet Fighter

The Navy also initiated jet engine and airplane development early in World War II. Its first jet engine did not rely on Britain's Whittle design. The Navy selected Westinghouse to develop a jet engine basically from scratch. Like General Electric, this was an appropriate choice because Westinghouse was very familiar with air compressors and turbines from the standpoint of basic principles. For the airplane itself, the Navy took the unusual step of contracting with a relatively new aircraft company, McDonnell Aircraft, which had no experience with US Navy carrier-basing requirements. (Having already demonstrated a flair for innovation with its batplane-like XP-67 fighter for the Army Air Forces and not being critical to the production of existing combat airplanes were probably in its favor.) Both companies proved to be good choices with the result being the McDonnell FD-1 (subsequently FH-1) Phantom powered by two small Westinghouse engines. Unlike the Whittle/General Electric engines, these had axial-flow compressors. The fundamentally different (and as time would prove, superior) compressor configuration for large jet engines was an unanticipated

benefit of the secrecy imposed on the program that precluded contact between General Electric and Westinghouse.

Like the P-59A and the P-80, the FH-1 was intended to be a combat airplane from the very first, not to mention fully compatible with carrier basing. After a relatively trouble-free development, Navy evaluation began that culminated with at-sea trials in July 1946 aboard *Franklin D. Roosevelt* (CV-42).

Production FH-1 Phantoms began to be delivered to the Navy's first jet fighter squadron, VF-17A, in August 1947. The squadron qualified at sea aboard one of the Navy's smaller carriers but never deployed with the FH-1. Marine squadron VMF-122 was also equipped with Phantoms. In both cases, the transition to jets was accomplished for the most part at the squadron level. According to reports from the pilots involved, it consisted of reading the flight handbook, a cockpit checkout, and assistance in starting the engine for the first time.

After a relatively short operational career, the surviving FH-1s (only sixty were built) were replaced by the next generation of jet fighters and transferred to a few reserve squadrons to provide them with jet experience.

The Navy's counterpart to the P-59A was the McDonnell FD-1 Phantom. It was far more advanced in design sophistication and performance than the Airacomet but not enough to justify more than a token production run while more capable jet fighters were being developed. *US Navy photo*

The FD-1 allayed the Navy's fears about the feasibility of operating jet airplanes from aircraft carriers with the at-sea evaluation aboard *Franklin D. Roosevelt* (CVB-42). *US Navy photo*

A Navy fighter squadron, VF-17A, was equipped with production Phantoms and qualified for carrier-based operation. However, the airplane was mainly used for familiarization and demonstrations. *US Navy photo*

D. The T-Bird

The Navy elected not to pursue a two-seat trainer of any of its early jets either because of budget priorities or a lack of concern about the need: "I can fly anything; just show me how to start it." Their contractors did not press to build one although Vought reportedly studied a two-seat derivative of its first jet, the F6U-1 Pirate. If McDonnell did any work on a two-seat FH it didn't proceed far enough to warrant the assignment of a model number. There is no record that Grumman or North American did so with their first jets, either.

Lockheed was more successful in proposing a two-seat modification of the P-80, its model 580, to the Air Force. In early 1947, reacting to reports of a high P-80 accident rate, Lockheed initiated a design study of a two-seat modification to the P-80. It was relatively straightforward: a 26.6-inch extension of the forward fuselage to add the second seat and a twelve-inch plug in the fuselage aft of the wing for balance. A long clamshell-type canopy covered the tandem seats. The fuel tanks in the wings were no longer self-sealing to minimize the loss of fuel capacity caused by the reduction in size of the fuselage tank required by the addition of the second seat.

The horrendous accident rate of the P-80 resulted in the development of a two-seat trainer that was a minimal modification. This early T-33 is still equipped with underslung F-80 tip tanks rather than the larger ones developed to restore the fuel capacity lost in providing a second cockpit. *USAF photo via Mark Nankivil*

In most other respects, the trainer was virtually identical to the P-80 fighter. It retained two of the .50 caliber machine guns in the nose as well as stores pylons for bombs and rockets. This would allow it to be used for "supervised" air-to-air gunnery and air-to-ground ordnance-delivery training in addition to jet transition.

The Air Force authorized the modification of a P-80C to be a two-seat TP-80C prototype in August 1947. Its first flight was accomplished on March 22, 1948 by Lockheed test pilot Tony LeVier at Van Nuys Airport, California. The performance and handling qualities were "practically identical" according to a Lockheed brochure.

Both cockpits were essentially the same, allowing for the student pilot to fly it from the rear seat on instruments under a cloth "hood" that restricted his outside visibility while the instructor flew in the front seat as safety pilot. However, the rear seat was also provided with a "lockout box" so the instructor could override the student's control of the electric trim tabs, wing flaps, and dive brakes if desired.

Even before the TP-80C prototype's first flight, the Air Force ordered 20 TP-80Cs from Lockheed in January 1948. It was equally clear to the generals that a two-seat jet trainer was essential.

The trainer actually gave up little in performance to the single-seat fighter. Some say it was a little bit faster due to the higher fineness ratio of the longer fuselage and the lighter weight resulting from the reduction in fuel capacity. According to the Navy's TO-1 and TO-2 Standard Aircraft Characteristics charts that corresponded to the Air Forces' P-80C and TP-80C respective:

The front cockpit of the T-33 was virtually identical to that of the F-80. In this example, the gun sight has been removed although the trainer retained provisions for machine guns. *USAF photo*

	P-80C	TP-80C
GROSS WEIGHT (LBS.)	15,336	14,442[1]
INTERNAL & EXTERNAL FUEL (LBS.)	5,060	4,576[1]
MAXIMUM SPEED (KTS.)	408	408
SERVICE CEILING (FT.)	36,000	37,000
RANGE (NM)	1,200	1,080[1]

[1]P-80C TIP TANKS

The TP-80C was redesignated the TF-80C on June 11, 1948 with the change in designation from P for Pursuit to F for Fighter and then to T-33A on May 5, 1949, as part of the simplification of trainer designations.

Since the T-Bird, as it became known, was developed from a proven airplane with minimal modification, its qualification was straightforward. The loss of internal fuel capacity was subsequently eliminated by the addition of larger tip tanks that were mounted on the end of the wing tips instead of under them like the F/P-80s.

The thrust of the Allison J33 engine in the T-33 was increased over time, increased over time to 5,400 lbs, a 17% increase. Like the P-59A, P-80A and the Navy's first jet fighters, the first two-seaters did not have ejection seats but these were subsequently incorporated in production and retrofitted.[10]

In June 1949, the T-33A began to be used for Air Force pilot training by the 3535th Flying Training Group at Williams Air Force Base in Arizona for the first time. The availability of T-33s was achieved just in time for the jet-pilot training buildup necessitated by the Korean War that began in June 1950.

It was one thing to transition a few very experienced, handpicked fighter pilots into single-seat jets with an informal cockpit checkout. (The first lowly Navy Ensign to check out in a jet was the 209th Naval Aviator to do so.) It was quite another to have to greatly expand the number of jet pilots in part with newly winged students who had little more than 200 hours total flight time solely in propeller driven airplanes.

Ejection seats and larger tip tanks were added early in the production of the T-33s. *USAF photo via Rich Dann*

T-33s quickly became the standard trainer in the USAF as shown in this August 24, 1971, taken at Peterson Field, Colorado Springs, Colorado by A1C James A. Edmundson. *USAF photo*

In the early 1950s, the Air Force basic training phase of sixteen weeks and 130 flight hours now included flight time in both the T-33 and the obsolescent F-80, providing a more solid foundation for the pilot's smooth and safe transition into single-seat high-performance jet fighters as well as an excellent platform for instrument training.

The T-33 replaced the last of the T-28s used in Air Force basic training on July 1, 1956.

The T-Bird proved to be a classic design for the purpose with an exceptionally long and worldwide operational career. Except for the fuel system[11], it was uncomplicated and the pilot's workload was low. The cockpit was quiet, well air conditioned once in the air, and roomy enough for the average-sized person. The visibility, particularly from the front seat, which was ahead of the wing, was very good. The early vintage powered-aileron design initially fostered over control in roll, particularly at takeoff speeds, that disappeared with experience and resulted in agreeably light controls at high speed. Approach to stall in either 1 g or accelerated flight generated unmistakable and progressive aerodynamic warning and the stall itself was benign with no roll off. It was reluctant to enter a spin but unlike some airplanes that were hard to spin, not reluctant to recover from one if finally forced to. The power-off glide ratio was good, more than two miles for every 1,000 feet of altitude, and drag was low. As a result, foresight was required for descent, approach, and landing. Speed stability on approach was very good. Its major vice was that of a typical jet of the time: deceleration was slow after a throttle reduction and if the throttle was reduced all the way to idle to kill speed, it took several seconds after the throttle was pushed forward before the engine produced much of an increase in thrust.

The T-33 provided a suitable transition between the Texan's replacement, the T-28, and not only the F-80 and F-84 but also the Air Force's next air superiority fighter, the swept-wing F-86. *USAF photo*

By the time that this picture was taken in 1955, the Air Force was only flight checking one in four of the T-33s that had been production flight tested by Lockheed pilots at Palmdale, California. Maj. Edwin Rackham (left) is picking one of these four T-33s for 1st Lt. Frank Hollingshead to fly for acceptance. *USAF photo*

E. Navy Jet Training

Compared to the US Air Force, the US Navy took a different approach to the introduction of jet fighters. It had to contend with a much higher degree of difficulty operationally, taking off and landing on the aircraft carrier, for which jets were initially unsuited. One prospective solution was the turboprop, which had an additional turbine in the exhaust turning the propeller via a gearbox. Another was combining a piston engine in the nose with a jet engine in the tail. The former was a non-starter due to the lack of gearbox durability; the latter proved to constrain the jet's speed potential.

The Air Force had one disappointment, the P-59A, which nevertheless provided valuable experience and then a success, the P-80, which was built in quantity along with the Republic P-84[12]. The Navy had obtained a few P-80s for evaluation, including at-sea trials of one. However, it was determined that incorporating required carrier-suitability changes would require substantial modification, eliminating any performance benefit it might have had over fighters that the Navy was developing and introducing into service.

The Navy's first jet, the FH-1 Phantom, was successful but like the P-59A, had a very short production run and was never deployed with a carrier air group. However, the

Although the Navy evaluated the P-80 for use as a carrier-based jet fighter, it proved to be inadequate from a structural and handling qualities standpoint for carrier takeoffs and landings. *US Navy photo*

The Navy had McDonnell develop a derivative of its successful FD with more powerful Westinghouse engines. It was designated the F2D, subsequently changed to F2H when Douglas resumed development of fighters. *T.H. Thomason collection*

Navy contracted for the development of three more fighters in early 1945, all of which were carried forward into production. These were the North American FJ-1 Fury, the Vought F6U Pirate, and the McDonnell F2H Banshee. Like the Phantom, the Fury and the Pirate were only produced in limited quantities. The Banshee, on the other hand (like the Grumman F9F-2 Panther that the Navy ordered a year later) went on to form the core of the Navy's carrier-based jet fighter capability through the Korean War. Before then, however, these jets provided Navy pilots with operational experience.

The Navy began taking delivery of a small quantity of North American FJ-1 Furies in 1948. These were assigned to VF-5A—soon to be redesignated VF-51—based in San Diego.

Incidents during the FJ-1's service with VF-51 suggested a more formal jet transition program would be appropriate. In one, the squadron was assigned a training exercise to locate a Navy destroyer at sea off San Diego using a flight of four Furies. Visibility was poor and the flight leader elected to extend the search a little too long. As a result, one airplane flamed out several miles out to sea and had to be ditched. Another flamed out after landing but before it could be taxied to the ramp. The squadron also entered six FJ-1s in the September 1948 Bendix trophy race from Long Beach, California to Cleveland, Ohio. Oversized tip tanks were installed that just barely met the range requirement. One pilot, trying to maximize his range by cruising at too high an altitude for his oxygen system (the FJ-1 didn't have a pressurized cockpit), became hypoxic.[14] As a result, he got lost. Low on fuel, he crash-landed in a field eighty miles southwest of Cleveland. Another of the pilots ran out of fuel fifty miles from the Cleveland Airport but was able to glide all the way there and make a dead-stick landing. One pilot who successfully reached Cleveland had his engine flame out from fuel exhaustion before he could taxi to the parking area after landing.

Grumman, late to jet fighter development but one of the Navy's long-standing providers of air-superiority fighters, was successful with its first one, the F9F Panther. This is a prototype without the tip tanks that quickly became standard to provide acceptable endurance for carrier operations. *US Navy photo*

Along with the McDonnell Phantom and the Vought F6U, the Navy contracted with North American for limited production of the FJ-1 Fury. This airplane is equipped with oversized tip tanks necessary for flying non-stop between Long Beach, California, and Columbus, Ohio, for the 1948 Bendix "race" for jets. The amount of extra fuel, twice that in the standard tanks, proved to be less than sufficient for one of the participants. *US Navy photo*

The Vought F6U Pirate saw very limited service. Production was delayed by development problems, the need to add an afterburner to provide adequate performance, and the move of Vought from Connecticut to Texas. As a result it was never qualified for carrier operation and saw very limited use by VX-3, a Navy Air Development Squadron that specialized in evaluation of fighter tactics and weapons employment. Most of the pilots who gained any experience from one were those who ferried it from place to place until it reached the destination where it would be stricken.

In 1948, a result of the delays in its fighter development programs and limited production, the Navy had to adopt a placeholder strategy to fill its jet-transition trainer needs. It bought fifty Shooting Stars from the Air Force to "train pilots and maintenance personnel in operation of jets." These were stock fifty P-80s (forty-nine P-80C-1-LO and one P-80C-5-LO). Since the Navy considered them to be

Three of the first four Navy jets were pictured in this formation. The two with XC on the tail are assigned to VX-3, a Navy evaluation squadron. Nearest the camera is the Vought F6U Pirate. On its wing is the McDonnell FH-1. The third airplane is the McDonnell F2H. *US Navy photo*

In order to reduce a shortfall in the number of jets required for operational and training squadrons in the late 1940s, the Navy purchased fifty Lockheed P-80s as its TO-1 trainer. *US Navy photo*

trainers, not fighters (for one thing, they were not carrier capable), the Navy designated them TO-1, its first trainer (T) from Lockheed (O). They were assigned Bureau Numbers 33821-33870. "To simplify problems of maintenance and logistic support," all were initially based on the west coast in the San Diego area, only about 130 miles south of Lockheed's plant in Burbank, California.

An existing Marine fighter squadron, VMF-311, received twelve TO-1s and operated them from MCAS El Toro, California. Similarly a Navy fighter squadron, VF-6A—subsequently redesignated VF-52—initially received twenty-four. The rest of the TO-1s were held in reserve for attrition and to replace airplanes going into overhaul.

A handful of VF-52 pilots completed Air Force jet-transition training in the P-80 at Williams Field, Arizona and returned to instruct the remainder of the squadron pilots; the squadron then functioned as the Navy's jet transition training unit. The first group of eighteen pilots completed the course in late November 1948. It consisted of fifty-two hours of classroom instruction and twenty-one hours of flight time in the TO-1. A Naval Aviation News article reported:

> After completing the prescribed course, all transition pilots said actual flying of jets is comparatively easy but that flight planning preparations and careful flight attention were much more critical than in conventional aircraft. Pilots also became 'believers' in maintaining a meticulous watch of fuel consumption.[13]

In addition to instituting a somewhat more formal transition program, the Navy also recognized the need for a two-seat jet trainer. It began to procure T-33s through the Air Force

Twelve TO-1s were assigned to USMC squadron VMF-311 at El Toro to begin Marine Corps familiarization with jet fighter operation and tactics. *US Navy photo*

Twelve TO-1s were assigned to US Navy squadron VF-6A (subsequently designated VF-52), which was to serve as an interim jet transition-training unit and be the basis for the first Navy jet fighter squadron operating Grumman F9F Panthers. *US Navy photo*

beginning in 1949. Its designation for the T-Bird was initially TO-2. In 1952, the TO-1 and TO-2 were redesignated TV-1 and TV-2 respectively when the Navy consolidated the designations of the two Lockheed manufacturing facilities, the former Vega plant (V) and the original Lockheed plant (O). With the change to a common designation system in 1962, the Navy's TV-2 became the T-33B since the Navy's T-Bird configuration had diverged somewhat over time from the Air Force's.

The Navy subsequently decided to transfer responsibility for its more or less formal jet transition training to its training command. VF-52 replaced its TO-1s with Grumman F9F-3 Panthers in 1949 and prepared to deploy with them on a carrier. Their TO-1s were sent to Advanced Training Unit SIX (ATU-6) at NAS Corpus Christi, Texas, with the first one arriving in July 1949. Two months later, ATU-6

was relocated to NAS Whiting Field, Milton, Florida, and redesignated Jet Transitional Training Unit ONE (JTTU-1). The squadron's mission was extended to include training of fleet pilots. (The unit transitioned the US Navy's Flight Demonstration Squadron, the Blue Angels, to its first jet aircraft.) On August 20, 1951, JTTU-1 moved back to Texas to NAS Kingsville and was redesignated Advanced Training Unit THREE (ATU-3).

Late in 1952, ATU-3 became ATU-200. The squadron's mission consisted of training newly designated aviators in familiarization, formation tactics, instruments and navigation using both TV-1s and 2s.

Surviving TV-1s were transferred to the reserves after sufficient numbers of obsolescent Grumman F9F Panthers became available for assignment to the advanced training squadrons.

Like the Air Force, the Navy almost immediately recognized the value of a two-seat jet trainer and purchased a quantity of Lockheed T-33s as its TO-2 trainer. The designation would be subsequently changed to TV-2 in accordance with a consolidation of Lockheed's two different factory designations. *US Navy photo via Mark Nankivil*

After initially being used by a Navy and Marine Corps operational squadrons on the west coast for jet transition training of their own pilots and others, the TO-1s were transferred to a training unit, ATU-3. *US Navy photo*

A snapshot of a transition: the pilot of this well-worn VF-94 Corsair might very well soon find himself in the front seat of the shiny TV-2 parked next to his F4U-4, learning the basics of jet flight. *US Navy photo via Mark Nankivil*

F. The T-Bird Legacy

In retrospect, the T-33/TV-2 probably saved the lives of many budding jet pilots around the world by keeping them out of the cockpits of single-seat fighters until they were more familiar with the aerodynamics and peculiarities of jet planes. Lockheed eventually built almost 6,000 T-33As and TO-2s through August 1959. Canadair built 656 more CT-33 Silver Star Mk 3s with the Rolls Royce Nene engine in place of General Electric/Allison J33. Kawasaki built an additional 210 on license.

After the T-33 began to be replaced by the supersonic T-38 beginning in 1961, it was still a significant part of United States Air Force trainer fleet for a few more years. Even after that, it continued in a training role with the USAF's Air Defense Command, equipped with electronic and physical jamming capability to imitate an intruder. It also provided instrument proficiency capability and served as a squadron or airbase hack.

In an unusual twist, a trainer derived from a jet fighter was used as the basis for a new fighter. An Air Force all-weather fighter, the F-94, was created from a T-33. A radar operator now occupied the rear seat and a radar filled the upper half of the nose. The additional weight was accommodated by adding an afterburner. *USAF photo via Alan C. Carey*

Chapter Four Endnotes

1. The Navy's Ryan FR-1 had flown in 1944 but it had a so-called "composite" or mixed power-plant arrangement, with a conventional piston engine in the nose driving a propeller and a turbojet engine in the aft fuselage. The first flight in June was actually made with only the piston installed.

2. The suffix letter A in the P-59A designation was part of the effort to conceal the existence of America's first jet airplane program. Bell had been under contract to design the P-59 (no suffix), a twin-boom, pusher-propeller-driven fighter. It was an unconventional configuration powered by a conventional reciprocating engine. The program was redirected, *sub rosa*, to be an airplane very conventional in configuration but decidedly unconventional with respect to its engine.

3. Cockpit pressurization was much easier to achieve in a jet airplane than in one powered by a piston engine because a source of compressed air, the engine, was already present. Since the jet range performance was significantly greater at altitudes well above the maximum that would be comfortable in an unpressurized cockpit, this was serendipitous.

4. Manual control of supercharging was undesirable because of the pilot workload and potential to damage the engine in combat maneuvering. As a result, the engine manufacturers added automation to power management. The shift from low blower to high was automatic in the P-51, for example. Vought incorporated additional powerplant-control automation features in the propeller-driven F4U-5 Corsair to reduce pilot workload. However, they proved to be unreliable and sometimes an annoyance, as when the cowl flaps opened automatically during formation flight, slowing the airplane relative to the others.

The turbocharged engine in the P-47 did not require pilot action with respect to power management with changing altitude either; a turbine in the engine's exhaust, not a gearbox turned by the engine crankshaft, drove air compression as dictated by a waste gate. (The pilot could also interconnect the throttle with the propeller and turbocharger controls for single lever operation in combat.) However, as with the supercharger, the pilot had to monitor his engine instruments to insure that engine operation was within limits.

5. The angle of attack for two critical flight conditions, stall and best range speed, did not change with altitude as did indicated airspeed. Unfortunately, the desirability of the display of angle of attack to the jet pilot took a few years to become obvious. It hadn't been as much benefit to pilots of propeller-driven airplanes (the landing weight did not vary as much due to the lower fuel fraction) or as straightforward to implement (the propeller wash had to be avoided).

6. With the earliest fuel controls, the pilot sometimes could not reduce thrust at high altitudes without flaming out the engine, and speeding up to descend might result in exceeding the Mach number limit. He was therefore forced to shut the engine down and restart it at a lower altitude.

7. E.T. Woolridge Jr, *The P-80 Shooting Star; Evolution of a Jet Fighter*, Smithsonian Institution Press, Washington DC, 1979, pg.20.

8. With the separation of the Air Force from the Army, Williams Army Airfield was re-named Williams Air Force Base on January 13, 1948.

9. Rhodes Arnold, Lt.Col. USAF (Ret.), *Shooting Star, T-Bird & Starfire*. Tucson, Arizona: Aztex Corporation, 1981, p.66.

10. None of the first US military jets had an ejection seat initially; the Airacomet was never fitted with one.

11. The T-33 fuel system consisted of several fuel tanks. There was a quantity indication for only one of them, the feed tank. The pilot was responsible for insuring that all of the tanks emptied into the feed tank and keeping track of his total fuel quantity remaining.

12. After the P-80, four of the next five Air Force fighters in numerical sequence—P-81, P-82, P-83, and F-85—were widely disparate ways to accomplish the long-range escort fighter mission. The P-81 was to have a turboprop engine in the nose and a jet engine in the aft fuselage, the P-82 was the Twin Mustang, the P-83 was a supersized P-59A from Bell, and the F-85 was a gnome of a fighter intended to be launched from and recovered to the bomb bay of a B-36. Only the piston-engined P-82 was put into production and used operationally.

13. "Navy Turns Out TO-1 Pilots," *Naval Aviation News* (February 1949): 24.

14. Although the Army Air Forces P-59A and P-80 cockpits were pressurized, the Navy FH-1 and FJ-1 cockpits were not.

Chapter Five
THE AIR FORCE ALL-JET TRAINING PROGRAM

A. The TX Program

After suffering through a period of severe austerity and demobilization while operating a fleet of obsolete trainers that had been developed in the late 1930s, the newly formed Air Force struggled to modernize its Training Command. This suddenly changed in 1948, one year after the Air Force became an independent branch of the military, when Congress responded to the Berlin Crisis and Soviet detonation of a nuclear device with a massive increase military spending.[1] Finally, two long-standing trainer programs were funded. The T-28A, a modern all-purpose trainer with tricycle landing gear, and the T-34A, a lighter, less complex primary trainer, were ordered. In 1952, a third, even more ambitious trainer program named TX was launched. The Air Force issued a Request for Proposal (RFP) for a high-performance trainer that would "teach students all maneuvers and techniques which are required of the military jet pilot with the exception of ordnances."[2] Trainer development, which had been dormant since the start of WWII, became a hotbed of activity.

The TX program was expected to produce a turbine-powered trainer with a cruising speed of 286 knots at 35,000 feet, two hours of endurance allowing for twenty take-offs and landings, the ability to clear a fifty-foot obstacle in 4,000 feet, a landing pattern speed of 113 knots, and an empty weight of not more than 4,000 lbs. Side-by-side seating was preferred since the Air Force was encouraged by European success with side-by-side seating in their trainers—it allowed the instructor to observe the student more closely. The RFP also provided a list of recommended turbojet or turboprop engines that would be provided as government supplied equipment, saving the airframe manufacturer the expense of maintaining an engine inventory. The Request produced fifteen proposals from eight manufacturers including North American, Ryan, Beechcraft, Temco, and Cessna. North American was considered the frontrunner because of its corporate size and experience in developing trainer aircraft. Cessna was regarded as a dark horse since it had no turbine experience and limited military experience (the UC-78 Bobcat and L-19 Bird Dog were Cessna's only military products up to that time). In fact, there was a good bit of ambivalence at Cessna over the RFP as engineer/test pilot, William D. Thompson, recalls:

Our top management and many in engineering were split, with many of us hoping we would not win. The reason was that it would change the whole character of our light plane company, making it vulnerable to the ups and downs (feast or famine) of the military airplane procurement business. The T-37, on the other hand would be a long-term stable production item that would fit into our production lines with minimum dislocations.[3]

Artist rendering of Cessna Model C-318, that evolved into the T-37. *Oswald Mall Collection*

While Cessna's senior management debated the wisdom of entering the competition, Cessna's Flight Test, Aerodynamics, and Preliminary Design group started to investigate configurations that would meet or exceed the Air Force specification. Harry Clements, a college senior and part-time intern, was working with the group under the guidance of an experienced aerodynamicist, Norman Crook. Clements recalls his early experience at Cessna:

We were disbursed within the administration building. Hank Waring was in charge of Flight Test and Aerodynamics, and another gentleman named Virgil Hackett was in charge of Preliminary Design. In January 1952, we all moved to a new office area in the back of the Experimental Hangar—for the first time, as far as I know, the desk people [aerodynamicists, structures, propulsion, and other engineering specialists] and board people [draftsmen] were located together. That sure was convenient for flight testing, since the airplanes were in the front part of the hangar and the aerodynamicists and designers were able to coordinate their work for the proposal activity. In January we embarked on an internal competition to evaluate potential TX configurations using some of the engines listed in the RFP. Hank was the lead in the proposal effort, but Virgil was in charge of the board engineers. As I remember, much was left to the individual board designers to lay out the various three-views and solve arrangement problems but we had an overall objective for each design to be small and readily accessible to ground crews for maintenance. Each board designer was responsible for just one configuration during our internal competition but joined with the others once the winning configuration was selected. During the internal competition a design could exceed any RFP specification—hoping to find one configuration that met or exceeded all requirements and provide the most performance for the least initial cost and lowest maintenance expense (the most bang for the buck). As I remember, the aerodynamicists were responsible for analyzing only one configuration each, while I did stability and control on a comparative basis for all of the configurations that we considered. The structures engineers, not located in our area, did work on all configurations. Once we presented the comparative capabilities, a management decision—I'm sure with a recommendation from Hank, and support from Virgil—for the twin jet, side-by-side approach was made. I don't remember how long that took but I am sure it was well into March. I'm also sure that Hank's successful management of the XT proposal led him to be selected Chief Engineer for the new Military Division when it was formed.[4]

Ryan's Model 59 was very similar in overall configuration to Cessna's proposal. The major difference was that there was a single tailpipe at the rear of the fuselage rather than one on each side of the fuselage at the wing root. *Craig Kaston Collection*

Ryan offered both single- and twin-engine installation. In both, the exhaust was on the centerline. This meant that there was no yaw as a result of an engine failure with the twin-engine alternative. *Craig Kaston Collection*

Fairchild M-178

North American J34

North American R-1820

Other MX-1962 Also Rans

Fairchild's TX proposal featured a split-nose intake that ducted the inlet air around the side-by-side cockpit. North American proposed two alternatives, one powered by the Westinghouse J34 engine and the other a side-by-side variant of the T-28 powered by the more powerful Wright R-1820. *Craig Kaston Collection*

Confident that the preliminary design group had developed an attractive response, Cessna management authorized the submission of a formal proposal for a small, easily maintained aircraft powered by two Continental J69 turbojets. The engines were buried in the roots of an otherwise conventional unswept wing that used a docile NACA 2400 series airfoil (the same airfoil used on Cessna's mild-mannered commercial aircraft) with high lift slotted flaps. The engine location allowed the use of short inlet and exhaust ducts that minimized thrust loss; the offset for the centerline was not ideal from a one-engine-inoperative standpoint but considered acceptable. The cockpit featured side-by-side ejection seats with a jettisonable clamshell canopy and an oxygen system. The landing gear was mounted with a very wide fourteen-foot tread and a steerable nose wheel for maximum safety and ease of ground handling. Cessna designated the design model C-318.

Cessna was noted for running a lean organization with limited engineering manpower so Harry Clements, now a full-time employee, was charged with much of the responsibility for preparing the proposal. The submission consisted of a five-volume technical description; each volume contained hundreds of pages. Clements produced two volumes on stability and control, and did much of the analysis on a third volume. The proposal for Cessna's C-318 design was submitted to the Air Force in June 1952. The other manufactures submitted multiple designs but Cessna submitted only one, and to the surprise of many, Cessna was declared the winner in January 1953. A contract was awarded for three flying prototypes with a separate contract for a non-flying static test article. Cessna's winning C-318 design received the Air Force designation XT-37.

B. XT-37 Development

With the development contracts in hand, Cessna established its new Military Division at the Wichita Municipal Airport. Chief Engineer, Hank Waring, and Project Engineer, Ozzie Mall worked on the detail design of the XT-37 prototypes, while Jim Slaughter, head of the Experimental Shop, assembled a preliminary wood mockup and started work on a more detailed metal mockup that would be displayed to the Air Force by the end of the year. Meanwhile, the Air Force sent a four-man delegation to France to study two twin-jet primary trainers, the Moraine Saulnier 755 Fleuret and the Fouga C.M.170R Magister. The evaluation team was tasked with identifying the problems of using jets in primary training, and determine the merits of side-by-side seating against tandem seating (the Moraine had side-by-side seating while the Fouga had tandem seating). The team concluded that the construction and operation of a high-performance lightweight jet was feasible, the use of such a jet in the primary training of inexperienced students was both sound and realistic, side-by-side seating was preferable to tandem seating, and the use of twin jet engines introduced a desirable safety factor that outweighed the complexity of two engines. In sum, the team concluded that Cessna's configuration for the T-37 was sound.[5]

On December 3, 1953, an Air Force Mockup Board inspected the T-37 display and approved it with several mandatory changes (narrowing of the cockpit being the major revision). At the same time the Air Force began to articulate a growing concern that became known as "The Century Problem." A new generation of complex supersonic fighters was coming on line and the woefully inadequate training system was expected to produce competent pilots for them in the space of one year.[6]

The F-100, first of the Century Series fighters, was expected to become operational in fiscal year 1955; therefore, it was imperative that T-37 development be accelerated. On June 30, 1954, almost four months before the first XT-37 flew; the Air force ordered eleven pre-production airplanes to speed up the testing process. Aware of the urgency, Jim Slaughter and his crew had already started working on the flying prototypes in early 1953. There was considerable overtime and lots of interface with the XT-37 engineers who were conveniently located next to the shop. Slaughter remembers fabricating the airframes with temporary fixtures and jigs that were assembled with erector set simplicity.[7] The speed of fabrication was remarkable for an airframe that was designed with slide rules and hand drawings—CAD (computer aided design) and CNC machining would not come into existence for several decades. Bruce Peterman joined the XT-37 project in August 1953 while the prototypes were being hand-built. Peterman recalls the heroic effort:

> Someone figured out that the average experience for each of the T-37 engineers was about two-and-a-half years, but the leaders were experienced, and what we might have lacked in experience we made up in enthusiasm and determination. We had our slide rules and information sources and standard references. The process was basically what it is today, except that we had to do without the benefit of a mountain of analytical data now available at the touch of a key.[8]

Wind tunnel tests to predict flight behavior had been planned early in the design program. The low-speed wind tunnel at Wichita University revealed that the XT-37 needed a larger horizontal tail and a smaller vertical tail with an increase in the wing dihedral angle and an alteration of the engine nacelles for better inlet pressure recovery. These tests consumed a large block of tunnel time, nearly 260 hours, as Cessna

The metal mock-up of Model C-318 built by Cessna's Experimental Shop. After this mock-up was approved by the Air Force in December 1953, work was started on the three flying prototypes that would differ in several ways from the mock-up: the inlet shape would change, the vertical fin would become shorter with a larger dorsal fairing, and the canopy frame would change. *Craig Kaston Collection*

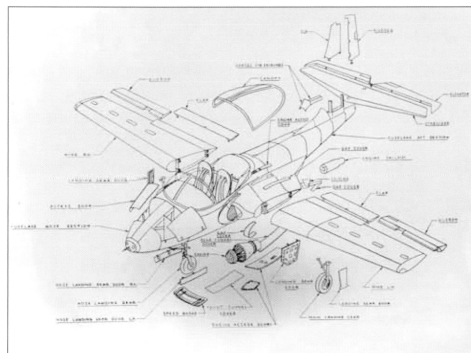

Airframe and engine cutaway drawing of the XT-37 prototype released shortly before the first flight. *NARA*

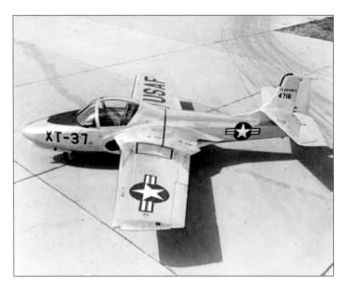

716 poses for a publicity shot before the maiden flight. The long test boom had not been installed on the left wingtip yet. *Hagen Family Collection via Robert F. Dorr*

Project Engineer Oswald Mall stands by the cockpit of the first XT-37 early in the test flight program. *Oswald Mall Collection*

optimized the configuration. Highspeed tests were conducted at Cornell Aeronautical Laboratory's tunnel in Buffalo, New York, to determine critical Mach number. This is the speed at which the airflow over some point of the aircraft reaches the speed of sound, a particularly important measure for a subsonic aircraft since control and stability deteriorate in supersonic airflow. The highspeed tunnel data predicted a critical Mach number of .75 (75% the speed of sound) where the airplane was expected to exhibit an abrupt nose pitch-down (a condition known as Mach tuck). The highspeed data also exposed the need for contour changes to the engine nacelles and an aileron gap seal to improve highspeed roll control. The high-speed tunnel test consumed 130 hours. Spin tunnel tests were conducted at the Wright Field twelve-foot vertical tunnel in late-1954 before actual spins were attempted in the flight test program. Results indicated that the XT-37 would exhibit prompt recovery characteristics, and that the airplane would spin steadily with no tendency to whip or wander. No airframe alterations were expected for spin behavior.

By September 1954, the first prototype, (serial number 54-716), was shop complete and ready for inspection by the Technical Compliance Board which approved it for its maiden flight scheduled for early the following month. Less than two years after receiving the contract, Cessna's first jet was ready for its first flight. Bob Hagan, a former Air Corps P-47 pilot in WWII who gained jet experience in F-84s when he was recalled for Korea, was selected as test pilot. He had been a test pilot in Cessna's Commercial Division and his F-84 experience made him the obvious choice for Cessna's first jet project. Once appointed, Hagan polished his jet flying skills and immersed himself in the XT-37 work at the Experimental Shop, studying its structure and systems.

On October 12, 1954, after a three-day marathon to meet the schedule, Hagan took off from Wichita Municipal Airport at 1:05 in sn. 54-716. The flight lasted sixty-five minutes and seemed uneventful to all on the ground. After landing, Hagan uttered the obligatory, "It sure is a honey of an airplane," to reporters covering the event, but in the cockpit Hagan had a problem. The fuel system was gravity-flow designed to draw equal amounts of fuel from each wing tank into a fuselage tank, but unequal vent pressure allowed fuel to flow from the right tank only. Throughout the maiden flight the XT-37 exhibited increasing wing heaviness on the left side. It became so pronounced that Hagan had to hold the stick with two hands to maintain level flight. The problem was serious enough that it had to be solved before the flight test program could continue. Several short flights around the pattern were made to find a fix. An interconnected vent system with fuel pumps on each wing tank seemed to be the answer, allowing the flight test program to continue.[9]

The XT-37 taking off on its maiden flight October 12, 1954, from Wichita Municipal Airport. *Hagen Family Collection via Robert F. Dorr*

C. Flight Test

By the mid-1950s, the Air Force employed a very rigorous process known as "Phase Testing" on low-rate production airplanes before ordering volume production. The testing often ran for several years, and consisted of eight phases:

Phase I): Contractor's exploration of the airplane's fundamental airworthiness conducted with contractor test pilots often at the contractor's facility;
Phase II): Verification of the contractor's phase I tests by Air Force test pilots at the Air Force Flight Test Center, Edwards Air Force Base;
Phase III): Contractor tests to insure that all deficiencies uncovered in phases I and II have been corrected;
Phase IV): Performance, control and stability, and general engineering evaluation conducted by Air Force test pilots at the Air Force Flight Test Center, Edwards Air Force Base;
Phase V): All weather testing at the Wright air Development Center to determine the reliability of the airplane in extreme weather conditions;
Phase VI): Functional development testing at the Air Force Test Center, Edwards Air Force Base where the airplane is flown frequently and for long periods to insure durability and reliability—during this phase handbooks and performance data references are prepared;
Phase VII): Operational suitability test conducted by the Air Proving Ground Command to determine the most effective way to operate and maintain the aircraft; and
Phase VIII): Service tests by the end user (the command that will operate the aircraft as part of its mission)—this phase is often conducted simultaneously with Phase VII.[10]

Cessna's Phase I responsibility was organized into three parts with each aircraft assigned to a specific part. The first prototype, 54-716, was assigned to demonstrate basic airworthiness, system functionality, structural integrity (up to 80% of the design limit), spin tests, high-speed characteristics, and stall characteristics. The second airplane, 54-717, was assigned to air load survey. It was instrumented to measure bending moment, shear and torque at the root section of each wing and tail surface at various airspeeds, altitudes, and attitudes with varying amounts of control deflection. The third prototype, 54-718, was to be used for propulsion tests, heat and ventilation system tests, and other systems and components tests that warranted investigation.[11]

Flight testing is intended to reveal problems, and the XT-37 exhibited several. Aileron effectiveness, landing gear uplocks, landing approach angle, engine inlet efficiency, fuel controls, stall warning, canopy gapping at high airspeeds, and spin recovery were the major deficiencies. Of these, erratic spin recovery was the biggest surprise, since spin tunnel tests predicted very benign characteristics. Test pilot, Bob Hagan, recalled the spin flights in a 1992 speech:

Prior to beginning the spin flights, a spin parachute was installed on the fuselage tail cone. Meetings were held with our aerodynamicists where it was explained that the spin chute was only a precaution—it wouldn't be needed. All of the model testing in the spin tunnel was successful, thereby proving that spinning the airplane and recovering from the spin would not be a problem. Despite this advice, we approached the spins very carefully. Our plan was to start out with ½-turn spins in both directions and then increase the number of turns in ½-turn increments. We discovered that the ½-turn incipient spins took 1½ turns to recover. A one-turn spin to the left resulted in no recovery until the spin chute was deployed—so much for theoretical predictions! The oscillograph records indicated that the spin was both faster and flatter than the scale model tested in the spin tunnel. We all did a lot of head-scratching and deep-thinking, but no real solutions came to mind. While obtaining more detailed spin characteristics data in the next fifty-three spins, we had to deploy the spin chute on four occasions to get a recovery. Finally, our luck ran out, and on that last chute deployment it pulled loose from the airplane. After trying (unsuccessfully) for about 10,000 feet, I used the ejection seat, which automatically deployed my parachute.[12]

The resulting crash destroyed 54-716, so the remaining prototypes, 54-717 and 54-718, were pressed into service, but not before their fuselages were lengthened twenty-five inches, their horizontal tails were raised six inches and two spin chutes were attached to each airplane. Several factors seemed to contribute to the erratic spin recoveries including persistent lateral imbalance from asymmetric fuel flow. But a significant cause was discovered by aerodynamicist Harry Clements who theorized that the wide forward fuselage, necessary for the side-by-side seating, was generating lift as it rotated in the spin. Clements reasoned that nose strakes (two-inch-wide, six-foot-long extruded angles of aluminum) would spoil this lift and allow a more positive recovery. It worked brilliantly; recovery could be achieved consistently in 1½ turns, meeting the Air Force specification. To ensure that the spin recovery problem was tamed Clements volunteered to try the maneuver himself:

> … it dawned on us that each and every one of those many, many spins had been done by a professional, jet qualified test pilot. Now, in a short order, novice trainees would be asked to routinely perform this maneuver. Even after all that development we still had some apprehension as to how well they would do. We hit upon an easily disguised and simple scheme to satisfy ourselves that those fledgling aviators could do a spin, thus hopefully alleviating the concerns we at the company continued to have. I was a certified Air Force Flight Observer so I could conveniently be scheduled on a test flight, and while I wasn't exactly a novice I had zero turbine, jet, multi-engine, aerobatic, or high performance time. If I could complete a 'regulation' spin, we'd all be relieved.
>
> We set the situation up with Bob Hagan as pilot … I took over at 20,000 feet, approached the stall and got plenty of warning buffet, put in the rudder and entered the spin through a couple of near horizontal 'roll' turns followed by a transition to vertical and a steady, not uncomfortable, five-turn spin. I executed what I felt was a normal recovery procedure and the airplane responded as I expected … the recovery to level flight was easy and uneventful, so our ad hoc spin test had been a success.[13]

Clements was not authorized to fly the XT-37 (which was government property under bailment to Cessna). Even though the "novice recovery test" was a success, Clements was grounded as a Flight Test Observer, but he was recommended for an Air Force commendation for his technical innovation of nose strakes that arguably saved the entire T-37 program from cancellation. Clements was also responsible for resolving another significant problem that became apparent during Cessna's tests. Stalls with the flaps retracted were preceded by noticeable airframe buffet—a desirable characteristic that warns of the impending stall. But with the flaps extended the pre-stall buffet disappeared. Clements found that the downwash from the extended flaps prevented turbulent airflow from striking the horizontal stabilizer (which causes the buffet). He devised a system that deployed spoilers (a flat plate) from the upper surface of each nacelle when the flaps were extended. Again it worked brilliantly, causing turbulent airflow over the tail at the onset of a stall which provided the warning required by the Air Force.

Several months into Cessna's Phase I test flight program the XT-37 takes off from Wichita Municipal still carrying the long instrument boom on its left wing. *NARA*

A flight test engineer, possibly Harry Clements, is in the right seat during this test flight. Qualified engineers would often accompany test pilots for data recording and flight observation. *NARA*

Early wind tunnel tests predicted that the XT-37 would have docile spin characteristics—flight tests proved the opposite. This is the remains of 716 after the spin mishap when Bob Hagen ejected successfully but aircraft continued to spin all the way down to the ground. A robust spin recovery program was started to prevent cancellation of Cessna's contract. *Hagen Family Collection via Robert F. Dorr*

The second prototype, serial 54-717, joins the test flight program. This XT-37 carried the instrument boom on its nose, the fuselage was lengthened by twenty-five inches, the vertical fin was made taller, and the dorsal fin was enlarged. *Baltzer via Nankivil*

Test pilot Bob Hagen prepares the second XT-37 for its maiden flight in this public relations photograph. *Hagen Family Collection via Robert F. Dorr*

The third prototype, 54-718, while at Wright Patterson Air Force Base. Nose strakes have been added to this XT-37 to improve spin recovery. *Baltzer via Nankivil*

A close-up shot of the nose strakes that improve spin recovery. This feature, developed by Cessna aerodynamicist Harry Clements, saved the program from cancellation. *Dan O'Hara*

Another feature developed by Harry Clements was the stall warning spoiler mounted on the upper surface of the engine nacelle. It was deployed when the flaps were fully extended to generate turbulent airflow over the tail for stall warning. *Mark Frankel*

A T-37 taxies at Hill Air Force Base with the stall warning spoilers extended as part of the pre-take off check. *Don Spering A.I.R. Collection*

D. T-37A

With Phase I tests under way, Cessna started work on the 11 pre-production airplanes that were ordered in June 1954. These airplanes, designated T-37A, would be more refined than the experimental XT-37, but they were still test articles subject to substantial modification. The first T-37A, 54-2729, rolled out of Cessna's Prospect Plant on September 3, 1955, and made its maiden flight three weeks later. After extensive factory testing it was delivered to the Air Force the following June along with five other pre-production examples. Three of these airplanes were assigned to Phase IV Functional Development testing which imposed prolonged, harsh use on every system to assess durability and reliability. The testing started June 8, 1956, and concluded on August 18. These airplanes were maintained on a sixteen-hour day, six-day work week schedule, flown by thirty pilots, accumulated more than 600 hours over 396 flights, and made 878 landings.[14] As expected, several new problems were revealed. The most serious involved the J69-T-9 turbojet engines that developed a history of turbine blade failures, starter-generator overheating, and combustion chamber cracking. The airframes experienced several nose gear torque link failures (a part that keeps the upper and lower sections of the nose landing gear aligned), and brake-disc warping. But the Flight Test Center expressed satisfaction with the T-37A:

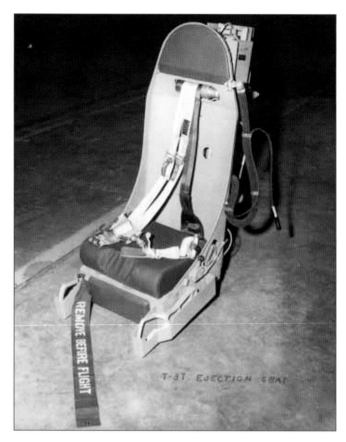

The T-37 was the first primary trainer to employ ejection seats. The design worked flawlessly for test pilot Bob Hagan in the spin mishap of first XT-37. *Baltzer via Nankivil*

A high utilization rate of 4½ hours per aircraft per day obtained for the entire 612-hour test program demonstrates the excellent reliability and ease of maintenance of the T-37A. Maintenance requirements are reasonable and most maintenance performed on the aircraft is simplified by excellent accessibility and simple layout. The limited requirement for ground support equipment and special tools is an excellent design feature.

All aircraft systems with the exception of the power plant and landing gear demonstrated satisfactory functional reliability during the program. The nine identical structural failures of the nose gear torque links indicate they are a definite weak point and are considered a safety of flight hazard. Poor brake feel and unsatisfactory nose wheel steering constitute the remaining difficulties with the landing gear system. Engine refinement and procurement programs are sufficiently behind the rest of the aircraft to establish them as the limiting parameter of the T-37 utilization at the present time.

The aircraft is easy to fly and performs well in all normal aerobatics. The ability to perform its designed training mission is greatly advanced by the side-by-side seating arrangement, simple layout, and good visibility.[15]

By mid-1957 the first T-37As were delivered to the primary flight instruction schools at Bainbridge AFB, Georgia, and James Connally AFB, Texas. At that time civilian flight instructors were used to provide primary training (a practice started before WWII). The civilians were carefully checked out in the new jets by Air Force pilots at Connally. On July 18, 1957, the first Air Force students received instruction in the T-37A at Bainbridge AFB under an evaluation program known as "Project Palm." The evaluation measured a test group of students who started with thirty hours in the propeller driven T-34A followed by 100 hours in the T-37A jet, against a control group who received all propeller training of thirty hours in the T-34A followed by 100 hours in the T-28A. 2nd Lt. Thomas W. Beaghan became the first student to solo in the T-37A. The purpose of the project was to measure the success of the jet-trained students against the propeller trained students in the advanced T-33 phase. Completed on December 29, 1958, Project Palm demonstrated that the jet group excelled in transitioning to the T-33.[16] The Air Training Command was so encouraged with the results that an expanded evaluation, known as Project All-Jet, was started on

November 19, 1958. All-Jet used the T-37A for the entire primary and basic syllabus, eliminating all propeller training. In January 1959, 2nd Lt. Gene McGinnis became the first USAF student to solo in a jet trainer with no prior propeller experience.[17]

By now, Cessna's Military Division was busy producing 534 T-37A-models to meet the Training Command's needs. At its peak, Cessna completed a new T-37A every eleven hours and twelve minutes. The last example rolled onto the flight line in October 1959, five years after the first XT-37 flight.[18] At some point, the T-37A earned the affectionate nickname "Tweety Bird" or "Tweet" because of high-pitched noise caused by the J69 centrifugal compressors in their short inlet ducts. Cessna experimented with several methods of lessening the "screech"—the most promising being a series of vertical vanes positioned in the inlet—but they caused an uneven distribution of pressure across the compressor resulting in some thrust loss, so the Air Force elected to live with high-pitched noise. Cessna also experimented with a thinner wing that showed substantial promise for increased performance. A wind tunnel model tested at the Cornell highspeed tunnel predicted a critical Mach number of .85 (the production wing was .75) with no change in the stall speed. But the Air Force saw no value in increased performance for a subsonic trainer and rejected the modification.

Increased service use of the T-37A exposed a new series of technical problems. One issue, random engine flameouts in the landing pattern, was particularly difficult to diagnose. The flameouts occurred when a fighter approach was used which imposed high G forces at the pitch out (a sharp ninety-degree turn over the runway). Usually one engine would flame out, but on occasion both would fail. After spending hours investigating inlet airflow under every conceivable condition, engineers failed to duplicate the problem. Finally it was noticed that the flameouts only occurred in early serial number aircraft. This led to the discovery that over time the grommets used in the engine mounts were softening in the high-heat environment of the engine bays. The softened grommets allowed the engines to shift slightly under the G load, which in turn allowed the throttle linkage to move to the idle shut-off position causing fuel starvation. Stiffening the engine mount grommets kept the engines running under all conditions.[19] Another powerplant issue was resolved with an equally simple but effective solution. The J69 turbojet engines required an unacceptably long time to accelerate from idle to full power, on the order of thirteen seconds. This risked an accident whenever a solo student was slow to recognize the need for more thrust on a landing approach. Cessna therefore added a "thrust attenuator." It was a retractable

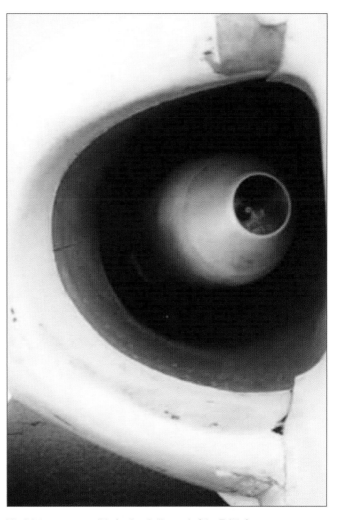

The inlet was responsible for the shrill sound of the T-37. Cessna experimented with several noise reduction designs but thrust loss made them impractical. The nickname "Tweet" was bestowed on the T-37 because of the inlet noise. *Dan O'Hara*

panel that extended into the jet exhaust to reduce the effectiveness of the engine thrust when the speed brake was extended and rpm was reduced below 68-70%. Deployment of the thrust attenuator therefore allowed the pilot to approach at a higher power setting than would otherwise be required for an approach. Retracting the attenuator resulted in an instant thrust increase; maximum thrust could be reached in only four seconds. Moreover, both extension and retraction were automatic so the student did not need to remember to do either.

T-37 Thrust Attenuator

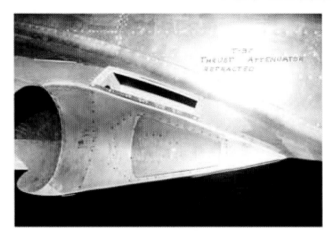

Retracted

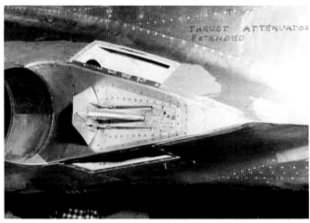

Extended

The thrust attenuator was incorporated to allow the engine to run at a higher rpm during the landing approach. Normally retracted, it extended during landing approach to diminish thrust so that the engine could operate at a higher rpm and provide a quicker response in the event of a go-around. *Baltzer via Nankivil*

The Air Force grew increasingly confident with the T-37; the primary school at Graham AFB introduced it in April 1958 followed by Bartow AFB in August 1958. Bainbridge AFB, which had been the first to use the T-37, became so reliant on the little jet that they phased-out their T-28 equipment by the end of 1958. Moore and Spence started using the T-37 in 1959, and by 1960 the T-37 was the only primary trainer in the Air Force as the T-34/T-28 phase out was complete. Also in 1960, the Air Force ceased using civilian flight schools and assigned military pilots to undergraduate pilot training. Detailed studies concluded that civilian training was more cost effective, but the introduction of the T-37 in primary training meant that active duty pilots could gain valuable jet experience while serving as instructors.[20]

The Air Force ordered eleven production T-37As while the prototype XT-37s were still being tested. This is the second production article, 54-2730, carrying a nose mounted instrument boom, and it was used in Phase IV Functional Development testing at Edwards AFB. *AFFTC History Office*

Later in the test program 54-2730 is pictured during a test sortie with its speed brake deployed. *Dann via Nankivil*

The Training Command was so pleased with the T-37 that they started phasing out the T-28A. By 1960, the T-37A was the only aircraft used for primary training. Here, a new T-37A and a soon to be replaced T-28A are pictured at Ellington Air Force Base. *A.I.R. Don Spering Collection*

A public relations photo from 1956 showing the range of jets in the Air Force inventory from the tiny T-37A to the huge B-52. *NARA*

Serial Number 60-0079, an early T-37B that featured engine and avionics improvements. *A.I.R. Don Spering Collection*

The T-37B improvements were so effective that the Air Force decided to upgrade 521 A models to the B Model standard. *Baltzer via Nankivil*

The T-37B instrument panel. Note that the instructor still did not have a full set of flight instruments on his side. *Baltzer via Nankivil*

E. T-37B

Shortly after the T-37A became operational, instructors began reporting occasional compressor surges during high altitude maneuvers. Initially, the Air Force lived with the problem but over time it became intolerable. A surge would cause an explosive bang during training flights—a condition not conducive to effective instruction. Continental redesigned the J69-T-9 compressor and turbine to eliminate the surge and in the process gained 105 pounds of thrust while eliminating six pounds of weight. The improved engine, designated J69-T-25, caused designer Eli Benstein to remark, "We jacked up the J69 nameplate and installed a new engine under it."[21] In April 1959, the Air Force ordered an updated T-37 with the new dash 25 engines and modernized avionics. The first example, designated T-37B (serial number 59-286), was rolled out on November 6, 1959 and went through phase I flight test at Cessna. The Air Force performed a phase II flight test on serial number 60-079 from October 24, 1960, to January 3, 1961, at Edwards Air Force Base and concluded:

> The performance of the T-37B is much improved over that of the T-37A. Take-off performance, climb rates and ceilings, and level flight speeds have been increased significantly. The increase in single engine performance is impressive and adds greatly to aircrew safety during the traffic pattern.[22]

Only the braking system, which was considered unsatisfactory in the T-37A, remained troublesome in the B version. But the Air Force was so pleased with the improved trainer that they converted most A-models to the B-model standard. Duane Moore, the Military Aircraft Division Production Manager, performed a masterful job in accomplishing all 521 "Project Turnaround" conversions in sixteen months. By the end of the project in July 1960 only thirteen A-models remained. In addition to the 521 conversions, 552 newly built T-37Bs were produced by 1973.

The T-37 fleet accumulated a large amount of flight hours in a short time—of course new problems emerged. Between 1965 and 1970, shattered canopies from bird strikes became an epidemic problem. An immediate solution was mandatory since the aircraft spent much time teaching takeoffs and landings at pattern altitude where bird encounters are likely. A thicker bird resistant Lexan polycarbonate windscreen was retrofitted, but visual distortion, fogging, and scratches made the transparency unacceptable. Finally, a solution was found in using a polycarbonate core sandwiched between two layers of Plexiglas.[23]

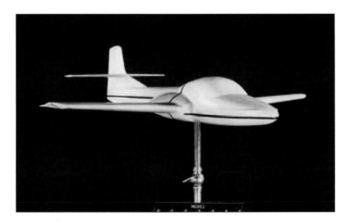

A rash of T-37B spin accidents caused a re-examination of spin characteristics. The Training Command wanted to find a standard recovery technique for all spin modes. Here a spin test model is being prepared for the NACA spin tunnel. *Craig Kaston Collection*

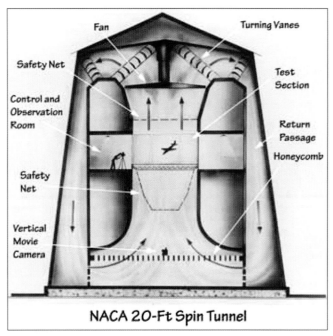

Fan   Turning Vanes

Safety Net

Control and Observation Room

Test Section

Return Passage

Honeycomb

Safety Net

Vertical Movie Camera

NACA 20-Ft Spin Tunnel

The NACA Langley twenty-foot free spinning tunnel was frequently used to evaluate the spin and spin-recovery characteristics of airplanes. Sometimes a second or third set of tests was required after actual spins revealed unacceptable characteristics. *Tommy H. Thomason*

T-37s also spent much time teaching spins. The nose strakes developed early in the XT-37 test program were thought to have made spins predictable and easily recoverable, but a rash of spin related accidents at the Training Command caused the Air Force to take another look at spin behavior. The T-37 exhibited three types of spins modes, erect normal (entered from a stall with full back stick and full rudder deflection in the direction of the spin), erect accelerated (entered at a higher speed than stall with less than full back stick), and inverted (entered from an inverted attitude with full forward stick and full rudder deflection in the direction of the spin).[24] In 1957, a fourth mode, the aggravated spin, was found by an instructor who was exploring botched recovery techniques. He was able to demonstrate that a normal erect entry spin, when allowed to develop beyond three turns, followed by very slow recovery inputs (at least four seconds), defied normal recovery techniques. The flight manual, at that time, described specific recovery techniques for each spin mode. But student pilots had difficulty recognizing the mode and applying the correct response. The Flight Test Center at Edwards AFB was asked to conduct a spin program with the objective of finding a single recovery technique that would work for any type of spin. The program made use of T-37B, serial 59-331, which was subjected to 270 spins over eighteen flights. The tests were started on September 13, 1961, and concluded on October 20 resulting in the development and demonstration of a simplified recovery procedure that worked for all spin modes.

Capt. Tracy Rhodes, a T-37 flight instructor at Webb AFB, TX in the mid-1970s, recalls the challenge of spin instruction and the simplified recovery procedure that the Training Command adopted:

The T-37 was a fun plane to fly. It wasn't a super-fast airplane, but in my opinion that made it much more fun to fly. Aerobatics took fewer gs and less altitude to complete than the T-38. Then there were the spins. The training syllabus in the T-37 included spin entry and recovery while the T-38 training only included various types of stalls.

When we practiced spins we first had to climb to at least 20,000' AGL. In west Texas where I was an instructor that meant climbing to about 23,000 feet MSL. Since the T-37 is an unpressurized aircraft, our maximum altitude was 25,000' MSL, so we were pushing our limits. The reason we had to be that high to enter a spin was that once the spin was fully stabilized the T-37 descended vertically at about 10,000 fpm. That gave you about two minutes to exit the spin or it would stop rotating on its own when it hit the ground. It was quite the ride.

It's amazing that after thirty-five years I can still recite the recovery steps. They were:

1) Throttles—Idle
2) Rudder and Ailerons—Neutral
3) Stick—Abruptly Full Aft and Hold
4) Rudder—Abruptly apply Full Rudder Opposite the Direction of the Spin and Hold
5) One Turn After Applying Opposite Rudder—Stick Abruptly Full Forward
6) Controls—Neutral and recover from the Dive

The first three steps were designed to get the aircraft in the same starting point for each recovery attempt. They establish the aircraft in a more or less stabilized spin condition. Between steps 3 and 4 you had to figure out which direction you were spinning. In theory you should know the spin direction since you're the one who started the spin in the first place, but as a student in the heat of battle, that might just slip your mind, especially when the aircraft starts whipping around. The intent was to provide a sequence of steps in case a spin was entered inadvertently. As I remember, in a stabilized spin the T-37 rotated at about three seconds per turn with the nose dropping to about thirty degrees down once it stabilized. The spin axis was on a vertical line that passed through the cockpit between the two seats. If you referenced the turn needle you could determine the direction of rotation, but if you looked at the slip/skid ball the instrument on the left side of the cockpit would have the ball to the left and the instrument on the right side of the cockpit would have its ball to the right. One thing that you needed to do at step 4 was to pick some point on the horizon or on the ground when you slammed in full rudder travel opposite the spin direction. The next step was to patiently (?) wait as the aircraft rotated until that point reappeared in front of you. This was an excellent way to experience time slowing to a crawl with an adrenaline rush. When your point finally reappeared you would immediately try to push the stick forward through the instrument panel: the nose would pitch down toward vertical and you would recover from the dive.

The application of the rudder opposite to the spin direction would start the recovery and, in some cases, could actually stop the spin rotation. Unfortunately, the students rarely noticed the rotation coming to a stop. On those planes, instead of accomplishing step 5 you could just move the stick to a slightly nose down position, the stall would be broken and the plane would recover. Again, in the heat of the battle, the student would be focused only on waiting for that rudder application point to reappear and wouldn't sense the spin rotation slowing. I remember one myopic student getting to step 5 just as the rotation stopped. I tried yelling "NO!" but I doubt if he heard me. He slammed the stick to the forward stop just as the aircraft had regained almost full control effectiveness. I had to check my helmet when we got back to the base to make sure I hadn't cracked it when my head hit the canopy. The average T-37 would merely slow its rotation slightly with the opposite rudder applied and then step 5 would pitch the nose down to vertical, breaking the stall. The requirement for step 6 would then be quickly obvious as the airspeed would build quickly if the nose wasn't immediately raised to the horizon.

In the T-37, if a student froze at the controls during a spin recovery we had two or three options for regaining their attention. We wore helmets and oxygen masks with an intercom system connecting the two headsets and sat side-by-side in the cockpit. If yelling as loud as you could didn't bring the student back to reality we could slap the student a few times on the side of the helmet. The half-inch thick aircraft checklist with its metal rings worked well. If that wasn't enough, our next-to-last resort was to grab the oxygen hose that leads to their mask and kink the hose. The inability to breathe would usually get their attention or transfer the student's fixation from the ground rushing up at them to finding air to breathe. The last resort was 'Handles-Raise, Triggers—Squeeze', the ejection sequence.

Unlike some civilian flight schools where students are assigned to instructors in an effort to even the workload (and income), the student/instructor pairing at UPT is done by an analysis of the student's performance in the previous phase of training. Stronger students were placed with the newer instructors and weaker students were placed with instructors with more experience. That meant that the longer that you were an instructor the worse your students became. The pilot screening process weeded out the really weak flyers, but there were always some individuals that took just a little bit longer or a needed little more help to see the big picture. By the time I had been instructing for three years, I was not being assigned the top members of the UPT class. I looked forward to the challenges but some days it was just plain frustrating. Then on this particular day one of the newer instructors in our flight called in sick and I filled in for a day instructing with one of the better students in the class. And it was spin training day.

We went through all the ground briefings and he seemed to have an entry-level understanding of the aerodynamics of the spin and a good handle on the entry and recovery procedures. With the ground training covered, we made our way to the equipment room to pick up our flight gear and headed for the airplane. The departure went fine and as we exited the airport area we contacted the controller to obtain a practice area assignment. At that time the practice areas for the T-37 fanned out to the north of the airport. I don't remember how many there were, but they were fairly large and were segmented into high and low areas with the bottom of the low area at 10,000´ MSL and the top of the high area at 25,000´ MSL. You could be assigned just the low or high segments or you could get both, depending on the traffic.

We were assigned a high area that day, called entering the area and proceeded to climb up to 22,000 ft. to begin our spin training. I demonstrated the first spin and recovery, talking our way through the steps and pointing out the aircraft reactions to each step. The student seemed to be following along and responded to the occasional question. After the demonstration we worked our way back up to the top of the area. Now it was the student's turn to give it a try. Since I had not flown with this student before and since it was his first attempt I was very alert to what may or may not happen. His spin entry went fine and the aircraft was reacting in a predictable manner as it stabilized in the spin. After a couple of turns I gave the 'Recover' command and the student performed the recovery almost perfectly. Great! It was going to be a really nice day of flying. Back up to the top of the area to try another one. I was relaxed. Boy, was that the wrong thing to do.

Second try. The spin entry was fine, the spin developed and I again gave the command to recover. He did a great job right up to step 5 when you apply full forward stick to break the stall. Step 6 is when you recover from the vertical dive that resulted from step 5. Without step 6 the controls are positioned so that the throttles are at idle, the rudder is at the full limit opposite the spin direction and the control stick is full forward. If you leave the controls there the aircraft pitches down and through vertical and back up to the horizon to put you inverted and in an aerodynamic stall with full rudder applied. You now find yourself in an opposite direction inverted spin.

As an instructor, you really should not ever let a student surprise you this much. I came back to full alert and instinctively grabbed the throttles and the stick and said 'I have the aircraft.' First challenge—both seats in the T-37 operate with right-handed stick and left-handed throttle and there is a difference between the student's throttles and the instructor's throttles. The instructor's set has the cut-off feature that shuts down the engine, accomplished by lifting the throttles up and back over the idle stop. On the ground or in normal flight, there has to be a conscious effort to raise the throttles. However, when you are inverted and you grab the throttles the weight of your arm will very easily pull the throttles up (down?) and aft. So, now I found myself inverted, rotating and watching the engines spool down.

When faced with multiple, overlapping emergencies you have to be able to prioritize. One way to do that is to determine which of the problems will kill you first. I knew that the airplane was not going to come out of the inverted spin by itself and I knew that it was only going to take about another minute and half to reach the ground, so that project seemed to jump out into the lead. As I said in the last episode, the first three steps of the spin recovery are designed to stabilize the spin so that the remaining steps are accomplished from the same point each time. I centered

the rudder and abruptly applied full back stick. That caused the aircraft to flip right-side-up and continue its spin from there. Things were now looking a bit more familiar. I methodically accomplished the remainder of the recovery steps and the plane came out of the spin gliding happily toward the bottom of our assigned area.

The next situation to consider was the possibility of running into traffic occupying the lower part of our practice area. I called the area controller and asked for the lower area in addition to our assigned upper area. We were about 1000′ from the bottom of our allotted airspace and would probably go into the lower area before we got an engine started. I managed to get the request out to the controller, but just after that the aircraft generators went off line due to the winding down of the engines. We no longer had radios to hear the reply and no longer had a working transponder that allowed the controller to see us. The only way to fix that was to restart the engines, our next project.

I had the student get out his checklist and read off the steps necessary to do an in-flight restart … twice. Both of the engines restarted and as the engines spooled up the generators came back on line. Our headsets were filled with radio calls from the area controller looking for a response from us. The controller had replied to our lower area request, was getting no response from us and had lost our radar return. They were starting to think about the possibility that they had lost an airplane. There was audible relief in the controller's voice when we finally responded. It turned out that the lower portion of our practice area was not being used and the controller assigned the airspace to us. We had descended about 1500′ into the lower area and were beginning to climb back up as fast as we could. Instead we leveled off and thought about what to do next. Both the student and I were a little unsettled, so we leveled off and just flew around the practice area for a while to relax. Then I transferred the controls to the student and had him fly us back to the airport and enter the pattern for a full-stop landing. We called the lesson incomplete and rescheduled it the next day.

What had I learned by the end of that day? First, as an instructor, don't for a minute believe that just because a student shows strong capabilities one minute that they can't have total brain fade the next and give you one of your worst nightmares. Second, at any level of your flying career, if you find yourself facing multiple emergencies/failures/ situations prioritize the individual problems and start methodically working through the list. You will eventually reach a point where things look familiar, the problems have been resolved or you are able to live with what remains.[26]

By the early 1960s, most of the T-37 development issues were corrected and the "Tweet" set a reliability record of 98% operational readiness. At the same time it was regarded as the safest airplane in the Air Force inventory, and it offered the lowest acquisition cost and operating cost of any jet. By the mid-1990s, more than 80,000 military pilots had received training in the T-37 with millions of flight hours logged.[27] The May 1995 issue of *Air Force Magazine* noted that 494 T-37Bs were still on the active roster, with an average age of 31.7 years making it one of the longest serving aircraft in Air Force history. The original design life of 10,000 flight hours was extended to 15,000 hours after a Cessna structural modification program in the early 1980s. In 1989, the Sabreliner Corporation conducted a Service Life Extension Program (SLEP) allowing the T-37 fleet to operate safely into the twenty-first century, for a total of 18,000 hours—nearly twice its original design life.[28] The final T-37 training sortie took place on June 17, 2009 from Shepard AFB, Texas, and the last T-37 was officially retired from active Air Force service on July 31 of that year, nearly fifty-five years after the first XT-37 flight.

By the early 1970s, many T-37s were painted white overall. This Tweet is wearing bi-centennial markings to commemorate the country's 200th birthday. *A.I.R. Don Spering Collection*

A

A Cessna Military Division publicity photo showing two T-37Bs in formation with a U-3B (Model 310), known in the Air Force as the *Blue Canoe* due to its white over blue paint scheme. *Harry Clements Collection*

B

Prior to the selection of an overall white scheme, several high-visibility schemes were evaluated such as this all-red one. These experimentally painted T-37s were referred to as the "Candy Cane Air Force." *Terry Panopalis Collection* 05-31aa CCC

C

In the early 1960s, when the T-37B was introduced, the fleet carried an unpainted aluminum scheme with high-visibility Day-Glo accents. *Terry Panopalis Collection*

D

Some T-37Bs remained unpainted. Aircraft operating in the dry climates didn't need corrosion protection. *Robert F. Dorr Collection*

E

A new dark blue and white scheme designed by artist Keith Ferris was applied to the T-37 fleet in the 1980s. *A.I.R. Don Spering Collection*

F

Capt. Jay Labrum (left) is congratulated by Col. Dave Gerber after completing the final T-37 Tweet student training sortie at Columbus Air Force Base, Miss. *US Air Force, Rick Johnson*

G

The last seven T-37 Tweets in the Air Force inventory, including the two pictured here, took off one final time July 31, 2009 as part of the aircraft's retirement ceremony. *US Air Force, Harry Toneman*

The Return of Props

All-Jet training proved to be a success for the Air Force. Students who were trained entirely on the T-37 and T-38 were better prepared to fly high-performance century series fighters in less time; however, the cost of wash outs (student failures) was enormous. The highest failure rate typically occurs in the early stages of primary training when deficiencies such as airsickness, fear of flying, or lack of proficiency are discovered. It is far less expensive to screen students in propeller aircraft than jets. Three years after implementing the All-Jet training syllabus, the Air Force considered purchasing a fleet of off-the-shelf propeller-driven civilian trainers to evaluate student aptitude inexpensively. Three general aviation companies, Beechcraft, Cessna, and Piper, responded to the Request for Proposal, each offered multiple variations of their civilian products. Cessna was the successful bidder with a unit price of $7000 for a basic Model 172. On July 31, 1964 the Air Force ordered 170 units and designated it the T-41A Mescalero. It was a simple 145 horsepower, fixed pitch propeller, light plane with basic flight instruments intended for day VFR operations. The cabin was very sparse with only front seats installed. Cessna was able to fill the order quickly—the first T-41A was delivered in September 1964 and the last in July 1965. A second contract for thirty-four additional units was awarded in July 1967. The Air Force returned to the practice of using civilian flight instructors and maintenance personnel for the T-41A fleet. The syllabus, which was conducted over a two-month period, provided thirty hours of instruction for students with no prior flight experience, and eighteen hours for those with a private pilot's license. The Air Force found the T-41A to be a safe (one fatal accident in thirty years of service), reliable, and inexpensive screening tool. After thirty years of hard use the last T-41A was finally retired from the active roster in November 1993.[29]

In 1992, the Air Force generated a new introductory syllabus known as Enhanced Flight Screening (EFS), which was designed to identify unqualified students and teach fundamental aerobatic maneuvers (the T-41A was not an aerobatic aircraft). The British Slingsby T67 Firefly (which was derived from the French Fournier RF-6B) was selected for the program. The Air Force ordered 113 units with the engines upgraded from a 4 cylinder 160 horsepower Lycoming to a 6 cylinder 260 horsepower Lycoming. Designated T-3A, the first example was built and flown in the UK on July 4, 1993, and was certified under Federal Aviation Regulation Part 23 as an aerobatic airplane on December 15, 1993. The majority of the T-3A fleet was assembled from Slingsby kits by Northrop employees at Hondo Texas. The first T-3A went into service in March

In 1964 the Air Force ordered "off the shelf" Cessna 172s for pilot screening and designated them T-41As. *NARA*

A civilian instructor leads an aviation cadet through a pre-flight check. *NARA*

The simple instrument panel of the T-41A, that was used only for daytime VFR flight. *NARA*

1994 and the last was delivered to the Air Force in 1995. But the program was marred by a series of unexplained engine failures and three fatal stall/spin accidents resulting in the loss of six lives. On July 29, 1997, the Training Command grounded the entire T-3A fleet until the cause of the accidents could be found. Several modified and unmodified T-3As were tested at Edwards Air Force Base, but no cause could be found. Aviation Week & Space Technology reported:

> After several hundred hours of rigorous flight testing that bordered on abuse of the aircraft, a US Air Force Team determined that there is nothing wrong with the T-3A Firefly pilot-screening trainer, and recommended it be returned to limited service.
>
> However, USAF leaders appear to have rejected the test team's findings, and are studying several potential safety-enhancing modifications. As of now, the T-3A remains grounded, and the Enhanced Flight Screening Program instructor cadre at Hondo Tex., and the Air Force Academy (AFA) here is being dispersed. Civilian employees—including flight instructors at Hondo—have been laid off.[30]

By October 1999, the Air Force decided to abandon the T-3A but the absence of an introductory screening aircraft caused the washout rate to soar. The Training Command engaged civilian contractors, Emory-Riddle Aeronautical University and Doss Aviation, to provide introductory flight training using the docile Diamond DA-20 and more powerful DA-40.[31] On July 6, 2011, it was announced that the Air Force was buying yet another off-the-shelf general aviation aircraft, the Cirrus SR-20, which was designated T-53A for the Air Force Academy's Powered Flight Program (PFP).[32]

The Slingsby T-3A was intended to provide pilot screening and initial aerobatic training, but three fatal accidents caused the Air Force to scrap the fleet. *US Air Force*

The Diamond DA20-C1 was leased by the Air Force after the T-3A fleet was grounded. The Diamond received the Air Force designation of T-52A. *US Air Force*

The Cirrus Aircraft T-53A is the latest screening aircraft. It went into service in the spring of 2012 and, unlike the Diamond T-52, it was purchased rather than leased indicating that the Air Force intends to use it for many years. *US Air Force*

Chapter Five Endnotes

1. For an excellent discussion of post WWII military programs see Elliott V. Converse, *Rearming For The Cold War 1945–1960,*(Washington, DC: Office of the Secretary of Defense, 2012) pp. 1-14.

2. Oral presentation of Oswald Mall, T-37 Project Engineer: *The XT-37 Training Airplane,* at the IAS-SAE meeting, Wichita Kansas, February 1955.

3. William D. Thompson, *Cessna Wings for the World II Development of the 300 Series Twins and Miscellaneous Prototypes*, (Maverick Publications, Bend Oregon, 1995) p.36.

4. E-mail correspondence from Harry Clements to Mark A. Frankel on 22 August 2013.

5. Air Training Command History, January 1954 – July 1954, pp.116-117.

6. Air Training Command History, January 1954 – July 1954, pp.113-114.

7. *Cessna Jets Celebrating Forty Years Of Achievement*. Cessna public relations pamphlet commemorating the 40th anniversary of the first flight of the T-37 "Tweety Bird."

8. Walt Shiel, *Cessna Warbirds*, (Jones Publishing, Iola WI., 1995) p.138.

9. Thompson, *Cessna Wings for the World II*, pp.38-39.

10. Col. Larry G. Van Pelt, *The Evolution Of Flight Test Concepts*. History Office Air Force Flight Test Center, 1982, pp.6-13.

11. Oswald Mall oral presentation.

12. Thompson, p.41.

13. Ibid. p.43.

14. T-37A Phase IV Functional Development Test, By D.E. Smith, 1/Lt., USAF, H.W. Trimble, Lt. Col. USAF, R.S. Martin, Captain, USAF. January, 1957. p.1.

15. Ibid. p.24.

16. Air Training Command History, July 1958—December 1958, p.50.

17. Ibid. p.37 and Shiel, p.142.

18. Shiel, p.143.

19. Thompson, p.43.

20. Air Training Command History, July 1955 – December 1955, p.38.

21. Richard A. Leyes II and William A. Fleming, *The History of North American Small Gas Turbine Aircraft Engines*, (American Institute of Aeronautics and Astronautics, Inc., Reston, Virginia, 1999), p.103-104.

22. T-37B Category II Performance Test. By F.W. Worthington, 1/Lieutenant, USAF and E.Sturmthal, Captain, USAF, April 1961 p.29.

23. Shiel, pp.156-157.

24. This is a simplification of the spin modes described in the T-37B Qualitative Spin Evaluation (Report No.FTC-TDR-61-59).

25. T-37 Flight Manual T.O. IT-37B-1, changed 31 May 1962 p.6-3.

26. Tracy Rhodes, *Spin Training I and II – the Cessna T-37*, 14 July 2009 and 22 July 2009 http://aroundpattern.sierrawebsolutions.com.

27. *Contract Flying Training In Air Training Command 1939–1980*, ATC Historical Monograph, by Barry H. Nickle, Sept. 1981,pp.16-19.

28. *Cessna Jets Celebrating Forty Years Of Achievement*. Cessna public relations pamphlet.

29. Shiel.pp.259-261.

30. Flight Test Report: "Nothing Wrong With T-3A" *Aviation Week & Space Technology*, November 9, 1998, p. 84.

31. "USAF Abandons Firefly Trainer," *Aviation Week & Space Technology*, 18 October 1999, p.37.

32. *Cirrus Aircraft News*, US Air Force Academy Selects Cirrus SR-20, www.cirrusaircraft.com, and EAA News, USAF Academy Buys Cirrus SR-20s, Designates. T-53A, www.eaa.org.

Chapter Six
SECOND-GENERATION JET TRAINERS FOR THE NAVY

A. Lockheed T2V-1 Seastar

For several years after World War II, the US Navy essentially piggy-backed on the Air Force trainer programs, adapting the T-28, T-33 (initially designated TO-2 and then TV-2 by the Navy), and T-34 in turn. It, however, needed to provide for a unique training requirement, carrier-based operation. That was relatively straightforward through the early 1950s. The low-performance propeller-driven trainers like the T-6 and T-28 were readily adapted to carrier approaches and arrested landings. It helped that they were originally designed to withstand a student's occasional

hard landing. Even then, the T-28C landing gear was modified to withstand higher sink rates.

The Navy eventually decided that a jet trainer designed for carrier takeoffs and landings was necessary. A jet fighter's approach speed and low-speed handling qualities, while acceptable for an experienced naval aviator, were likely to represent a challenge to a low-time pilot making his first landing in a jet after qualifying aboard with two touch and goes and four arrested landings in a T-28. What was needed was a jet that did not approach a speed quite as fast as a fighter and was relatively easy to fly at low speed.

Obsolete jet fighters like this Grumman F9F-2 Panther were used by the US Navy training command for advanced training in gunnery, tactics, etc. *Mark Nankivil Collection*

Carrier-landing capability was a Navy-unique requirement that the Air Force could not be expected to accommodate in a jet trainer. The features and performance necessary in a carrier-takeoff and landing airplane would have imposed a significant weight and cost penalty on one intended to operate solely from land bases. For one thing, maximum touchdown sink rates required for land-based trainers are on the order of ten feet per second; carrier airplanes are designed for sink rates of somewhat more than twenty feet per second, which is a bone-jarring vertical speed of sixteen miles per hour.

For example, the Navy evaluated the Army Air Forces Lockheed P-80 fighter for carrier operations. It was only able to approve it for at-sea trials without external fuel tanks due to structural and performance shortcomings. On internal fuel only, it posed a significant problem for carrier operations because of its very limited endurance. The Shooting Star was also marginal from the standpoint of controllability at carrier approach speeds and the ability to take a last-moment wave off.

Another example of the penalty involved in modification of a jet originally limited to land-based operation was the North American FJ-2/3 Fury. Due to delays with its own high-performance fighter programs, the Navy turned to North American to modify its F-86 Sabre to be carrier-capable with catapult provisions, a tail hook, wing folding, Davis barrier compatibility, etc. The weight increase was about 1,000 lbs. The FJ-2's performance (and carrier suitability) with the F-86's J47 engine suffered to such a degree that it was only assigned to US Marine Corps squadrons that principally operated from land bases. The substitution of the higher-thrust Wright J65 in the follow-on FJ-3 resulted in a satisfactory interim solution, along with the Grumman F9F Cougar, to the Navy's immediate need.

Nevertheless, the Navy chose not to initiate a carrier-capable jet trainer program in the early 1950s. Its first one was yet another iteration of an Air Force airplane. In 1953, Lockheed again decided to fund a trainer demonstrator, this time modifying a T-33 for lower speed takeoffs and landings along with a raised rear seat to improve the instructor's forward visibility. [1]

The purpose of the H-tail with a larger horizontal stabilizer on this T-33 has been speculated to be an evaluation of an empennage to provide better directional stability for low-speed carrier approaches (the presence of a spin chute and its deployment provisions may have been mistaken for a tail hook in low-resolution pictures). Or, Lockheed may have been addressing an Air Force desire to improve the T-33's post-stall handling qualities. *Robert Dorr Collection*

The Lockheed Aircraft Corporation demonstrator was created from a T-33A that was purchased from the Air Force while it was still on the production line. It was radically modified with redesigned engine inlets, wing, empennage, rear cockpit, and canopy. Most of the modifications were focused on low-speed performance and handling qualities. Aerodynamically actuated slats were added to the wing leading edge and a boundary layer control (BLC) system was incorporated to improve the effectiveness of the trailing edge flaps. BLC had recently been demonstrated on a Navy F9F-4 Panther. It used high-pressure air bled from the engine compressor to delay separation of the airflow over the wing flaps to higher angle of attacks. (Lockheed originally expected to reduce takeoff stall speed by ten knots and landing stall speed by eight knots.) The empennage was also modified to provide adequate control power at low speeds: the vertical fin was enlarged; the horizontal tail was raised farther above the fuselage and its span was increased by twelve inches.

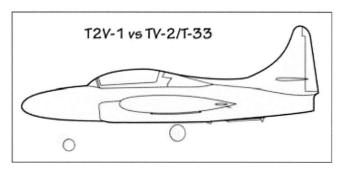

The "T-33B" that became the T2V featured a raised aft seat and a significantly larger vertical tail compared to the TV-2/T-33 that it was derived from. *Tommy H. Thomason*

The Lockheed-funded prototype of an improved T-33 was civil registered as N125D and identified as the "Lockheed Trainer" or "T-33B." No tailhook was fitted originally. *Mark Nankivil Collection*

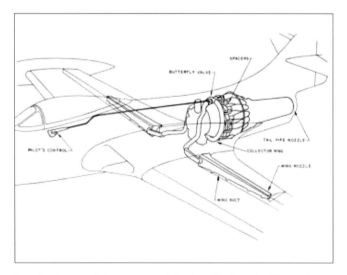

Boundary layer control was a concept developed in the early 1950s and demonstrated on a Grumman F9F-4. High-pressure bleed air from the jet engine's compressor was ducted out along the leading edge of the wing flaps and "blown" over them to increase the angle of attack (and therefore lift) that could be reached before wing stall. *Tommy H. Thomason*

Up until then, the instructor's seat in tandem-seat trainers was usually mounted at the same height as the student's. The head of the student in the front seat and the side of the forward cockpit therefore restricted the view forward from the rear seat, particularly at the angles of attack used for approach and landing. Raising the rear seat in tandem-seat trainers subsequently became standard.

The resulting L-245 was marketed as the Lockheed Trainer and also referred to informally as the T-33B.[2] Lockheed obtained a civil registration, N125D, for its demonstrator, which first flew on December 16, 1953. The major changes resulting from initial Lockheed flight test was the addition of a larger dorsal fin to provide adequate directional stability and development work to optimize the engine inlet. Lockheed then took it on a tour of Air Force and Navy bases.

The Air Force passed on the L-245. It's likely that it did not provide enough improvement over the T-33 to justify the investment in new airplanes. Moreover, a T-37 first flight was imminent and the "T-33B" was probably deemed too big for the Basic training role and too slow for the forthcoming advanced training requirement.

The Navy, however, liked the idea of a carrier-capable jet trainer and ordered eight as the T2V-1 in May 1954. It received the popular name Seastar in accordance with Lockheed's preference for ones ending in "star." In addition to the changes introduced as a result of flight test of the demonstrator, the T2V landing gear was designed for higher-sink-rate landings and catapult and tail hooks were added to the airframe. Nose gear extension for a higher angle of attack during launch was incorporated. Self-boarding with integral steps was provided so that boarding ladders would not be required on the carrier. However, to minimize the weight increase associated for carrier operations, the L-245 did not have folding wings. Folding was considered unnecessary for a trainer since deck-parking capacity was not a problem even if the airplanes stayed on the carrier overnight.

One BLC drawback, in addition to the added complexity involved in shutoff valves and ducting for piping hot air from the engine to the wing cove, was that the engine thrust was reduced about 5% when the system was in operation. A J33-A-22 rated at 6,100 lbs of thrust with BLC operating was to be substituted for the T-33's J33-A-16 that had 5,400 lbs of thrust in order to offset the higher weight and provide better wave-off response.

Once the Navy was identified as the primary customer for the new Lockheed trainer, a tailhook was added to the demonstrator and it was repainted with Navy markings. The Navy designated it T2V-1 as the second trainer from Lockheed, with the single seat TV-1 and TV-2 (shown flying on its wing) counted together as the first one. *Mark Nankivil Collection*

Inlet optimization was an early flight test requirement. The inlets on the demonstrator for this evaluation flight had been cut back severely to evaluate the effect of the change on the airflow to the engine and duct losses. *Mark Nankivil Collection*

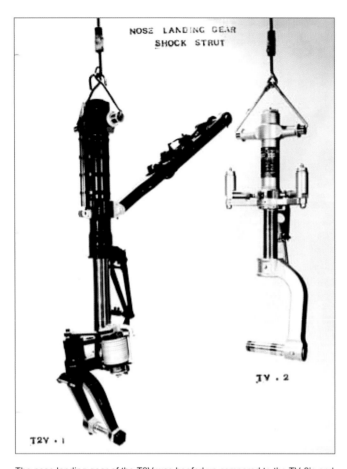

The nose landing gear of the T2V was beefed up compared to the TV-2's and an extension feature was incorporated to raise the nose for a higher angle of attack when being catapulted. *Tommy H. Thomason Collection*

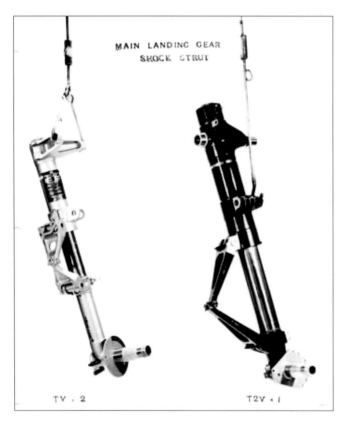

NACA Ames test pilot Robert Innis made two evaluation flights in the L-245 to evaluate its BLC system. He noted that the stall speed reduction was dependent on the thrust being used: "With the flaps set at 55°, a six-knot reduction was realized at eighty-percent rpm, while 90-percent rpm resulted in an eight-knot decrease in stall speed." One concern was that the throttle reduction to idle then used for landing on an axial deck resulted in an abrupt and significant increase in the rate of descent due to the loss of lift from BLC. One benefit was a more nose-down attitude during the approach, which provided better visibility for the instructor in the rear cockpit.[3]

The first production T2V-1 flew for the first time on January 20, 1956. After initial development at Lockheed and evaluation by the Navy, carrier suitability testing began with shore-based testing of T2V-1 BuNo 142267 on October 29, 1956. As a result, the Navy deemed the BLC effectiveness to be inadequate and required its redesign. There were also the usual shortcomings with tail hook bounce, directional problems during arrested run out, and landing-gear rebound on touchdown.

Following modification to improve the T2V's carrier compatibility and shore-based testing to confirm its effectiveness, at-sea testing was accomplished aboard the Essex-class carrier *Antietam* (CVS-36) and the bigger *Saratoga* (CVA-60) in June 1957. These were satisfactory and the T2V-1 was cleared for day and night carrier operations with the first Seastars to be delivered to ATU squadrons in early 1958.

One additional production change was not available in time for the at-sea evaluation. The T-33 speed brakes located on the underside of the fuselage had been determined to be inadequate and were therefore augmented by two mounted on either side of the fuselage just aft of the wing. The Navy still did not consider this configuration to be effective enough at low speeds but decided that it was "uneconomical to continue further investigation."[4]

The main landing gear of the T2V was beefed up compared to the TV-2's and provided a much longer strut stroke to soften the impact of a high-sink-rate landing. *Tommy H. Thomason Collection*

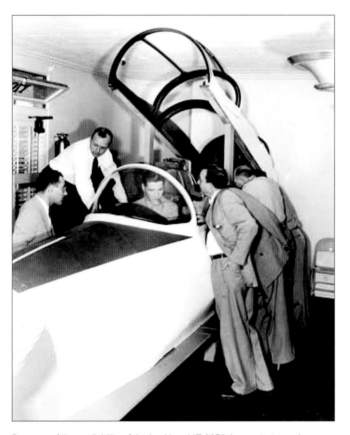

Because of the availability of the Lockheed "T-33B" demonstrator, only a cockpit mockup and detail change items like the landing gear and tailhook was necessary for the Navy's review on October 27-28, 1954. *Tommy H. Thomason Collection*

Two T2Vs from the first production lot were finally evaluated at-sea aboard *Antietam* (CVS-36), the Navy's training carrier at the time, in June 1957. *US Navy Photo*

The first production T2V-1, BuNo 142261 shown here, incorporated all the changes developed on the demonstrator as well as Navy-specific requirements like self-boarding with integral steps. *Courtesy of Mark Nankivil Collection*

The pilot could extend the T2V nose strut to provide a higher angle of attack and therefore more lift at the end of the catapult stroke. The black nonskid area on the top of the engine inlet was part of the self-boarding arrangement that included a pull-down step and the two kick-in steps on the side of the fuselage. *US Navy Photo*

The emphasis the Navy placed on safe spin training was evident in the NATC comments on the Lockheed proposed spin test program:

1. Exhaustive attempts should be made to develop inverted and erect spins from stalls in a near vertical attitude (80° to 100°) with particular emphasis on developing high yaw rates near stall speed.

2. Attempts should be made to enter left and right spins from steep climbing turns at altitudes above 30,000 feet with sufficient normal load factor to stall the airplane in a near-vertical attitude. Full pro-spin controls should be applied near the stall.

3. Attempts should be made to enter spins from an uncoordinated rapid reversal of turn in the buffet region of 0.60M or higher at altitudes of 40,000 feet or higher.

4. Attempts should be made to enter spins from rapid wind-up turns at speeds of 0.60M or higher and at altitudes of 40,000 feet or higher.

5. Attempts should be made to enter spins from normal stalls with lateral control held full with and against the spin.[5]

The Navy determined that the T-33 speed brakes provided inadequate speed reduction, particularly at low speed, so a second set of speed brakes was added on the fuselage just aft of the wing. *Tommy H. Thomason Collection*

Introduction of the T2V to the training command got off to a bad start when one of the flight instructors being checked out in it, Lt. Jay D. Higgs, was killed on January 31, 1958. After two dual flights, he was on his first solo flight doing touch-and-goes at the Pensacola Municipal Airport when he attempted a steep climb out on takeoff. He appeared to stall at about 600 to 800 feet and then dove into the ground. BLC was probably a factor, since the flight manual stated, "A power-on stall with the boundary layer control operating and with the airplane in the landing configuration may result in a sharp nose pitch down if the stall is allowed to penetrate beyond the mild airframe buffet condition." A loss of 1,000 feet was to be expected as a result of the pitch down. Nevertheless, T2Vs continued to be delivered to NAS Memphis, Tennessee and NAS Pensacola, Florida. ATU-205 and its sister squadron ATU-105 at Memphis had been flying T-28s. They were equipped with T2Vs and combined to form BTG-7 in July 1958. The T2Vs delivered to Pensacola were assigned to the newly formed BTG-9 at Forrest Sherman Field with students first flying them in July 1958 as well.

BTG-9 T2V-1s in the break at NAS Pensacola. The speed brakes have been extended on the airplane at the top of the picture. *National Museum of Naval Aviation*

B. Grumman Plays Catch-Up

In August 1954, shortly after the Navy contracted with Lockheed for the T2V, Grumman submitted a proposal for its Design 105 to the Navy. It was a two-seat modification of its swept wing F9F-8 Cougar. The -8 was one of the Navy's deployed day fighters at the time. It had only just begun reaching operational squadrons a few months earlier. (Higher performance fighters were, of course, beginning development but would not be in production for a few years.)

Up until this point, unlike the Air Force, the Navy had not considered it necessary or beneficial to have a two-seat version of any of its fighters. The F9F-8T was to be the first, and for a long time the only one that the Navy would put into service.

The changes to create a two-seat jet trainer from the F9F-8 were similar to those that resulted in the TO-2/T-33A. The forward fuselage was extended by about thirty-four inches to accommodate a second complete cockpit. However, no extension of the fuselage aft of the wing was considered necessary. The forward shift in the center of gravity was minimized by the retention of only two of the fighter's four cannons, which were also relocated farther aft and provided with almost one-third less rounds per gun. The armor plate and IFF electronics, neither of which was required for a trainer application, were also removed. (IFF capability was subsequently restored.) The six stores pylons were retained for air-to-ground training missions as was provision for inflight refueling.

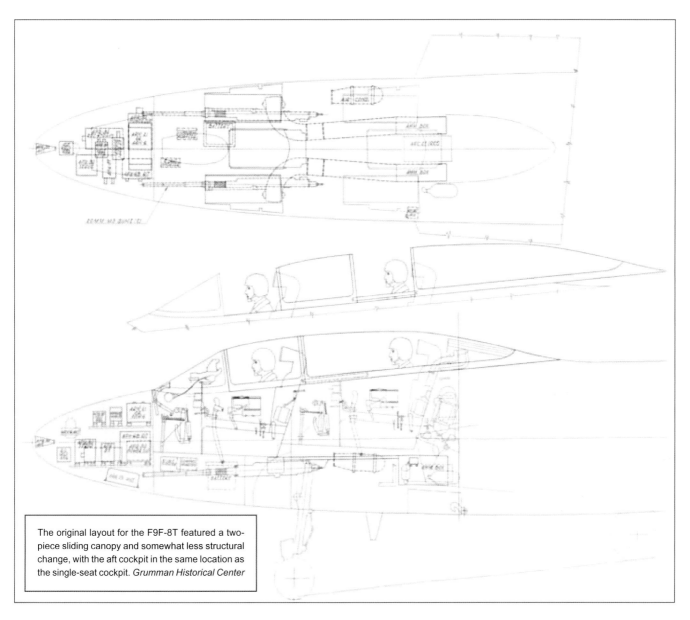

The original layout for the F9F-8T featured a two-piece sliding canopy and somewhat less structural change, with the aft cockpit in the same location as the single-seat cockpit. *Grumman Historical Center*

The fuel capacity remained the same as did the basic gross weight, potentially avoiding any need for structural beef up or requalification. (As it turned out, some beef up was required of the arresting hook carry-through structure and the main landing gear.) While the center of gravity did shift forward, the loaded cg was still within the limits that had been established for the F9F-8.

Like the T2V, the instructor in the rear cockpit sat higher than the student to provide him with better visibility forward. Instead of having a clamshell type canopy like the T2V, however, the canopy over the two cockpits slid aft. This allowed it to be opened for carrier takeoffs and landings, the preferred configuration at the time.[6] A small windscreen was located in front of the aft cockpit to reduce windblast when the canopy was slid back in flight.

The first F9F-8T, converted from a production F9F-8, BuNo 141667, flew on February 26, 1956, only a month after the T2V-1. After the customary development and

evaluation requirements were complete, at-sea carrier-suitability testing was accomplished aboard *Saratoga* (CVA-60) in June 1957, the same month as the T2V went aboard it. Lockheed had lost all of its initial lead.

During carrier-suitability tests, the field of view from the aft cockpit was determined to be unsatisfactory for at-sea carrier approaches and landings. However, it was deemed adequate for demonstration of shore-based approaches and monitoring the student's field-carrier-landing practice. Since the student's at-sea qualification was accomplished solo after many hours of dual and solo field-carrier landings, this limitation was acceptable.[7]

Grumman delivered the first F9F-8T of the first production lot of 155 airplanes in July 1956. Service Acceptance Trials began in March 1957 and concluded in July. Deliveries to ATU-223 at Chase Field in Beeville, Texas began in late 1957 although fleet units had begun receiving F9F-8Ts as early as March for proficiency training.

The F9F-8T retained the inflight refueling capability, two 20 mm cannon, and all six external stores pylons of the F9F-8 fighter and was supersonic in a dive, making it an ideal advanced trainer. *Grumman Historical Center*

Consistent with the practice at the time, the F9F-8T's canopy could be opened in flight, providing quick egress in the event of a water landing. *Grumman Historical Center*

The final BIS report was complimentary: "All the BIS deficiencies are being corrected where feasible. The F9F-8T is an excellent Navy jet trainer with high maintainability and economy of operation. Of particular note are its wide operating-strength envelope and its ability to be used in a wide variety of training functions."

In parallel with the evaluation of the F9F-8T for service use, it was used for a demonstration of the Martin-Baker ejection seat that the Navy was considering to replace all the different contractor-furnished ejection seats in its existing fighters, both in service and development. The early ejection seats simply provided bailout assistance. Even after features like automatic seat separation were added, a survivable ejection had to be initiated at least 500 feet above the ground, much more if the airplane had a high sink rate. Surviving an ejection during takeoff or final approach was unlikely.

At-sea qualification of the F9F-8T were initially accomplished aboard *Saratoga* (CVA-60) along with the Grumman F11F Tiger, which was intended to be the successor to the single-seat F9F-8 fighter that the two-seat Cougar was derived from. *Grumman Historical Center*

The F9F-8T was used to demonstrate the ground-level ejection capability of the latest version of the Martin-Baker ejection seat. The Navy elected to retrofit the training command's Cougars first. *Grumman Historical Center*

C. A Fresh Start: OS-141

Although Lockheed and Grumman were developing jet trainers based on existing airplanes, the Navy also decided to pursue a clean sheet of paper approach to its basic trainer requirement. The Bureau of Aeronautics issued an RFP (Request for Proposal) on December 2, 1956 against its Outline Specification 141 for a jet basic trainer. Seven proposals were received on January 30, 1956. The specification required the capability to operate to and from an aircraft carrier like the T-28C but with the benefit of a catapult launch. The airplane was to be easy to fly visually or on instruments. It had to have provisions for limited weapons training, both guns and rockets/bombs, including an APG-30A ranging radar installation for a gun sight. In-flight refueling, a requirement for jets that was just being introduced in the fleet, was the only notable omission of an operational capability. Like the Air Force's T-28 program, reliability and maintainability received equal emphasis with performance. The gross weight was expected to be 10,500 pounds or less.

The new trainer was to have a stall speed of not more than 65 knots (with 20% of internal fuel) and a maximum speed of at least 400 knots (at 25,000 feet and military thrust). The maximum takeoff and landing distances over a fifty-foot obstacle were to be 3,000 feet and 3,500 feet, respectively. A service ceiling of at least 35,000 feet was required. Two missions were defined, at least 1.5 hours of endurance (internal fuel) and 700 nm range (with external fuel if required). Speed brakes were required to decelerate from Vmax (level flight, military thrust) to 0.8 Vmax in level flight in not more than sixteen seconds.

Two acceptable engines were listed, the Westinghouse J34-WE-46 and the Allison J33-A-24. All but one of the proposals were powered by the J34; it provided less thrust than the J33 but had a better thrust-to-weight ratio and used less fuel for the defined missions so the resulting design had lower empty and gross weights.

North American had promoted a "Jet T-28" that resembled the propeller-driven T-28. Its wing (with substantially less dihedral), landing gear, and windscreen were similar if not identical, but the rest of the airframe was new. The substitution of the J34 jet engine in the aft fuselage for a heavy radial engine in the nose required a substantial shift in the position of the fuselage on the wing, with the cockpit positioned well forward; the empennage moved closer to the wing and was enlarged to provide adequate control power.

Martin-Baker was dedicated to improving ejection seat capability. In the mid-1950s, it succeeded in qualifying a seat system that resulted in a survivable ejection even when the airplane was on the runway if its speed was at least 100 knots.[8] In 1956, BuAer contracted with Grumman to install the new Mk4 M-B seat in the rear cockpit of an F9F-8T for a demonstration. Flying Officer Sidney Hughes, RAF, successfully ejected himself from the rear cockpit at Patuxent River in August 1957 while the airplane was still on the runway at a speed of 120 knots.

This successful demonstration resulted in a Navy contract with Martin-Baker for the Mk 5 seat, which was a strengthened version of the Mk 4 from a crashworthiness standpoint. (An actuator loop was also added at the front of the seat pan to expedite ejection if required, such as an emergency during catapult launch, or when g levels made reaching the face-curtain loops difficult.) The changeover started with the single and two-seat F9F Cougars in the training command. Most in-service Navy fighters were retrofitted with the new seat and new production fighters were delivered with it as soon as qualification of the seat in each could be accomplished.[9]

Although the improved ejection envelope was to be desired, the Martin-Baker seat as initially installed in the Cougar proved to be very uncomfortable because the seat had to be installed somewhat more upright than it was intended to be. As a result, the pilot sat hunched over in the cockpit. At least two modifications to the seat were subsequently incorporated.[10]

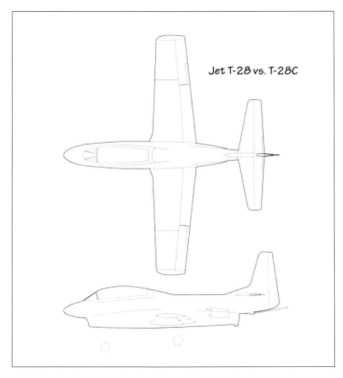

Jet T-28 vs. T-28C

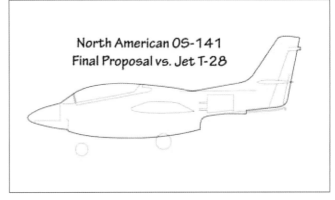

North American OS-141
Final Proposal vs. Jet T-28

In the end, North American's OS-141 proposal bore very little resemblance to the Jet T-28 that was based on its T-28C, the incumbent. *Tommy H. Thomason*

In responding to the Navy's interest in a new jet basic trainer, North American first elected to promote a design, the Jet T-28, which maximized commonality and appearance with its T-28C propeller-driven trainer. *Tommy H. Thomason*

One of the Navy's objections to the Jet T-28 was its relatively low critical Mach number. At least in part as a result, North American submitted an all-new design in response to the December 2, 1955, Request for Proposal (RFP). Virtually all that remained of the T-28 configuration according to the proposal were "the same conservative design principles." The wing planform was similar but in order to raise the critical Mach number, it was reduced to a 12% thick section and aileron boost was incorporated. It featured what North American called a "superposed" arrangement of the equipment and power plant under the wing the cockpit above, creating the shape that caused generations of student pilots to refer to it as the War Guppy when used for armament training.

Lockheed's CL-330 proposal was basically a T2V with some internal weight reduction changes; its CL-340 was a clean sheet of paper approach to the OS-141 requirement that bore little resemblance to the T2V. *Tommy H. Thomason*

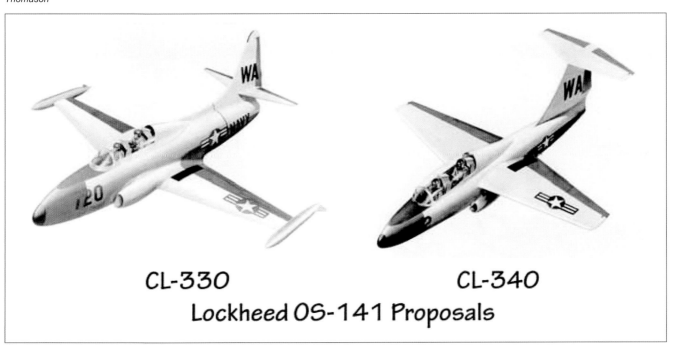

CL-330   CL-340
Lockheed OS-141 Proposals

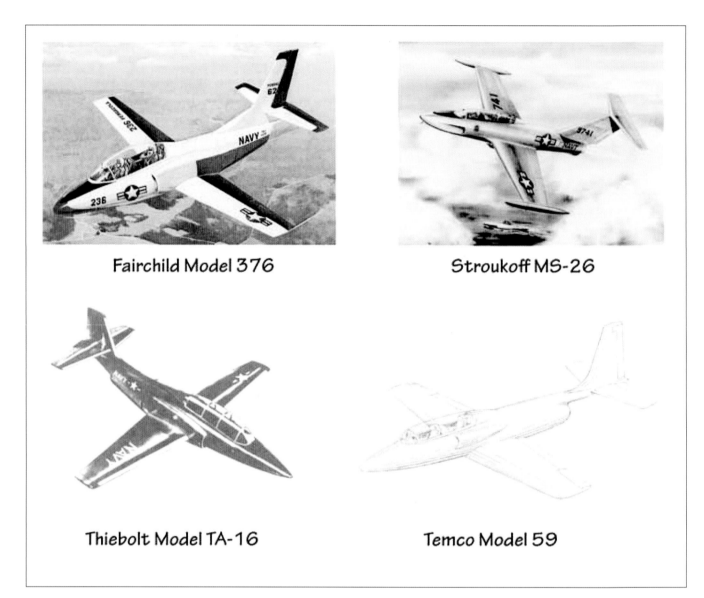

Fairchild Model 376

Stroukoff MS-26

Thiebolt Model TA-16

Temco Model 59

These four OS-141 proposals could be charitably described as long shots, if there was any likelihood that the Navy would contract with an airplane company that had no experience with carrier-based operations. *Tommy H. Thomason*

Lockheed proposed two variations on the T2V, the CL-330 and the CL-340. The former was a relatively minimum change from the T2V while the latter was an all-new design with the J34 engine substituted for the much heavier J33. As a result the CL-330 significantly exceeded the maximum gross weight limit as well as stall speed. (Some of the BuAer division evaluations didn't even bother to consider the CL-330.) The smaller CL-340 still bettered the performance requirements but providing enough fuel for a 1.5-hour mission resulted in it being 700 lbs heavier than the desired maximum weight of 10,500 lbs.

Cessna did a predesign study of a tandem version of its T-37 in its ongoing campaign to make the Tweet attractive to the US Navy as a primary trainer in place of the T-34. *Mark Frankel Collection*

The T2J mockup did not include the right wing or horizontal stabilizer to reduce cost and the space required. Note the large pictures of carrier decks that could be rolled into place to evaluate the view over the nose on approach. *Mark Nankivil Collection*

Proposals were also received from Fairchild Aircraft Division, Stroukoff Aircraft Corporation, Temco, and Thieblot Aircraft. The Temco proposal resembled its TT-1 Pinto (to be discussed in Chapter 7).[11]

Some of the usual Navy suppliers—Grumman, Vought, Douglas—elected not to bid. Cessna and Beech, among others, considered submitting a proposal against the OS-141 requirement but decided not to. Cessna did suggest to the Navy that it consider its T-37 for its primary training requirement. Ironically, it had won a stiff competition for the Air Force trainer that included a proposal from North American for an airplane similar to one proposed for OS 141 albeit with side-by-side seating. This time North American's design won; the Navy was no longer piggybacking on Air Force trainer programs.

North American's winning entry, which the Navy designated T2J-1,[12] represented a continuation of a source for Navy trainers stretching back to the prewar SNJ through

the T-28. Every Naval Aviator in training to fly jets between November 1959 and 2004 almost certainly flew a T2J (or T-2 after November 1962) at some point before receiving his wings. It was produced in three variants, each with a different engine.

The T2J development risk was low. The engine, always a critical success factor particularly in a single-engine application, was a Westinghouse J34 first run in January 1947. It was rated at 3,400 pounds of thrust. Although differing in detail, the unswept, non-folding wing was arguably a direct descendent of the one on North American's first jet fighter (and one of the Navy's first carrier-capable jets) the FJ-1 Fury. The control system was based on the T-28's with hydraulic boost added. Reliability, durability, and ease of maintenance were emphasized as the Navy had desired. For example, almost all replaceable items were located at waist level or below for ease of access. A higher rear-seat position and ground-level ejection capability at speeds over 75 knots (with a North American-designed seat) were other proposal features.

The Navy ordered six preproduction airplanes with the June 1956 contract rather than the usual one or two prototypes. A second contract for 121 production aircraft was received at the end of 1956, well before the first flight, which was accomplished on January 31, 1958, by Richard Wenzell at Columbus, Ohio. Development was relatively trouble free, although the North American test pilots considered the T2J to be underpowered and a loud duct rumble was disconcerting. The duct problem was finally addressed with an extended intake lip. More troubling was a low pre-stall buffet that didn't provide adequate stall warning and a tendency to roll off at the stall. A ten-inch stall strip was added to provide acceptable stall characteristics.

Even though it was a very conventional, low-risk configuration and its handling qualities had been acceptable to North American and Navy test pilots (for example, at-sea carrier suitability testing was accomplished in May 1959 aboard *Antietam* (CVS-36)), its stall characteristics were deemed to be unsatisfactory during BIS testing in April 1959 and early in Fleet Introduction Program.[13] The stall during a power approach was considered to be abrupt and inconsistent, resulting in an unsatisfactory roll-off.

North American quickly modified four airplanes (one had also been modified with the extended engine intake duct) at Columbus with the leading-edge spoiler strip relocated to the inboard section of the wing. It was triangular in shape, ten inches long, and mounted about two feet outboard of the fuselage. The flap shroud was also modified

This photo of the first T2J-1, BuNo 144217, shows the large access door on the lower fuselage under the rear seat that provided easy access to the avionics and other equipment located on either side of the engine-air intake ducting. *Mark Nankivil Collection*

The carrier-capability features of the T2J consisted of a good field of view for the student and instructor, large flaps for low-speed approach, long-stroke landing gear to cushion the impact of high-sink-rate landings, and a tailhook. *Mark Nankivil Collection*

to act as a flap seal with the flaps retracted. Navy pilots evaluated these airplanes in mid-July 1959. The improvement was judged to reduce any roll-off at stall to an acceptable level but it was noted that the degree of roll-off varied between airplanes when the flaps were down. Careful rigging of the flaps during production or post-maintenance flight test was therefore required to be accomplished to eliminate any significant inconsistency.

The Navy had NACA Langley conduct a spin test evaluation of the T2J-1 with a 1/20 scale dynamic model in the Langley 20-foot free-spinning tunnel in 1957. Based on the results, the Langley engineers predicted that different control positions should be used depending on the distribution of disposable load and spin type. For erect spins at the flight design gross weight, i.e. with no wingtip tanks or external stores, the recovery was optimum with simultaneous rudder reversal against the spin and aileron applied with the spin. With full wingtip tanks and internal fuel while carrying rockets, rudder reversal was to be followed by downward movement of the elevator. For the flight design gross weight condition with partially full wingtip tanks, recovery "should be attempted" with simultaneous rudder reversal against the spin, movement of the ailerons with the spin, and jettisoning the wingtip tanks. And finally, for inverted spins the optimum recovery technique was predicted to be rudder reversal against the spin and the stick maintained longitudinally and laterally neutral.[14]

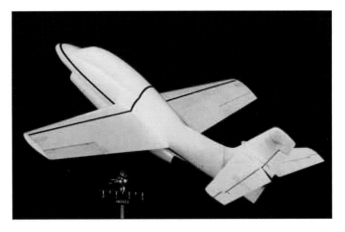

The Bureau of Aeronautics had NACA Langley conduct spin tests of most of its airplanes. The models were fairly large (this T2J has a wing span of 21½ inches), dynamically scaled for mass distribution, and had remotely movable flight controls. They were tossed into a vertical wind tunnel with pro-spin controls set; spin-recovery controls were applied after a spin had developed. *NASA Langley*

In this instance, the NACA spin-tunnel test results proved overly pessimistic and the recovery recommendations unnecessarily situation and configuration dependent. North American test pilots conducted extensive spin testing of the T2J—including the vertical-entry testing required by the Navy—without serious incident (rockets were mounted on the tip tanks to "break" the spin when all else failed but weren't used). The resulting T2J flight manual spin recovery instructions simply stipulated that the power control lever be retarded to idle and full opposite rudder be applied with the stick held neutral in pitch and roll in all aircraft configurations. When rotation ceased, the rudder was to be neutralized and aft stick used to recover from the ensuing dive. Although intentional inverted spins were prohibited because the negative g limit might be

exceeded, the recovery process was the same, even with the tip tanks partially full. Jettison of the tanks was not required. It turned out, as North American test pilot Ed Gillespie noted, "a great airplane for unusual attitude recoveries."

Armament training with the T-2 was somewhat realistic for the time because it was equipped with an AN/AWG-6 Fire Control System that included the AN/APB-30A Ranging Radar. The Mk 6 Mod 9 gun sight could be used for air-to-air gunnery, or to drop bombs on, fire rockets at, or strafe ground targets. An AERO 15D bomb rack could be mounted on a removable pylon on each wing. The T-2 could therefore be armed either with bombs, rockets, or a .50 caliber gun pod. Alternatively, the pylons could be used to carry sleeve or banner-type tow targets that could be streamed in flight.

The first squadron to receive the new trainer was BTG-9 (its designation was changed to VT-4 on May 1, 1960) at NAS Pensacola in July 1959, replacing the T2Vs.

For many years, the Navy had the funds to operate a dedicated training carrier and the naval aviator training volume to justify it. This is *Antietam* (CVS-36) in April 1961 preparing to launch T2J-1s and AD Skyraiders for student-pilot carrier qualification. *US Navy*

VT-7 was one of the first squadrons to train student pilots and provide jet transition or familiarization in the single-engine T-2A. *Mark Nankivil Collection*

The T2J had been formally named "Buckeye" by the Navy the month before in recognition of its birthplace in Ohio. BTG -9 was primarily responsible for air-to-air gunnery, field carrier landing practice, and at-sea carrier qualification. At that time the gunnery phase consisted of ten flights, four of which were live fire using gun pods slung under the wings. Only ten hops were devoted to Field Carrier Landing Practice prior to at-sea qualification since the students had already carrier qualified in the SNJ/T-28. If all went well, the students then made takeoffs from and landings on the carrier designated for qualification at the time. Takeoffs via catapult were not very demanding but exciting. Approaches were much more challenging and consisted of two touch-and-goes (the hook remained up) followed by four successful arrested landings. The first student to qualify in the T2J aboard the training carrier *Antietam* was 2nd Lt J.B. Hammond, USMC, on June 2, 1960.

The last of 217 T2J-1s was delivered in April 1961. At that point, it equipped VT-4 and VT-7 of the Naval Air Basic Training Command (NABTC) in the Pensacola, Florida area and the Naval Air Technical Training Unit (NATTU) at Olathe, Kansas.

The T2J did not meet a few of the OS-141 performance metrics as determined by Navy flight test but it bettered most significantly. Stall speed was determined to be 68 knots against the original requirement of 65. Service ceiling was only 30,000 feet compared to the specification of 35,000 but it was adequate to the task. Maximum speed was 28 knots faster than the 400-knot requirement and takeoff and landing distances were on the order of 1,000 feet less than stipulated. Maximum range was 99 nautical miles greater than the 700-nm requirement and minimum endurance fell short by only 90 seconds. The Training Command got the airplane that the Navy was looking for.

The three training squadrons flying TF-9Js at NAS Chase Field, TX were VT-24, VT-25, and VT-26. In accordance with the marking convention at the time, they were assigned a tail code with the number 3 for that naval air station and letters J, K, and L respectively for the individual squadrons. *Mark Nankivil Collection*

D. And the Winners and Losers Are

Lockheed originally had orders from the Navy for 390 T2Vs. Unfortunately, it proved to be too big and expensive for basic/intermediate training and not capable enough for advanced training. As a result (and because of delays in its development), only 150 were delivered; orders for 240 were cancelled.

The T2V was flown in the training command for less than two years. By May 1960, the Seastars were being replaced in the basic training squadrons by Buckeyes to reduce flight-hour cost and increase availability. The advanced training squadrons never flew it because the two-seat Cougar was being delivered to them in early 1958, replacing its forebear, the TV-2. North American eventually delivered more than 500 T-2s, as the T2J was redesignated in September 1962. Grumman delivered 399 F9F-8Ts.

Even if the T2V had been delivered earlier to advanced training squadrons, the two-seat Cougar would have soon displaced it there as well. The F9F-8T was more operationally representative of day fighter and light jet-attack airplanes than the T2V. It was therefore better suited for advanced training, which consisted of low-level navigation, instruments, tactics, air-to-ground weapons delivery (up to and including the Low Altitude Bombing System (LABS) delivery of a simulated nuclear weapon), night flying, and carrier qualification. Moreover, unlike the T2V, it provided an introduction to in-flight refueling and the handling quality peculiarities of the swept wing, so it took over the advanced training role.

The F9F-8T was redesignated TF-9J in 1962. In 1965, the two-seat Cougars began to replace the aging single-seat Grumman F-11A Tiger in VT-23, the advanced training squadron at NAS Kingsville, Texas, and those in VT-26 at NAS Chase Field in 1967.

The F-11A, as the F11F, had been the loser in a head-to-head competition with the Vought F8U Crusader for the Navy's day fighter mission. Only 200 were built as a result. After a very short career with operational squadrons, the Tigers were relegated to the advanced training role beginning in 1961. The F11F was the only airplane ever assigned in strength to the Navy's training command that had an afterburner and was capable (just) of supersonic speed in level flight.

Some T2Vs were retained at Pensacola by VT-10 to provide flight experience and mission training for Naval Flight Officers The remainder were distributed to various Navy and Marine Corps bases to be used as station hacks, instrument proficiency, and the hours required each month to qualify for flight pay. A few were used for systems and equipment test.

Carrier qualification did not always go well, as evidenced by this VT-25 TF-9J dangling by its tailhook from the deck of the training carrier *Lexington* (CVS-16) in May 1966. *US Navy*

The units to which the T2Vs were assigned undoubtedly appreciated them because they served in those secondary roles for another decade. The airplane was sturdy and easy to fly. The BLC system, which was reportedly a maintenance burden in its brief stint in the training command and adversely affected availability, was not a factor for land-based operations and in any event, was reportedly deactivated.[15] The last of the T2Vs, redesignated as the T-1A in 1962, was flown off to storage in 1971. A few avoided the eventual scrapping. One, BuNo 144735, was even restored to flight status in the civil experimental category. One is on display at the Pima Air and Space Museum. However, an indication that it didn't make much of an impression is that its 1962 redesignation, T-1A, was recycled twenty years later for the Raytheon Jayhawk, an off-the-shelf cabin-class executive jet, used as a trainer by the Air Force. (Reuse of a designation is rare and might have been inadvertent.)

E. Scooter for Two, Super Cougar, or Twosader?

One change that affected the Navy's trainer program from 1958 on was the establishment of the Replacement Air Group concept that year. Although created using existing squadrons for the most part, the RAGs, one on the east coast and one on the west, were actually training units. Naval aviators fresh from receiving their wings, senior aviators who had been designated as Air Group Commanders, and aviators returning to flying duty after a two-year assignment behind a desk would be sent to the appropriate RAG depending on their next fleet-squadron assignment. Upon completion of the RAG training, they would be fully qualified and proficient in the aircraft that they were to fly in the fleet. All they needed to do after arrival at their new squadron was to get up to speed on local procedures and the operating area.

Before the creation of the RAGs, training of the newly minted Naval Aviator in fleet aircraft had been accomplished at the squadron level in the air groups/wings. The quality and completeness of the training could vary significantly.

This VT-23 F-11A carried Sidewinder launch rails on its outboard pylons. It was the only afterburner-equipped, supersonic airplane to see any significant utilization by the Navy training command. *US Navy*

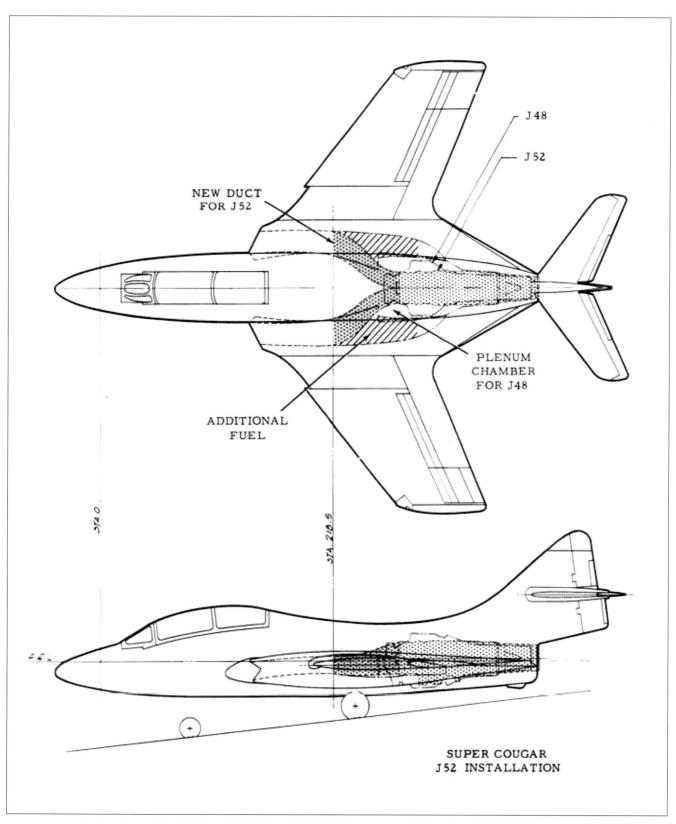

NEW DUCT
FOR J52

J48

J52

PLENUM
CHAMBER
FOR J48

ADDITIONAL
FUEL

SUPER COUGAR
J52 INSTALLATION

The Super Cougar was to be powered by an axial-flow Pratt and Whitney J-52 replacing the centrifugal-flow Pratt and Whitney J48. Relatively minor internal modifications were required to change the inlet ducting from a plenum-chamber arrangement to straight-in flow. *Grumman History Center*

There was little standardization and dissemination of best practices and lessons learned between squadrons. Accident statistics demonstrated that this approach was not appropriate, particularly as the complexity and performance of tactical airplanes increased.

The training command still needed to provide a pilot to the RAG who had achieved a level of proficiency in the combat arts of air-to-air maneuvering, weapons delivery, low-level navigation, formation flying, in-flight refueling, etc. This had previously accomplished in advanced training units that utilized obsolescent fleet fighters and bombers. As the high rate of new fighter development began to slow and production rates fell farther and farther from even Korean War levels, fleet airplanes were overhauled and upgraded rather than being replaced. There were therefore fewer and fewer "used" fighters and bombers available for advanced training. What's worse, the RAGs were first in line for the airplanes that did become available. As a result, Douglas, Grumman, and Vought identified sales opportunities for advanced trainers.

Douglas had proposed a two-seat version of the A4D-5 (A-4E) to the Navy in 1959 specifically for use by the A4D squadrons in the fleet replacement air groups. The A4D-5T was to be fully mission capable in accordance with the requirement for combat tactics and weapons-employment training. In this role and for shore-based carrier-landing familiarization, it allowed an instructor to more closely observe the student pilot's actions and also demonstrate maneuvers to him or her. The trainee pilot could then use the same aircraft for his carrier qualification landings, albeit solo in accordance with the established practice. In the instrument-training phase, it obviated the need for a second Skyhawk or other airplane to fly along with the student to ensure that he did not run into other airplanes or terrain. At the time, though, the Navy was still buying the two-seat F9F-8T (TF-9J) for its requirements for both an instrument refresher/proficiency trainer for fleet pilots and an advanced, carrier-capable jet trainer for the Naval Air Training Command. As a result, it passed on the two-seat Skyhawk.

Grumman delivered its last F9F-8T in December 1959. In 1961, it was in the process of developing the A2F Intruder, which had made its first flight in April 1960, powered by two Pratt & Whitney J52 engines. The J52 was a new engine that was a little lighter and smaller around than the J48 in the Cougar but already produced 1,000 pounds more thrust. Its specific fuel consumption, moreover, was dramatically less than that of the older engine. The J52's normal rated thrust was the same as the J48's military thrust and it was burning 30% less fuel for the same thrust.

Grumman marketing credibly claimed that an F9F-8T engine change would be straight forward, particularly since the J52 was in flight test at Calverton in the A2F. Because of the greater thrust, the Super Cougar, as it was called, would have better takeoff performance and fly somewhat faster and higher than the J48-powered F9F-8T. The main benefit, because of the better fuel efficiency, was 100% more endurance at sea level and almost 80% more range.

According to a Super Cougar marketing brochure dated October 1961:

> In the near future, the Navy will require additional trainers. Increased training activity and normal attrition of aircraft will soon render the existing supply of aircraft inadequate.
>
> The most logical course to follow would be to order more of the types now in service. Recent discussions with CNATRA, CNAVANTRA, AirLant, AirPac, the 2nd MAW and the RCVG's disclosed an impressive vote of confidence in the F9F-8T. The consensus of opinion was that it is the only logical airplane for the Navy to buy at this time of all available trainers or training adaptations of current fleet aircraft.

Reading between the lines, Grumman considered its competition to be a two-seat derivative of the Navy's front-line day fighter at the time, the Vought F8U Crusader.

> With CNAVANTRA graduates already flying two fighter models in the Mach 2 class, with no "quantum jump" in fighter or attack airplane speeds foreseen, and with the emphasis shifting to more subsonic airplanes, there appears to be little reason to conceive and introduce a more sophisticated, higher speed trainer for Navy use. This would raise the cost of training and the pilot attrition rate out of proportion to any benefits that can be foreseen. CNAVANTRA has stated that the F9F-8T is sufficiently challenging to use as a trainer for all existing fleet aircraft.

Moreover, because of the importance of the two-seat Cougar to the training command and the need to provide for attrition and service life limits, the Navy was in the process of taking 190 F9F-8Ts from fleet squadrons, where they had been used for instrument and navigation proficiency/training and administrative missions, and putting them into storage. They were to be replaced by single-seat A4D Skyhawks, which required two airplanes, particularly for instrument proficiency. Grumman therefore marketed the Super Cougar as a better alternative.

The Navy chose to pass on the Super Cougar but took a closer look at the supersonic Vought F8U Twosader as described in Chapter 8.

F. Making a Good Trainer Even Better

Although the T2J-1 had adequate performance for its basic training role, it was considered to be underpowered with its Westinghouse J34 engine, which was also no longer in production. As a result, North America suggested what amounted to a complete redesign to the Navy in April 1956, a T2J variant powered by either the new Pratt & Whitney J52 or a Westinghouse J50.[16] The new airplane would have a gross weight of 12,500 pounds with a J52 engine providing 7,600 pounds of thrust, more than double that of the J34. The fuselage was similar to the T2J's but wings and tail surfaces were somewhat swept to increase the critical Mach number. Combat ceiling was predicted to be in excess of 50,000 feet. Maximum speed at 35,000 feet was Mach .95; at sea level, just over 600 knots.

Instead of buying more single-engine T2Js with either modest or high performance, the Navy instead issued a contract to North American in January 1962 to convert two T2J-1s, one of the original prototypes (BuNo 144218) and one of the first production airplanes (BuNo 145997), to be T2J-2 prototypes powered by two Pratt & Whitney J60-P-6 engines derated to 2,905 lbs of thrust. The change consisted of a redesign of the lower fuselage to widen it, an increase in the size of the engine intakes, and mounting structure and systems for two engines instead of one.

Because the T2J-1 was somewhat underpowered with the Westinghouse J34, its high speed and altitude performance were underwhelming. North American proposed to install a higher-thrust Pratt and Whitney J52 and also sweep the wings to raise the critical Mach number. *Tommy H. Thomason Collection*

T-2A BuNo 145997 was one of two modified to be twin-engine T-2B prototypes. The engine intakes were enlarged and the lower fuselage squared off to accommodate the replacement J60 engines. *Mark Nankivil Collection*

This T-2B has a side number of 000 and a multi-colored rudder in accordance with the tradition of markings on an airplane in a squadron nominally assigned to its commanding officer, even though other pilots would usually fly it. *Mike Wilson Photo*

Going to two engines provided the increase in thrust desired, an early introduction to flying a twin-engine jet with one engine out, and a hoped-for reduction in airplane loss and fatal crashes in the event of an engine failure. The first prototype flew on August 30, 1962. In September 1962, the T2J-1 and T2J-2 were redesignated T-2A and T-2B respectively.

In the basic training configuration with full fuel, including tip tanks, the T-2A had a takeoff gross weight of 11,580 lbs. The T-2B was about 1,000 lbs heavier, but the total thrust from its twin engines almost doubled the thrust available from the T-2A's single engine. The 34th and subsequent T-2Bs received a 100-gallon internal fuel capacity increase with a fuel tank in the wing leading edge to offset the loss in specific range resulting from twin-engine operation. The change was retrofitted to the T-2Bs built earlier.

After a Navy evaluation of the T-2B prototypes, North American received an initial contract for ten production T-2Bs in March 1964.

The first production T-2B flew on May 21, 1965. Except for some avionics and the engines and associated systems, it was otherwise virtually identical to the T-2A. NATC began qualification tests of the T-2B in August 1965. In August 1966, three T-2Bs and a few T-37Bs were assigned to VT-7 for a three-month comparative evaluation of their suitability for the basic training role except, in the case of the T-37B of course, carrier operations. VT-7 subsequently received T-2Bs as replacements for its T-2As beginning in November. Some

were subsequently delivered to VT-4, also part of the Basic Training Command, at Pensacola for air-to-air gunnery and carrier qualification. The last T-2A in the training command departed VT-9 in February 1973.

Ed Gillespie has fond memories of the twin-engine T-2:

The J60-powered "Bs" were so much improved over the As with the J34 that they were night and day. From the first flights of the T2J-1, we NAA pilots wrote internal memos criticizing the lack of performance with the single J34. The J60 was so much better and with two of them, WOW! During a climb to service ceiling, (for T2B handbook data) we had previously decided to continue to absolute ceiling, if things were looking good at service ceiling. After climbing for another almost half hour after the service ceiling was reached, I finally "zoom" climbed the last 500 ft. and topped out in a stall at over 50,000 ft. We got it all on data but NAA decided not to advertise the fact. The airplane would also really turn (preferably below 20M") in a dogfight if a good pilot asked.

In early 1967, Secretary of Defense Robert McNamara almost introduced the T-37B into the Navy primary training program by fiat. For the Fiscal Year 1968 budget, he proposed that T-37Bs be substituted for most of the Navy's basic flight training requirements as they were half the cost of the T-2Bs. Only enough T-2Bs would be procured to provide for the gunnery and carrier qualification phases. Congress did not agree with his approach.

One reason for the cost differential was that Pratt and Whitney had increased the price of the J60 for T-2B production. In response, the Navy elected to reengine the T-2 with two less expensive, slightly lighter, but also less fuel-efficient General Electric J85-GE-4 engines with the same thrust rating as the J60s. The only performance penalty was a 5% decrease in specific range. As a result, North American built only ninety-seven T-2Bs. T-2B BuNo 152382 was modified to be the prototype for the T-2C. First flight was accomplished on April 17, 1968.

There were 231 T-2Cs produced with the first one closely following the last T-2B on the production line. First delivery was to VT-9 at NAS Meridian in April 1969. The T-2C eventually replaced all the T-2As and Bs, with the last of them being phased out in 1973.

However, because of a subsequent and temporary shortfall in the number of T-2Cs versus training requirements, several T-2Bs were reclaimed from MASDC storage in the early 1980s and refurbished at the Naval Air Rework Facility at Pensacola. These were assigned to VT-10 and other units that were operating T-2Cs in a non-pilot training role to free them up for pilot training. The T-2Bs were retired for the second time in 1991.

The T-2C prototype, BuNo 152832, is shown here configured for an evaluation of the training provision for weapons pylons. *Mark Nankivil Collection*

The last class of students to train in the T-2C accomplished their carrier qualification aboard *Truman* (CVN-75) in July 2003. It was also the last carrier airplane to be catapulted with a bridle rather than the nose-tow system that had been introduced with the Grumman A-6 Intruder and E-2 Hawkeye in 1963.

North American T-2C *Buckeye*s wait behind the blast deflector on the flight deck of the aircraft carrier USS *Lexington* (AVT-16) in April 1989 for their turns at the catapult during carrier qualifications in the Gulf of Mexico. *US Navy*

The T-2 was equipped with provisions for a gun pod for gunnery training. It could also be fitted with a tow target so a squadron could provide its own air-to-air training. *Mark Nankivil Collection*

G. TA-4

Although the Navy had passed on Douglas's original two-seat A4D trainer proposal in 1959, in 1964 the concept provided a means to address a Navy light attack fleet planning concern that was not shared by the Department of Defense. Vought was in the process of developing the A-7 Corsair II that was intended to replace the Douglas A-4 Skyhawk and single-seat A-1 Skyraider for carrier-based light attack and interdiction. Secretary of Defense Robert McNamara had made Navy's ability to have enough light-attack airplanes to meet operational requirements in the late 1960s and early 1970s dependent on the all-new A-7 being delivered on schedule. In fact, he had stated to Congress that the A-4E with its higher-thrust J52 engine was only marginally better than the J65-powered A-4C so no more Skyhawks would be procured after the 500 A-4Es on order were completed.

The admirals—who had more experience than McNamara with the uncertainties involved in aircraft development—were concerned that production of A-4Es then on order was going to end before the A-7 was proven and in production at high enough rate to maintain the light attack fleet at the required size. It therefore wasn't hard for Douglas to convince the Navy to order a two-seat A-4 that would 1) fulfill an existing OSD-sanctioned requirement for a two-seat combat trainer, and also 2) keep the A-4 production line "warm" in the event that more single-seat A-4s were required. Douglas received authority in June 1964 to convert the last two production A-4Es on order, BuNos 152102 and 152103, to a two-seat configuration, to be known as the TA-4E. According to detail specification SD-495-5-5, the two-seat Skyhawk was to be "capable of training pilots in all phases of naval operational flying."

The fuselage of the two-seat variant was only lengthened by twenty-eight inches ahead of the wing compared to the recommended length for a seat and rudder pedal controls of at least fifty inches. Any greater stretch, since the 20 mm cannon were to be retained, would have required a more extensive redesign to rebalance the airplane, such as extending the fuselage aft of the wing to compensate for the added weight forward. In order to provide the space required for the second cockpit, Douglas had to reduce the capacity of the fuselage fuel cell by 140 gallons. In its place, Douglas proposed the addition of a 300-gallon fuel tank in a dorsal fairing aft of the canopy. It more than replaced the fuel capacity lost in reduction in the size of the fuselage fuel cell and was also positioned over the center of gravity so there was no trim change with fuel burn.

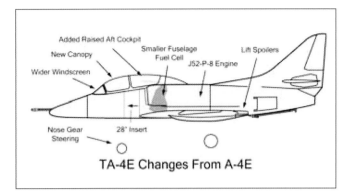

The changes to create the two-seat TA-4E were similar to those that had been used for the conversion of single-seat fighters to trainers or two-place airplanes. *Tommy H. Thomason*

The Navy decided that since the two-seater was a trainer, it did not require an endurance of more than two hours or so for a given flight. The reduction in fuel capacity was therefore acceptable, considering the increase in development and unit cost associated with the dorsal tank. It may have also taken into account the increase in the height of the center of gravity that would result from the change, which would have increased the A-4's existing and marginally acceptable top heaviness (the increase in the height of the cg, if any, due to the second cockpit was offset by the shift of the nose landing gear forward with the fuselage extension; there was therefore no increase in the A-4's already high turnover angle.) The reduction in the internal fuel capacity of the two-seat Skyhawk approximately offset the 1,000-pound increase in empty weight plus the weight of the second crewman. As a result, when carrying the same external stores, the TA-4's gross weight was only slightly more than the single-seat A-4E (A4D-5). There was a notable reduction in range and endurance, of course, due to the smaller internal fuel capacity of the TA-4, but relatively less when external tanks were carried. In any event, the TA-4 proved to have adequate range and endurance for training missions.[17]

Since a redesign of the canopy/fuselage interface was required, Douglas and the Navy decided to take the opportunity to address the cramped shoulder room and limited headroom of the original A4D design. The distance between the canopy rails was widened, which resulted in a new, wider windscreen with a rectangular, rather than oval, center panel. The canopy was not only wider, but also angled up in back so that the aft cockpit could be higher than the front cockpit and thereby provide better forward visibility for the instructor. Because it was a much larger and heavier structure than the single-seat canopy, it was now power actuated.

The mockup of the TA-4E was displayed at the 1965 Paris Air Show complete with dummy bombs and rocket pods.
T. Panopalis Collection

The latest version of the Douglas ejection seat, the Escapac 1C-3 with zero-speed, zero-altitude escape capability, was introduced on the TA-4. A larger, more powerful rocket eliminated the need for a minimum speed of ninety KIAS when on the deck for a successful ejection. It also reduced the size of the sink-rate/roll-angle-versus-altitude envelope where a successful ejection was unlikely. Inflating bladders in the seat pan and back provided positive pilot/seat separation for the quickest possible parachute deployment.

Since these aircraft were to be primarily shore-based as well as flown by student pilots, the crosswind-landing shortcomings of the basic Skyhawk design were finally addressed with the addition of nose wheel steering and wing lift spoilers. Douglas had evaluated a simulated lift spoiler in high-speed taxi tests followed by the modification and flight test of an A-4C with spoilers and nose wheel steering. Both were fairly straightforward modifications that proved to be retrofittable to existing aircraft.

The lift spoiler was essentially a duplication of the split flap on the upper surface of the wing, pivoting upward to reduce lift. Deployment was automatically triggered when

the system was armed, the engine RPM was less than seventy percent, and the left main landing gear oleo was compressed on touchdown. The immediate reduction in wing lift significantly increased braking effectiveness immediately after touchdown and reduced the risk of blowing a tire when the brakes were applied. The spoilers also provided increased aerodynamic braking after touchdown for a shorter landing roll, a capability not previously available to the Skyhawk pilot due to the lack of elevator effectiveness at landing speed. The changes resulted in an increase in the crosswind landing limit from a maximum of fifteen knots to a more acceptable twenty-five knots.

A full-size mockup of the TA-4E was created by adding a wooden forward fuselage to a surplus airframe. After completion in April 1965 and review by the Navy, it was taken on a marketing tour to Europe and displayed at the Paris Air Show.

Although not really necessary since the increase in gross weight of the two-seater was not significant, a more powerful J52 engine, the -8A with 9,300-lb thrust was installed in the production two-seater rather than the -6A with 8,500-lb thrust in the A-4E (A4D-5).

The first version of the two-seat Skyhawk, the TA-4F, was assigned to Replacement Air Groups that provided type training or to naval aviators prior to their assignment to a fleet squadron. Here, a VA-127 TA-4F flies on the wing of a single-seat VA-127 A-4F. *T. J. "Jeff" Brown Collection*

Since it was a relatively straightforward change from the basic airframe and an existing A-4E (A4D-5) engine was installed initially, the first TA-4E, BuNo 152102, flew on June 30, 1965, only eight months after the authority to proceed. Because of the detail changes that had been made to the basic A-4E (A4D-5) configuration, including the use of the more powerful J52-P-8A engine, the two-seater designation was subsequently changed to TA-4F. TA-4F production totaled 241 airplanes, including the first two TA-4Es.

Two-seat Skyhawks were not initially delivered to the Navy Training Command, *per se*. The first ones were delivered to VA-125, the west coast A-4 fleet replacement training (formerly replacement air group) squadron based at NAS Lemoore, California, in May 1966. Its east coast counterpart, VA-44 at NAS Cecil Field, Florida, received TA-4Fs in August. Four RAG squadrons—VA-43 at NAS Oceana, Virginia; VA-45 at NAS Jacksonville, Florida;

VF-126 at NAS Miramar, California; and VA-127 at NAS Lemoore, California—all received TA-4Fs to replace their TF-9Js for instrument training in mid- to late 1967. VF-127 at Lemoore also utilized TA-4Fs for instrument training in addition to providing jet transition training to Naval Aviators from other non-attack communities like VP (patrol squadron) pilots being assigned to A-4 squadrons due to the shortage of attack pilots. TA-4Fs were also delivered to the Marine Corps. VMT-103 at MCAS Yuma, Arizona, which was the west coast Marine Corps squadron responsible for advanced training as well as swept-wing refresher/transition, received its first TA-4F in November 1966, replacing TF-9s. Its east coast counterpart, VMT-203 at MCAS Cherry Point, North Carolina, received its first TA-4F in July the following year. The Marine Headquarters & Maintenance squadrons, which provided logistics support and intermediate level maintenance within a Marine Air

In mid-1971, the TA-4Js were replacing the aging TF-9Js for advanced jet training. Here, two VT-23 Skyhawks (3H) flank two VT-26 (3L) Cougars. *Terry Panopalis Collection*

Wing, also received a few TA-4Fs each. TA-4Fs were also parceled out to Navy test and evaluation units for chase, air-to-air photography, and logistics support.

The two-seat Skyhawk program not only kept the single-seat production line open,[18] it provided a timely replacement for the Navy's aging fleet of two-seat TF-9J trainers in the training command at minimal investment. This new procurement, designated TA-4J, was almost identical to the TA-4F except for a cost and weight reduction decision to eliminate armament, which also allowed the use of lower thrust J52-P-6 engines—the 20 mm Colts, the two outboard wing pylons, and weapons sights and associated hardware were therefore deleted from the configuration. Provisions for operating as an inflight refueling tanker were also to be removed, although the receiver capability was retained. In practice, however, some of the deleted mission equipment was subsequently incorporated in some Js to increase their usefulness as an advanced trainer. A total of 281 TA-4Js were produced, not counting the thirty-three similar TA-4s built for non-

US military requirements. (This fleet was subsequently augmented by the conversion of many TA-4Fs to the TA-4J configuration.) The first TA-4J, originally ordered as a TA-4F, flew on December 17, 1968. It was introduced in the Navy's training command beginning in June 1969 with deliveries to VT-21 at NAS Kingsville, Texas. By the end of 1970, the two-seat Skyhawk had replaced all the Cougars in all three advanced training squadrons there: VT-21, -22, and -23. VT-24 and -25 at NAS Chase Field near Beeville, Texas, also transitioned to the TA-4J. The last TF-9J in the training command left VT-4 for long-term storage in Arizona in May 1973.

The Js also replaced Fs in the Marine Corps readiness training squadrons, now designated VMAT-103 and -203, in the early 1970s. VA squadrons, whenever they weren't deployed, also tried to get a TA-4 assigned for use as a support and cross-country aircraft. Other units such as NATC and the Navy Test Pilot School at NAS Patuxent River also found the TA-4 to be useful for chase, photography, and other requirements.

The deck crew of the *Carl Vinson* (CVN-70) positions a VT-7 TA-4J Skyhawk for launch in April 1984. By this time, fleet airplanes were equipped with nose-tow launch catapult shuttles, while the T-2C and TA-4J still had to be hooked up with separate bridal and holdback arrangements and in the case of the TA-4J, manually positioned with a steering bar. *US Navy*

H. Training Squadron Realignment and Re-Equipment

The replacement of the TF-9Js with TA-4Js roughly marked the beginning of a relatively stable phase of Navy training of jet pilots, at least from an equipment standpoint. There was also a realignment of the Navy's jet training syllabus to increase training effectiveness and reduce the time and cost associated with moving students between training bases. Prior to 1970, each of the Navy's training bases was primarily, if not exclusively, devoted to only one phase of the overall pilot training process. As a result, a student Naval Aviator would travel a circuit around the American southeast in the year or so it took to complete his flight training. For example, a student would go through pre-

flight training at NAS Pensacola and then move up the road to NAS Saufley Field to receive primary flight training in the Beech T-34B Mentor. If selected for jets, he would travel to NAS Meridian, Mississippi, for basic flight training in the North American T-2 Buckeye and then go back to Pensacola for gunnery and initial carrier qualification in T-2s with VT-4. The final step in the process (before training in a specific deployable-airplane type at a replacement air group squadron) was advanced jet training in Grumman Cougars or Douglas Skyhawks accomplished at either NAS Chase Field or NAS Kingsville in Texas.

Beginning in 1971, each of the three jet training bases—Meridian, Kingsville, and Chase Field—was assigned both T-2 and TA-4 squadrons for basic and advanced jet training, respectively. VT-23 at Kingsville traded its

Skyhawks for Buckeyes while VT-7 at Meridian assumed the advanced jet-training role with TA-4s in place of its T-2s.[19] The TF-9Js were retired over the next few years. The T-28s used for primary training were eventually assigned to a single squadron, VT-27 based at NAS Corpus Christi; the last of these, BuNo 137796, was ferried to the Naval Support Facility at Anacostia, District of Columbia, to be put on display.

The T-2s and TA-4s would remain in the training command until the next major change in training aircraft accomplished with the McDonnell-Douglas T-45 Goshawks (to be described in Chapter 10) beginning in 1992.

As the TA-4s began to be replaced by T-45s in the early 1990s, the number of advanced strike training squadrons flying the TA-4J was eventually necked down to one really big one, VT-7 at NAS Meridian. At one point, it was assigned more than 100 two-seaters as well as a few A-4Es for instructors to provide chase for student solo flights. Its thirty-three-week advanced flight-training syllabus included weapons training at NAF El Centro and carrier landing qualifications. VT-7 eventually transitioned to the T-45 as well. The last carrier qualification in a TA-4J was in September 1999 from *George Washington* (CVN-73).[20]

This VT-7 TA-4J is en route to the bombing range with practice bombs loaded on the center pylon. Although tiny, they have the same ballistic characteristics of actual bombs, providing the student pilot with the appropriate feedback on his delivery accuracy. *T.J. "Jeff" Brown Collection*

Sometimes It Requires Teaching More Than Stick and Rudder Skills!

In the early 1990s, Lt. Tom Kalfas, an F-14 fighter pilot with the VF-84 "Jolly Rogers," was assigned to advanced jet training after his carrier tour. He learned an unexpected lesson as an instructor pilot in the TA-4J Skyhawk during his shore assignment:

As a fleet LSO (Landing Signal Officer), one of my primary areas of instruction "specialty" was carrier qualification, teaching the procedures and techniques for landing on an aircraft carrier (in Naval Aviator terms, "the boat"). The advanced jet syllabus was broken into numerous phases of training, built in a fairly specific succession, with carrier qualification slated to be the final phase before a student earned his "Wings of Gold." This made sense since every flight built time, experience and comfort in the aircraft and the completion of every phase of instruction built confidence, a quality that is critical … especially "behind the boat.

While the syllabus sequence called for carrier qualification to be the final phase of training, the reality was that things didn't always work out that way. In fact, it was rare that a student's last flight would be carrier qualification. A variety of factors such as carrier availability often caused the last two phases, carrier qualification and air combat maneuvering (dog fighting), to be conducted simultaneously.

While the *USS Lexington*, CVT-16, was the designated "training carrier," it was not always available and we would frequently detach (travel to and operate from another base) from Chase Field to utilize fleet carriers. It was during one such detachment that I would learn … and teach … a valuable lesson.

Carrier qualifications require that the student fly solo to the ship. No instructor sits in the back seat of a student's plane; the student is alone in his aircraft while facing the greatest challenge in aviation. It's a true testament to the program that these relatively inexperienced aspiring aviators, many with only a couple hundred hours of flight time when they first "see the boat," successfully meet the challenge.

Getting to the boat is relatively easy since student pilots fly formation on a "Lead-safe" instructor who takes flights of two, three, or four students all the way into the pattern at the carrier. Once established on downwind at the proper distance abeam the carrier with all students properly spaced behind him, the Lead-safe instructor departs the pattern and takes an observation position overhead the ship, remaining on-station to chase or escort back to the beach any students that might develop an aircraft problem. At that point, each student is on his own.

Hook dangling well below the wheels, a VT-7 TA-4J nears touchdown and a "trap." *US Navy*

Each flight to the boat is exhaustively briefed by one of the beach-bound LSOs. One subject always discussed in-depth is the need to strictly adhere to standard procedures. Students who carrier qualify understandably experience euphoria unparalleled to that point in their careers and there is an ever-present temptation for the successful student to celebrate his accomplishment by "flat-hatting" … operating the aircraft in a non-standard fashion while flying back to the beach. It is only natural for the newly minted carrier qualified student to feel like "King Kong."

As a matter of practicality, the shipboard LSOs need a way to get back to the beach so the last qualifying student in the group has the added responsibility of flying the LSO back to the beach. No LSO wants to ride in the back of a student's jet coming off the carrier … so it is routine that the student unstraps from the front seat and moves to the back allowing his LSO to take the front seat, all done while the engine is running and the aircraft is being refueled while chocked and chained to the deck. This is always a big let down after qualifying, the last thing a student wants is to relinquish command of the jet and be shoved into the back seat.

My students were progressing well. On the last day (it typically took 2-3 days to qualify each squadron) my last student was in the pattern and I was geared-up, ready to jump into the jet once he successfully trapped for the last time. Every now and then, for reasons no Training Command LSO could ever understand, "The Boss," the Commander in charge of flight deck activities, would-dictate that time constraints did not allow for the seat swap and the LSO would have to ride the student's back seat to the beach. This was my fate on this lesson-filled day and I reluctantly strapped into the back seat for my ride to the beach.

With refueling complete and me strapped into the back seat, my student taxied to the catapult and we were airborne in short order. It was immediately apparent to me that I was flying with "King Kong." He did not climb to the required 500 feet, he accelerated past the standard 300-knot departure speed within ten miles of the ship and he commenced his climb to altitude well inside the ten mile minimum distance for executing altitude changes outside the landing pattern.

I debated with myself about speaking-up. Here I was, riding the back seat of a student who had minutes earlier completed every phase of navy flight training and was for all intents and purposes a Naval Aviator. I was not supposed to be in that back seat and was only there due to timing. A week later he would be a winged, full-fledged Naval Aviator and off to train in a tactical fleet aircraft. I decided to not say anything and continued to sit back and observe … even though he was still a student and I was (supposed to be) an instructor.

He continued to violate all sorts of rules and regulations, climbing to non-standard altitudes, making non-standard radio calls … and I continued to sit back and say nothing. Approaching NAS Key West, he entered the overhead break at a lower than standard altitude and substantially exceeded the student's standard break-entry speed of 300 knots.

Entering the downwind he started to configure the aircraft for landing, dropping the landing gear seventy-five knots above its airspeed limit. Now concerned for the physical state of the aircraft, I had finally seen enough. Just as I was about to take control of the aircraft and communicate this to the student, I observed that he raised the landing gear handle in an attempt to "catch" the gear … while it was still in transit!

I took control of the aircraft and proceeded to properly configure the plane for landing. There is no doubt that the student, at that point, believed that he had earned himself a "down" for the flight; successful in carrier qualifying but failing the return flight, a flight that should have found him alone with no one to observe his mistakes or "down" him.

Once I established the aircraft abeam the landing area, properly configured at the proper altitude and airspeed, I gave control back to the student, stating, "Let's see if we can get the airplane on the ground and parked without breaking any more rules."

The brief remainder of the flight was uneventful and by-the-book. Our walk together back to the hangar was done in solemn silence. Once inside the hangar, the student turned to me and said, "I'll get the pink-sheet, sir" (a grade sheet used to document a failure). I told him that he didn't need to do that. With a puzzled look on his face, he listened to me blame myself and take full responsibility for the events of the flight. I told him that if I had done the "right thing" and said something the very first time he violated a procedure, none of the subsequent "mistakes" would have happened. I stated that we were fortunate to safely return uninjured and with our aircraft undamaged. I thanked him for helping me learn a valuable lesson that day and hoped that he would always remember it as he embarked on the beginning of his career. I then had to explain to the maintenance personnel why I had allowed a student to overspeed the landing gear and cause many hours of work in the hot sun for our mechanics.

There's a saying that every accident is usually preceded by a chain of events and that breaking any link in that chain might have prevented the accident. On a beautiful, sunny, hot day operating in the skies off Key West, Florida, one fortunate student and his instructor were lucky to have a chain that had at least one more link before reaching its end.

Carrier qualifications were accomplished solo but the aft cockpit was sometimes occupied when the trainer was being flown by a carrier-qualified aviator. *US Navy*

Chapter Six Endnotes

1. The L-245's raised rear seat may have been Lockheed's counter to the Air Force preference for side-by-side seating in a trainer if improved instructor's visibility forward had been the Air Force's goal. However, the primary reason was reportedly better instructor/student communication and the ability of the instructor to monitor the student.

2. The T-33B designation was eventually applied to the Navy's TV-2s in the DoD consolidation of the Navy and Air Force designation systems in 1962. The suffix letter was not the same as the Air Force T-33's because the configurations of the Air Force and Navy T-birds had diverged over time.

3. Memorandum for the NACA Ames Director from Robert C. Innis: Visit to Lockheed Aircraft Corporation, Palmdale, California to evaluate the T2V airplane dated 6 September 1955.

4. Bureau of Aeronautics Memorandum from Director, Airframe Design Division to Director, Aircraft Division: Final Report, Service Acceptance Trials of Model T2V-1 Airplane dated 29 May 1958.

5. Memorandum from Commander, Naval Air Test Center to Chief, Bureau of Aeronautics: Demonstration of Model T2V-1 Spinning Characteristics dated 31 July 1957.

6. The practice of leaving canopies open for takeoffs and landings was to insure a rapid ingress in the event that the pilot had to ditch the airplane in the water. As it happened, the practice was subsequently discouraged following incidents with barricade engagements that resulted in the upper strap entering the cockpit and injuring or killing the pilot.

7. The Landing Signal Officer was often quicker to discern a bad trend on a carrier approach then even an experienced carrier pilot. He could be counted on to keep the student relatively safe. In any event, few instructors would be willing to ride along for a student pilot's first carrier landings. Even fewer would be capable of only taking over just in time to avoid catastrophe. Any sooner and the student could not demonstrate that he had recognized the error and started correction himself.

8. Although a survivable ejection from the runway at speeds above 100 knots was likely with the Martin Baker Mk 4 seat, rates of sink and angles of bank required that ejection be initiated at higher altitudes.

9. The Grumman F11F Tiger was an exception to the retrofit of US Navy fighters with the Martin Baker seat. Its production had been curtailed because of the clear superiority of the Vought F8U Crusader. Even though seats had been procured for the fleet and it continued in service with the training command and the Blue Angels flight demonstration team, none of the Tigers operated by the Navy were ever retrofitted, unlike the F9F-8Ts.

10. According to Tom Weinel "There were also at least three different MB seats in the Cougar when I flew it in 1966-67. Most had the USN harness arrangement but some had the RAF style. You had to know which seat type the aircraft you were going to fly had, because with the RAF seats you didn't wear a torso harness. One of them, I don't recall which one, was the absolutely most uncomfortable ejection seat I ever sat in. I was always glad I never had to eject with one, it was no wonder they were back breakers, the position they had you in."

11. Three of the competitors had prior relationships: Fairchild, Stroukoff, and Thiebolt. Armand Thieblot had been Fairchild's chief engineer at Hagerstown, Maryland for many years. He had been hired in the late 1930s by Sherman Fairchild to design a primary trainer for the Army Air Corps. Designated the PT-19, it was procured in quantity. He subsequently struck out on his own after World War II. He founded and was president of Thieblot Aircraft in Bethesda, MD, and Martinsburg, WV. (In the mid-1950s, Thiebolt was acquired by the Vitro Corporation.) Michael Stroukoff had been chief engineer and president of Chase Aircraft until the Air Force cancelled its C-123 production contract, reportedly over production costs at the Kaiser facility where it was to be built. (Kaiser was a majority shareholder in Chase.) The Air Force selected Fairchild to complete its C-123 production requirements. Following the cancellation of its production contracts, Kaiser closed down Chase. Stroukoff acquired the Chase production facility in 1954 and formed a new company, Stroukoff Aircraft Corporation, that specialized in developing advanced variants of the C-123 Provider. However, none of the company's designs resulted in a production order. The company folded in 1959.

12. The T2J designation has a convoluted background. Navy had ordered 240 SNJ-8s from North American that were similar to the T-6G. These were subsequently redesignated TJ-8 when the trainer designation was changed to T. Although the TJ-8 order was subsequently canceled, as a general rule a designation once issued was not reused. The Navy's next trainer from North American would therefore have normally have been designated T2J. However, the Navy had agreed in principal in 1952 to begin to use the Air Force designation for airplanes that it procured that were initially developed and put into service by the Air Force. As a result, the next North American trainer became the T-28B instead. When the Navy contracted with North American for a new jet trainer, the Navy picked up where it had left off and designated it the T2J.

13. NATC report AC-67101.3, T2J-1 Fleet Introduction Program, Report No.1, Final Report of July 12, 1959

14. Free-spinning-tunnel investigation of a 1/20th scale model of the North American T2J-1 airplane by James S. Bowman, Jr. and Frederick M. Healy, Langley Research Center NAS TM SX-245

15. In addition to the poor availability caused by the BLC system, it is likely that the instructors and students also didn't like the T2V as a basic trainer. BLC complicated the handling qualities on approach, the maneuvering control loads were considered to be high, and the airframe buffet above 15,000 feet at high speed and load factor "severely hindered" performance of aerobatics like loops and Immelmanns.

16. It probably wasn't a coincidence that North American submitted a proposal for a high-performance trainer just as Grumman was about to make the first flight of the two-seat Cougar.

17. One shortcoming of the TA-4 that carried over from its initial development as a small, low-cost jet bomber was its lack of self-boarding capability. Since boarding ladders or stairs were not always available at the airfields these airplanes might utilize, this required some agility on the part of the aviators to dismount and climb back into the cockpits. The fairing over the in-flight refueling probe provided precarious access to and from the front cockpit (The move around the engine inlet from the strake to the wing was another challenge in the process.) Access to and from the top of the wing was relatively straightforward using the fins on the external fuel tanks.

18. In part as a result of the two-seat A-4 program, the Skyhawk production line remained open for another thirteen years. More than 300 single-seat A-4Fs and Ms were delivered to the US Navy and Marine Corps in addition to foreign sales.

19. For a brief period in the mid 1970s there was also a Jet Transition Training Unit (JTTU) at NAS Kingsville, which provided a tailored ground-and-flight training syllabus for the benefit of experienced non-jet pilots who were headed for jet assignments. The JTTU was only a separate unit from late 1974 to August 1975, when it was folded into VT-21.

20. Even when a training carrier was assigned fulltime for student carrier qualifications, it would sometimes be out of service and a fleet carrier would fulfill the requirement. *Forrestal* (AVT-59) was the last dedicated training carrier and served in that role for less than a year. All carrier qualifications were subsequently accomplished on an available fleet carrier, sometimes on the west coast.

Chapter Seven
NAVY PRIMARY JET TRAINERS

A. The Navy All-Jet Experiment

The Navy, like the Air Force, acquired increasingly high-performance tactical jets after Korea, and the Naval Air Training Command faced the problem of producing pilots competent to fly them. One approach to produce a new crop of proficient pilots was to introduce jets in the earliest phase, primary training. However, because of budgetary limitations the Navy could only watch the Air Force T-37

primary jet program with interest—until the fall of 1954 when the Temco Aircraft Corporation submitted an unsolicited proposal to the Naval Bureau of Aeronautics (BuAer) for an inexpensive jet trainer. Temco offered to modify their Model 33 Plebe (which had been unsuccessful in the Navy's 1953 competition against the T-34) into a jet primary trainer.[1]

The Model 33 Plebe was the first tricycle landing gear aircraft built by Temco. It was built for the Navy primary trainer competition in 1953 but lost to the Beechcraft T-34B. In the fall of 1954, Temco proposed an inexpensive jet version of the Plebe to meet the Navy's interest in evaluating an all-jet program. *Vought Heritage Foundation*

Beechcraft also proposed an inexpensive jet conversion of the T-34. This is the sole prototype on a test flight in late 1955. Known as the Model 73 Jet Mentor, this airplane was owned by Beechcraft and flew under a civilian registration. Its similarity to the T-34 is apparent, the wings and tail are essentially unchanged, but the fuselage is lengthened 4½ feet. The Jet Mentor had a gross weight of 4,500 lbs. compared to the T-34s gross weight of 3050 lbs. *Naval History and Heritage Command*

Prior to the Navy evaluation in the spring of 1956 the Model 73 received an overall re-painting. At this point Beechcraft was able to demonstrate the Jet Mentor's ceiling of 28,000 feet and maximum speed of 295 mph. *Beechcraft via Mark Nankivil Collection*

Temco, a respected subcontractor for several major airframe manufacturers, had attempted to win a primary contract on several occasions—first with the TE-1A in a 1949 Air Force competition, then with the TE-1B Buckaroo in a 1951 continuation of the Air Force competition, and most recently with the Model 33 Plebe in a 1953 Navy competition. In each case Temco failed to receive a production contract, but Temco's current proposal generated serious interest at BuAer. It also awakened the Navy to the possibility of simply adapting a jet engine to their current primary trainer. Temco objected loudly to the T-34 conversion idea requesting that the Navy evaluate their airplane in an open competition. BuAer decided that it was a good idea and issued a Request for Proposal (RFP) that specified a stall speed of no more than fifty-five knots at landing weight, a maximum speed of at least 250 knots, minimum endurance of 1½ hours, the ability to operate from a 3,000-foot runway over a fifty-foot obstacle, and be suitable for training up to 15,000 feet altitude. Temco, Beechcraft, and Carma Manufacturing Co. responded, each company proposed a single-engine, light jet powered by the Continental J69 turbojet (the same engine that powered the Air Force T-37).

The Navy's program was quite distinct from the earlier Air Force TX program since the Navy was not certain that a jet primary trainer was practical. The Navy offered a limited contract for only 14 off-the-shelf aircraft to the winner, while the Air Force committed to a full-scale production contract for hundreds of aircraft. Furthermore, the Navy's evaluation aircraft were required to be privately funded, while the Air Force funded three XT-37 prototypes. Motivated to win the contract, Temco abandoned the modified Plebe idea and started work on a new design that featured a pod and boom fuselage to minimize the jet tailpipe length. It was assigned the factory designation Model 51 and was first flown on March 26, 1956.[2] Beechcraft had the advantage of simply modifying an existing T-34, and was able to fly their prototype on December 18, 1955, four months before Temco. Carma flew their prototype on March 25, 1956, but withdrew from the competition one month later when their Weejet Model 880 was lost in a spin accident.

In July 1956, the Jet Mentor was also demonstrated to the Air Force at Edwards AFB. Noted Air Force test pilot Frank Everest is seated in the cockpit. Beechcraft test pilot, Tom Gillespie, is standing at the far right. *Beechcraft via Michael Machat Collection*

The Temco prototype, which carried the civilian registration number N78856, was hurriedly prepared for the Naval Air Test Center (NATC) evaluation at Patuxent River Maryland, scheduled for mid-April. Beechcraft had been flying their prototype, which carried the civilian registration N134B, for five months generating over 100 hours of experience. Only two days before Temco was

scheduled to fly their airplane to Patuxent River it suffered a structural failure performing a rolling pullout from a dive. This maneuver imposed a high load on the airframe causing the left horizontal stabilizer to detach. The test pilot, Marty Collis, was able to maintain control with the remaining tail surface and landed safely, but Temco had to fix the problem (lack of stiffness in the elevator trim tab) and repair the damaged tail. The Beechcraft Model 73 arrived at Patuxent River on April 14; the Temco Model 51, on April 27. Pilots from the Naval Air Test Center and the Naval Air Training Command flew both aircraft putting twenty-four flights totaling 29.9 hours on the Beechcraft, and thirty-two flights totaling 39.5 hours on the Temco. Both aircraft were evaluated for flying qualities, performance capabilities, trainer suitability, safety of flight, reliability, and ease of maintenance.[3] During the evaluation the Beechcraft suffered two mishaps. The first was an explosive compressor stall that damaged the inlet ducts; the second was a failure of the tailpipe clamp that allowed the tailpipe to separate from the engine damaging the aft fuselage. The Beechcraft Model 73 was repaired after both mishaps and completed the evaluation on May 31. The findings, summarized in a NATC Flight Test Division report, found numerous cockpit deficiencies in both airplanes. Both displayed unsatisfactory wave-off characteristics (because of the thirteen-second spool-up time between idle and maximum thrust for the J69 engine). The engine start

The Carma Manufacturing Co. submitted a small V-tailed jet named Weejet Model 880, but it was lost in a spin accident during contractor test flights and Carma was forced to withdraw. Like Beechcraft and Temco, the Carma was powered by an early version of the Continental J-69 turbojet. *NARA*

Temco abandoned the turbojet conversion of the Plebe when Beechcraft announced its plans to offer the Navy a turbojet conversion of its T-34 Mentor. Instead Temco designed a totally new airplane to optimize it for the competition. The result was this pod and boom mid-wing design known as the Model 51, shown here during its rollout. *Vought Heritage Foundation*

Temco Model 51

Beechcraft Model 73

Inboard profile drawings show differing approaches to jet engine installation in the Temco and Beechcraft designs. The pod and boom fuselage allowed Temco to use gradually curved bifurcated inlets with a short tailpipe, while Beechcraft employed sharply curved wing root intakes with a long tailpipe. *Tommy H. Thomason*

Model 51 in April 1956, as it is prepared for departure to the Naval Air Test Center, Patuxent River, Maryland. Three factory technicians, a senior engineer, Cotton Condor, and a parts truck were assigned to accompany the airplane to Patuxent River. *Cotton Condor Collection*

system and taxi characteristics of the Beechcraft were considered inferior to the Temco. However, both airplanes displayed excellent stall characteristics, and satisfactory spin recovery. Both were declared satisfactory for primary training, but the Beechcraft proved more suitable for maintenance. While the report expressed a slight preference for the Beechcraft flying qualities, it concluded:

> In view of the nearly equal balance between flying qualities and those maintenance aspects considered in the evaluation, it is recommended that the contract for fourteen aircraft be awarded on the basis of cost and those additional considerations under the purview of the Bureau of Aeronautics.

Temco submitted a dramatically lower price quote than Beechcraft based on Temco's willingness to amortize the fourteen aircraft over an anticipated production run of 500 aircraft (Temco expected foreign sales also). Beechcraft's bid was $6,185,023 for fourteen aircraft, while Temco's was $1,978,939—the contract was awarded to Temco on June 29, 1956, and the aircraft received the Navy designation TT-1. [4]

Model 51 photographed at the Temco factory in its experimental test flight scheme of natural aluminum with red trim and markings. This photograph illustrates the limited amount of ground equipment needed to service the aircraft, an important consideration for training aircraft. *Vought Heritage Foundation*

The Temco Model 51 after being painted for the Navy evaluation. The original natural aluminum and red trim has been replaced with an overall orange-yellow finish typical of the Naval Air Training Command scheme of that period. *Vought Heritage Foundation*

This demonstration flight photograph shows the upper surface of the Model 51. The aircraft was still owned and maintained by Temco and carried a civilian registration. The US Navy marking on the upper right wing is non-standard. *Vought Heritage Foundation*

B. TT-1 Production

In a fit of exuberance the Temco public relations staff arranged a public christening of the TT-1 by actress Jayne Mansfield who would confer the name "Pinto" on the airplane. Jim Stanfield, a Temco engineer, remembers the event vividly:

> Jayne Mansfield was a movie actress in the 1950s. She had no discernible talent but possessed a body shape that was popular at the time. Someone in senior management decided that Jayne would be the perfect person to christen the Pinto. I'm sure that the meeting between the PR folks and Ms. Mansfield's agent was one for the books. It was decided that Ms. Mansfield would require a pinto pony for the photo "op." The pony was to be clean and odor-free. The Temco purchasing department bought alfalfa hay and a pint of perfume and rented a horse. This may have been the first time a horse rental expense appeared on the books of an aerospace company. After his bath and perfume spray the horse got very sick and was taken to the vet. I heard later that he died.[5]

On July 23, 1956, while undergoing additional contractor testing at the Temco plant the prototype suffered a second tail failure pulling out of a dive at 343 knots. This mishap was almost identical to the April 13, 1956, incident and resulted in yet another redesign of the elevator and trim tab. But production proceeded smoothly and the first unit, BuNo.144223, was accepted by the Navy on September 3,

1957. The last, BuNo.144236, was accepted on 14 July 1958. Production aircraft featured an improved canopy shape, sequenced landing gear doors, and the addition of a third section to the speed brake array. Three Pintos, 144226, 144228, and 144229 were sent to the Naval Air Test Center (Service Test Division) in the spring of 1958 for service suitability trials. These aircraft made a total of 305 flights for 289.5 flight hours. They were piloted in a rigorous manner by forty-five pilots with a large portion of the flight time spent on aerobatics and landings to simulate primary training service; however the tests were limited to airspeed of 350 knots (or 0.7 Mach) and load factor of +5.5g to -2.0g. They were maintained by Temco personnel during the initial trials phase, then by Navy personnel for the remainder of the trials. The report concluded that the TT-1 was considered an adequate primary trainer and was well liked by all pilots who flew it. A number of deficiencies were discovered such as engine flameouts from water ingestion and landing gear failures, which were fixed. But some deficiencies, such as slow throttle response and inadequate thrust for wave offs, could not be resolved with the limited power available from the J69 engine. On May 5, 1959, flying qualities and performance testing was begun by the Flight Test Division of the Naval Air Test Center on BuNo. 144225. This airplane was flown to 450 knots (0.73 Mach) with a load factor of 7.5g but was lost in an unrecoverable flat spin on June 13, 1959. Flight Test Division trials were completed with BuNos 144223 and 144228 at NAS Pensacola on August 15, 1959.[6]

After winning the Navy contract for fourteen aircraft the Navy conferred the designation TT-1 on the Model 51. Temco public relations department adopted the nickname "Pinto" and actress Jayne Mansfield was hired for a christening event. The event did not go well. *Jim Stanfield Collection*

A photograph of the ramp area at the Temco factory as the first production Pintos were being prepared for delivery to the Navy. The prototype is in the foreground with the N51X markings. The prototype landing gear doors differed from the production aircraft, and the canopy profile was less arched. *Vought Heritage Foundation*

The first TT-1 accepted by the Navy was Bureau Number 144223 on September 3, 1957. *Vought Heritage foundation*

The third production Pinto, 144225, being prepared for delivery. This photograph shows the landing gear door system that differs from the prototype. This aircraft was lost during spin tests at Patuxent River. *Vought Heritage Foundation*

Wearing NATC (Naval Air Test Center) on its vertical fin and ST (Service Test) under the windshield, 144228 is pictured here at a Flight Test Center open house. The Service Test Division evaluates a new aircraft's durability and verifies maintenance procedures. *Don Spering A.I.R. Collection*

The same aircraft, 144228, with FT (Flight Test) under its windshield. The Flight Test Division measures performance and evaluates flight characteristics. *Vought Heritage Foundation*

In May 1958, while the TT-1 was undergoing evaluation at NATC, Temco proposed a carrier-capable TTX to the Navy with a tailhook installed under the tail boom and catapult hooks under the fuselage. It was to be powered by an uprated J69 engine. A fairing was added behind the canopy to house TACAN avionics. The endurance and range was to be increased with additional fuel tanks in the wings and external tanks mounted under the wings. Since the Navy's new basic trainer, the North American T2J, was fully carrier capable and had already flown in January, the prospects for the TTX depended on a disappointing T2J and a pleasing TT-1 experience. Neither was in the offing and the TTX never evolved beyond the planning stage.

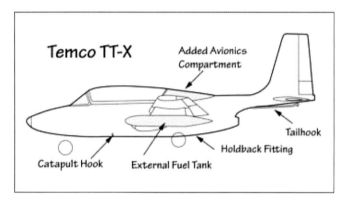

In May 1958, as the TT-1 was being evaluated at the Naval Air Test Center, Temco proposed a carrier-capable variant known as the TTX. The Navy rejected the proposal and the TTX never progressed beyond the planning stage. *Tommy H. Thomason*

The last batch of Pintos on the Temco factory ramp being prepared for delivery to NAS Pensacola. *Vought Heritage Foundation*

C. TT-1 Training Service

The Training Command received its first Pintos at Saufley Field on July 15, 1958. Lt. Wayne Fox, a Basic Training Unit (BTU) instructor, was one of the first Navy pilots at Saufley to fly the Pinto. He recalls his overall impressions:

> I first flew the Pinto on July 18, 1958. I had time in 144231, 232, 233, and 234. I flew the TT-1 22 times and had a total of 19.3 hours with a total of sixty-three landings. I do not recall being restricted from spins [the spin accident at NATC occurred the following year] so I assume we ran it through all the paces. I do not recall any adverse flight characteristics and, as I remember, it was a very stable and easy airplane to fly. The wide main gear and high visibility made it very comfortable in landings and also in taxiing. There was a big lag in acceleration when advancing the throttle but I had a lot of jet time so I had learned to cope with this on a minor scale. It only required some adjustments in my reaction time. I did not like the stick shaker [a stall warning device]. I feel that a good pilot should be able to feel what the plane is going to do before it does it. The stick shaker hides and takes away that last ounce of performance that could be critical in some situations. In the specifications the flight duration was given as 1.5 hours. This must have been achieved in other than normal flying. The longest I was up was 1.2 hours and my fuel state was critical. This, to me was the biggest fallacy that the TT-1 had.[7]

As the flight instructors at Saufley became familiar with the new jet and developed a training syllabus, a number of deficiencies in addition to the limited fuel supply became apparent. On wet runways the low-slung air inlets would ingest water and cause a flame out. A bicycle-like fender was added to the nose landing gear as a result. The J69-T-2 provided only 880 pounds of thrust, but did so at 22,600 RPM, a very high rotational speed that imposed extreme stress and reduced engine reliability. On July 31, 1958 Lt. Fox experienced the lack of reliability when his engine shed a turbine blade during takeoff in 144231. With only 100 feet of altitude Fox could not eject and there was a solid forest of pine trees straight ahead. The only option was to attempt a return to the field. That is not a standard procedure, but Fox felt that he could maintain control of the Pinto. Unable to make the field, he saw a clearing with a road but there was a car in his path. He landed alongside the road with the landing gear still retracted. The nose gear, which retracted forward, acted as a bumper and the cockpit remained intact despite the tail and wings having been torn off. There was no post-crash fire even though both fuel cells ruptured and Fox did not have time to shut

The last batch of Pintos in formation during their ferry flight to Pensacola. *Vought Heritage Foundation*

Lt. Wayne Fox, an experienced flight instructor, survived the crash landing into a wooded area when his engine failed shortly after takeoff. The nose gear acted as a bumper absorbing some of the energy from the impact. *Wayne Fox Collection*

the engine down. BuNo 144231 was stricken with only twenty-eight hours of total flight time.

In early 1959, the first class of BTG-1 (Basic Training Group One) students trained in the Pinto. The broadest possible cross-section of candidates was assigned to the new jet to evaluate its effectiveness. Pinto students were taken from the top, middle, and bottom of their pre-flight classes. Some had no prior flight experience, while others were accomplished pilots. Some were college graduates while others were not. Their progress was measured against conventionally trained T-34 students at various milestones such as solo. Skills such as formation flight and aerobatic proficiency were carefully studied. NAVCAD Earland R. Clark of East Stroudsburg, PA, who had no prior flying experience, was the first student to solo in the Pinto on March 13, 1959.

In December 1959, Lt JG Lacey Collier was assigned to BGT-1 as a Pinto flight instructor.

The Flight syllabus for the TT-1 program tracked that of the well-established T-34B," recalls Collier, "Pre-solo included all of the basic maneuvers, from the fundamental flight attitudes to precautionary emergency landing approaches and touch-and-go landings at ALF Santa Rosa. Of real importance to the Pinto were lessons in fuel management … As the TT-1 hop was a maximum of 1.0 hour, and the T-34 usually 1.3+, the syllabus was less than three total hours more than the T-34, and most of that was wasted in transit to and from the training area.[8]

The tail boom and the outboard end of the port wing were sheared off from the impact. *Wayne Fox Collection*

The post-crash examination revealed that the engine turbine wheel failed. *Wayne Fox Collection*

The evaluation of jet primary training proceeded at Saufley Field. The Navy found that there were some advantages to an all-jet syllabus, but the disadvantages were considerable. *Don Spering A.I.R. Collection*

VT-1 Pinto 144229 with student and instructor take the active runway at NAAF Saufley for departure. *Tailhook Association via Cdr. Doug Siegfried*

Late in the evaluation 144234 cruises above the beach at Pensacola. Pilots loved the Pinto's handling but its lack of fuel capacity made flight duration a serious problem. *Robert F. Dorr Collection*

During the T-34 solo check ride, notes Collier, the instructor simply got out of the airplane after determining that the student was safe to solo and watched him make several touch-and-go landings from the side of the runway. The TT-1's limited fuel supply required that the Pinto student fly alone from engine start to shut-down. In the precision stage the Pinto students were taught the same maneuvers as T-34 students—wingovers, loops, rolls, Cuban eights, and Immelmans, but it required eighteen flights versus fifteen in the T-34. The loss of 144225 during spin trails at Patuxent River forced the Training Command to prohibit spin training in the Pinto; instead Pinto students were given spin indoctrination in the T-34. Collier recalls the animosity caused by the Pinto's limited endurance:

> … those of us in the Pinto program were not exactly beloved by the T-34B instructors and students. For some reason they resented us calling for taxi and receiving priority over all other aircraft as we hurried to the duty runway and were immediately cleared for takeoff—all T-34s had to move over as we taxied by or circle overhead as we launched. The same was true on our return. We called in at the appropriate checkpoint, and the tower cleared the pattern for our arrival and landing. You make a lot of friends that way! It made no difference to an overheated (summer) or frozen (winter) T-34 instructor who had to pull over or wave-off that we usually were returning with 100 lbs. or less of fuel remaining."[9]

Aside from its limited endurance, the TT-1 proved to be a fine teaching platform; students and instructors admired its stability and crisp handling. Capt. R.G. Hanecak was the Flight Training and Standardization Officer on the staff of the Chief of Naval Air Basic Training when the Pinto was being evaluated. His logbook shows that he flew five of the BTG-1 Pintos. Capt. Hanecak considers the TT-1 a better formation and aerobatic trainer than the T-34, "It was more precise due to the higher airspeeds and students had to do more 'head work' to keep up with the airplane." But the Pinto had quirks. The engine fire warning light would come on for no apparent reason, "We would get to the nearest field and land. As long as the engine temp and rpm remained constant we lived with it, but with caution!"[10]

D. End of the Experiment

According to Capt. Hanecak the Training Command's data showed that Pinto students had a slight edge over T-34 students at the start of advanced training, but the advantage was short lived. The propeller students caught up to the jet students within a few weeks. The jet program was clearly more expensive than the propeller program, the fuel costs were higher, the maintenance costs were higher, and flights often had to be repeated to cover the planned lesson because of the Pinto's limited fuel capacity. In addition, five of the fourteen Pintos were lost during the program.

Lacey Collier remembers that the end of the of the TT-1 program came suddenly:

Without warning, at least to those of us on the flight line, notice was received in May/June 1960 that there would be no allocation of funds for fuel to fly the TT-1s after 31 July … Eventually we were told to finish those students we could, transfer the others to the T-34 program and begin to refresh ourselves on T-34 maneuvers.

This turn of events was very disappointing. The program, at this time was cruising—maintenance and aircraft was excellent, and there was lots of flight time with good students in a great little airplane.

Someone somewhere had decided that there was no benefit to an all-jet flight syllabus. Whether this conclusion was correct or not, I suggest we will never know as I do not believe the program was evaluated over a long enough period of time to support any decision, one way or the other. [11]

The Navy's all-jet experiment was abandoned after only eighteen months. The nine remaining Pintos were ferried to NAS Litchfield Park, Arizona, for long-term storage or disposal, and the Training Command returned to exclusive use of T-34Bs in primary training.

144233 and 144234 pictured at Litchfield Park Arizona where the nine surviving Pintos were stored when the Navy terminated the program in the spring of 1960. The nose tire shroud that prevented water from being splashed into the air intakes can be seen in these pictures. *Naval Aviation Museum*

The J69 Engine

The common thread among all of the jet primary trainers was the engine. All used a form of the Continental J69 turbojet that was a license-built derivative of the Turbomeca Marbore II developed in France. The original application for the J69 was the pilotless Ryan Q-2 Firebee target drone, but a long life, man-rated version was selected by Cessna for its XT-37. The initial man-rated engines were given the designation J69-T-2 and provided 880 pounds of thrust, but the Air Force climb specification required a minimum of 920 pounds of thrust. Continental spent two years improving the output and complying with another Air Force requirement that the fuel control provide automatic starting and acceleration in response to throttle movement—an advanced feature for its time. The uprated prototype engines installed in the XT-37 were designated J69-T-15. The standardized production version installed in the T-37A was designated J69-T-9. A total of 1,189 units were produced by 1959. When the T-37A fleet began to encounter high altitude compressor surges the Air Force insisted on a fix. Continental undertook an extensive redesign of the J69-T-9 compressor and turbine that resulted in the J69-T-25.

This new engine eliminated the compressor surge problem, increased the thrust by 105 pounds, and decreased the engine weight by 6 pounds. The Air Force was so impressed with the solution that they ordered the J69-T-25 for the improved T-37B and retrofitted most of the T-37A fleet with it. By the time production ended in 1976 a total of 1,804 J69-T-25s had been produced. The Temco TT-1 used the earlier J69-T-2 that was simply an Americanized Marbore II capable of only 880 pounds of thrust.[12]

The J69 architecture consisted of a single-stage centrifugal compressor, a through-flow annular combustor, and a single-stage axial-flow turbine. A unique feature of

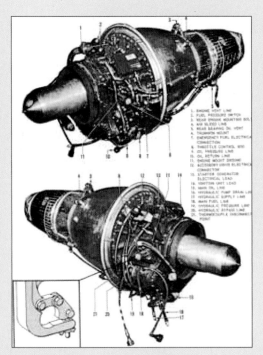

The Continental J69-T-2 turbojet engine that powered the TT-1 Pinto. *US Navy TT-1 Maintenance Manual*

the engine was its slinger-type fuel injector that was developed by Turbomeca. Fuel was supplied at moderate pressure to the interior of the hollow main-rotor shaft. The centrifugal force generated by the rotating shaft caused the fuel to be ejected through small holes where it was "slung off" and atomized by the shaft's tangential velocity. This eliminated the need for any high-pressure fuel pump. The J69 grew from the original 880 pound thrust T-2 to 1,920 pounds in the T-406 version. It was produced from the early 1950s into the 1990s and became Continental's most successful jet engine series.[13]

The Beechcraft Jet Mentor J69 engine installation with its long tailpipe removed. *NARA*

An improved higher thrust version, J69-T-25 used in the Cessna T-37B. This engine provided an additional 105 pounds of thrust. *Gerald Baltzer Collection via Mark Nankivil*

E. The Turbo Mentor

The Navy finally acquired a primary jet trainer (albeit a turboprop) when, in the late 1960s, the piston engine T-34B was showing its age and limitations and many airframes were reaching their service-life limits. In addition, a Pentagon study concluded that the cost of Navy flight training was well in excess of the Air Force. The Chief of Naval Operations expressed serious concern that the Navy could be relieved of flight training—a devastating blow to Naval Aviation. In this environment the Navy sought better and less expensive ways to train its aviators. A plan known as the Long Range Pilot Training System (LRPTS) was devised which focused on the acquisition of a new training aircraft that would serve both primary and basic needs, replacing the T-34B and T-28B/C. The new trainer would have flying characteristics similar to tactical jets, and it would be supported by new simulators, training aids, and programmed instruction based on the latest educational advances. Under LRPTS, the aircraft manufacturer would be required to supply contract maintenance:

> Under the new system, training wings would provide the facilities and services, monitor the work and perform functional check flights. The manufacturer would be responsible for each level of maintenance. No longer would plane captains help service aircraft on the line or strap pilots in. Civilian technicians would provide total maintenance and supply support during normal workdays from 0600 to 2400.
>
> LRPTS also included an overall revision of the training syllabus, the first in 20 years, known as the Navy Integrated Flight Training Syllabus (NIFTS). It consisted of extended primary training (where the costs were lowest) with heavy reliance on modern simulators and self-study. It also introduced increased instrument training allowing for better evaluation of the student before selection for the advanced pipeline. [14]

John Jenista was, as much as anyone, the godfather of the T-34C. He joined Beechcraft as a marketing executive and engineering test pilot while the Navy was wrestling with dramatic changes in flight training. One of his early assignments involved presenting T-34 replacement proposals to the Navy. Beechcraft management favored developing a four-place trainer based on its aerobatic F-33C Bonanza that, according to Jenista, they offered to sell for $47,000, but the Navy requested numerous modifications making the concept cost prohibitive. In 1973, a Pentagon planner, Capt. Dan Mealy, suggested that a turboprop powered T-34 would be the ideal new trainer. After all, the Navy

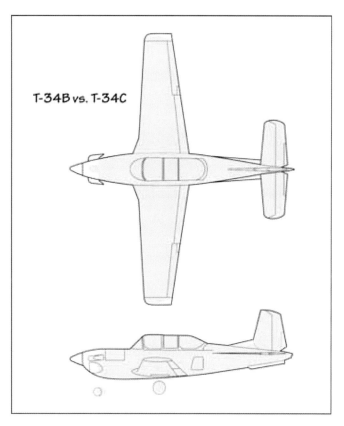

An illustration of the external differences between the T-34B and C. The strakes and ventral fins on the T-34C were added to aid spin recovery. *Tommy H. Thomason*

had over twenty years of experience with the Mentor and it had proven to be a durable, reliable, and effective. With a turboprop engine it would have the performance to provide jet-like training to students from pre-solo until advanced training. In short, argued Capt. Mealy, the turboprop T-34 could be used to do the job of the T-34B and the T-28. The idea received serious attention when some T-28s developed structural issues, illustrating the problems of an aging training fleet.

The Chief of Naval Operations was impressed with Capt. Mealy's concept and issued a research and development contract for "Turboprop Feasibility Evaluation" to the sole bidder, Beechcraft. Two flying prototypes and one static test article were ordered and given the designation of YT-34C. The contract provided that Beechcraft would convert three existing T-34Bs from the Navy's inventory and the prototypes were expected to fly within six months. John Jenista traveled to Pensacola, Florida to select three airframes for conversion. He chose BuNos 140784 and 140861 to become the flying prototypes, and 140862 as the static-test article.

The first of three T-34Bs (two for flight test and one for static test) converted to turboprop power under a Chief of Naval Operations "Turboprop Feasibility Evaluation" contract. This aircraft, Bureau Number 140784, made its maiden flight on September 21, 1973. *Naval Heritage and History Command*

The first prototype on a contractor test flight piloted by Beechcraft test pilot, Bob Stone. This photograph was taken early in the test program since the strakes and ventral fins have not been added yet. *Naval Heritage and History Command*

O784 prepares for another test flight late in the program. By this time Beechcraft has installed the strakes and ventral fins to augment spin recovery. *Don Spering A.I.R. Collection*

Actual work was started in May 1973. Allison and Garrett turboprops were considered for the conversion, but Beechcraft engineers chose the Pratt & Whitney PT6A-25 (military designation, T74) as the most suitable engine. The PT6 offered 715 shaft horsepower but only 400 shaft horsepower was needed to meet Navy specifications. Thus the engine could be torque limited to provide very fuel efficient power with exceptional longevity. Furthermore, the PT6's aluminum case was preferred by the Navy over the magnesium cases of other engines, and an inverted oil system could be fitted to the PT6 permitting more than two minutes of inverted flight. From the outset Beechcraft designers wanted the new turboprop to mimic the behavior of a pure jet, so the engine was mounted with considerable side and down thrust (three degrees right and two degrees down) to offset the torque effect of the propeller. Even the throttle response of the PT6 was adjusted to produce a lag similar to the response of a jet engine.

In addition to the new power plant and cowl, the converted T-34Bs received Beechcraft Baron wings in place of their original Bonanza wings (increased spar strength and six inches more span), new landing gear from the Beechcraft Duke, and a larger vertical tail from the Beechcraft Travel Air. These off-the-shelf components expedited the project and saved enormous cost. The cockpit was designed to replicate the T-2 Buckeye jet trainer that students would fly after graduating from the Turbo Mentor. Jenista remembers his frustration trying to achieve consensus on the cockpit design, "We spent hours debating the placement of meaningless items like ashtrays while we took only minutes to decide on switch placement. This is typical of committee decisions that are not made by aviators."[15]

The first prototype YT-34C (Buno.140784) made its initial flight on September 21, 1973, but spin tunnel tests at NASA Langley conducted before the initial flight predicted serious issues. Scale models of the Turbo Mentor displayed spin behavior quite different from the benign T-34B. The elongated nose allowed it to spin in a manner that was unpredictable. In technical terms the aircraft had a neutral inertia yawing moment parameter that made recovery control impossible to predict. The NASA report stated in part:

The spinning motion is very complicated and involves simultaneous rolling, yawing and pitching while the airplane is at high angles of attack and sideslip. Since it involves separated flows in the region beyond the stall, the aerodynamic characteristics of the airplane are very non-linear and time dependent: and hence at the present time, the spin is not very amenable to theoretical analyses.[16]

Both YT-34C prototypes in formation. 0784 is piloted by Bob Stone and 0861 by John Jenista. *Don Spering A.I.R. Collection*

Demonstrating aerobatic ability, the two YT-34Cs pose in a mirror image with John Jenista flying 0861 inverted. *Don Spering A.I.R. Collection*

NASA recommended two aerodynamic devices—stabilizer strakes and ventral fins—to promote more moderate spin behavior. Beechcraft fitted both to the prototypes prior to the spin trials. Bob Stone, the senior Beechcraft engineering test pilot, completed 175 spins in 140784 during the initial flight test phase with John Jenista flying chase in 140861. The YT-34C prototype was then submitted for its first Navy Preliminary Evaluation (NPE). The evaluation consisted of fifty-five flights with only one spin flight. The evaluation report concluded:

> The YT-34C exhibited excellent potential to perform the primary training mission … Installation of a turboprop engine, angle-of-attack indicator and upgraded avionics package makes the YT-34C a superior trainer to the present trainer airplanes.

The Navy was still apprehensive about the spin behavior and declined to award a production contract. Beechcraft embarked on a seven-month program to overcome the Navy's concern. Test flights included 1,200 spins with several difficult dynamically oscillated recoveries demonstrated. Finally, consistently reliable rudder-primary recoveries were achieved in all conditions. The YT-34C spin characteristics were compared to those of the T-34B, T-28, and T-37 in flight evaluations and found to be superior to all. The Navy conducted a second NPE consisting of forty-eight flights (over half included spins) and found that all of the earlier deficiencies had been corrected. Then the two prototypes were flown to NAS Pensacola for an Operational Evaluation (OPEVAL) that was to consist of 120 hours to be flown over six weeks. But the entire program was concluded in only 97.4 hours flown over three weeks

thanks to the 100 per cent availability of both airplanes and the enthusiasm of the participating instructor pilots.[17]

In the spring of 1976, the Navy placed an initial order for 184 production T-34Cs with first delivery scheduled for November 1977. Delivery was delayed when production flight testing revealed an aileron-flutter problem. While the Turbo Mentor ailerons had been beefed up, they retained the two-hinge installation of the original design. This allowed the ailerons to bow in the center at higher airspeeds causing flutter. The condition was fixed by adding a third hinge at the center of the aileron, but the Navy was forced to hold the first sixty-three aircraft in storage insisting on further high-speed testing. On July 15, 1977, these high-speed tests resulted in the structural failure of a production T-34C and the death of Chief Test Pilot, Bob Stone, when he attempted to recover from a 20,000-foot dive at 330 knots—well above the normal speed regime of the airplane. The horizontal stabilizer failed (the elevator trim tabs departed according to one account).

Finally on January 16, 1978, the T-34C was placed in training service with the first student solo occurring on March 19, 1978. By mid 1982, the Turbo Mentor fleet had logged over 500,000 flight hours with a ninety-three per cent availability rate at a cost of less than $50 per hour. By comparison the A-4 Skyhawk, a reliable tactical jet, had an availability rate of seventy percent at more than $600 per hour. Each of the two T-34C squadrons at NAS Whiting Field were flying 45,000 flight hours, or 30,000 sorties per year—a typical fighter squadron flew only 7,000 hours per year. The T-34C also established a remarkable safety record with only 1.62 strike (unrepairable) damage accidents per 100,000 flight hours compared to 5.97 strike damage accidents per 100,000 hours for all Naval aircraft combined.[18]

In May 1987, the Navy ordered its final block of 19 T-34Cs to be delivered between June 1989 and April 1990. Total Navy production amounted to 352 aircraft. On September 27, 2011, the last Turbo Mentor training flight was completed at NAS Whiting Field, flown by 2nd Lt. Michael Harper under the instruction of Lt. Cdr. Tom Healy.[19] The Turbo Mentor continued to instruct students in VT-27 and VT-28 at the Naval Air Station Corpus Christi, Texas, until April 28, 2015, nearly thirty-eight years after it entered service. ENS James Butz and 1st Lt. William Parker flew the final training T-34C sorties. The remainder of the T-34C fleet has been dispersed to various locations to serve in utility roles. MCAS Miramar received several to serve with VMFAT-101 as a range-spotting aircraft monitoring FA-18 pilots during low-level bombing practice. Others were sent to NAS North Island for Navy Reserve Officer Corps training or Davis-Monthan for storage. The phase-out of all T-34Cs from the Navy's inventory is scheduled for some time after the fourth quarter of 2017. Then, for the first time in sixty-three years, no Beechcraft Mentor will be serving in a US military unit.[20]

Production of the Turbo Mentor at the Beechcraft factory, Wichita Kansas. Total production amounted to 353 aircraft delivered under three orders between November 1977 and April 1990. *Naval Heritage and History Command*

By January 1978, the Turbo Mentor was placed in service and the flight line at Whiting Field was filled with new T-34Cs. The propellers are restrained with straps to prevent them from rotating like windmills. *Navy Heritage and history Command*

The front cockpit instrument panel of an early production Turbo Mentor. The general layout retained similarity to the T-34B but included features such as an angle of attack indicator, fuel flow gauge, turbine tachometer, interstage turbine temperature gauge and torquemeter. The tubes between the center console and the outside edge of the rudder pedals were part of the rudder pedal positioning mechanism. *Beechcraft via Don Spering A.I.R. Collection*

A T-34C taxies under the spray of fire hoses on September 27, 2011, to mark the last training Turbo Mentor training sortie at Whiting Field. *US Navy*

The darkened sky highlights the modified color scheme applied to T-34Cs in the mid-1980s. The original factory scheme used International Orange on only the fin and the outer wing panels. Now the entire fin, rudder, and rear fuselage along with a large portion of the wing surface was painted International Orange for increased visibility. *Paul Minert Collection*

The last T-34C training flight of VT-27 at NAS Corpus Christi, Texas, was flown by Ensign Mary McGhee on July 25, 2013. By the end of 2015, it is expected that the T-34C will be fully retired from its training role, however it is scheduled to remain in the inventory as a chase plane and range spotter for strike aircraft beyond 2017. *US Navy*

For enhanced visibility the Navy experimented with a new color scheme. Two Turbo Mentors, 162648 and 162649, were painted orange-yellow with a black pin stripe in lieu of International Orange but the scheme was not adopted. *Rich Dann Collection, Paul Minert Collection*

Nearing retirement, some T-34Cs received commemorative color schemes. This Training Air Wing 5 Turbo Mentor is painted to resemble the standard Navy/Marine scheme of the 1930s for the Centennial of Naval Aviation. *US Navy*

Chapter Seven Endnotes

1. Gerald P. Moran, *The Corsair, and other Aeroplanes Vought 1917-1977*, Terre Haute, IN, Aviation Heritage Books, 1978, p.134.

2. Project TED No. PTR AC-67101.1/.2 Navy Evaluation and Demonstration of the Beech Aircraft Corporation Model 73 Primary Trainer; Report No.3, final report, p.I.

And Project TED No. PTR AC-67101.1/.2, Navy Evaluation and Demonstration of the Temco Aircraft Corporation Model 51 Primary Jet Trainer; Report No.2 p.I.

3. Project TED NO. PTR AC-67101.1 Navy Evaluation Of Primary Jet Trainer Aircraft Report; No.1, p.17.

4. June 18, 1956, Confidential Memorandum To: Chief, Bureau of Aeronautics, From: Assistant Chief, Research and Development, Subject: Primary Jet Trainer Aircraft—Recommendation.

5. E-mail correspondence from Jim Stanfield to Mark A. Frankel, September 11, 2005.

6. Project TED No. BIS 21222, Service Suitability Trials of Model TT-1 Airplane, Report #2, Final Report, and Project TED No. BIS 21222, Combined Stability and Control and Aircraft and Engine Performance Trials of the Model TT-1 Airplane Flying Qualities and Performance Phases, Report No. 2, Final Report.

7. E-mail correspondence from Wayne Fox to Mark A. Frankel, October 23, 2012.

8. The Honorable Lacey A. Collier, *Temco TT-1 Pinto The Navy's forgotten Trainer*, Foundation Volume 33 Number 1, Spring 2012, p.20.

9. Ibid. p. 21.

10. E-mail correspondence from R. Hanecak to Mark A. Frankel, November 14, 2005, November 17, 2005, and January 6, 2006.

11. Collier, pp.22-23.

12. There are several references to the J69-T-2 having a thrust rating of 920 pounds, but this is probably in error. Navy technical reports confirm that the J69-T-2 output was approximately 880 pounds (some tested higher or lower than the rating).

13. Richard A. Leyes II and William A. Fleming, *The History of North American Small Gas Turbine Aircraft Engines*. American Institute of Aeronautics and Astronautics, Inc., Reston, Virginia, 1999, pp.91-106.

14. Cdr. Douglas Siegfried, USN (retired), "Long-Range Pilot Training System and NIFTS," *Cleared for Solo* (unpublished manuscript), pp.14-20.

15. Interview with John Jenista at the Palm Springs T-34 Fly-In, March 11, 2011.

16. "T-34 Charlie: A Better Mentor," *Air International*, May 1976 (unattributed), p.229.

17. Ibid pp.229-230.

18. News Release, NAS Whiting Field Public Affairs Office, July 26, 1982, "A Navy Aircraft and a Taxpayer's Delight."

19. "Turbo Mentor Sunset at NAS Whiting Field," The Hook, Winter 2011, pp.61-62.

20. Association of Naval Aviation, Hampton Roads Squadron, August 1, 2013, T-34C Training Aircraft To Serve Beyond 2017.

Chapter Eight
TACTICAL TRAINERS

A. The Looming Crisis

The transition from trainers to high-performance combat-capable fighters has always been one of the most challenging aspects of flight training. During WWI, the performance differential between trainer and fighter was not great, but it increased dramatically in WWII when new pilots were expected to fly tactical aircraft capable of speeds in excess of 450 mph after training on aircraft that could barely reach 200 mph. In the primary, basic, and even advanced phases of flight training the military pilot learned to fly and navigate and was introduced to the fundamentals of formation flying and air-to-air gunnery with an instructor

in a two-seat trainer of relatively low horsepower. But the transition to tactical aircraft was often accomplished in a single-seat fighter, generally an obsolescent one no longer suitable for an operational unit. After a rudimentary period of cockpit familiarization and ground-based instruction, the newly winged pilot would take off—solo. For some training flights, an instructor in another airplane would accompany him for evaluation and in-flight direction and correction. Instrument proficiency in a single-seat airplane would be accomplished by providing another pilot flying escort in another airplane who would look out for conflicting

A few dual-cockpit tactical fighters were built during WWII for advanced training. This is one of two TP-47Gs built by Curtiss Wright under license from Republic. The second cockpit was added ahead of the original one. *Mark Aldrich Collection*

North American built a limited number of dual-cockpit P-51Ds in 1944. This is a post-war example converted by Temco, which was designated TF-51D. The dark area under the canopy was part of the modification for the additional cockpit and different canopy. The aft half of the canopy incorporated a hood for instrument proficiency flights. *Robert F. Dorr Collection*

traffic and egregious navigation errors. These precautions seemed perfectly adequate until the early 1950s. During WWII, some two-seat versions of front-line fighters were evaluated, but none were produced in significant numbers for transition training. The Curtiss factory, for example, added a second cockpit to thirty P-40 Warhawks which were assigned the designation TP-40N-6 and several similar conversions were completed in the field by USAAF maintenance units. The Curtiss-Wright factory built two P-47G Thunderbolts under license from Republic as dual-cockpit TP-47Gs. Bell Aircraft built one P-39Q-5, a dual-control training version of the P-39 fighter with its armament deleted. Kits were made available for field conversion to this configuration under the designation TP-39, but few aircraft were converted. In 1944, North American built ten dual-control P-51Ds designated TP-51Ds; the rear seat displaced the fuselage fuel tank and required relocation of radio equipment. Some additional Ds as well as a few B and C models were converted to two-seaters in the field but these rarely included the addition of dual controls.[1] After the war, Temco produced fifteen Mustang conversions under the designation TF-51D.[2] Unlike the North American two-seat P-51s, these had an elongated canopy for more headroom in the aft cockpit, which was configured for instrument flight training. Most were assigned to the 3615th Pilot Training Wing at Craig AFB, Alabama, to augment its fleet of F-51s used for advanced training. US Air Force Aviation Cadet Class 51H was the first to receive instruction in these TP-51D trainers which were used for initial checkout and instrument proficiency, including takeoffs under the hood from the rear cockpit.

During World War II, the Navy, in contrast to the Army Air Corps, appeared to have had no interest in the dual-control versions of its fighters nor did its contractors. However, in late 1945, after the WWII Armistice, Chance Vought Aircraft proposed to modify surplus F4U-1D/FG-1D fighters, of which there were many, into a "High Speed Corsair Trainer." Vought assigned project number V-354 to the two-place F4U. The proposal brochure stated in part:

> The need for high-powered training planes was great during the war, but the emphasis was necessarily placed on the production of combat airplanes. With the cessation of hostilities, it is anticipated that a very large part of naval air activity will consist of training—training on a budget—and it is therefore believed that the need for a good, high-powered transition trainer is still great. To provide an airplane which will permit smooth, safe, and efficient transition from low and medium-powered trainers to high performance single-place fighters is the prime purpose of the Corsair Trainer offered in this presentation.[3]

Bell Aircraft built one dual-cockpit TP-39Q-5. Field conversion kits were made available but few P-39s were modified. *Paul Faltyn*

Curtiss built thirty dual-cockpit P-40s which were designated TP-40N-6s. A standard single-place P-40N is seen in the background. *Paul Faltyn*

The airplane would be used for advanced instrument, gunnery, and bombing instruction. The cost was projected to be $15,000 per airplane, approximately that of a basic trainer of lesser capability and performance. A second seat, instruments, and flight controls would be substituted for the Corsair's only internal fuel tank, which was located ahead of the existing cockpit. It was replaced with four fuel tanks, two in the belly of the fuselage and one in each of the outboard wing panels, which displaced two of the three guns and their ammunition. As a result, total internal fuel capacity was reduced from 237 gallons to only 175.

The student was to occupy the front seat with a full set of instruments and controls: "Familiarization with these instruments and controls in the company of an experienced instructor or check-pilot will imbue the pilot-trainee with a feeling of confidence and security which should make his transition to a high-powered single-place airplane rapid and pleasant."[4] Only basic flying instruments and minimal engine controls (i.e., a throttle and ignition switch) were provided to the instructor in the aft cockpit.

Because of the reduced fuel capacity and armament, the Corsair Trainer was to have a somewhat lower empty weight. The gross weight with full internal fuel and ammunition was significantly lower, 10,800 lbs. versus 12,086 lbs. for the single seat F4U/FG. This translated to a better rate of climb and higher ceiling. Maximum range was reduced to 820 miles versus 1,070, but this was considered to be acceptable for a trainer.

With the exception of the number of guns and the reduction in internal fuel, the Corsair Trainer was otherwise to be identical in capability to the fleet F4Us, including carrier compatibility. Maintenance and replacement parts could be drawn from existing stocks and no significant

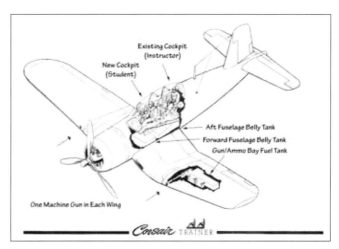

An illustration of the dual-cockpit features from the Chance Vought Corsair Trainer Project, V-354. *Tommy H. Thomason Collection*

changes to manuals or additional maintenance training would be required.

The Bureau of Aeronautics was not initially interested but Vought built a base of support within the Naval Aviation Training Command, which now appreciated the value of a two-seat transition between the existing advanced trainers and the higher performance single-seat fighters. The Naval Air Advanced Training Command at Jacksonville, which was slated to be a training base for dive-bombing using F4U/FG-1D Corsairs, was particularly enthusiastic about the project, according to memoranda from Vought marketing to management.

The Navy considered this offer in a January 25, 1946, conference in Washington involving representatives from the Office of the Chief of Naval Operations and the Bureau of Aeronautics.[5]

A rough estimate of the requirement for the training command was forty-four airplanes (thirty on the line and fourteen for attrition and the overhaul pipeline) with an additional fifteen or twenty to be utilized by fleet squadrons for instrument proficiency.

The Bureau of Aeronautics was critical of the fuel system complexity, the fuel capacity, and the small size of the cockpits. The center of gravity was also predicted to be too far aft. These were, however, not believed to be difficult to correct:

> It was suggested that we develop a policy regarding the need for high-performance trainers. A discussion followed during which it was determined that it was necessary for training types to keep pace with service types in performance and characteristics. Converting F4U-1s was a quick way of accomplishing this but such a procedure could not always be counted on to produce satisfactory training types.[6]

The conference concluded with a recommendation to BuAer to work with Vought to resolve the concerns identified. If the major objections were eliminated, then a cockpit mockup should be authorized. However, no commitments were to be made "beyond an adequate number of prototypes for trial by Advanced Training Activities."

The Navy subsequently took steps to allocate fifty freshly overhauled Corsairs to the program and assigned F4U-1D BuNo 82538 to Vought for the conversion to a two-seat mockup.

The V-354 two-place trainer mockup was reviewed in late May 1946. In July, the Navy was planning to convert 100 FG-1D airplanes to "Two-Place Trainers" with 1948 funds. Vought, however, had just won a jet-fighter competition with what was to become the F7U Cutlass and taxi testing of its XF6U jet fighter was in progress. As a result, Vought's engineering department was overloaded. Although the Navy initially thought the two prototype conversions and subsequent production would be accomplished by the Naval Aviation Material Command at Philadelphia or Goodyear, a second source for the F4U during the war, Vought proposed to accomplish the program by subcontracting the engineer design effort to Edo Aircraft.

By December 1946, however, the Navy had decided not to proceed with two-seat F4U conversions. According to a Vought internal memo dated December 11, Sales Manager John J. Hospers stated, "this project is cancelled because of the economy slash in Navy department funds."[7]

While the Corsair trainer program only resulted in a single conversion (which appears to have been a non-flyable mockup), the requirement for a two-seat advanced trainer continued to have supporters in both the Air Force and the Navy. Vought reportedly did some preliminary design work on a two-seat F6U but none were ever built. Several months later Lockheed proposed a two-seat conversion of their P-80 jet fighter to the Air Corps. Initially designated TP-80C it was enormously successful, evolving into the iconic T-33/T2V (as described in chapter 4) and serving both services in large numbers for decades.

The sole product of the V-354 Project was this static airframe of the dual-cockpit Corsair Trainer. *Tommy H. Thomason Collection*

B. The Air Force Faces the Century Problem

By 1954, the Air Force was poised to introduce a new generation of fighters with performance that couldn't have been imagined a few years earlier. However, the training aircraft used to produce pilots for these advanced fighters was woefully inadequate. A 1954 Air Training Command History describes this as the "Century Problem":

> Within the foreseeable future, Air Training Command was going to be expected to train pilots competent to fly supersonic jets in the space of one year. The use of the T-34/T-28 combination of conventional aircraft in primary flying training and the T-28/T-33 conventional/jet combination in basic single-engine training was not going to suffice for the training of such pilots. Students were going to have to be introduced to jet aircraft at an earlier stage of training and the aircraft used in basic flying training were going to have to be faster in order that the jump from training aircraft to combat aircraft would not be too great for the student to accomplish.[8]

The gap between the straight-wing, low-thrust T-33 and the swept-wing, high-thrust F-100 was expected to be unmanageable for many new pilots and since the F-100A was a single-place supersonic jet the use of an instructor to oversee the transition was not possible. The new pilot's first flight in an F-100 would be his solo flight. Unfortunately, the Training Command's concern was very prophetic: the F-100 accident rate was appalling. During the first months of tactical training at Nellis Air Force Base, three of the first ten F-100s were lost; as a precaution the remaining aircraft were grounded. Even as the F-100 fleet matured it suffered ninety-five major accidents in the first 100,000 hours of aggregate flight time; this grew to 471 major accidents (287 aircraft destroyed) in the first 750,000 hours of aggregate flight time, the worst safety record of any aircraft in the Air Force inventory.[9]

Lt.Gen. C.T. Myers, Commander of the Air Training Command proposed a two-fold solution. First, the TX trainer (Cessna T-37) should be purchased in quantity and employed at the earliest possible time in the primary training phase; and second, the TZ trainer (an undefined supersonic replacement for the T-33) should be developed as soon as possible and employed in the advanced training phase. But there was strong opposition to Lt. Gen. Myers's strategy at Air Force Headquarters. The T-37 was experiencing early teething problems (poor spin recovery and lack of stall warning) that some viewed as incurable, and there was growing support for a two-place dual-controlled F-86 for advanced training that would avoid the development cost of a totally new airplane.

C. TF-86, a False Step

The success of the Lockheed P-80 Shooting Star conversion into the two-seat T-33 jet trainer generated interest in a similar conversion of the North American F-86 Sabre. This two-seat Sabre, it was argued, would be a cost effective means of introducing new pilots to the handling qualities and transonic flight peculiarities of a swept-wing jet that the straight-wing T-33 could not demonstrate.

North American proposed a TF-86 to the Air Force in February 1953 and began design work on its NA-204 in April. The conversion was based on the F-86-F-30 wing (with slats reinstated for good low-speed handling qualities), nose, aft fuselage, and empennage. The center section was stretched sixty-three inches to incorporate a tandem cockpit under a clamshell canopy. This required that the wing be moved forward eight inches to rebalance the airplane. To minimize the weight increase and center of gravity shift associated with the second cockpit, the armament was deleted but otherwise the systems and engine were the same as the single-seat F-86.

In September, the Air Force provided F-86F-30 serial number 52-5016 to North American for conversion to a TF-86 prototype. North American accomplished the modification in short order, with a first flight on December 14, 1953. The Air Force evaluated it in three different roles—first, as an instrument and transition trainer for F-86D interceptor pilots, second, as a fighter-bomber trainer, and third, as an overall T-33 replacement.

In February 1953, North American proposed a two-placed version of their highly successful F-86F. This is the cover of the brochure that accompanied the proposal. *Tommy H. Thomason Collection*

The first TF-86F, 52-5016, was flown on December 14, 1953 but before it could be formally evaluated it was lost during a demonstration at Nellis Air Force Base. *Tommy H. Thomason Collection*

After the loss of 52-5016 the Air Force ordered a second TF-86F that carried the serial number, 53-1228. This example had more wing and vertical stabilizer area. *Tommy H. Thomason Collection*

After the Air Force terminated the TF-86F evaluation it assigned 53-1228 to chase plane duties at Edwards Air Force Base where it received new markings. *Tommy H. Thomason Collection*

The initial flight test was promising but the formal evaluation, scheduled to begin on April 1, 1954, was delayed for several months when the only prototype was destroyed during a flight demonstration at Nellis Air Force Base, Nevada. North American test pilot Joseph Lynch crashed while attempting a roll on takeoff (the takeoff occurred in a severe crosswind and the airplane had reportedly been fully, rather than partially, fueled causing it to be heavier than Lynch expected). Within days, the Air Force authorized the conversion of a second F-86F, serial number 53-1228, as North American's NA-216.

The second TF-86 differed in detail from the first. It had the 6-3 leading-edge extension in addition to slats and a two-foot increase in wing span. Two .50-caliber machine guns and a pair of under-wing pylons were retained to allow for weapons training. The height of the vertical fin was increased and a small ventral fin was also added to the aft fuselage to increase directional stability. It flew on August 5, 1954.

Inestimable North American test and demonstration pilot Robert (Bob) Hoover began a tour of Air Force training bases with the TF-86 in early September 1954, providing impromptu air shows and breaking the sound barrier with selected pilots flying along. Among these were five senior Training Command pilots who flew the converted fighter and damned it with faint praise. They were unanimous in declaring it to be a good to excellent trainer with respect to transonic flight preparation but not good enough to prepare students for the anticipated supersonic fighters with more challenging handling qualities.

The formal TF-86 evaluation began at Tyndall Air Force Base, Florida, in late September and a similar conclusion was expressed by the assigned test pilots. The evaluation ended at Nellis in January 1955 when the Director of Flying Training terminated the test program early stating that, "further evaluation would be a waste of time since the end result is obvious."[10] The Air Force decided to forego using the TF-86 for advanced training. The airplane was transferred to Edwards Air Force Base in March for use for chase. It was retired in November 1958 and subsequently scrapped in 1961.

With the TF-86 proving to be a dead end, Air Force Headquarters gave the Air Research and Development Command the authority to proceed with a design study on the long anticipated TZ airplane. After more than two years of thought and discussion, the first major step had been taken toward the realization of a purpose-designed supersonic training aircraft. However, this supersonic trainer was not expected to be operational before 1960, and the "Century Problem" needed an immediate solution as tactical squadrons faced the task of transitioning new pilots from the docile subsonic straight-winged T-33 into supersonic afterburning jets with severely swept wings.

D. An Interim Solution—Two-Seat Century Fighters

As an expedient, Air Force Headquarters approved the acquisition of two-place dual-control Century fighters. These would not be trainers in the pure sense, but conversion airplanes with some weapons delivery capability that would serve alongside their single-cockpit counterparts in tactical units.

The first example of the two-place strategy, the TF-102A, did not go well. It was a modification of the Air Force's first fighter with a delta wing and no horizontal tail. The delta wing had some unique handling quality features. Most notably, it did not stall in the conventional sense and could reach a significantly higher angle of attack than achievable by an airplane with a swept wing and horizontal tail. The high angle of attack was, of course, accompanied by a corresponding increase in drag. A high sink rate could therefore develop on landing approach so high, according to the Flight Manual, T.O. 1F-102A-1, that it was "beyond the capability of the engine to overcome." The TF-102A, unlike the other Century Series trainers that would follow, used side-by-side seating. The Air Force, at that time, was impressed with the success of several European trainers that featured side-by-side cockpits. Widening of the fuselage eliminated the ability to reach supersonic speed in level flight, which wasn't much of a drawback from a training standpoint because the more unusual aspects of the delta wing configuration were apparent at high angles of attack and while maneuvering. One peculiarity of the side-by-side configuration in the TF-102A was that, unlike the T-37 trainer, the throttle for the pilot in the left seat was located on his left side whereas the throttle for the pilot in the right seat was located on his right side, requiring him to hold the control stick in his left hand.

Development of this combat trainer, from the outset, was not encouraging. A Mock-Up Board meeting at the Convair plant in September 1954 revealed that its estimated performance would fall far below expectations. The aircraft needed to shed substantial weight, yet the weight reduction would diminish the airframe's ability to withstand the stress of combat maneuvers. Nevertheless, the Air Force ordered the TF-102A into limited production, and first example flew on November 8, 1955. In addition to reducing supersonic capability, the widened TF-102A cockpit introduced another problem, severe buffeting of the canopy at transonic speeds. Adding two lines of vortex generators, one at the leading edge of the canopy and the other at its trailing edge, reduced the buffet by increasing the energy in the airflow over the canopy and thereby eliminating the intermittent separation that caused the buffeting. However,

the Flight Manual, T.O. 1F-102A-1, still noted that there was a canopy buffet between Mach .90 and .95 in 1-G flight. Moreover, it "may be quite startling when first experienced." The vertical fin was also increased in size to restore suitable directional stability. The TF-102A retained the full fire control and armament capability of the single-seat F-102A, "if conditions make such use necessary" according to the Flight Manual. The higher drag and increased gross weight of about 800 pounds did affect its capability as an interceptor due to reduced acceleration, maximum speed, rate of climb, and combat ceiling (the Flight Manual required that the second seat always be occupied in flight, unless a chase or pacer airplane accompanied the TF-102A because of the restricted view to the right of a pilot in the left seat). Convair produced only 111 examples of the TF-102A. While the single-seat F-102A was affectionately nicknamed "The Deuce" the two-place version, in recognition of its less sleek appearance and performance shortfall, was branded "The Tub."

Development of a two-place F-100 Super Sabre did not start until late 1954 when the recommendations of a privately funded North American Aviation study on the elongated fighter were approved. The initial example (serial 54-1966) was converted from a standard F-100C and designated the TF-100C. It acquired the enlarged tailfin of the F-100D while retaining the flapless wing of the F-100C. It was intended as a transition trainer only and carried no operational equipment. It was flown for the first time on August 3, 1956, by North American test pilot Alvin White, who demonstrated level supersonic flight proving that, unlike the widened TF-102A, the lengthened TF-100C cockpit did not diminish performance. The Air

A Convair concept drawing prepared for the TF-102A program. This would become the first dual-cockpit Century Series Fighter. *NARA via Mark Aldrich*

The prototype TF-102A parked to the left of a single-seat F-102A. For weight and balance reasons, the TF-102A had a shorter nose. *NARA via Tommy H. Thomason*

Photograph of the prototype TF-102A taken at the Air Force Flight Test Center on June 22, 1956. The tufting around the cockpit was used to study airflow at transonic speed to determine the cause of buffeting. *NARA via Mark Aldrich*

Force issued a contract for 259 TF-100Cs but rescinded the order when it was decided to develop a two-place F-100 with full operational capability that could provide weapons training in addition to transition training. This new variant, designated the F-100F, was closely based on the F-100D with the enlarged tailfin and wing flaps. No prototype was ordered since the Air Force was already satisfied with the flying qualities of the TF-100C and those of the F-100F, with more wing area and flaps, were expected to be even more benign. The first F-100F to fly was the first production article (serial no.56-3725) that made its maiden flight on March 7, 1957. Meanwhile, the sole TF-100C was lost during a spin test on 9 April 1957. Production of the F-100F ended in October 1959 after 339 units had been produced.

In 1955, both the Training and Tactical Commands requested that the Air Force Chief of Staff acquire two-place, dual-control versions of all the new Century Fighters. Dual-control fighters were expected to be particularly useful for pilots transitioning to the McDonnell F-101 Voodoo and Lockheed F-104 Starfighter, airplanes with unusually small wings requiring abnormally high takeoff and landing speeds. The F-101 was also prone to violently pitching up in an accelerated stall and then going into an unrecoverable spin.

The two-seat F-101B Voodoo was initially developed for the Air Force Air Defense Command as an all-weather interceptor incorporating search and track radar. It first flew on March 27, 1957 and entered service in January 1959. Some of these B Models were completed as two-seat operational trainers with dual controls receiving the new designation of TF-101F. Subsequently the T was deleted and they were re-designated F-101F. McDonnell built seventy-nine dual-control F-101Fs; later 152 earlier B models were retrofitted to include dual controls.

A front view of the TF-102A showing the turbulators mounted on the canopy to solve the buffeting problem. At best the turbulators reduced transonic buffet but did not remove it *NARA via Mark Aldrich*

54-1966 was the first and only TF-100C seen here taking off on an early test flight at Edwards Flight Test Center. This aircraft was modified from a single-seat F-100C and had no operational systems. It served as a proof-of-concept for the F-100F that was built in large numbers and could perform both as a trainer and operational aircraft. *NARA via Tommy H. Thomason*

The F-100F performed as an effective trainer for the unforgiving Super Sabre; however the mishap rate for the type remained unacceptably high. *NARA via Tommy H. Thomason*

The TF-100C retained the supersonic performance of the single-seat F-100s. It used the flapless F-100C wing but inherited the tall F-100D fin. *NARA via Tommy H. Thomason*

This F-100F painted in the Vietnam era S.E. Asian camouflage scheme was frequently used for Wild Weasel missions in addition to its trainer role. *Don Spering Collection*

This dual-controlled F-101F Voodoo was assigned to a Kentucky Air National Guard where it provided transition and currency training for the squadron. *Jack Morris Collection*

This dual-cockpit F-101B displays its operational capability firing an AIR-2A Genie missile. *NARA*

The dual-cockpit Voodoos had increased performance over the single-cockpit variant. Powered by two J57-P-55s, the highest thrust example of that engine, the F-101F was over 100 knots faster than the A model at 35,000 feet. *Don Spering A.I.R. Collection*

The prototype F-104B, 63719, parked next to another Lockheed trainer project of the day, the T2V-1 intended for Navy carrier training. The F-104B had reduced fuel capacity, a 25% increase in vertical tail area, was 183 knots slower than the single seat A model at 40,000 feet, but it retained full operational capability. *NARA*

The Air Force bought a handful of two-seat F-104 trainers: 26 B models and 21 D models. The F-104B was essentially a two-seat F-104A interceptor with the cannon deleted. The F-104D was a two-seat version of the F-104C, a Tactical Air Command fighter-bomber, also with its cannon deleted. The vertical tail of both trainer variants was enlarged by 25% and a full- powered rudder was adopted to compensate for directional instability caused by the additional area of the longer forward fuselage and higher canopy. The relatively small quantity of these trainers was consistent with the small quantities of the single-seat F-104s procured by the Air Force; however, other two-seat variants, F-104Fs and TF-104Gs, were built in large numbers for foreign customers.

The Republic F-105 Thunderchief was a large, single-engine, supersonic fighter-bomber flown by the Tactical Air Command. A total of 833 were built with the last 143 being two-seat F-105F tactical trainers. The forward fuselage of the F-105D was extended by thirty-one inches to provide for the aft cockpit and the fin was taller; otherwise it was similar to the F-105D, including performance capability. The F-105F first flew on June 11, 1963, and had full combat capability. Some F-105Fs were converted to the Wild Weasel configuration with the mission of air defense suppression. On these missions the aft cockpit was occupied by an Electronic Warfare Officer.

By the time the Convair F-106 was developed the value of tactical trainers had become so obvious to the Air Force that the two-seat TF-106A was ordered into production five months before the first single seat F-106A flew. The F-106 evolved from the F-102 but unlike the wide cockpit TF-102A, the TF-106A seats were in line, so it retained the narrow cross section of the single-seat F-106A and its Mach 2 speed capability. Since it carried all of the operational equipment of the A model, it weighed 500 lbs. more. As a result, it had a longer takeoff roll with a lower rate of climb and service ceiling. It also had somewhat less endurance and range because the aft cockpit was accommodated by reducing the fuel capacity and some of its avionics had to be relocated to the weapons bay. Originally, the two-seat variant was designated the TF-106A, but since it had full combat capability, the designation was changed to F-106B. First flight was accomplished on April 9, 1958. Convair only built 63 F-106Bs in what was to become the last of the Century Series produced. The final two examples were delivered in December 1960.

The F-104D was a dual-controlled version of the F-104C fighter-bomber. It had additional hard points, boundary layer control for improved slow speed handling, and a retractable probe for probe and drogue refueling. This aircraft is the export version of the F-104D known as the TF-104G used to train foreign pilots at Luke AFB, Nevada. *Don Spering A.I.R. Collection*

The tactical trainer version of the F-105 was the F model that was thirty-one inches longer with a taller vertical tail than the single-seat models. Like the other Century Series tactical trainers, the two-seat F-105F retained full operational capability. *Don Spering A.I.R. Collection*

The value of dual-controlled tactical fighters was well established by the time the F-106 was under development. The dual-cockpit B version was built as part of the initial order and flew less than eighteen months after the prototype single-seat A model. This is the first publically released photograph of the F-106B taken a week after its first flight in April 1958 *NARA*

A unique feature of the dual-cockpit F-105F was the twin clamshell canopies. All other two-seat Century Series aircraft used an elongated single piece enclosure. *Don Spering A.I.R. Collection*

The prototype F-106B takes-off on its maiden flight from Edwards AFB. Piloted by Convair test pilot John M. Fitzpatrick, the aircraft was taken above Mach 1 on this flight. *NARA*

Although deliveries of the F-106B began in early 1959 they were not operational until mid-1960. Typically each F-106 squadron was assigned two B models for transition and proficiency training. *Don Spering A.I.R. Collection*

E. After the Century Series

While the Air Force became reliant on two-seat derivatives of their tactical fighters, the Navy rarely ordered them. The Grumman F9F-8 Cougar was purchased as a two-seat, dual control version F9F-8T (described in chapter 6), and some attack aircraft such as the A-4 and A-7 were acquired in two-seat versions, but budget constraints forced the Navy to focus on operational aircraft production. Yet in 1961, presumably with the encouragement or at least the acquiescence of the Navy, Vought used corporate funds to build a two-seat F8U Crusader demonstrator nicknamed the Twosader.

Vought modified the F8U-2NE prototype to a two-seat configuration conferring model number 408 on the project. It was originally the seventy-seventh F8U-1, Bureau Number 143710. As a two-seater it was designated F8U-1T although it retained the larger radome, ventral fins, and afterburner scoops added to make it the F8U-2NE prototype. Although the more powerful J57-P-20 engine was also installed for this purpose, it was derated to produce the same thrust as the J57-P-4A engine in the F8U-1.

The second seat was added without stretching the airframe, minimizing the structural changes and those associated with maintaining the location of the center of gravity. However, some equipment had to be relocated and two 20 mm cannons and the ventral rocket pack were deleted. The aft seat was raised by fifteen inches above the front seat, providing both visibility forward and more fuselage volume. Both cockpits were covered by one long canopy that was hinged at the rear like the single-seat Crusader's. A parabrake installation was added at the base of the vertical fin to reduce the landing roll at shore bases. In line with its intended purpose as an advanced trainer for fighter pilots, it retained the Sidewinder missile capability.

The first flight of the prototype F8U-1T was accomplished on February 6, 1962. It was subsequently redesignated TF-8A in September in accordance with the DoD aircraft designation-system consolidation. The Navy accomplished an extensive evaluation of the TF-8A including at-sea trials aboard *Independence* in June 1963. It was also evaluated by VT-22 with student pilots. Four reportedly received training in the TF-8A. One became the first (and probably only) 1,000-mph student pilot. The Navy placed an initial order for twelve F8U-1Ts (BuNos 145648-145659) with Vought but subsequently canceled the contract because of budget priorities.

None of the other countries to which the Twosader was proposed elected to buy it either. The one and only TF-8A was assigned to the Navy Test Pilot School for several years. Vought eventually used it again for its original purpose, flight training, for a short while when the

Philippines bought Crusaders for its Air Force. It crashed on July 28, 1978 following an engine failure during a training flight from Vought's facility at Grand Prairie, Texas. The Vought instructor and the Philippine Air Force student ejected safely.

The Navy also elected to evaluate a dual-control version of its supersonic F4H Phantom II, accepting an early McDonnell engineering change proposal, ECP 85, to add provisions for flight controls to the aft cockpit of the F4H. The installation consisted of several removable items:

1) Control stick with pitch and lateral trim capability
2) Non-adjustable rudder pedals without brakes
3) Throttles for power control in the basic thrust range
4) An instrument panel with additional flight instruments and engine tachometers.
In addition to the removable items, linkages were to be permanently installed between the control stick, pedals and throttle installations.

McDonnell's reasons for the dual-control option were:

1) Maintenance of proficiency
2) Pilot checkout at the squadron level
3) No chase required for pilot checkout
4) No chase required for instrument training/proficiency
5) Demonstration and evaluation of intercept techniques

For airfield landings the TF-8A could deploy a drogue chute. The long nose boom was used to obtain test data. *Tommy H. Thomason Collection*

The Navy was reluctant to order dual controlled versions of their tactical fighters but in 1961 Vought used corporate funds to build this Crusader demonstrator. Originally designated F8U-1T and unofficially nicknamed the Twosader, this one-off tactical trainer is pictured here during its Naval Air Test Center evaluation in 1962. *Tommy H. Thomason Collection*

The TF-8A retained two of its cannon and also the fuselage-mounted Sidewinder missiles for use in air-to-air gunnery and missile training. *Tommy H. Thomason Collection*

After the evaluation, the Navy ordered twelve TF-8As but cancelled the order for budgetary reasons. The sole Twosader was assigned to the Test Pilot School at Patuxent River, Maryland. *Don Spering A.I.R. Collection*

Only a handful of Navy Phantom IIs incorporated ECP 85 as a result of a brief Navy flight evaluation of BuNo 148263, the thirty-fifth F4H-1, on January 13-14, 1961. The evaluation team was unimpressed with McDonnell's first three reasons but focused on the last two. In particular, they assumed that the "design intent was to place the pilot being instructed in intercept techniques in the rear seat." The evaluation criticized the placement of the removable controls from a comfort standpoint and the access to the CNI control panel. The view forward from the rear cockpit was considered to be unacceptable for a pilot to function as a safety observer and the rear cockpit was inadequately instrumented for simulated flight by instruments. The team's summary concluded:

> Experience gained in flying the F4H-1 airplane during Board of Inspection and Survey Trials has shown the F4H-1 to be a relatively easy airplane to fly. Pilot familiarization flights under the supervision of an experienced pilot in the rear seat of a standard F4H-1 have been carried out at the Naval Air Test Center with good results after the natural initial reluctance on the part of the instructor pilot to serve in that capacity without controls was overcome. This procedure has proved markedly superior to the chase plane procedure. Therefore, the dual control installation, as presently configured, does not offer a significant increase over the basic airplane in training effectiveness. The team recommended that "the dual control installation be deleted from F4H-1 airplanes with the earliest practicable production effectively.[11]

This early F4H-1 Phantom was used by the Navy to investigate dual controls for the F4H-1 Phantom but unlike the Air Force the Navy canceled the requirement after a flight evaluation. *Robert F. Dorr via Tommy H. Thomason*

Nevertheless, when the Air Force decided to procure the Navy's F4H instead of additional F-105s and F-106s, it reinstituted dual controls in the aft cockpit. Early examples of the Navy F4H-1 had drawn international attention when they set an unparalleled series of world records including: absolute altitude (98,557 ft.); 500 km and 100 km closed circuit speed (both over Mach 2); transcontinental speed (two hours forty-eight minutes); low-level speed (902.769 mph flown under 328 ft.); and the world absolute speed record (1,606.3 mph). These achievements were particularly notable since Naval aircraft are typically hampered by the additional weight of folding wings, heavier landing gear, and arrestment structure. In 1961 the Department of Defense ordered a series of competitive evaluations between current Air Force fighters and the Navy Phantom. The results were startling. The F4H-1 proved to be faster, climbed higher, detected threats at longer range, carried heavier loads, and proved easier to service than anything in the Air Force inventory. As a result the Air Force ordered this exceptional Naval fighter and designated it the F-110A Spectre (later changed to F-4C Phantom in 1962 when the Department of Defense adopted a common tri-service designation system). The F-110A/F-4C was a two-place, dual-controlled aircraft from the outset since the Air Force initially assigned rated pilots to the rear seats. In later service when Weapons Systems Operators, who were not rated pilots, occupied the rear seat the dual controls were retained nevertheless.

The next "fighter" program was the DoD-directed F-111. Initiated in 1961 by the Secretary of Defense, Robert S. McNamara, it was intended to combine an Air Force long-range, supersonic (at sea level!) nuclear-strike requirement with the Navy's for a Fleet Air Defense missile-truck that was to be subsonic and loiter at altitude 100 miles or more from its carrier. Like the F-4, the F-111 was designed as a two-seater from the outset; however, it used a side-by-side seating arrangement. While the Air Force F-111A employed dual controls, with both seats occupied by pilots, the Navy F-111B did not have a second set of controls for the crewman in the right seat, who was dedicated to operating the radar and missile control system. In any event, the F-111B variant was short lived, with only seven examples delivered. The admirals, who bitterly resented that the Department of Defense dictated the joining of its requirements with an Air Force program, were eventually able to convince Congress to terminate the F-111B on the arguably spurious claim that it didn't meet their requirements. (Left unsaid was that the F-111B's *raison d'être*, the Phoenix Missile System, was at least two years behind schedule with production F-111Bs nearing completion.)[12]

The Phantom II was developed for the Navy. A Department of Defense evaluation confirmed that it outperformed anything in the Air Force inventory. In a rare procurement decision the Air Force ordered the Navy's spectacular new fighter but insisted on rear seat controls. *Don Spering A.I.R. Collection*

Initially designated F-110A Spectre by the Air Force, the Department of Defense common nomenclature policy of 1962 caused a redesignation to F-4C Phantom II. *Don Spering A.I.R. Collection*

The Air Force F-111A, on the other hand, was built in quantity and served for decades. Its dual controls were easily adopted for training and its safety record confirms the effectiveness of the dual-control tactical training. The first example flew in December 1964 and by December 1977 the entire F-111 fleet had accumulated 750,000 hours of aggregate flight time with the best safety record of any tactical aircraft. It suffered only seventy-three major accidents over the thirteen years it took to accumulate 750,000 hours. By comparison the F-100 suffered 471 major accidents over the six years it took to acquire 750,000 hours.[13]

The first Air Force post-Vietnam fighter program was the F-15. Its development contract called for ten single-seat models and two dual-seat models to be evaluated simultaneously. The first-production F-15 accepted by President Gerald Ford at Luke Air Force Base on November 14, 1974 was a two-seat TF-15A. Christened "TAC 1," it introduced the F-15 into service and underscored the importance of tactical trainers. Likewise, the two-place F-16B was part of the initial development contract awarded to General Dynamics on January 13, 1975.

The prototype F-111A. This fighter/bomber had dual controls from the outset and was easily adaptable for training. Its safety record was quite favorable when compared to early Century Series aircraft. *Don Spering A.I.R. Collection*

The developmental contract for the F-15 included two TF-15As intended for transition training. This is one of the dual-control aircraft, serial 71-290, during flight test at Edwards AFB. *Jack Morris Collection*

The first operational F-15 delivery was this dual-controlled TF-15A model, which was dubbed TAC-1. *Jack Morris Collection*

This F-16D, like the earlier F-16B, is a dual-controlled version of the Fighting Falcon with full operational capabilities. It is used for transition and proficiency training by the Illinois Air National Guard. *Mark Nankivil Collection*

A rare example of a Navy dual-control tactical fighter is this TF-18A assigned to VFA-125. Only thirty-nine examples of this type were built and they were later redesignated F/A-18Bs when used by Marine squadrons in fast-forward air-control missions. *Craig Kaston Collection*

The Air Force practice of procuring dual-control versions of its fighters ended after the F-15 and F-16 programs. There were never any plans for a trainer version of the F-117 even though it had very quirky flight characteristics. The two-seat F-22B was canceled even before the first flight of the production F-22A. There are currently no plans for a two-seat F-35 version but one may yet be initiated; however, it would almost certainly be for a workload-heavy mission like ECM (Electronic Counter Measures), not for pilot-transition training. Instead, highly realistic simulators have become a cost-effective means of providing almost all of the training for these advanced aircraft. A small number of specific training events/ qualifications like air-to-air refueling and air-to-air combat maneuvering are currently required to be accomplished by F-22 pilots with an instructor in two-place F-15s and F-16s before they are cleared to do them in the Raptor.

The Navy continued its practice of not employing dual-control variants of its fighters with the F-14, the successor to the F-111B. However, its next fighter program, the F-18, did include a dual-control trainer version originally designated TF-18A. Thirty-nine examples were acquired specifically for training use by Fleet Replacement Squadrons. It was subsequently redesignated F/A-18B, partly in recognition of its application by the Marine Corps to its Fast FAC (Forward Air Control) mission. A follow-on two-seat version, the F/A-18D, which appeared in the late 1980s, was usually configured with only one set of controls but like the newest generation two-place F/A-18F Super Hornet, could be quickly reconfigured with a second set of controls. [14]

The current generation of Air Force fighters, F-117, F-22, and F-35 have no dual cockpit versions for transition training. All training is accomplished by simulator systems. *US Air Force/Staff Sgt. Joshua Strang, Jared Romanowicz*

Rise of the Simulators

The Wright Brothers, credited with the first successful powered flight, can also be credited with developing the first flight simulator. They provided ground based control familiarization on a primitive simulator. Simply an old airframe, without landing gear or tail assembly, mounted on two saw horses, which allowed the student to experience the effect of control inputs. Another early flight simulation device was the British Sanders Teacher, an aeroplane replica mounted on a universal joint that was free to move in the wind. It was used to teach students appropriate control movements to maintain equilibrium. Slightly later the French developed a rig to simulate the controls of the Antoinette monoplane that consisted of a half barrel mounted on two universal joints manually moved by two instructors (one for pitch and the other for roll). In 1917 the need to train large numbers of pilots for WWI led to the creation of the Ruggles Orientor in the United States. This device consisted of the cockpit section of a fuselage mounted on a gimbal ring that could be moved in three axes by electric motors in response to a student's control inputs.[15]

In the late 1920s Edwin Link, a young engineer whose family manufactured pianos and organs, developed a training device that used pneumatic organ bellows to move in pitch, roll, and yaw. The Link Trainer, as it was called, was patented and sold in small numbers but was ignored as a "toy" until the Air Mail scandal of 1934. The Army Air Corps had been assigned the task of carrying airmail after it was discovered that the airlines had been overcharging the Post Office Department, but Army Air Corps pilots were not experienced in night and instrument flying. Within a seventy-eight day period twelve Air Corps pilots were killed from lack of instrument familiarity. Edwin Link, who had been trying to sell his trainer to the Air Corps for instrument instruction, was summoned to a hastily arranged meeting at the Newark New Jersey airport on February 11, 1934. The morning of the meeting was so foggy that it was assumed Link would postpone his demonstration. To the surprise of the assembled generals, Link piloted his airplane to Newark on instruments proving the training value of his invention as an instrument trainer. Air Corps assistant chief of staff, Brigadier General Oscar S. Westover, was highly impressed with the Link trainer; but the Army had no funds. Link and Westover appealed to the chairman of the House military affairs committee, Congressman Howard McSwain, who backed an emergency appropriation bill for six Link trainers, is credited with

An early attempt at synthetic flight was this device known as the Ruggles Orientor. It was used to observe student pilots' responses to unusual attitudes. While not an actual training device, it was useful in screening students with orientation difficulties. *Tailhook Association Collection via Cdr. Doug Siegfried*

launching the simulator industry.[16] The Link Company expanded rapidly producing over 10,000 instrument Trainers during WWII. The "Blue Box" as it was nicknamed, became standard equipment at every flight school in the United States and most allied nations. It rotated on three axes and used a complete array of flight instruments. It could simulate stalls and spins and it could be operated with an opaque canopy for blind flight training.

A major breakthrough in synthetic flight occurred when Edwin Link developed this simulator that could replicate flight. It operated by a mechanical pneumatic system. *Binghamton University Library*

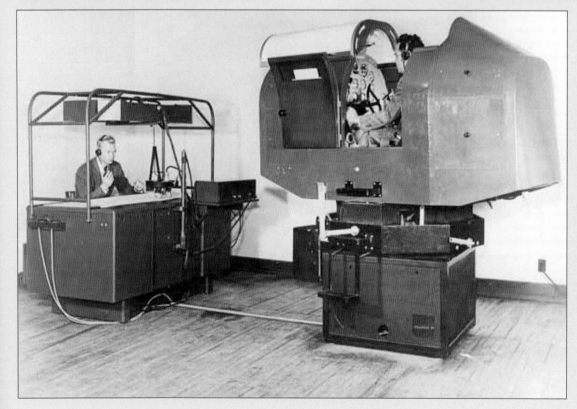

The Link Trainer became a very effective instrument training device. The student could be completely enclosed in an opaque covering and taught to navigate solely by reference to instruments without risk to the aircraft or student. *Binghamton University Library*

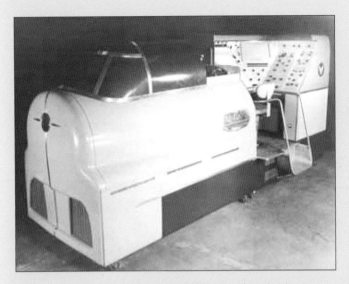

After the war Link modernized the mechanical pneumatic system to an analog electrical system. This is the first jet trainer known as the Link C-11. Unlike the earlier pneumatic Link trainers, the C-11 was a fixed based simulator that had no motion feature. *Binghamton University Library*

Early Link Trainers were generic and did not represent a particular aircraft but during WWII an aircraft-specific trainer was developed in England for the Halifax Bomber, known as the Silloth Trainer. It consisted of a nose section from a Halifax airframe with all of the instruments and switches found in the actual bomber and it featured a flight control system that mimicked the bomber's "feel." The British also employed the center section of a Spitfire fuselage in the Hawarden Trainer to acquaint pilots with the high performance of that airplane. By the end of WWII Link developed an aircraft-specific simulator, the ANT-18 (Army Navy Trainer Model 18), a replica of the AT6/SNJ cockpit and flight characteristics.

Up to this time the flight simulators employed pneumatic-mechanical systems to replicate flight, but the Silloth Trainer exposed the limits of that technology for large multi-engine aircraft. After the war analog electronics emerged as the preferred technology and a new generation of simulators was developed. The transition to electronics drew the interest of companies such as Bell Telephone Laboratories, who built an operational flight trainer for the Navy's PBM-3 and Curtiss-Wright, who built two simulators for the AAF. Link was motivated by this increased competition and in 1949 adopted an analog electronic system for the first jet simulator, the C-11.

By the late 1950s, Link had adapted their simulator to replicate specific aircraft. This is the link simulator for the Northrop F-89 Scorpion interceptor. *Binghamton University Library*

In *Flight Simulation,* authors Rolfe and Staples conclude that the modern simulator had arrived by the late 1960s. While there have been refinements—some very significant—the basic principles had been established by then.[17] Walt Fink, a former Naval Aviator, recalls training in a simulator of that vintage:

All students were required to complete a Link syllabus prior to beginning Basic Instrument (BI) stage at VT-2 (NAAS Whiting Field). Ours were located in a simulator bay with several machines there; they were only the "fuselage" cocoon, without the wings or tail surfaces that the original ones sported. They were equipped with basic controls of stick, left-hand throttle, and rudder pedals, and as I recall, switches for gear and speed brake actuation. The simulator would pitch and roll a limited amount in response to control inputs, but rotated 360 degrees on its pedestal. An electric/electronic cable connection from the Link to the "spider" (on the instructor's desk) was provided, as well as repeaters of the cockpit instruments so he/she could tell what the student was looking at while the spider tracked the progress of the flight on a map.

The purpose of the Link was simple ... it taught SCAN, period. It didn't really perform like a T-28 nor fly like one, but the instrumentation was similar. Good instrument scan is absolutely essential in IFR flying—failure to master this technique can have disastrous results.

We flew many different patterns in BI Links, but they all had similar characteristics: timed turns, changing altitudes, and changing speeds. The most challenging (and feared) pattern as I recall was the Yankee Pattern, which was several minutes in length and involved lots of turns, climbs and descents, and configuration and/or speed changes. A pattern with standard rate turns (3 degrees per second) meant it'd take one minute to turn the Link 180 degrees in heading. If it called for a simultaneous descent of 1000 feet per minute, you watched the clock and each time the second hand passed a 'cardinal' mark (:00, :15, :30, and :45), you wanted the Link to have turned 45 degrees and descended 250 feet. You had to watch your attitude, meaning angle of bank and nose attitude, the turn and bank indicator to keep the needle on the SRT mark, the Vertical Speed Indicator to monitor your descent rate, and the airspeed indicator to keep it where it was supposed to be, meaning you had to also watch your power setting. The fledgling aviator had to juggle a lot of balls in the air during these "flights." Scan, scan, check, scan, double-check, scan. And sweat.

Once the students completed BI stage, we went on to Radio Instrument stage at VT-3, where we integrated navigation aids with the training we already learned. When we went to Advanced Training, our first flights were back to Basic Instruments again. Why repeat something we'd already had in Basic? Because if some dark night you fly off the sharp end of the boat and put it in the water, it ain't because you didn't know your radio procedures.

In retrospect, as in all aviation-related things, there were comical things with the Links. It wasn't uncommon for us to be sweating out a pattern inside the box, trying our level best to make all the right corrections, when the instructor would decide we needed his intervention and would just walk over and snatch the door open. You get a little caught up in the moment anyway, and are "flying" along with all your mental faculties focusing on the task at hand, when suddenly the side of your "airplane" falls off. It caused a little adrenaline rush there for a second.

The instructors could really fly those Links, let me tell you. I had a WAVE instructor who could stand on the external step of the sim and pilot that thing like nobody's business. She'd just whack the throttle to "about there" and with her hand on top of the stick (not even holding the grip) fly a perfect, precise pattern without hardly looking at the instruments and then tell me, "See? It's simple. It's just like that. Try it again."

The Links were "activated" by an air pressure-bellows system, so they'd make hissing sounds rather than engine noises as they operated. The rotation on their pedestals was done by the same system so there wasn't a hard connection, and thus a hand to the outside of a Link could slow or even stop its rotation. Your fun-loving fellow students could have a field day during after-hours sim practice by slowing down your turn while you were in the box trying to hit all your marks. That would result in your putting in some more aileron (hiss) to catch up, and they'd slow it down some more. More aileron (HISSSSS) until you had a whole bunch in it, then they'd release their hand pressure and you'd whip through sixty degrees before you knew what hit you.[18]

Motion, which had been provided by pneumatic bellows on earlier simulators, was deleted from Link's C-11 jet simulator so it was characterized as "fixed-based." The use of motion has become a topic of great debate. The Air Force concluded by the 1980s that there was no reliable evidence of motion affecting training transfer and purchased predominantly fix-based trainers, yet the FAA insisted on motion in civil airline simulators that is realistically achieved with hydraulic jacks. Ian Strachan notes in a "Military Simulation and Training Magazine" article that the current industry is dominated by L-3 Link (successor to the original Link Company), Boeing, and Lockheed Martin. He argues that realistic motion; even simulated G forces can now be incorporated for maximum training benefit. Strachan notes that visual displays have become very sophisticated and highly realistic. The F-35 Full Mission Simulator display consists of a 360-degree two-meter diameter dome with twenty-five liquid-crystal-on-silicon (LCoS) projectors. Image generation is from twenty-three Rockwell Collins EPX channels.[19]

It is clear that all phases of modern military flight training are highly dependent on simulators, so much so that procurement decisions are now based on the simulator system as well as the actual aircraft. A student Naval Aviator going through the advanced-strike pipeline spends more than half of his cockpit time in a simulator. Furthermore, the current generation of fighters has become so expensive that it is unlikely dual-cockpit versions will ever be built for training. Synthetic flight is essential in transitioning

Modern military synthetic flight training takes place in fixed-base simulators with high-resolution visual displays. The cost versus benefit (limited g-force changes, buffeting) of motion simulation is still a subject of debate. *US Air Force*

pilots to advanced aircraft like the F-22 or F-35. Simulators provide the added advantage of not being affected by weather, not consuming fuel, not requiring routine post flight maintenance, and not exposing the pilot or aircraft to risk even in the most dangerous situation.

Chapter Eight Endnotes

1. F.G. Swanborough, *United States Military Aircraft Since 1909*, London and New York, Putnam, 1963, pp.48, 50, 192, 363-364, 410.

2. Gerald P. Moran, *The Corsair, and other Aeroplanes Vought 1917-1977*, Terre Haute, IN, Aviation Heritage Books, 1991, p.133.

3. Vought Proposal Brochure (undated) to the Bureau of Aeronautics submitted late 1945.

4. Ibid.

5. Office of the Chief of Naval Operations memorandum, Proposed Conversion of F4U-1's to Two-Place Trainer, dated January 28, 1946.

6. iIbid.

7. Vought SMM-162 Departmental Correspondence dated December 11, 1946.

8. Air Training Command History, January-July 1954 Chapter V: The Crisis In Training Aircraft, pp.113-114.

9. Martin W. Bowman with Mattias Vogelsang, *Lockheed F-104 Starfighter*, Ramsbury, Marlborough Wiltshire, England: Crowood Press Ltd. 2000, p.21, and Peter E. Davies with David W. Menard, *North American F-100 Super Sabre*. Ramsbury, Marborough, Wiltshire, England: Crowood Press Ltd. 2003, p.33.

10. Air Training Command History, July-December 1954, Chapter IV: *Continuing Crisis In Training Aircraft*, pp.129-130.

11. Speedletter Report dated February 27, 1961 from Commander, Naval Air Test Center to Chief, Bureau of Naval Weapons; subject Brief Evaluation of Dual Control Installation In Model F4H-1 Airplane.

12. Tommy Thomason, *Naval Fighters number Forty-one, Grumman Navy F-111B Swing Wing*. Simi Valley, CA: Steve Ginter, 1998, pp.52-54.

13. Bowman with Vogelsang, p.21.

14. Brad Elward, *The Boeing F/A-18E/F Super Hornet & EA-18G Growler, A Developmental and Operational History*. Atglen, PA: Schiffer Publishing Ltd., 2012, pp.29-30.

15. J.M. Rolfe and K.J. Staples, Editors, *Flight Simulation*, (Cambridge, England: Cambridge University Press, 1986) pp.14-17.

16. Lloyd L. Kelly (As Told To Robert B. Parke), *The Pilot Maker*, New York, New York: Grosset & Dunlap, 1970, pp.51-53.

17. Rolfe and Staples, p.35.

18. Lt. Walt Fink, USN (Retired) e-mail correspondence to Tommy H. Thomason, December 24, 2013.

19. Ian Strachan, "Military Flight Simulators Today" *Military Simulation & Training Magazine*, January 2008.

Chapter Nine
THE SUPERSONIC TRAINER

A. The Number One Priority

Dual-cockpit fighters proved enormously helpful in dealing with the "Century Problem" allowing tactical units to prepare new pilots to operate high-performance airplanes with skills and techniques that were impossible to teach with trainers of the mid-1950s. However, Lt.Gen. C.T. Myers, commander of the Air Training Command, was still very outspoken about the need for a supersonic basic trainer. He was adamant that student pilots had to be exposed to the take-off and landing speeds, high-altitude characteristics, sink rates, climb performance and acceleration of the Century Fighters during the basic training phase. On November 22, 1954 he advised the Air Force Chief of Staff, Gen. N.F. Twining, that the number-one priority of the Training Command was development of the TZ trainer.[1] Lt.Gen. Myers was probably unaware of it at the time, but two companies, Northrop and General Electric, were working on independent privately funded projects that would blend into the perfect solution.

In 1952, Northrop was a troubled company with only two major programs, the F-89 Scorpion interceptor and S-62 Snark ballistic missile—both were experiencing serious problems. The F-89 had been grounded due to structural problems and the Snark was found to be unreliable. In this environment company founder, Jack Northrop, who was growing increasingly discouraged by the cancellation of his cherished YB-49 flying wing bomber and a contentious relationship with board Chairman Oliver P. Echols, announced his retirement. Heading for possible corporate oblivion, the company was forced to undertake a major reorganization. Echols assumed the responsibilities of president with the understanding that product development and government contracts would be his first priority. To this end Edgar Schmued, recently hired by Echols and legendary for his work at North American Aviation as the designer of the P-51, F-86, and F-100, was elevated to vice-president of engineering. In turn Schmued was able to recruit Dr. William F. Ballhaus from Convair as his chief engineer. Ballhaus brought along Welko E. Gasich, a wizard of preliminary design. The team was rounded out by two respected RAND Corporation consultants, Ward Dennis and Thomas V. Jones. Dennis was a noted weapons system analysis, while Jones was an engineer with an interest in economics and industrial management. With a new technical team in place Echols's quest for contracts began in earnest. The Century Series fighter programs were already under development at North American, Convair, McDonnell, and Lockheed so the Northrop team focused on other opportunities such as long and medium-range interceptors. They also began to investigate light, inexpensive fighters that would cost roughly half as much as a Century fighter. Jones, who would ultimately become the president of Northrop, was an outspoken advocate for a small airplane since he saw fighter development in economic terms. He brought a procurement concept from RAND that he called "life-cycle cost." It was a simple, clear-eyed way of analyzing the true value of an airplane (or any weapon system) by determining the total cost over its entire life span. Most defense planners considered only the research and development cost and purchase price of an airplane, but Jones argued that maintenance and operation expense over the life of an airplane must be added for the true measure. This meant that less complex, easily maintained, aircraft offered maximum value over time.

The team's initial attempt at designing a light supersonic fighter was in response to an Air Force General Operating Requirement released on December 12, 1952. Using company funds, Schmued and Gasich defined a small butterfly tailed delta winged aircraft known as Model N-102 Fang—a name selected by Schmued to distinguish his work from the earlier "insect" named Northrop products

(P-61 Black Widow, F-89 Scorpion).[2] The Fang clearly reflected Ballhous' Convair heritage—the delta wing and butterfly tail were reminiscent of Convair's experimental XP-92. The Fang emerged as a small airframe wrapped around a large engine—the Pratt & Whitney J57, Wright J65, and General Electric J79 were all proposed.

Ultimately, the butterfly tail was abandoned in favor of a conventional tail when the mock-up was completed in 1953. Very ambitious performance estimates were published (Mach 2 speed, 59,300-foot service ceiling, and 2,030 mile ferry range).[3] In addition to its compact size the Fang offered exceptional maintenance accessibility. Internal components were easily reached through removable hatches and doors, cockpit instruments could be accessed when the forward hinged windshield was raised, even the entire lower fuselage could be removed as a module and a different engine could be substituted to suit changing mission requirements. The designers estimated that the aircraft could be fully serviced in six minutes from landing to re-launch. But the large engine consumed most of the airframe interior; there was little room for anything else and little chance for growth.

The design team was forced to return to the drawing board when the Air Force selected the Lockheed for the XF-104 to fill its General Operating Requirement and the Fang failed to produce any orders. Corporate funds were used to continue work on the Fang but Thomas Jones was convinced that the design was flawed by its expensive engine which limited the customer base.[4] Undeterred, Northrop dispatched a team of management and technical personnel to Europe and Asia to study the needs of NATO and SEATO air arms and found that the lightweight, inexpensive, supersonic fighter concept had merit. Data generated from this trip resulted in a new family of designs under the Northrop project name N-156 that was expected to be attractive to the United States and its allies.

Meanwhile a development was taking place at the General Electric that would have a major impact on Northrop's plans. Edward Woll, engineering manager of the Small Engine Department, was convinced that General Electric possessed the technology to produce a high-thrust lightweight engine. He anticipated that a 2,500 lb. thrust turbojet weighing 250 pounds would fill a huge gap in the market. In the fall of 1953, there was no specific application for such an engine, but Woll ordered an advanced design study for three possible layouts at 5:1, 7:1, and 12:1 pressure ratios. He presented the study to Air Force Headquarters to determine if there was any interest and was pleased to find considerable interest in the 7:1 version. Independent of Woll's presentation to Headquarters, the Air Force Training Command expressed a need for an engine that weighed less than the Continental J69 used in the T-37.

The N-102 Fang mock-up which was built with corporate funds. The compact airframe size is apparent. *Gerald Baltzer Collection via Mark Nankivil*

Sideview of the N-102 mock-up showing the engine bay panels removed allowing for multiple engine installations. Northrop imagined that Fang could change engines to meet changing mission requirements. *Gerald Baltzer Collection via Mark Nankivil*

Legendary designer Edgar Schmued displays the N-102 Fang mock-up to a Department of Defense official. Schmued had spent most of his career at North American where he was recognized as the designer of the P-51, F-86, and F-100. *Gerald Baltzer Collection via Mark Nankivil*

A cutaway display of the General Electric J85 turbojet. This small, high-thrust engine was originally designed as a non-man rated missile engine. It provided the breakthrough that Northrop needed to develop a practical lightweight supersonic aircraft. *National Air and Space Museum*

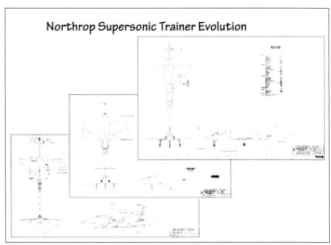

The lightweight supersonic aircraft program was designated N-156 at Northrop. These general arrangement drawings show the evolution of the concept from the twin podded engine design favored by Edgar Schmued (left rear), to the internal engine design that was presented to the Navy as the "Tally Ho" fighter designed by Joe Talley (center), to the two place area ruled design by Welco Gasich which became the T-38 Gerald *Baltzer Collection via Mark Nankivil*

In addition the XQ-4, a new supersonic target drone being developed by Radioplane a Northrop subsidiary, required a high thrust-to-weight ratio engine in the 2,000 lb. thrust class. Woll's design study was proving to be a shrewd investment. On November 28, 1954, the Air Force issued a contract to General Electric for two XJ85-GE-1 demonstrator engines. The engines were built and bench run successfully. The first airborne application for the J85 was in the GAM-72 Quail decoy missile, an air launched expendable missile designed to protect B-52 bombers. But a significant turning point occurred in mid-1954 when Woll called on Northrop's chief engineer, William Ballhaus, to present a full-size mock-up of the seventeen-inch-diameter, 36-inch long turbojet capable of producing 2,500 pounds of thrust.

The sales call was intended to present the J85 as a powerplant for the new Radioplane drone, but when Woll explained that the engine could be refined into a man-rated engine, and that it could be fitted with an afterburner that would increase thrust by as much as 40%, and two J85s would weigh less than a single engine of equal thrust allowing twin engine safety, Ballhaus became highly enthused. Schmued and Gasich were informed of the new G.E. engine and all agreed that now the small, cost effective, supersonic aircraft concept was feasible.

Initial work on the N-156 was aimed at the Navy's interest in a lightweight supersonic fighter that could operate from the decks of their small jeep aircraft carriers left over from WWII. Early configuration studies sparked a sharp conflict between Schmued and Gasich. Schmued advocated under wing pods for the engines for ease of maintenance, while Gasich argued that the podded installation would cause too much drag and insisted that the engines be mounted side-by-side in the fuselage. It is reported that these highly respected engineers had some very contentious exchanges and Gasich expected to be fired, but further studies proved Gasich's point and Schmued relented—the N-156 proceeded with the engines mounted internally. The jeep carrier design became known as the Tally-ho fighter named after one of its designers, Joe Talley, but it proved another dead-end when the Navy decided to mothball its entire jeep carrier fleet.

Another marketing initiative was launched in January 1955 when a team headed by John R. Alison, vice president of Marketing, with designers Edgar Schmued and Welko Gasich staged a series of briefings for Air Force commanders on two new variations of the N-156, the F fighter and the T trainer.

The Air Force showed little interest in the lightweight fighter but displayed substantial enthusiasm for the trainer. Lt Gen. Myers was highly impressed and said that the N-156T was exactly what the Air Training Command needed. Finally, in January 1955, Air Force Headquarters gave the Air Research and Development Command the authority to proceed with a design study on the long-anticipated TZ airplane. After more than two years of thought and discussion, the Air Force took its first major step toward the realization of a training aircraft specifically designed to prepare student pilots for supersonic flight. On May 31, 1955, after the design study was completed, Air Force Headquarters published General Operating Requirement (GOR) 94 that states in part:

This Basic Trainer, Jet, Aircraft will bridge the transition training gap between the T-37 aircraft in the undergraduate training phases and the projected 1959-1970 first line aircraft in the combat crew training phase.

This aircraft will be used to train pilots to a level of proficiency whereby required transition in the first line aircraft will be reduced to a minimum. It will operate day or night, in moderately Adverse (sic) weather, and will provide training in subsonic and supersonic speed ranges in instruments, formation, acrobatics, navigation, and cruise control.

The Requirement specified a cruise endurance of 2½ hours, a service ceiling of 50,000 feet, the ability to fly an entire mission at supersonic speed, side-by-side seating if practicable or tandem seating with good visibility, and service availability by 1959.[5]

In response to the General Operating Requirement Northrop management instructed Gasich to commence a specific design study which was submitted to the Air Force as the N-156T Supersonic Trainer Proposal in March 1956. Northrop felt confident that they had the inside track since the Requirement was derived from their earlier presentation. North American submitted a proposal for a two-seat version of the F-100 and Lockheed offered a two-seat F-104, but these aircraft were far too complex and expensive to serve the Air Training Command and Gen. Myers, remained steadfast in his enthusiasm for the Northrop proposal. On June 15, 1956, the Air Force issued a letter of intent to Northrop for two flying prototypes and one static test article.

The N-156 project benefited from being on the crest of a new wave of second-generation supersonic aerodynamics that was exploited by the talented engineers reporting to Gasich. Robert Katkov and Art Nitakman were the aerodynamicists, Art Ogness engineered the structure, George Gluyas dealt with propulsion and Lee Begin laid out the configuration. The area rule principle developed by NACA scientist, Dr. Richard Whitcomb, was now widely understood and applied to the N-156 fuselage to mitigate transonic drag, giving it a "wasp waist" appearance. To provide the minimum frontal area, the student and instructor cockpits were on the same level enclosed by a low profile canopy. Provision was made for the nose to droop for instructor visibility during takeoff and landing, but weight and complexity forced Gasich to rethink this feature. A simple and effective solution was found: elevating the rear cockpit ten inches giving the instructor unobstructed vision over the student. The undersurface of the forward fuselage received a subtle convex curve to reduce both forebody drag and the pitch-up moment that resulted from the arched canopy shape, while the remainder of the

undersurface received a shallow concave curve. In profile the fuselage took on the elegant look of a lady's slipper.[6] The wing used a remarkably thin cross section that was considered unthinkable a few years earlier, but new structural techniques made it possible, and a cambered leading edge gave it docile subsonic characteristics. The horizontal stabilizer was placed low to eliminate the pitch-up tendency that plagued high-tailed Century Series fighters such as the F-101 and F-104. The original vertical stabilizer was tall and swept but this was replaced by a large trapezoidal fin of low aspect ratio (wide base with low height) to provide increased stiffness and avoid the roll coupling problem experienced in early F-100As and F-102As. The application of these solutions to difficult aerodynamic problems promised remarkable flight characteristics, but maintainability was given equal emphasis. Internal component arrangement was carefully thought out by Gerald Huben who employed a "one component layer" design philosophy so that systems could be easily accessed in minimal time. Approximately twenty-five percent of the aircraft skin was made removable for ease of servicing. A simple means of removing the aft fuselage for access to the engine bays was also devised by Huben. Engines could be removed without the need to remove the attached accessories allowing both engines to be replaced in just ten man-hours.

The mockup was completed and received a Developmental Engineering Inspection on August 15, 1956, a Cockpit Standardization Inspection on September 6, 1956, and a formal MockUp Board Review on October 16-17, 1956. Legend has it that when Lt.Gen. Clarence "Bill" Irvine, head of Air Force aircraft procurement, inspected the N-156 mockup he was escorted by Schmued and Gasich. Unaware of their earlier dispute, the general praised Schmued for the elegance of the design. Fully acknowledging that it was Gasich who deserved the praise, Schmued gave Gasich a wink behind Lt. Gen. Irvine's back. The mockup was approved with several changes and work was started on the first three articles.

Now designated YT-38, the first aircraft (serial 58-1191) rolled off of the advanced production assembly line on August 15, 1958, and the second (serial 58-1192) was shop complete on 15 November. Pleased with Northrop's progress, the Air Force issued a follow-on contract for four production models that were assigned the designation T-38A. After meticulous inspection by the Air Force, the first prototype was approved for flight on December 10, 1958. It was disassembled and trucked to the Air Force Flight Test Center at Edwards AFB in preparation for its maiden flight.[7]

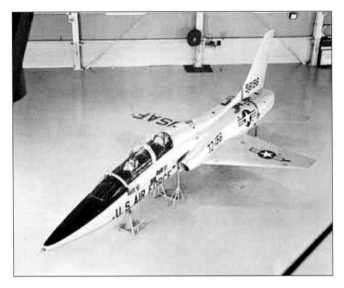

The mock-up presented to the Air Force in late summer and fall of 1956 differed from the flying prototype in only a few details. The tall swept vertical is one obvious difference. *Tony Chong Collection*

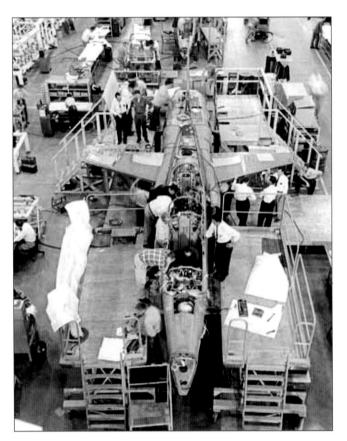

Construction of two prototype YT-38s started in late 1956. Both were completed by the second half of 1958, but problems with the afterburning YJ85 engine delayed test flying and threatened the entire program. *Tony Chong Collection*

However, things were not going well at General Electric. The afterburning J85 engines were far from ready, and the interim non-afterburning engines were experiencing compressor stalls during ground runs. The erratic compressor behavior prevented the engines from producing full power and often caused an over temperature condition requiring engine shutdown. The YT-38s couldn't fly until the compressor issue was resolved, and the Air Force was threatening to cancel the J85 program. Ed Woll and his engineers at General Electric found the problem impossible to diagnose until Woll decided to remove all of the compressor blades from a particularly sub-standard engine and carefully measure them against the blueprints. These blades had been designed with a high aspect ratio (long and narrow) and their cross-section (airfoil) was especially critical. Woll found that the blades did not have the correct airfoil shape. They were manufactured in the same manner as G.E.'s larger engines where the excess material (known as flash) from the forging process was chopped off. This process was tolerable on large blades, but on the J85's small blades the process was unacceptable: it distorted the critical airfoil by making the leading and trailing edges blunt. The blades were recontoured to the exact shape specified in the blueprints by a specialized tool and die shop then reinstalled in the 7-stage compressor. This cured most, but not all of the problem, and Woll was relieved to learn that the erratic performance was the result of a fixable manufacturing problem. But time was running out, and the compressor was still not providing sufficient airflow to prevent occasional engine malfunctions. So in July 1957,

Northrop prepared public relations booklet commemorating the rollout ceremony. This reproduction of the booklet cover illustrates the event. *Craig Kaston Collection*

At the time of the rollout Northrop took the opportunity to display the F-5 mock-up alongside the airworthy YT-38 prototype. The F-5 had not been awarded a contract yet. *Craig Kaston Collection*

Northrop publicity photos taken at the time of the rollout show test pilot Lew Nelson in a pressure suit and high altitude helmet that he probably never wore for actual test flight. This gear was extremely uncomfortable and severely restricted the pilot's range of motion *Tony Chong Collection*

The pilot's cockpit of the YT-38. During most of the test flight program the rear cockpit would be filled with flight test instrumentation. *Tony Chong Collection*

Throughout the entire test program the external features of the YT-38 remained unchanged. Its appearance at rollout is substantially identical to its appearance at the conclusion of the test program—a tribute to the designer, Welko Gasich and his team. *Tony Chong Collection*

The Air Force approved YT-38 1191 for flight on December 10, 1958, but General Electric was experiencing serious compressor stalls with the installed engines. The Air Force issued a strict deadline of April 11, 1959, for the maiden flight, and on April 10, the prototype finally flew for forty-two minutes, reaching Mach 0.9 at 35,000 feet with no major problems. *Tony Chong Collection*

The speed brakes are extended during the first flight. Test pilot Lew Nelson dubbed it "the cleanest first flight in my experience." The white covering over the rear canopy protected the test instrumentation. *Don Spering A.I.R. Collection*

The prototype YT-38, 1191, parked on the Edwards ramp early in the test program. The entire program was flown without a mishap—a remarkable achievement for a new supersonic aircraft. *Air Force Flight Test Center*

while work continued on the original 7-stage engines that would power the YT-38s, Woll decided to design an 8-stage compressor. The Air Force, now on the verge of canceling the J85 program, set a firm first-flight deadline of April 11, 1959. When reinstalled in the YT-38 airframe the "fixed" J85s continued to experience compressor stalls during ground runs. The GE team at Northrop joined Woll in a redoubled their effort to find the cause. Finally it was discovered that hot gases were being drawn forward into the inlet duct during high-power ground runs. The hot gases expanded the compressor casing that increased the clearance between the casing and the rotor blade tip allowing the engine to stall. This condition was fixed by installing suck-in doors near the compressor face that prevented the recirculation of hot gases during ground runs. But the interim engines were only producing 2,180 pounds of thrust on the test stand (and had to be de-rated further to avoid compressor stalls in the airplane), this was less thrust than the predicted 2,500 pounds, and far less than the 3,600 pounds expected from the afterburning engines. With the deadline at hand Woll urged test pilot Lew Nelson to "just get air under the wheels," and Nelson managed to fly the YT-38 on April 10, one day before the deadline.[8] The first flight lasted forty-two minutes, reached Mach 0.9 at 35,000 feet and Nelson declared it, "the cleanest first flight in my experience. And the first with no squawks."

The flight went so well that Nelson was able to make a second flight the same afternoon. On April 14, during its third flight Nelson exceeded the speed of sound while still flying with the thrust-limited interim engines.

Recounting the early test flights, author Steve Pace wrote:

By April 22, YT-38 number one had flown four times. It had reached specified altitudes, exceeded the speed of sound, and made life difficult for its F-100 chase plane and utterly impossible for its T-33 escort. Nelson reported a few minor squawks, but no significant malfunctions.[9]

In October 1959, six months after the first flight, with the test program going smoothly, the Air Force issued a letter contract for thirteen additional T-38As to be used in the flight test program.

The second prototype YT-38, 1192, joined the test program shortly after 1191. By the fall of 1959, both airplanes had completed over 100 flights with no aerodynamic changes needed to either aircraft. The second YT-38 has tufting attached to its tail surfaces to observe airflow in flight. *Don Spering A.I.R. Collection*

The spin chutes attached to the YT-38 tail during spin testing. The T-38 proved very spin resistant and had to be aggressively forced into a spin. *Craig Kaston Collection*

B. The Flight Test Program

Less than eight months before the YT-38 maiden flight the Air Force changed its entire flight test procedure. A regulation titled: Testing/Evaluation of Systems, Subsystems, and Equipment, Air Force Regulation 80-14 established a new process for evaluating airplanes and the YT-38 would be the first aircraft tested under this new process.[10] The former process, called Phase Testing, was replaced by Category Testing, which marked a fundamental shift in the responsibilities of the contractor and the Air Force. Phase Testing evolved in the late 1940s as an unofficial means of evaluating new airplanes. The process began with the contractor's investigation of airworthiness and flying characteristics (Phase I). This was followed by an Air Force verification of the contractor's results (Phase II). Deficiencies found by the Air Force were corrected by the contractor and re-tested by the Air Force (Phase III). The program concluded with a thorough evaluation of all operating characteristics to obtain data for the flight manual (Phase IV). At the conclusion of Phase IV the airplane was released to the operating commands, but this often led to the delivery of airplanes that were not fully suitable. In 1949 a study was commissioned by the Air Force Chief of Staff resulting in a regulation that officially codified and expanded Phase Testing.[11] Additional Phases were added to the process to deal with severe weather, durability and maintainability under field conditions, and operational suitability. By the mid-1950s, Phase Testing was increasingly criticized for the length of time it consumed and the disappointment of end users who were still receiving unacceptable airplanes. The new process, Category Testing, was designed to put an end to this by combining contractor and Air Force participation at an early stage, and evaluating the airplane with all of its systems as an entire package. The new test program consisted of just three categories that could be conducted simultaneously. Category I was still a fundamental investigation of airworthiness and flight characteristics, but as both contractor and Air Force test pilots shared the responsibility, this eliminated the redundancy of Phase II in the former process. Category II evaluated the airplane and all of its systems in an operational configuration. In this Category the aircraft was demonstrated in an all-weather environment and Air Force personnel assumed an increasing role in maintenance. Category II tests were not considered complete until the using command demonstrated effective preparation, operation, and maintenance. Category III tested the entire system under the sole control of the using command under field conditions. This category allowed for the development of operational tactics, and the refinement of logistics, personnel, maintenance, and training requirements.[12]

A detailed memorandum titled "Test Plan T-38 Category I/II/III" was prepared by the Air Force in preparation for the new program. The stated purpose of the plan was, "to accomplish complete weapon system testing which will insure timely and effective integration of the T-38 trainer into the Air Training Command inventory." The plan scheduled the testing to begin in January 1959 (the actual testing was delayed until April because of engine problems) and conclude in September 1961. It was anticipated that fifteen aircraft would be required for Category I/II testing and an undetermined amount of additional aircraft for Category III testing.

The YT-38 test program was remarkable for its lack of problems that is particularly notable since it combined a new testing process with a new supersonic airplane. Historian Fred Anderson characterizes early Category I tests:

> By fall the two prototypes had completed 100 flights … Milt Kuska, director of Flight Test Engineering, reported that the T-38 had encountered none of the major problems usually experienced in flight testing supersonic aircraft; not a single aerodynamic change was indicated throughout the program. The T-38 was rapidly achieving a reputation for outstanding flight handling qualities with 'forgiving' flight characteristics. Maintenance was likewise proving very low.[13]

The Category I Flight Test report published in January 1960 concludes:

> Within the present flight envelope of the YT-38, this aircraft demonstrates excellent potential as a trainer. However, it should be noted that the rear cockpit has not been evaluated because of the instrument package.

The report praises the fundamental characteristics of the airplane but recommends several changes in the cockpit layout, nose gear steering, and flight controls. However, the low thrust available from the interim engines receives serious criticism:

> The performance of the aircraft with the low thrust YJ-85-GE-1 engines is poor and under some conditions makes the airplane marginal, even for use as a test bed vehicle. The low thrust (1,625 pounds per engine installed static thrust) of the prototype engines was partially the result of a requirement to derate the engines upon installation by increasing the tailpipe area to provide adequate engine stall margin for operation. Installation of the J85-GE-5 engines should provide adequate thrust for operational use.[14]

The afterburning engines were expected to provide 3600 pounds of thrust, more than doubling the available thrust from the interim engines, but afterburner development had been delayed by the erratic compressor performance on the core engine. General Electric's Engineering Manager, Ed Woll, must have felt like he had bitten off more than he could chew, for it was Woll who suggested the possibility of an afterburner to Northrop during his sales call. To save weight and allow the engine to fit in the T-38, Woll had to scale down the successful J79 afterburner design. Work on the first afterburning J85 was started in July 1956 but test runs were not conducted until January 1959. Ten months later, G.E. shipped the first afterburning engines to Northrop for installation in the first production T-38A (serial 58-1194). As it happened, the afterburner became the most important accomplishment associated with the J85. Surprisingly, in its ultimate production form the J85-GE-5 provided 3,850 lbs. of thrust, 250 lbs. more than originally expected. In November 1959, the afterburning engine powered the production T-38A on its maiden flight. By now much of the Category I testing was over and the Air Force was visibly pleased, issuing a letter contract in October 1959 for fifty additional T-38As to be used in Category III testing.

A significant portion of Category I included a full year of spin testing that began in April 1960. Initial spin flights were conducted by Northrop, with the Air Force participating in mid-August. The spin tests were completed in April 1961 and the Flight Test Center reported: "The T-38 will not enter a continuing spin except following an abrupt application of aft stick at close to maximum possible rates. This aft stick rate required is abnormal." When forced into a spin, the T-38 exhibited an unstable inverted mode, a continuing oscillatory erect mode, or a continuing erect smooth flat mode that could develop from the oscillatory mode. Recovery from the inverted spin mode was very fast and positive with application of full opposite rudder, full back stick, and full aileron in the direction of the spin. Recovery from any of the erect spin modes was found to be less predictable and often resulted in engine flameouts. The Flight Test Center recommended: "Due to the uncertainty of recovery, intentional spins in the T-38 should be prohibited and an appropriate warning placed in the Flight Manual."[15]

While Category I tests concluded Category II tests started with ten production T-38As flown by eight Air Force pilots. As planned, Northrop's participation was substantially reduced and the Air Force's was increased since Category II was intended to be an extensive systems evaluation in a realistic military environment. The tests were performed at Edwards by the Air Research and Development Command with participation from the Air Training Command. Performance data from these tests was used to develop the Flight Manual. By now the entire test fleet was powered by

58-1196 the third production T-38A in liberal Day-Glo markings parked on the Edwards dry lake. The G.E. logo on the fin indicates that it was being used for powerplant testing by the engine contractor, General Electric. *Mark Nankivil Collection*

J85-GE-5 afterburning engines, and Category II was completed on schedule in February 1961 with over 1,320 hours flown. The Category II Performance Test report states:

> The T-38A is an excellent trainer for transition into high performance aircraft. It has excellent handling characteristics, maximum speed is in the low supersonic range, and takeoff and subsonic climb is comparable to the latest Century Series fighters.
>
> With maximum power, the aircraft can readily takeoff in 2,500 feet at 12,000 pounds gross weight, can climb from sea level to 40,000 feet in 2.5 minutes, and can attain a combat ceiling (500 feet per minute rate of climb) of 51,000 feet.[16]

After accumulating more than 2,000 flight hours in Category I and II the Air Force was ready to proceed with Category III Testing. On March 17, 1961, Col. Arthur W. Buck, director of the USAF T-38A operational testing program, delivered a T-38A to the Headquarters of the Air Training Command, Randolph Air Force Base, San Antonio, Texas. Col. Buck marked his arrival with a sonic boom, a sound that would become routine at Randolph. By the mid-year a task force of twenty-eight production Talons had arrived at Randolph and instructor training was started. In September a group

High visibility from the Day-Glo markings is very apparent in this image. *Don Spering A.I.R. Collection*

of primary-phase graduates who had just completed training in the T-37 at Webb Air Force Base were the first students to fly the T-38. They formed Class 62-FZ, and received 140 hours in the new supersonic trainer. Later classes received only 130 hours because of aircraft shortages that was further reduced to 120 hours when engine and airframe problems limited T-38 availability. The Air Training Command conducted the entire Category III program, verifying the training syllabus and thoroughly evaluating all aspects of T-38 operations in an actual training environment. Testing was concluded in March 1962 and the Training Command was delighted with its new trainer, it proved to be very effective for all students regardless of assignment and its safety record was remarkable. The Flight Test Center at Edwards reported that all Category I, II, and III test sorties were flown without a single major accident—a record unequalled in supersonic aircraft test programs. The Air Force was proud to announce that the T-38 test program was the most successful ever conducted at Edwards.[17]

When the T-38A was placed in training service during category III testing the aircraft were used hard and often as evidenced by the chipped paint on the cockpit rails and the forward fuselage markings. *Don Spering A.I.R. Collection*

59-1597 was part of the second block of eight T-38As. It is seen here in May 1961 after category III testing was under way. *Craig Kaston Collection*

C. Operational Service

At the conclusion of Category III testing the T-38 was deemed fully operational and introduced to ten Air Training bases: Randolph; Reese; Webb; Laughlin; and Laredo in Texas; Williams in Arizona; Moody in Georgia; Vance in Oklahoma; Craig in Alabama; and Columbus in Mississippi. Ultimately the Training Command ordered 1,114 Talons that were produced between 1959 and 1972 (Northrop built a total of 1,187—some going to operators other than the Air Training Command). During the 1960s the training syllabus focused on high performance flying skills (aerobatics, stalls, unusual attitudes, slow flight, and traffic pattern work), formation training, instrument flying, and navigation.

In early 1975, a course was established for new tactical fighter pilots known as Lead-In Fighter Training (LIFT), designed to teach newly winged pilots the basics of air-to-air and air-to-ground sorties. LIFT was conducted at Holloman AFB, New Mexico, where Talons modified to carry a weapon system provided realistic fighter tactics experience. These modified Talons, re-designated AT-38B, carried a gun pod or practice bombs on a centerline pylon mounted under the rear cockpit. But the added weight

By 1964 all pilot candidates in the Air Force trained in the T-41, T-38, and T-37 (pictured left to right) regardless of career path under a philosophy of generalized flight training. However this was later deemed inefficient and training became more specialized. After 1988 not all pilots were assigned to the T-38. *Don Spering A.I.R. Collection*

In 1975, the Lead In Fighter Training was started to give newly winged pilots experience with operational techniques. Some T-38As were modified to carry a centerline gun pod or practice bombs and were redesignated AT-38Bs. This AT-38B has a large travel pod mounted on its pylon. *Don Spering A.I.R. Collection*

This AT-38B is the flagship of the 49th Flight Training Squadron, Columbus Air Force Base, MS. It wears a typical Lead In Fighter Training camouflage scheme known as "Special Lizard." *Don Spering A.I.R. Collection*

and aggressive maneuvering of Lead In Fighter Training took its toll. In 1978, two armed AT-38Bs suffered wing failures forcing the Air Force to retrofit new wings with thicker skins. This work was performed by Lear Siegler between 1981 and 1986. Before the re-winging was complete, a new AT-38B structural concern emerged. The dorsal longeron—the structural backbone of the airframe that runs from the rear cockpit to the tail providing rigidity to the vertical stabilizer—was showing signs of fatigue. A new steel longeron was inserted alongside the original aluminum member to prevent stress-induced fractures. By 1985, the same issue was beginning to appear in the unarmed T-38A fleet. Since all USAF student pilots flew the T-38, a life-extension program to strengthen the fleet was essential. Officially named "Pacer Classic," the work was performed by Lear Siegler at Randolph AFB at a cost of $500,000 per aircraft (in 1988 dollars). The program was expanded to "Pacer Classic I" in 1990 to replace cracking magnesium flight control components and further expanded in 1991 to replace wheels and brakes. In 1993, upgrades continued under "Pacer Classic II," which included improved electrical wiring, and installation of bird resistant windshields and new canopies.

This AT-38B in the "Purple Grape" camouflage scheme is attached to Holloman Air Force Base, NM, where Lead In Fighter Training was originated. *Don Spering A.I.R. Collection*

By the early 1990s, many T-38s had been in service for more than thirty years and required repainting. A number of color schemes evolved as seen in this photograph. The two Talons in the foreground, used for B-2 bomber flight proficiency, wear an overall gunship gray scheme. The aircraft in the center still wears its original ATC high visibility scheme. The two T-38s in the background, used for F-117 training support, are painted gloss black. *Craig Kaston Collection*

The most ambitious improvement, however, was the Avionics Upgrade Program (AUP), which was started in 1996. This program was designed to modernize instrumentation and add features found on modern tactical aircraft. Installation of a head-up-display (HUD), hands-on throttle-and-stick (HOTAS) controls, liquid crystal displays, embedded GPS inertial navigation, and numerous other modernizations made the upgraded T-38 cockpit resemble the digital cockpit of an advanced fighter/bomber. Meanwhile a comprehensive Wing Life Improvement Program started in 1997 resulted in a redesigned wing built with modern fatigue resistant materials that was expected to double the life of the original wing. Also, General Electric received a $600 million contract to improve the compressor, turbine, afterburner, and exhaust nozzles of the J85-GE-5 turbojet. The result was an upgraded airplane that was reintroduced into service as the T-38C with a service life extended beyond 2020.

T-38 useful life was further extended by a fundamental change in training philosophy. From the late 1950s until the early 1990s all Air Force pilots, regardless of assignment,

This is a rare gray scheme on a Talon from Holloman Air Force Base assigned to R&D test at the White Sands Missile Range. *Craig Kaston Collection*

A T-38A attached to the 25th Flight Training Squadron at Vance Air Force Base, OK has been repainted in the new "Orca" scheme which is being applied to up-graded T-38Cs. *DACO Publications*

The gloss gray scheme on this T-38A from the 509th FTS at Whiteman Air Force Base highlights the Talon's elegant lines. In more than fifty years of service the Talon has received structural, avionics, and engine modifications but its fundamental shape has never been modified for aerodynamic reasons. *SrA Holston, US Air Force Photograph*

trained in the same aircraft (T-37s and T-38s) under the same syllabus. This practice, known as "Generalized Training," was an outgrowth of the All-Jet strategy designed to accelerate jet pilot training. The goal was to breed pilots competent to fly anything in the Air Force inventory. In practice, it became apparent that Generalized Training was a flawed concept. Using only T-37s and T-38s to train all students consumed useful life at a prodigious rate. Equally troubling was the realization that students assigned to transport or tanker aircraft didn't need the aerobatic or formation skills taught in the T-37/T-38 syllabi. In 1988, Congress mandated that the Air Force develop a plan to achieve a more cost-effective means of providing pilot training. The Air Force re-examined its training philosophy and conceded that: "Specialized Undergraduate Pilot Training (SUPT) provides the highest quality graduate for the lowest expenditures in procurement, operations, and support."[18] In the early 1990s, the Air Force acquired a fleet of 180 off-the-shelf Beechcraft Jayhawk business jets to provide more appropriate training for tanker and transport students. Reese AFB, was the first base to receive T-1 Jayhawks where the first specialized class, 93-12, began on July 20, 1992.[19] Other changes in Undergraduate Pilot Training included the "One Base—One Wing" concept to provide a complete undergraduate pilot curriculum at each training base so that students wouldn't be shuffled around the country. By 1995, Lead In Fighter Training,

As T-38A Talons are converted to the new T-38C standard the cockpits receive an avionics upgrade program. The new cockpits contain digital instrumentation found in modern fighters like the large multi-function display in the center of the instrument panel. *DACO Publications*

The forward cockpit of an older Talon shows the analog gauges of the T-38A instrument panel. *DACO Publications*

A top view of A Talon undergoing maintenance shows the area rule or "wasp waist" of the fuselage. This aerodynamic feature was common among supersonic aircraft of the 1950s. *SrA Holston, US Air Force Photograph*

The T-38C employs an improved J85 with a new compressor, turbine, and afterburner. It can be recognized by the new ejector exhaust nozzle. *DACO Publications*

which had been conducted exclusively at Holloman, was dispersed to Columbus, Laughlin, Sheppard, Randolph, Reese, and Vance. The training became known as Introduction to Fighter Fundamentals, which evolved into a six-week course, spread over sixteen to twenty missions. The new weaponized Talons are designated AT-38Cs and for the first time in thirty years the universal experience of T-38 training for all Air Force pilots has ended. Now only some pilots fly the trainer affectionately nicknamed "White Rocket." [20]

T-38 Tales

Douglas Barbier, a former T-38 instructor pilot at Williams AFB, with over 1,200 hours in the Talon, recalls his experiences in one of the most important training airplanes in history:

I last flew the T-38 in 1978, before the jets were modified to glass cockpits and visual simulators were just coming on line. In my tactical flying career, which included 1,250 hours of flying the F-4, I spent maybe one hour supersonic and most of that was on maintenance test flights which required a max speed check, so the fact that the T-38 was only marginally supersonic really wasn't a factor. It had the afterburners and performance equal to or better than the early Century Series—with climb, descent, maneuverability and landing speeds to match. On a no flap final approach, it was zipping along at about the same speed as an F-104 or an F-106.

By the time students reached the T-38, they knew how to fly, and had had an intro to formation, etc. The biggest challenge was to get the hand-eye coordination and more importantly, to get the brain going fast enough to stay ahead of the airplane. We lost most students to being unable to solo—and that from being unable to land safely. The T-37 was like a horse and buggy—a jet powered Cessna 172. The T-38 was like driving a Ferrari with your foot to the floor—everything happened A LOT FASTER and you couldn't just keep up with the jet, you had to be ten miles in front of it because when something happened, there wasn't time to stop and think. When you are moving ten miles per minute, taking thirty seconds to think is putting yourself five miles downstream with no clue—and now you are well behind the jet—which is continuing to race along with you falling farther and farther behind.

It was a brilliantly basic joy to fly—it had a higher roll rate than most Century Series aircraft and as long as you honored the corners of the flight envelope it was very forgiving. The biggest threat was getting behind the power curve—low and slow. Northrop reduced the stabilator authority so that you could not really stall the jet, but you could get it to the point where the induced drag exceeded the thrust available from the engines. In fact, one of the demos we did was to go to altitude, configure the jet with gear and flaps, and let it slow down while trying to maintain level flight. Eventually you reached full aft stick—the jet wouldn't stall in the classic sense, but it would behave like a falling leaf with the wings rocking back and forth, descending with the vertical velocity indicator pegged at over 10,000 feet per minute down. You could go full afterburner and it did not matter. The only way to recover was to unload—

Doug Barbier in December 1974 while still a T-38 student at Williams AFB. Flying was cancelled on that day because of the dense cloud layer that posed an icing threat. The J85 engines were very intolerant of ice. *Doug Barbier Collection*

reduce back-pressure on the stick—and dump the nose to reduce the drag and get the thing flying again. When you got into a situation like that close to the ground—a heavyweight single engine approach was where you were most likely to see it—it was almost impossible to force yourself to push the stick forward and point the airplane towards the ground. The instinctive reaction is to pull back—which only makes the situation worse. If you did that, the jet would most likely roll on its back and land inverted. If you pushed forward, you would probably ruin the jet, but at least you would crash upright and survive. The key was to recognize the situation in time to go full afterburner, relaxing the back-pressure while still having enough altitude to get a hard touch and go in the worst case. That was one of the hardest parts of being an IP in the jet—knowing how long you could let a student go before taking control. Things happened quickly down low and you couldn't always accurately anticipate what the student was going to do. Most landing accidents happened right before the student was supposed to solo, where the IP ended up letting him go too far while trying to see if he or she would recognize the situation and correct in time. The low and slow, high induced drag problem caused a great many accidents—the infamous F-100 "Sabre Dance" was a perfect example of this.

In addition to getting your brain up to speed, another real difficulty was learning to fly the jet in formation. Everyone instinctively thinks of "up and down" in terms of the earth. In formation that is no longer true. "Up and down" is all relative to your leader and if he is inverted, "down" means going farther away from the earth—i.e. "up." That is not instinctive and it was not unusual to have several hairy moments in close formation while students tried to understand that. The other key was to not have a death grip on the control stick. As sensitive as the jet was, you could not think in terms of "moving" the stick. It was how much pressure you needed to get the jet to do what you wanted. THINK it, not move it. And of course, when a student got stressed, the instinctive reaction was to grab the stick harder—the dreaded "death grip." That was time for the IP to take the jet for a little, have the student relax, wiggle his fingers, etc. Then I would have them take the stick using only their thumb and index finger. Anything more was too much—even in 5 G wing work.

In the late 1970s, students started with a month of academics, egress training and simulator before getting in the jet. For the T-38 phase, Supersonic Aerodynamics was one of the bigger courses in academics. The simulators let the students practice normal procedures like starting the engines, going through the checklists and learning to fly on instruments—which also gave them a feel for how fast things were going to happen in the jet. Of course endless hours of emergency procedures training was emphasized. "Your left generator just failed, or your right engine just failed. What still works? What doesn't? What checklist are you going to do first?" And of course, the mantra "Fly the jet, analyze the situation and take proper corrective action" was constantly drilled with the unstated caveat that if you didn't have time to do that, it was time to either eject or die. Even with all of that, the first ride was a thrill. It was called the "Boom Ride" and was an unrestricted full afterburner climb to 45,000 feet, followed by a supersonic speed run—usually out to Mach 1.1 or 1.2 (which was about

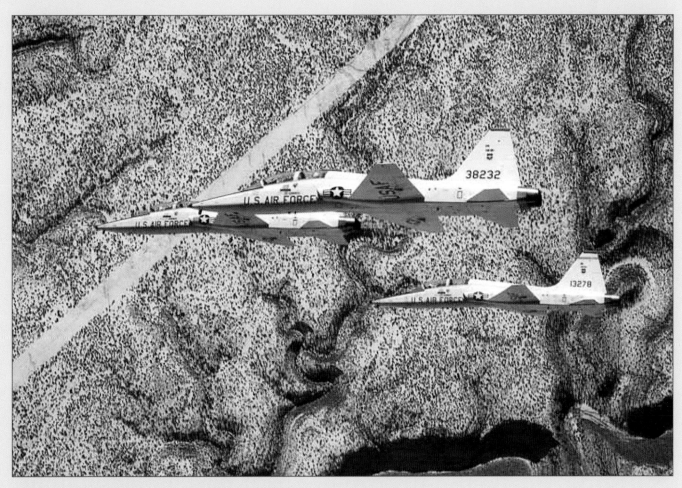

A tight four-ship formation flown over the Mogollon Rim near Williams AFB. The only student on this flight was in the number 2 position who was working up to a four-ship solo flight which is required for graduation. *Doug Barbier Collection*

This shot was taken from a rare three-ship formation. Doug Barbier recalls, "We were high and slightly 'behind the line' to get some space from the other two T-38s. I cannot remember why we had only three jets … either somebody aborted out of the four-ship or it was another IP [instructor pilot] proficiency ride." *Doug Barbier Collection*

This shot of 10422 was taken in April 1978. Doug Barbier remarks, "Undoubtedly another IP proficiency ride as I never carried the camera while I was instructing a student. The colored bands near the tip of the vertical fin indicated which maintenance flight the jets were assigned to—Echo through India were the T-38 flights, if I remember properly after all of these years." *Doug Barbier Collection*

Another shot of 10422 in the lead of a four-ship, "…on another IP proficiency flight," recalls Barbier, "you can tell the back seaters (IP seats) are flying because of where the helmets are pointed—the guys in the back seat are boresighted on the leader while the front seaters are looking any which way. *Doug Barbier Collection*

as fast as it wanted to go), followed by a local area orientation, pointing out landmarks on the ground so you could stay in your assigned working area and a normal recovery to an instrument landing approach, touch and go and then an entry to the overhead traffic pattern—all the while pointing out landmarks to use for reference. The IP made the takeoff from the back seat because the student was never going to get the landing gear retracted in time to avoid over speeding it—never having been exposed to staying in full afterburner and seeing the incredible rate of acceleration. Generally speaking, you had made the departure turn at 2DME, contacted departure control, got handed over to Albuquerque Center, passed 10,000 feet, and accelerated to 0.9 Mach before the student was mentally at the end of the runway. The jet would be level at 45,000 feet before the student had mentally made it to 10,000 feet. The early non-visual simulators just did not prepare you for the visual sense of speed, the chatter on the radio, or the G forces. All of that had to be learned in the jet.

A T-38 on short final at 155 knots for a touch and go landing. The landing phase is the most difficult part of T-38 training and the largest cause of washout. Many students who performed well in the T-37 cannot master the T-38's landing characteristics in the required amount of time. *Doug Barbier Collection*

The early part of flight training was a mixture of instrument and contact—either flying in the back seat under the instrument hood or in the front seat learning aerobatics and traffic patterns and landings. Once the student soloed, the instrument training turned into navigation (or cross-country) flights and 2-ship formations with the occasional solo flight to practice aerobatics and patterns. One weekend was spent on a minimum four-leg cross country flight to learn flight planning, practice getting out in the "real world" and see different locations. Usually at least one or two "out and back" missions were flown to fairly nearby fields in order to practice instrument procedures and strange field approaches. Later in the syllabus one or two weeks was spent night flying with at least one dual instructional mission, one night solo flight, one night solo "round robin" navigation sortie and then a dual 2-ship formation mission and a night solo formation flight. A fair amount of time was spent in 2-ship formation and the final part of the program was 4-ship formation. And of course there were the check rides—the contact check, the instrument check and the 2-ship formation check.

One vice the T-38 did have was its inability to tolerate ANY icing—even to whisper "frost" to it was to have the engines quit. That meant at Willy in Arizona, you never were allowed to fly into a cloud—either you had the stratus in the winter—which meant ice, or you had the towering cumulus—which meant thunderstorms in the summer. Either way, it was unwise, even trying to cruise in cirrus at altitude was not smart. The first time I ever actually flew in real weather was at Randolph AFB, Texas when I was going through the T-38 Instructor Upgrade program. I went out with another rated "student" on a typically hot and humid overcast day and flew an hour and a half of actual weather approaches to minimums at Kelly AFB. That was the first time I really felt like I was a pilot.

A solo student holds the correct attitude at 130 knots. Barbier describes the technique, "power in idle as you come up to the overrun and then it was slowly bringing in back pressure to reduce the decent rate to zero and bleed off airspeed to 130 simultaneously with the wheels touching down (and if you did it well, you should barely feel them start to roll)." *Doug Barbier Collection*

My experience with pilot training and the T-38 was unique in several ways. Every nine months or so, the airplane did its utmost best, if not to kill me, then at least to get my serious and undivided attention. The first incident came in the middle of the night when some of those "hours of boredom" became "instants of terror."

Part of the training syllabus was a night solo round-robin flight. From Williams AFB, southeast of Phoenix AZ, we took off, did an instrument departure that was basically a climbing 270-degree turn and headed west to Yuma AZ, then over to Blythe, CA, up to Prescott AZ and back to Phoenix before heading to our initial approach fix and shooting the instrument penetration and approach back to Willy. It was basically a confidence builder for the student pilots and another chance to get some night landings in. Half the class would do it on the first night and the second half the second night. On the first night I flew it solo and while en route to Yuma, the guard (emergency) channel on the radio came alive—that night an F-111 from Nellis had a mid-air collision with a twin Cessna, thinking it was his aerial refueling tanker. While I cruised along, I listened to the other F-111 calling about fireballs on the ground and trying to mark the location for ATC. Other than that rather unnerving reminder that you had better pay attention to what was going on around you, the flight was utterly routine. The following night I had to go do it all over again, but this time in the back seat as an instrument sortie with an instructor. They didn't trust a sky full of students to be out there without an instructor around somewhere, so there were three jets with instructors in the air. An instructor was in the first, middle and last jet to take off. That gave Air Traffic Control (ATC) an instructor to give advice or chase the problem ship in the event of an emergency. And since there was no way they were going to waste a sortie, those instructors went up with a student on an instrument training ride. In my case, we were the middle "control ship."

After takeoff, I duly pulled the instrument hood over my head as the gear came up and droned around the route again. Somewhere in the middle of the circuit, ATC called us to relay that the tail end Charlie (the last jet) had ground aborted due to some maintenance problem and that the squadron was asking us to conserve fuel and stay airborne until the last of the students had made it around. We climbed up to FL420 (42,000') and Albuquerque Center gave us the entire Williams High MOA (military operating area) to wander around in—which basically meant that we had the entire central eastern part of Arizona to ourselves. With the throttles pulled back to max endurance, the instructor let me come out from under the bag (instrument hood) and we drilled aimless holes in the sky while watching the flares over the Gila Bend Gunnery Range as the guys from Luke and Davis-Monthan practiced night bombing. Finally the last of the students was inbound to Phoenix and our fuel was down to the point where it was time to head home. In an attempt to get some useable training out of all of this, the IP had me go back under the bag, close my eyes and he set me up for a nose low unusual attitude recovery. The fact that he took his arms off of the canopy rails and took the stick probably saved his life; because just after he said "you have the jet" we had an explosive decompression as his (front) canopy exploded into a million pieces. Had his arms still been up on the rails, the 0.9 Mach windblast and pressurization leaving the jet would probably have ripped his arms right out of their sockets. As it was, I was under the instrument hood, trying to recover a jet that was nose low, inverted, doing nearly the speed of sound and trying to figure out why he had ejected without warning me that something was wrong. It took a second to realize that if he had ejected, I would have gone first, so after getting the jet upright and level I tore the hood back and checked to see what was in front of me. I could still see his seat and helmet, but the windblast and pressure breathing made it absolutely impossible to communicate. Since he had not shaken the stick to take the jet back, it was now my problem to solve. I pulled the throttles to idle, pointed the jet towards Willy, slowed down as much as I could, put the speed brakes out, tried to lose some altitude, and figure out what was working and what wasn't. All of the lights in the cockpit had gone to "full bright," the air conditioner went to "full hot" since it was detecting the fifty below outside air temp but the thing that bothered me was that the altimeter had frozen and was stuck with the hands at twelve o'clock. Here I was in a jet over some serious terrain, in the middle of the night and descending rapidly with no idea how high I was. Fortunately, we were nearly over San Carlos Lake at that point and I could see it reflecting in the moonlight. And as we got lower, the pressure breathing from the oxygen regulator reduced and the noise got somewhat less. After whacking at the altimeter several times, it finally broke free, spun around in a blur for what seemed like a dozen times and started working again. I leveled off at 15,000 feet, dropped the flaps, slowed as much as I could while making a beeline for Willy and for the first (and only time) in my life, called "Mayday" on the radio. I finally got Albuquerque to figure out what was going on and they gave me direct and a handoff to Willy Approach control. About that point we finally re-established communications between the IP and me. He had run his seat full down, crouched down as far as he could in his seat and waited for the windblast to go down enough to be able to move. At that point our plan was for me to fly an ILS (instrument landing approach) down to as low as I could and he would take the jet for the landing. As a student, I had never attempted a back seat landing in the jet, much less one at night.

The rest of the recovery was pretty straightforward, RAPCON (radar approach control) vectored me to a ten-mile final, I got the jet configured and flew the needles down to the point where I was starting to wonder whether I was going to end up landing it myself—we didn't have enough fuel left for a go around at that point—but just about the point where I was going to reduce power and have a go at my first back seat landing, the IP shook the stick and took the jet. Once we got back to the chocks and parked, I could finally see what had happened. The canopy rail was still in place on the jet but there was literally nothing left of the Plexiglas except a few shards still attached to the rails. We were loaded into an ambulance and hauled off to the base hospital where we promised the Flight Surgeon that if he wouldn't keep us there overnight, we would come in instantly if we had any signs of the bends from the decompression. We called home to tell our wives not to listen to any bad news about us—we were OK. We returned our helmets and parachutes to ops, did a quick debrief on the mission, and headed home. I seem to recall getting an "Excellent" on Emergency Procedures on that grade sheet.

The very next morning, another T-38 took off from Willy on a FCF (Functional Check Flight) with a jet just out of heavy maintenance. As he passed 35,000 in the afterburner climb, the pilot heard a loud "crack," looked over his shoulder and saw that his front canopy was cracked from side to side. He pulled the throttles to idle, did a split-S back to the field and maintenance went looking for what on earth was going on. It turned out that both canopies were newly installed and both from a new manufacturer—both were defective—Caveat Emptor!

As the war in South East Asia wound down, military budgets were cut drastically. Those cutbacks hit Air Training Command hard and one of the responses was a reduction in maintenance standards. Fatigue issues were beginning to make themselves felt as the T-38 fleet aged. The White Rocket had never really had any serious mechanical problems except for a rare aileron that became disconnected and randomly went full deflection. That had killed a couple of people, but then the wing tips started falling off in flight. The outboard two feet or so of the wing was a separate piece of aluminum honeycomb with skins on top and bottom. They contained the navigation lights and were held onto the main portion of the wing with a line of screws across the top and bottom. I do not recall the exact source of the problem—whether the honeycomb was starting to delaminate or whether it was simply fatigue stress that caused the skin to fail around the screws, but whatever the reason, wingtips would suddenly depart the jet while in-flight with no warning whatsoever—and usually while you were under high "G" loadings. The resulting snap roll into the now shorter wing was absolutely eye watering and guaranteed to bounce your helmet off of the side of the canopy. My Flight Commander lost a wingtip while he was leading a four-ship formation flight and only through pure luck or divine intervention, was no one killed. They were in echelon formation doing wing work and the wingtip on the side opposite the rest of the jets came off so he snap rolled away from the flight. If it had been the inner one, eight pilots would have died instantly.

My turn came when I was instructing a student who was on an Advanced Contact ride. We had been out in the MOA (military operating area) doing air work and it was time to head for home. In Arizona in the summertime, the cumulus started building over the mountains to the East of Phoenix by mid-morning. By late afternoon they were usually thunderstorms. Our mission was in the middle of the afternoon and we were going to have to go over the top of one of those big towering cumulus clouds to get back to the base. With my typical IP planning and foresight (or conniving and cunning), I had taken the jet from the student and was going to set him up for a vertical recovery. My plan was to get a good 500+ knots, while pointing at that big old cloud, do a 5 G pull to the vertical, followed by one and a half vertical rolls with a little G on the jet and give it to him to recover from the unusual nose high attitude. If he did it right, we would be over the top of the cloud and pointed pretty much straight at the recovery fix. If he did it wrong, it was going to be instantly obvious. So much for the plan— as we raced toward the cloud, I started the pull-up. Just as the G loading started, the left wingtip departed. A split second later, I was trying to stop the roll, we were twenty degrees nose low and blasting into the cloud headed down at over 500 KIAS. Not good! I caught the roll at about 135 degrees, rolled back upright and tried to pull again to get us headed away from the ground—since we were now headed right for the mountains. I knew we either had a disconnected aileron—which would mean ejecting, or we had lost a wingtip. As I pulled straight back, the jet rolled back to the left and I countered with full right aileron. That slowed the roll down so I knew we had lost a wingtip. So I unloaded, rolled about sixty degrees right and pulled again, all the while holding full right aileron. About that time we were twenty degrees nose up, climbing and we blew out of the far side of the cloud into brilliant sunshine. A couple more of the roll and pull exercises got us headed towards Willy, we declared an emergency with center and asked for someone to join up on us to see what damage we had. I could see that we were missing the left wing tip but wanted to know if any other part of the jet was damaged. Another jet eventually joined up with us—it was a dual ship with a student on his first flight in the jet. Welcome to T-38s! They said we had a few holes in the aft fuselage and fin but were otherwise no worse for wear. Then I had to do a controllability check to see if we were going to be able to land and how much extra airspeed we were going to have to hold on final. The T-38 doesn't have much wingspan to begin with and

it was now a couple of feet less than we started with. It turned out that we had to add about fifteen knots on final. I think we came down at about 185 KIAS (a little over 200 mph), and I timed the flare so that I put it on the ground just as I was running out of aileron control.

For a time, there was serious talk about taking both wingtips off of the entire fleet, which would have made an F-104 look slow on final, but in the end the FAA refused to let us fly at night that way, since there would be no position lights. I left for another assignment before the whole saga ended and have no idea how they ever fixed the problem. After that, I was very careful to look very closely at all those screws on the wingtips while preflighting the jet. Sure enough, one day I was following a student around on a preflight and lo and behold, there were half a dozen screws with stress cracks radiating out on the left wingtip. I let the student finish up his preflight and asked him if he thought it was a good jet. His preflight grade went to "Unsat" (unsatisfactory) when he said "yes." I showed him the cracks, told him that the wingtip would not have survived the ride and that the preflight was his chance to check the jet to make sure it wasn't going to try to kill him, not an excuse to take a relaxing walk in the afternoon sun. The crew chief said something like, "golly, nobody has ever found them cracked before flight before." I asked if they had ever really looked. We took a spare jet.[21]

Chapter Nine Endnotes

1. *Air Training Command History*, July-December 1955, Chapter II: Summary of Flying Training, p.44.

2. Ray Wagner, *Mustang Designer Edgar Schmued and the P-51*, London and Washington; Smithsonian Press, 1990, p.195.

3. Ibid. p.196.

4. Jerry Scutts, *Modern Combat Aircraft 25: Northrop F-5/F-20*, Shepperton, Surrey, Ian Allan Ltd., 1986, p.7.

5. Department of the Air Force Headquarters United States Air Force Directorate of Requirements G.O.R. No.94 (SC 2c-1-59), May 31, 1955.

6. Robert D. Archer, "Northrop N-156F Freedom Fighter," *Flight*, January 8, 1960, p. 43.

7. Program Progress Report T-38 Support System For Period December 15, 1958 to January 15, 1959, p.1.

8. Richard A. Leyes II and William A. Fleming, *The History Of North American Small Gas Turbine Aircraft Engines*, Reston, Virginia: American Institute of Aeronautics and Astronautics, Inc., 1999, pp.267-271.

9. Steve Pace, "Northrop And The Light-Heavyweight Legend," *Wings*, August 1989, p.16.

10. Col. Larry G. Van Pelt, "The Evolution Of Flight Test Concepts" (History Office Air Force Flight Test Center, June 1982), p.15.

11. Ibid. p.7.

12. Ibid. pp.15-17.

13. Fred Anderson, *Northrop An Aeronautical History*, Century City, CA. Northrop Corporation: 1976, p.181.

14. *YT-38 Category I Flight Test*, Charles C. Crawford Jr. and Swart H. Nelson, January 1960, p.22.

15. *T-38 Spin Evaluation*, William A. Lusby, Jr., Swart H. Nelson, and Norris J. Hanks, August 1961, p.iii.

16. *T-38A Category II Performance Test*, Lawrence F. McNamar, Henry C. Gordon, November 1963, p.9.

17. Don Logan, *Northrop's T-38 Talon, A Pictorial History*, Atglen, PA, Schiffer Publishing Ltd., 1995, p.9.

18. Michael D. Hays, *The Training of Military Pilots: Men, Machines, And Methods.* Alabama, Air University Maxwell Air Force Base: June 2002, p.23.

19. Robert F. Dorr, "The White Rocket," Combat Aircraft Monthly, July 2013, p.84.

20. Jamie Hunter, "Talon Turns 50," *Combat Aircraft Monthly*, January 2010, p.28.

21. Douglas R. Barbier e-mail correspondence to Mark A. Frankel, March 16, 2014.

Chapter Ten
NEW TRAINER PROGRAMS

Trainers are characteristically durable aircraft with reliable systems and well-proven flight characteristics. They don't require advanced technology in their structure or systems for combat survivability or mission effectiveness. While they receive hard use from inexperienced students and accumulate flight time at an accelerated rate, the airframes, engines, and systems are regularly overhauled to keep the airplanes safe and mechanically reliable. Avionics updates are accomplished periodically although budget constraints sometimes dictate the pace of change. As a result, a trainer

from the 1950s could still be in service more than sixty years later. However, the time eventually comes when a trainer fleet has to be replaced because it is too small; increasingly uneconomical to operate, maintain or overhaul; or lacks the avionics and cockpit instrumentation to support a service's training requirement. Surprisingly, even so-called non-developmental trainer procurements proved to be almost as difficult to bring to fruition as all-new trainer developments. One all-new trainer program was even canceled, although not for technical reasons.

North American had a long tradition of providing trainers to the USAF as depicted in this artist's concept of them flying in formation with its proposed Next Generation Trainer. *Darold Cummings*

A. VTX-TS

The Navy's VTXTS[1] program was initiated in 1978 to provide a training system to replace both the aging T-2Cs (intermediate) and TA-4Js (advanced) with one airplane type. One of the challenges was that it had to be carrier-capable. Based on the age and remaining service life of its existing trainers, the Navy wanted to have the system in service by 1988. The Navy contracted with four companies in March 1978 for VTXTS studies: Douglas Aircraft Company, Northrop Corporation, Vought Corporation, and General Dynamics.

The Navy also considered existing jet trainers from other countries. It awarded British Aerospace (BAe) a contract in 1979 to define the modifications required to its Hawk jet trainer to make it carrier compatible. Similarly, Dassault/Dornier received one for their Alpha Jet.

The inclusion of the phrase "training system" in the title of the program was significant. Instead of the government functioning as a general contractor and separately purchasing all the various elements of a training program, the successful bidder was to provide both an airplane and a complete, turnkey, ground-based training system, both hardware (cockpit procedure trainers and flight simulators) and software (manuals, lectures, computer-assisted instruction, training management system). What the Navy wanted to buy from an airplane manufacturer was not just an airplane, but also a system that produced a competent pilot at affordable cost.

These T-2C and TA-4J fuselage hulks were photographed at NAS Meridian, Mississippi on October 8, 1999. Although a Navy Repair and Rework Facility could probably have restored them to flightworthiness, by then the Buckeye and the Skyhawk had both been replaced by the T-45A. *John Bennett Photo*

Simulators in particular had proved to be of value, increasing safety and reducing the cost of training, but heretofore their development and delivery had not generally been bundled with the procurement of the airplane itself.

The performance requirements were not particularly challenging:

1. Maximum speed at 30,000 feet: more than 0.8 Mach
2. Critical field length: less than 8,000 feet
3. Sustained Load Factor at 15,000 feet: more than 3.0 g
4. Maximum sink off bow on 90° day: less than five feet
5. Approach speed: 105 knots

Two engines were not a requirement, but if a twin was proposed, the one-engine-inoperative rate of climb on a hot day with 60% of internal fuel was to be more than 500 fpm and axial acceleration, 0.065 g on two engines, 0.0152 g single engine.

The design requirements included carrier catapult and arrested landing capability. This included the nose-tow-launch nose landing gear with dual wheels, good handling qualities and forward visibility at approach speed, structure and landing gear designed for high-sink-rate landings, a tailhook, etc. Low operating costs were to be a significant evaluation metric. Low fuel consumption and maintenance man-hours per flight hour were demanded along with high reliability and availability. In order to better prepare student pilots for the airplanes that they would be flying in the fleet, state-of-the art head-up and multi-function "glass" displays were required.[2]

The request for proposal was finally released to industry in March 1981. After separately accomplishing design studies for the Navy of all-new airplanes, Northrop and Vought (N-350/351 and V-532 respectively) subsequently teamed for the program. However, in the end they elected not to submit a proposal, probably in the belief that the Navy would not be willing to fund development of a new airplane for this training requirement.

North American, now Rockwell International, did not receive a study contract but elected to not only bid, but to propose both an upgrade of the existing T-2C, identified by Rockwell as the T-2X, as well an all-new design that was also powered by two engines.

Artificial Horizon Instrument

Electromechanical

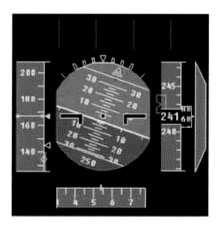

"Glass"

Multi-Function

The substitution of cathode ray tube and then LED screens for the electromechanical cockpit instruments had begun in the 1970s. The first "glass" cockpit instruments were not reconfigurable but presented more information in the same panel space. These were subsequently developed into multifunction displays that could be modified by the pilot using switches on the bezel to suit his needs for data. *Tommy H. Thomason*

After doing individual studies, Northrop, which did not have carrier-based airplane experience, and Vought, which built the first airplane to land on a US Navy aircraft carrier, teamed for a VXTXS proposal. *Bill Spidle Collection*

The T-2X, an upgraded T-2C—one of the trainers being replaced, was one of two North American VTXTS proposals. Except for the substitution of a dual-wheel nose landing gear, all of the improvements were internal like uprated engines. *Darold Cummings*

North American also proposed an all-new twin-engine design for the Navy's VTXTS competition. The wings were slightly swept; reductions in the size of electronics and engines resulted in the elimination of the prominent belly of the T-2 that had previously housed them. *Darold Cummings*

Beech and Grumman did not receive design study contracts either but they teamed to propose an all-new twin-engine design, the D-730. Beech brought a long-standing reputation for training airplanes to the partnership and Grumman, the bona fides for the all-important carrier compatibility. Link (part of the Singer Company) was a team member for the simulator requirement.

Like North American, McDonnell Douglas submitted proposals for an all-new airplane and one modified from an existing jet trainer. Its Douglas division submitted its twin-engine D-7000 while St. Louis was the US lead contractor for the modified BAe Hawk proposal. The Hawk was originally developed by Hawker Siddeley as a company-funded jet trainer and had first flown in 1974. It was a single-engine airplane powered by the Rolls-Royce/Turbomeca Adour engine.

Lockheed California acted as the US lead for the modified Dassault/Dornier Alpha Jet. It was the result of collaboration between Dassault-Breguet of France and Dornier of Germany to develop a jet trainer and light attack airplane to be used by the air forces of both countries. It first flew in 1973. It was a twin-engine airplane powered by Snecma LARZAC 04 turbofans.

There were other companies interested in the new program as well that did not propose formally. Alenia Aermacchi reportedly accomplished design studies of its single-engine MB-339 with US Advanced Technology Systems. General Dynamics considered submitting a proposal of its Model 603E with American Airlines providing the training system expertise. Gulfstream contemplated the proposal of a tandem-seat, twin-engine derivative of its "Peregrine" single-engine executive jet.

After the Navy reviewed the proposals, the selected finalists in the competition were the modifications of the Alpha Jet and the Hawk that were in production.

Grumman, another long-standing supplier of US Navy carrier-based airplanes, and Beech, equally well known for its Navy and Air Force trainers, teamed to propose the D-730. *Grumman History Center*

The Douglas division of McDonnell Douglas proposed its D-7000 for the VTXTS program. Along with North American, it was an incumbent supplier for the airplanes being used by the Navy training command. *Tommy H. Thomason Collection*

The Dassault/Dornier Alpha Jet was aggressively promoted by Lockheed-California for the VTXTS program. It was on the short list but lost to the McDonnell proposal of a modified British Aerospace Hawk. *Tony Buttler Collection*

Alpha Jet: The French began using the twin-engine Alpha Jet for pilot training in 1979 as did Belgium. The Germans, who relied on the US for pilot training, procured it for light attack missions and advanced weapons training. It was also on order by, if not yet in service with, five other countries at the time of proposal. For the VTXTS program, Lockheed was to develop and manufacture a carrier-capable US variant under license. Teledyne CAE would produce the engine under license from Snecma. Logicon and its subcontractors would provide the ground-based training elements. Since an existing design was the basis for its proposal, Lockheed projected an Initial Operational Capability in 1986, well before the Navy's need date.

Modifications required included:

1. New nose landing gear with dual wheels and launch bar for the nose-tow launch system.
2. Modified and reinforced main landing gear.
3. Carrier-type arresting hook.
4. Structural modifications for arrested landing and catapult takeoff.
5. US Navy dictated avionics and instruments.

Lockheed conducted a demonstration tour of most of the Navy's training bases with an Alpha Jet in September 1980 beginning with a three-day visit to Andrews AFB, Maryland to brief government officials, key military officers, and representatives of the media. The support aircraft was a Lockheed L-1011 TriStar. Its forward cabin was utilized as a briefing room.

A nose-tow launch system replaced the cumbersome straps and separate holdback attachment previously used for catapult launches beginning in the early 1960s. It required a dual-wheel nose landing gear equipped with a launch bar and a holdback attachment point. The mounting structure for the nose gear also had to withstand the resulting loads and properly transfer them into the airframe. *Tommy H. Thomason Collection*

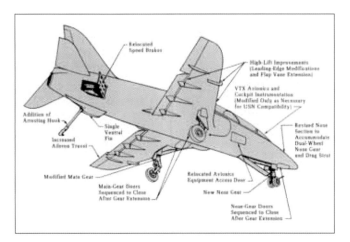

As would be expected, significant changes were needed to convert an airplane for carrier-based operation. *Tony Buttler Collection*

Hawk: Like the Alpha Jet, the Hawk was in production and proven as a trainer. The two were in head-to-head competition for trainer and light attack sales around the world. Deliveries to the Royal Air Force began in late 1976, the same year that an export version with weapons delivery capability flew. The Sperry Aerospace was to provide the ground-based portion of the training system as a subcontractor to Douglas, which would be the VXTXS prime contractor. (Sperry would be acquired by Honeywell in 1986.)

Configuration changes from the BAe Hawk included:

1. New dual-wheel nose gear with integral launch bar and hold back.
2. Modified main landing gear with longer stroke.
3. Wider wheelbase to accommodate the additional main landing gear stroke.
4. MLG inner doors and forward nose gear doors closed after gear extension.
5. Tailhook added with mounting serving as one ventral strake replacing the two original ones.
6. Speed brake relocated to sides of fuselage.
7. Modified instrument panel and cockpit including addition of head-up display.

In June 1981, as part of its VTXTS marketing effort, BAe conducted a tour of US training bases with a Hawk that was flown across from England. More than 100 flights were made during the tour with only one canceled due to an aircraft problem.

In November 1981, the Navy announced that the Douglas/BAe team had won the competition. It was to become known as the T-45TS, for Training System. All anticipated a relatively trouble-free development program based on the well-proven Hawk design. Unfortunately, that was not to be the case. It wasn't for haste in implementing the program. Although an initial contract was awarded to Douglas in November 1981, the next few years were taken up by refinement of the Navy's acquisition strategy to better define the program and reduce its projected cost. This included essentially forcing McDonnell Douglas to accept a firm fixed-price contract for what had been proposed as a cost-plus program.

One outcome of the program definition phase was the deferral of the advanced Electronic Flight Instrument System that had been an RFP requirement. Another was a two-phase production plan intended to recover some of the program schedule that had been lost in restructuring

A British Aerospace-owned Hawk was used for marketing demonstrations in the United States in support of the McDonnell VXTXS proposal. *Terry Panopalis Collection*

the program. This was to be accomplished by first building fifty-four T-45Bs, which were essentially off-the-shelf BAe Hawks that would not be carrier capable but would have a cockpit modified to US Navy standards. However, Congress directed in late 1983 that only carrier-capable airplanes would be procured so the T-45B "Dry Hawk" placeholder was stillborn.

McDonnell was finally awarded a full-scale engineering contract in October 1984. Fortunately, there were enough TA-4s and T-2s with enough service life remaining to accommodate the delay, although some T-2Bs had to be resurrected from Davis Monthan and TA-4Js and T-2Cs reassigned to the training command from other operating units.

The winning proposal had come from McDonnell Douglas' St. Louis division but the program was assigned to its Long Beach, California facility, where the work was needed and engineers familiar with the Navy's TA-4 trainer were available. The formal rollout was accomplished there on March 17, 1988. It included starting the airplane's engine and a short taxi.[3] First flight was accomplished from the Long Beach airport the next month.

One change to the original configuration proposed in 1981 was the addition of a fixed horizontal strake, aka SMURF (Side-Mounted Unit-horizontal-tail Root Fin). It was located on the fuselage just ahead of the leading edge of the stabilator, the all-moving horizontal stabilizer. During the flight test of the RAF T.1, BAe had determined that the downwash from the wing with the flaps down and landing gear up resulted in the stabilator stalling with full aft stick, resulting in an abrupt nose-down pitch. At the time, removing the outer section of the flap vanes between the wing cove and the flap solved the problem. This reduced the wing's maximum lift and therefore downwash. The resulting increase in stall speed was considered acceptable. The T-45, however, needed as much lift as possible to achieve the required stall speeds for carrier takeoffs and landings. The shape and location of the strake generated a vortex of high-energy airflow over the stabilator at high angles of attack that kept it from stalling, allowing the outer section of flap vanes to be reinstated.

The only major exterior change to the T-45A at the March 1988 rollout from the proposal was the addition of a fixed horizontal strake on the fuselage in front of the horizontal stabilizer. *Mark Nankivi Collection*

Cost and the confidence in the adaptability of a proven design continued to dictate program planning. For example, the number of development airplanes had been cut from four to two. The impact on the length of the flight-test program was exacerbated in late 1988 when Navy test pilots first flew the T-45A and declared it unsatisfactory from a performance and handling qualities standpoint.

The major problems were:

1. High-speed longitudinal stability.
2. Engine response and hot-day thrust.
3. Speed-brake-induced pitch up at speeds above 270 kts.
4. Lateral/directional stability on approach.
5. High approach speed,[4] lack of stall warning, and roll-off at stall.

Douglas management disputed that the company was responsible for improvements (and in some cases the need for them) but a horrific landing accident on *Lexington* (CVT-16) in October 1989 provided a vivid reminder of the necessity for the best possible low-speed handling qualities and stall warning. A VT-19 student pilot stalled his T-2C just short of the ramp. The airplane rolled inverted and crashed into the island. He was killed as were three of the deck crew and a civilian contractor.[5]

T-45A flight test began in April 1988 with BuNo 162787 shown here. Note that the rear cockpit is filled with orange-painted test instrumentation equipment. *Mark Nankivil Collection*

245

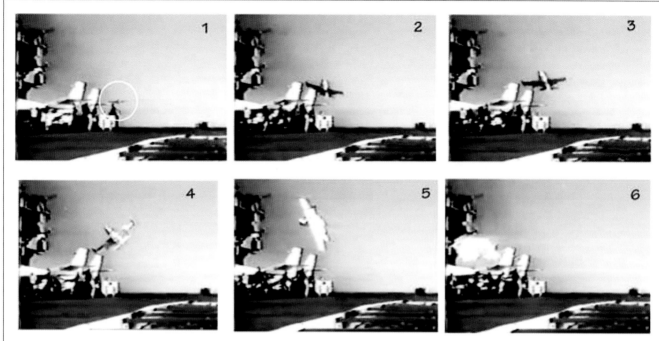

T-2C Crash on Lexington October 1989

The horrific crash of a T-2 into the island of the training carrier *Lexington* reinforced the Navy's T-45A requirement for low stall speed as well as excellent handling qualities and stall warning at approach speeds. *Tommy H. Thomason*

One of the last changes required to make the T-45A satisfactory for the Navy was the addition of leading edge slats to lower the approach speed. Simpler and lighter modifications like a cambered leading edge were evaluated first. *Mark Nankivil Collection*

In part as a result of the problems with the program, responsibility for completion of development and production (at Douglas' Palmdale facility) was moved from California to McDonnell's St. Louis, Missouri facility in 1990.

Another year of modifications and flight test evaluation resulted in the following changes to the production T-45A:

1. Full-span leading-edge slat.
2. Squared-off wing and horizontal stabilizer tips.
3. Four-inch extension on each horizontal stabilizer.
4. Six-inch taller vertical fin.
5. Higher thrust engine for hot-day wave-off and bolter performance.
6. Speed-brake pitch compensator.
7. Ventral fin.
8. Flight control system and engine control modifications.

Initial at-sea trials were finally accomplished aboard *John F. Kennedy* (CV-67) in December 1991.

After correction of the deficiencies identified by Navy evaluation flights in late 1988, the T-45A was finally evaluated at sea on *John F. Kennedy* (CV-67) in December 1991. Visible additions to the prototype include the leading edge slat, a six-inch taller and squared-off vertical fin, and the ventral fin just ahead of the tailhook attach point. *Mark Nankivil Collection*

The first T-45A to go to the Navy Training Command was delivered to VT-21 at Kingsville, Texas in December 1992. Embarrassingly, it and the next several T-45As delivered there had to undergo a modification program after arrival that required removing the wing and engine to make thirteen different structural and component location changes. (The twenty-fourth and subsequent T-45As were to be delivered from St. Louis with these changes incorporated.) VT-21 students finally began flying the T-45 in February 1994, more than three years late to the plan in place at full-scale-development award.

A colorful T-45A Goshawk from Training Air Wing 2 lands on the flight deck of the aircraft carrier USS Theodore Roosevelt (CVN 71) off the Atlantic Coast.
US Navy photo by Mass Communication Specialist 2nd Class Katie Lash

All's well that ends well, however. As delivered, the T-45 Goshawk proved its acceptability as an intermediate and advanced trainer. The advanced cockpit originally desired was introduced with the T-45C, the seventy-third production Goshawk. The T-45A's "steam gages" were replaced by two multi-function displays on both front and rear cockpit instrument panels. The addition of GPS and INS facilitated navigation. The first T-45C was delivered in December 1997, and the last of 221 in October 2009. The T-45As were converted to the T-45C configuration when they went through overhaul.

Ironically, the Air Force's next military trainer program, which resulted in an all-new design, suffered fewer development problems after a troubled start but nevertheless floundered and did not go into service.

LTJG Jon Michael Chombeau, a flight student assigned to Training Air Wing (TRAWING) 2, Squadron 21, conducts ground flight training in the T-45C visual simulator at Naval Air Station Kingsville. The T-45C simulator produces a 180-degree video in a dimensional perspective for realistic flight perception. *US Navy photo by Richard Stewart*

B. Next Generation Trainer Program

By 1980, the time had come for the Air Force to replace the aging T-37.[6] It was not only approaching the end of its 15,000 hour service life, but suffered from a litany of shortcomings:

1. Excessive fuel consumption.
2. Excessive maintenance man hours per flight hour.
3. Engine noise (two times FAR 36 limits).
4. Limited range and endurance.
5. Inadequate takeoff, climb, and altitude performance.
6. No cockpit pressurization or air conditioning.
7. Restricted crosswind takeoff and landing capability.
8. Outdated instrument displays.
9. No ice protection for the wings and tail.
10. Poor ejection seat altitude/airspeed envelope.
11. Inadequate bird-strike protection.
12. Inability to maintain level flight on one engine in the landing configuration at moderately high-density altitudes.

The Air Force issued a request for concept definition studies in February, suggesting three alternatives: a modernized T-37, an off-the-shelf trainer, and an all-new design.[7] The emphasis was to be on low life-cycle cost while meeting the performance requirements of the Air Training Command.

As with the Navy's VTXTS program, several companies were interested in a contract that was to result in 600 to 650 airplanes for the Air Force with follow-on international sales to be expected. The Air Force provided four-month study contracts in June 1980 to five of them: Cessna, Fairchild, Rockwell International, Vought, and General Dynamics.

The program was formalized in 1981 as the Next Generation Trainer (NGT). Among the requirements were pressurization, a major shortcoming of the T-37 that limited its altitude and weather-avoidance capability, and a lower life-cycle cost and a higher utilization rate than provided by the T-37. The Air Force also expressed a preference for two "podded" turbofan engines, side-by-side seating, and conventional (i.e. no major use of composites) structure.

The children of students who had learned to fly in the T-37 in the late 1950s could have learned to fly in it when the Air Force decided it was time to replace it in 1980. *US Air Force Photo*

The desire for a "podded" engine turned out to be a misleading description. What was desired was not necessarily one actually located in an externally mounted pod. The intention was to insure maintainability (readily accessible engine accessories as well as quick removal and replacement of an engine) and also allow for an upgrade with a more efficient and/or powerful engine if desired.

Unlike the Navy, the Air Force did not seem receptive to an off-the-shelf solution. In any event, the only side-by-side jet trainer in production or development at the time was the single-engine Hindustan Aeronautics Kiran Mk 2.[8] There were DoD and congressional attempts to force the Air Force to use the Navy's T-34C for primary training. The generals successfully defended their plan for a different trainer in part by arguing that the T-34C would not address all of its primary training requirements. The resulting shortfall would have had to be made up with more T-38 flight hours, resulting in a higher overall training cost and an earlier need to replace the White Rocket.

Cessna initially tried to convince the Air Force to simply reengine and update the T-37, guaranteeing it the

business. That was a non-starter, however, so its proposal was all-new design, the "T-37D" (not to be confused with the later armed AT-37D), which still bore a strong resemblance to the Tweet except for its T-tail.

Fairchild-Republic went all-out to win the program since production of its A-10 Thunderbolt II was coming to an end. It needed a new project to sustain its business and had focused on the T-37 replacement as a likely and worthwhile prospect since the late 1970s. As part of its proposal and marketing effort, in 1981 it commissioned a single-seat 62%-scale flying demonstrator (the size was arrived at by the thrust available from two readily available FAA-certificated jet engines) from the Ames Industrial Corporation to loft lines furnished by Fairchild-Republic. Detail design and flight test of the airplane were accomplished by Burt Rutan and Dick Rutan respectively at the Rutan Aircraft Factory (RAF)[9] located at Mohave, California.

The demonstrator was flown eighteen times for about twenty-one hours total flight time beginning with a first flight on September 10, 1981. Flight test included evaluation of deep stall, accelerated stall, and post-stall characteristics.

Cessna frequently proposed replacement engines and other updates to the T-37 in order to provide for future business and avoid a competition for its replacement. For the NGT competition, it chose to emphasize low risk by proposing a T-37 lookalike modernized externally with a T-tail version. *Mark Frankel*

Although spins were not accomplished, the twin-tail layout appeared to be spin resistant. Wind tunnel test predictions of stability and damping were also confirmed along with a tendency to Dutch roll at high altitude.

Rockwell had initiated a T-37 replacement project in 1975 and worked closely with the Air Training Command (ATC) headquarters at Randolph Field to define the design requirements. The result was its Near-term Optimum Value Aircraft (NOVA). Company-funded preproposal activities included the construction of a mockup demonstrating the NOVA's features and wind tunnel spin testing. Based on the early and close working relationship with ATC, Rockwell management was confident that it had the winning design.

Vought accomplished design studies and wind tunnel tests based on the VFW Eaglet, a RFB Fantrainer. The ducted fan was to be driven by two small Allison 250 turboshaft engines. However, Vought subsequently decided not to submit a proposal to the RFP issued in October 1981. Neither did General Dynamics, another of the original five primes that had received study contracts.

Although the Air Force had not provided either Gulfstream American or Ensign Aircraft with a study contract, they submitted proposals.

In its full-court press to win the NGT competition, Fairchild commissioned a sub-scale, single-seat, flying demonstrator as a risk reduction and marketing vehicle. The pilot seems oversized because the Rutan Model 73 was only 62% of the size of the proposed airplane. *Mark Nankivil Collection*

Rockwell built a full-scale mockup of its all-new design for the NGT competition, NOVA (Near-term Optimum Value). It featured engines mounted at waist level just behind the wing for easy accessibility. *Darold Cummings*

The Gulfstream American Peregrine 600 was on static display at the 1981 Paris Air Show, having just flown for the first time the month before. *Terry Panopalis*

Gulfstream American proposed the Peregrine 600, a single-engine jet that was a derivative of its Hustler 500 executive transport that was powered by a turboprop engine in the nose and a jet engine in the aft fuselage. A prototype with side-by-side seating had been flown in May 1981.

Ensign Aircraft was a small aerospace subcontractor located near Long Beach, California, that had provided engineering services to bigger companies. Its EA-12 proposal, which was powered by two Williams Research WR44 turbofan engines, emphasized advanced automated manufacturing concepts to reduce cost and provide flexibility in production rate planning.

Rockwell had a 1/6th scale spin model tested at NASA Langley in March 1982 in support of the its NGT proposal. The aft fuselage was lengthened relative to the mockup in order to provide the tail arm required for excellent stall/spin/spin recovery characteristics. NASA reportedly kept the model as a bench mark for future spin testing because it had the best spin and recovery characteristics that they had seen. *Darold Cummings*

Evaluation and Selection

The Request For Proposal (RFP) stated that the following factors would be evaluated in descending order of importance:

1. Operational utility.
2. Readiness and support.
3. Life-cycle cost.
4. Design approach.
5. Manufacturing/Program Management.

After the proposals were initially reviewed, any deficiencies were made known to the offerer, who was allowed to submit a revised proposal for consideration. After the review of those, Gulfstream and Ensign Aircraft were eliminated from the competition as not being within the competitive

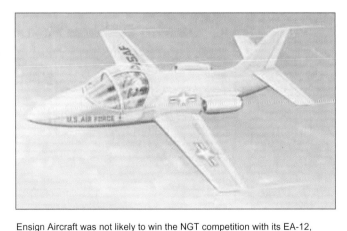

Ensign Aircraft was not likely to win the NGT competition with its EA-12, since it had no track record of aircraft design and development. *Tommy H. Thomason*

range.[10] Definitive fixed-price incentive contracts were then negotiated with each of the three remaining offerers, Cessna, Fairchild-Republic, and Rockwell. After all that, there wasn't much differentiation in the proposals from a performance, life-cycle cost, or design/manufacturing capability standpoint. Any of them was acceptable.

Other factors therefore influenced the Air Force to select Fairchild-Republic for its NGT program in July 1982, with the airplane designated the T-46. First, there was the claim of risk reduction that had been provided by Fairchild's flying demonstrator. Second, A-10 production at East Farmingdale, Long Island would be winding down in 1985 when the NGT was to begin production, both providing the requisite manpower and facilities and avoiding layoffs on Long Island.[11] By contrast, Rockwell had just had its B-1 production program reinstated and Cessna was of no industrial base importance to the Air Force.

In announcing the selection of Fairchild-Republic, the Secretary of the Air Force stated that the selection was based on:

1. Evaluation criteria established in the RFP.
2. The secretary's integrated assessment of the Fairchild proposal.
3. The terms and conditions agreed on in negotiations.
4. The Evaluation Board's Summary Evaluation Report.
5. The Advisory Council's Proposal Analysis Report, and
6. The capability of Fairchild to fulfill requirements.

Rockwell was surprised in addition to being disappointed. They believed that the Training Command favored their design and thought Fairchild's to be inferior for a small trainer: the high wing meant that landing gear loads had to be absorbed by fuselage structure, not the wing, and the H-tail had higher drag but was of no benefit. Rockwell production capacity was not a constraint but it was at the Navy plant at Columbus, which was not an Air Force concern. They considered a protest but feared that one would have an adverse effect in Congress, since Congressman Joseph P. Addabbo from a district on Long Island was the chairman of the House Appropriations Subcommittee on Defense and intent on Fairchild-Republic getting the contract.

Unimpressed by the source-selection justification and having no major government program to protect, the Senators from Kansas and the Congressman from Cessna's district asked for a General Accounting Office (GAO) review of the Air Force's evaluation and selection. The GAO report[12] did note that most probable total life-cycle cost of the Fairchild NGT was not the lowest, but it was the second lowest and only 1.5% higher than the lowest. In its opinion, the difference was more than offset by the superior characteristics of the Fairchild NGT airplane. Furthermore, there were thirty-six operational, logistical, technical, and manufacturing/management items that were established for evaluation before the proposals were received. An overall acceptability rating was given to each of the thirty-six items for each proposal. The Fairchild proposal received more exceptional ratings than those from Cessna or Rockwell.

In summary, the GAO concluded that the NGT source evaluation and selection was done in accordance with the relevant DoD and Air Force instructions and the evaluation criteria in the RFP.

The Air Force ordered two T-46 prototypes along with two structural-durability-test airframes. Fairchild was projecting a first flight in 1984. The initial contract included production options for up to sixty-five aircraft, since production orders were to be placed even before first flight so that pilot training in the T-46 could begin in early 1988.

The Air Force also awarded the Garrett Turbine Engine Company a contract for the development and initial production of its F109 engine that would power the T-46.

Although low risk, except possibly for the engine, the T-46 was expected to provide a significant improvement in the training role compared to the T-37. It was pressurized so it could be flown at much higher altitudes. It was to have much greater range. Those two features meant that, unlike the T-37, it didn't have to fly around en route weather and if weather at the intended landing field was a problem after a 1.5-hour training mission, it could divert 300 miles as opposed to the 100-mile diversion capability of the T-37.

The twin-engine climb rate was twice that of the T-37's and at 25,000 feet, which was above the usual operating altitude for the T-37, it could sustain a 2.5 G turn. On a hot day from a high-altitude airfield, the climb gradient on one engine was predicted to be 3.7%. The student and instructor would be sitting on Weber-built Aces II zero-zero ejection seats. The frameless windscreen was stressed for a four pound bird strike at 370 knots.

The T-46 design emphasized simplicity within the limits of the Air Force requirement. The only powered flight control was the rudder to insure good spin recovery characteristics as well as crosswind landing capability up to 30 kts. It also provided for stability augmentation if needed to avoid Dutch rolling at altitude that had been indicated by subscale demonstrator flight test. The low-mounted Garrett engines were readily removable among other maintenance features.

Reflectone was to update the existing T-37 simulators with T-46 cockpits and new computers, with the first one to be available even before the new trainer was on the flight line to begin checkout of T-46 flight instructors.

In accordance with the plan for flight training to

Fairchild Republic was all but desperate to replace the military business it had enjoyed with its A-10, even if the T-46A, here represented by the full-scale mockup, was clearly a smaller and less imposing product.
John Sandford Collection

commence in January 1988, ten production airplanes and associated support equipment and data were ordered in November 1984, well before first flight of a prototype, with the first to be delivered in April 1986. It was, in short, a well-planned procurement of a low-risk airplane tailored for the Air Force training requirement. Unfortunately, Fairchild had been overly optimistic about its weight and cost, in addition to initially bungling the program's implementation.

By 1984, it was already apparent that the T-46 was overweight and more expensive than estimated. According to Darold Cummings, who was the NOVA Chief Engineer, Fairchild representatives visited Rockwell that year, asking for an independent review of the design. The major weight and cost driver proved to be the use of a large five-axis machined bulkhead that carried pressurization, landing gear, and wing loads and provided a frame around the inlet. It couldn't be simplified without increasing weight or a major change to the configuration.

Fairchild staged a formal rollout of the first flight test airplane on February 11, 1985, which was consistent with the scheduled first flight date that was expected to occur by early May. On close inspection, however, the airplane was obviously incomplete and in no way ready for the extensive ground checkout required prior to first flight.

To begin with, it was missing many internal components. Some of the exterior skin consisted of fiberglass panels in place of metal parts. The result was a rarely invoked Contractor Operations Review (COR) accomplished by the Air Force Contract Management Division of Fairchild's management systems and ability to complete the T-46 contract. Their conclusions from their on-site evaluation in June 1985 were scathing, totaling 279 findings in the eight functional areas reviewed. In August, the Air Force began withholding 50% of Fairchild's progress payments.

Fairchild responded with a list of underlying causes and corrective action plans for each of the findings. A vice president was appointed to accomplish the action plans. He reported directly to the division president and worked directly with the Air Force commander who headed the procurement office at Farmingdale.

The major corrective actions were:

1. Appointment in July 1985 of a new division president, John Sandford, with experience in running aerospace companies.
2. The sale of $200 million of corporate assets to provide funds for the program.
3. An increase of $46 million in its investment in the T-46 program.

Normally a cause for celebration, the roll out of the T-46A became a *cause célèbre* when it became known that it was not even close to complete from a functional checkout standpoint and some of the exterior was not airworthy. *John Sandford Collection*

4. Assigned additional personnel to the program.
5. Improved communication from top management to middle management.
6. Provided additional skills and supervisory training to program personnel.
7. Increased emphasis on quality, safety, and schedule rather than on cost only.
8. Strengthened the quality function.

In September 1985, in recognition of Fairchild's "substantial progress" in correcting the deficiencies, the Air Force restored half of the withheld progress payments.

The T-46 empty weight was also significantly greater than Fairchild's original proposal of 4,725 lbs.[13] At first flight, the prototype's empty weight was reportedly more than the proposed takeoff weight of 6,460 lbs (it was not a big airplane). This is a possibility. The airplane was certainly overweight: a subsequent GAO report stated that the production T-46 was 900 lbs heavier than the Fairchild proposal and that was after planned changes and redesign for weight reduction. For example, the prototypes had metal ailerons that were twice as heavy as the production

ailerons constructed using Kevlar skins over Nomex honeycomb. Moreover, the prototypes were burdened by flight test instrumentation. So the empty weight was probably in the vicinity of 6,000 lbs.

Ironically, the biggest risk in the program would likely have been considered to be the engine. It wasn't quite all new, but it was a significant modification of an existing Garrett Research turboprop engine, the TPE33. Its propeller and associated gearbox were to be replaced with a new low-bypass fan module, thereby creating a turbofan engine. The result was a jet engine with relatively low fuel consumption, a significant portion of life-cycle cost. As it happened, Garrett successfully completed initial accelerated-service testing before the first engine deliveries to Fairchild in January 1985; all that was required for flight test was a much less challenging qualification test run. The engines were first run in the T-46A prototype in August 1985.

The first flight by Fairchild-Republic test pilot Jim Martinez finally occurred at Edwards Air Force Base on October 15, 1985, six months behind the original contract schedule. As is customary—unless the pilot had to make an emergency landing or worse—it was reported to have been trouble free.[14] Nevertheless, disappointing flight test results were quick to be reported by those who had reason to wish ill on the program. The drag was said to be 50% higher than expected so that the predicted maximum-level flight speed supposedly could only be achieved in a forty-degree dive and altitude could not be maintained with one engine shut down and the landing gear down. These were very unexpected results given the risk reduction supposedly furnished by the subscale demonstrator but its primary purpose had been to provide data on handling qualities and stability and control, not performance.

Former Fairchild-Republic employees who may or may not have had been closely involved in the program claim that the reports of weight and performance were exaggerated and shortfalls remediable.[15] The drag problem was caused in part by an inlet-lip redesign introduced after a scale-model wind-tunnel test of the inlet indicated unsatisfactory airflow distortion at the front of the engine compressor at high angles of sideslip and angle of attack, i.e. during spins. (A fan-type engine was more susceptible to compressor stalling than the less fuel-efficient axial-flow engines.) The change, however, resulted in excessive inlet spillage drag in cruise flight.

The resulting performance shortfall was exacerbated by the overweight condition of the prototypes and the need to install flight test instrumentation, which could not be significantly offset. Since it was a trainer, mission equipment or external stores represented a negligible portion of the useful load. Therefore, the only way to reduce the gross weight of an instrumented airplane to that of the production airplane was to fly it solo, a reduction of about 200 lbs. (more if the ejection seat was not installed) or not completely fill the fuel tanks that had a capacity of about 1,300 lbs.

Fairchild had no reason to count on any goodwill with the Air Force System Program Office (SPO) due to the attempt to hide a behind-schedule status with a premature rollout, the unsatisfactory COR, and poor cost control. In addition to the weight and performance shortfalls, there were other smaller setbacks like a failed bird-strike test or an ill-conceived aileron-balance-weight experiment that causing an in-flight flutter incident.

On a happier day at Edwards AFB in late 1985, Jim Martinez, Fairchild Republic's Chief Test Pilot and Director of Flight Operations, walked out to the T-46A for a flight test. *John Sandford Collection*

T-46A flight test was relatively trouble-free for a new airplane, but its performance relative to the proposal was disappointing. Nevertheless, it was deemed adequate for the training requirement by both the Air Force and the General Accounting Office. *John Sandford Collection*

Nevertheless, by the end of 1985, Fairchild had made a substantial recovery in the eyes of the SPO. Its manufacturing assessment review of the plant in December 1985 concluded that Fairchild was adequately prepared to continue low-rate production. A second General Accounting Office report[16] requested by Kansas Senator Robert Dole, again with the expectation that it would document major T-46 shortcomings to Cessna's benefit, included the following statement:

> The Air Force SPO and Edwards Flight Test Center officials, as well as the contractor test pilot, said that the T-46A's performance tests have been successful. They also said that technical tests have been outstanding and reliability and maintainability significantly better than predicted. They believe the T-46A's airworthiness is excellent.

It's possible that there was some self-serving weasel wording from the SPO and contractor test pilot (both generally don't disparage the airplane that they are responsible for to auditors) in response to the GAO's inquiry. Stating that the tests were successful doesn't necessarily mean that the airplane achieved the predicted performance, only that the tests were accomplished without reportable damage to the airplane. However, the Edwards Flight Test Center was under no obligation to gloss over an airplane's problems and by the conclusion of the test program, the drag had been established to be 24% higher than predicted, not 50%, still disappointing but resulting in an acceptable cruise speed and range for a side-by-side trainer.

Moreover, the Air Force-generated estimate as of early 1986 for the T-46A performance at maturity indicated that it would meet or better almost every one of the original Air Training Command requirements, if not the Contract Specification negotiated with Fairchild. (Range wasn't included in the GAO report.)

CHARACTERISTIC	ATC REQUIREMENT	T-46A SPECIFICATION	ESTIMATED PERFORMANCE
CRITICAL FIELD LENGTH (FT.)	5,000	4,800	4,260
LANDING DISTANCE (FT.)	5,000	4,930	4,870
RATE OF CLIMB[1] (FPM.)	2,000	2,390	2,010
SUSTAINED G[1]	2.5	2.7	2.3
CRUISE SPEED[1] (KTS.)	300	376	345
CRUISE CEILING (FT.)	35,000	42,000	39,800
CLIMB GRADIENT[2] (%)			
TAKEOFF	3.5	3.7	3.2
GO-AROUND	2.0	2.7	NOT ESTIMATED[3]

Notes
[1]At 25,000 ft.
[2]Single Engine.
[3]Fairchild estimated 2.63.

There were only two shortfalls to the original ATC requirement, sustained G at 25,000 feet and takeoff climb gradient. If the Air Force had deemed either to be unacceptable, Garrett would probably have been able to boost the F-109 engine's thrust enough to eliminate it. Range and endurance weren't mentioned but presumably they were notably better than the T-37's even if they didn't meet the original requirement.

The absence of a powered flight control system, a maintenance benefit, did not affect handling qualities. Cockpit pressurization and air conditioning were welcome changes from the T-37's instruction environment that provided neither.

The Air Force and Fairchild allowed several guest pilots—including General officers and politicians—to fly the T-46 prototype in 1986 so it must have had at least satisfactory handling qualities and performance. By the time it had accumulated 100 flight hours, 21 different pilots had flown it. The second T-46A flew in July 1986.

Unfortunately for the Air Force Training Command and Fairchild, in 1986 there were other, higher priority Air Force programs completing for budget. The Northrop B-2 needed redesign for low-altitude ingress and the Advanced Tactical Fighter program was entering its next and more expensive phase, the design, manufacture, and test of the YF-22 and YF-23. (The usual difficulty with the budget planning process that year was further exacerbated by the Gramm-Rudman-Hollings Balanced Budget and Emergency Deficit Control Act of 1985.) As a result, in March the Air Force announced that it did not plan to exercise the option for the second T-46 production lot. In order to maintain a near-term training capability, it approved a T-37B structural life extension program in July for an additional 3,000 hours of airframe service life to allow time to evaluate longer-term options.

If the GAO report[17] is to be believed, the Air Force decision was almost certainly not the result of problems with the T-46 in flight test: "An Air Force Air Training Command official said that based on actual flights by their personnel the T-46A's performance was excellent, met the Command's needs for a modern trainer, and would save millions of dollars in yearly maintenance cost." It was

There were briefly three T-46As on flight status when the program was terminated, the two prototypes shown here in formation over Edwards AFB on an infrequent overcast day and the first production airplane. *John Sandford Collection*

instead the result of budget priorities and possibly put forth in the belief that Congress would continue to provide funding for the program.

The House of Representatives was initially inclined to do so, 213 to 190, but Fairchild's powerful supporter Congressman Addabbo—who had told the Secretary of Defense, Casper W. Weinberger, that his top three priorities were T-46, T-46, T-46—had died in April. The Senate, on the other hand, had sided with the Air Force's T-46 budget decision, 79-14. Matters came to a head on October 16, 1986, when Senator Barry Goldwater, then Chairman of the Senate Armed Services committee, spoke in favor of not only eliminating Fiscal Year 1987 funding for the program but also withdrawing the 1986 funds not yet spent. Senator Dole of Kansas, where Cessna was based, supported his position. (Cessna latest unsolicited trainer proposal, the New Technology T-37, would provide the life-extension and performance improvement upgrade to the Tweet necessary in the event of a T-46 cancellation.)

Goldwater had been one of the guest pilots who flew the T-46 at Edwards and praised it at the time. In his biography, however, he wrote, "It's not a bad airplane, but the Air Force was right. We didn't need it, so why spend the money?"[18]

Senator Alphonse (Al) D'Amato of New York tried to save the program for Fairchild immediately following Goldwater's unusually public rejection of a military program. After his filibuster on its behalf had shut down the Federal government for a day, October 17, 1986, he agreed to a compromise that provided for a 1987 fly-off between the T-37 and T-46, which the newer airplane would likely have won.[19] His attempt at rescue failed, essentially because the new Chairman of Fairchild Industries insisted on a guarantee to build all 630 T-46As originally planned in order to recoup the company's financial investment in development and production startup. If true, his was not a realistic demand since one Congress cannot bind a future one. In any event, Fairchild had decided to cut its losses and withdraw from the aerospace business.

The fly off with the T-37 never occurred. When the first production T-46 flew on January 14, 1987, almost a year behind schedule, the program was a dead man walking; on March 13, 1987, Fairchild-Republic announced that it would cease operations at the Farmingdale plant by the end of the year. Other aerospace companies, including nearby Grumman, had considered the acquisition of the Fairchild-Republic facility and its contracts. A group of former employees made an offer to take over the T-46 program. In the end, however, no single proposition acceptable to all the entities involved—a purchaser, Fairchild Industries, and Fairchild-Republic's commercial and military customers—was forthcoming. The existing

As a result of the termination of the T-46A program and Air Force budget priorities, the aging T-37s were forced to soldier on with periodic trips to repair and overhaul facilities. By the time they were finally replaced, the grandchildren of some of the pilots who first learned to fly in the *Tweet* could be learning to fly in them. *US Air Force Photo*

subcontracts were individually settled and the A-10 support business was sold to Grumman. The Air Force quietly acquiesced to a cancellation of the existing T-46 production contract for ten airplanes. The Farmingdale plant was closed.

The Air Force had various options after suspending Fairchild's T-46A production. It could restart T-46A production with another airframe manufacturer, contract with Cessna for a major upgrade of the T-37, purchase an off-the-shelf trainer (there were several candidates in development or production worldwide), or keep patching up the existing T-37 fleet for several more years.

The New Technology T-37 proposal would have retained the T-37B airframe but rebuilt and reengined it with the Garrett F109 engine that had been developed and qualified for the T-46. The structural modifications to the existing airframe would restart the clock on a 15,000-hour service life. New ejection seats, avionics, flight instrumentation, and pressurization would have been incorporated. A larger vertical fin would have been added to improve its crosswind takeoff and landing capability. That must have been tempting but still involved development expense and the resulting airplane would not meet all the NGT requirements that had been established by Systems Operational Concept (SOC) and Mission Element Need Statement (MENS) that the training command had created.

None of the other jet trainers in or nearing production worldwide met the Air Force's NGT requirements either. Lower cost was not enticing; it had already rejected the notion of turboprops when it was suggested that the T-37 be replaced with the Navy's T-34C.

The Air Force therefore elected to stand pat with the existing T-37 Service Life Extension Program (SLEP). It did not include any performance or capability improvements.

C. JPATS

The Service Life Extension Program for the T-37 was clearly a temporary expedient. In the late 1980s, the average age of a Tweet was approaching thirty years, the upper limit of the most recent modifications and repairs. Although flight trainer procurement is not a high priority relative to that of state-of-the-art fighters and bombers, at some point replacement is necessary and in the case of the T-37, well overdue. The Air Force therefore initiated the Primary Airplane Training System (PATS) in 1988. To reduce the cost and expedite availability, the Air Force decided that rather than initiating a program requiring an all-new design, it would buy an existing trainer that could be minimally modified to meet its requirements, preferably a jet with a turbofan engine.

In response to the Air Force's plan, Congress requested a Department of Defense (DoD) plan that included the Navy's future trainer requirements, with the expectation that the Navy and Air Force would procure a "similar trainer aircraft and take advantage of the associated cost savings of joint-service procurement and development"[20]. Although the Navy's T-34Cs were relatively new, they were based on a 40-year old design.

The DoD directed the Air Force to work with the Navy and create a Trainer Aircraft Master Plan that included what was to become the Joint Primary Aircraft Training System (JPATS). The plan resulted in a T-37 maintenance program that relied on replacing two fatigue-critical components and identifying three others for replacement as required during periodic inspections.

In December 1988, the Air Force and the Navy agreed to jointly establish specifications a primary aircraft training system, or JPATS. Like the VTXTS and the NGT, it was to result in not only a new common trainer but also the associated ground-based training hardware and software. The Air Force would lead the program, since it needed trainers to replace the T-37 beginning in 1997 while the Navy's T-34Cs were projected to not require replacement before 2004.

Flight training is hard on airplanes. And generally, for the sake of economical production, all the ones needed for the next twenty years or so are built in the span of a few years. Eventually, it is necessary to start a new production line when the fleet, through attrition or increased need, becomes too small. The Navy's T-34C was an exception because the Air Force was overdue for a T-37 replacement as part of their joint primary trainer program. *Mark Nankivil Collection*

To minimize cost, the airplane itself was to be "off-the-shelf" to the extent possible, with the term-of-art being a non-developmental effort. This also would expedite its availability and reduce the likelihood of a production schedule slip.

The procurement, as once again emphasized by the term Training System, was to include all training devices; computer-based and/or aided instruction; courseware; a training-management system; a training system support center; and logistic support.

From a crew station requirements standpoint, the cockpit was to be pressurized, have zero-zero ejection seats, and be equipped with a "glass" cockpit. Contrary to Air Force preference but with its concurrence, the seats were to be tandem and not side-by-side. The meant that the student would have the same field of view left and right and the fuselage would have less drag. It was also more similar to fighter cockpits. From a psychological standpoint, it tended to promote self-sufficiency on the part of the student, since his instructor's presence was not nearly as obvious as it was in a side-by-side arrangement. The Air Force and the Navy signed a memorandum of agreement including that decision on December 12, 1989.

The question of the number and type of engines took somewhat longer to resolve. Air Force, which had insisted on a twin-engine jet for NGT, finally agreed to consider a single-engine turboprop airplane that was the Navy's preference. As a result, some of the metrics were significantly changed:

CHARACTERISTIC	NGT REQUIREMENT	JPATS GOAL	JPATS REQUIRED
CRITICAL FIELD LENGTH (FT.)	5,000	5,000	7,000
LANDING DISTANCE (FT.)	5,000	5,000	7,000
SUSTAINED G	2.5[1]	3.0[2]	2.5[2]
CRUISE SPEED[1] (KTS.)	300	NONE	NONE
CRUISE CEILING (FT.)	35,000	35,000	NONE

Notes
[1] At 25,000 ft.
[2] At 15,000 ft.

A maximum speed of 400 knots and 2,000 fpm rate of climb at 25,000 feet was subsequently reduced to 270 knots at 1,000 feet and 3,000 fpm rate of climb at sea level. Cruise speed was to be at least 250 knots. Maximum G capability was to be +6 to -3. The sustained G was reduced to 2 at 22,000 feet. The crosswind takeoff and landing capability was to be at least 25 knots. The ejection envelope at ground level was now a minimum of sixty knots rather than zero.

Because the Air Force needed the new airplane first and even joint programs are best headed by a single service, the Navy agreed that the Air Force was to have the JPATS program lead. In October 1991, the services agreed to a Joint Services Operational Requirements document. At that time, the schedule called for source selection in fall 1993, contract award in early 1994, and first Air Force delivery in October 1996 with the first training squadron equipped in 1998. The Navy program would follow the Air Force's by about three years. A total of 813 airplanes were to be procured, 465 for the Air Force and 348 for the Navy. Production deliveries would continue through early 2005.

Evaluation of candidate airplanes was to have been accomplished at Wright-Patterson AFB between July 6 and August 28, 1992 by Air Force and Navy Training Command pilots. However, only two had gone through the process when the Under Secretary of Defense for Acquisition halted it over concerns about the definition of non-developmental among other things. A debate subsequently arose between the Defense Department and Congress about the best way to insure that the winning prime contractor was paired with the best ground-based training system. The result was a delay in the initiation of the procurement phase of the program.

Although several interested companies eventually dropped out, JPATS source selection would not lack for choice or variety to choose from. Because of the subsequent delay in the issuance of the RFP, two companies were able to propose airplanes that first flew the year after the aborted trainer evaluation. In the end, seven responded to the RFP: Raytheon (Beech), Cessna, Grumman, Lockheed, Northrop, Rockwell, and Vought. All but one, Cessna, had teamed with a European or South American manufacturer because of the lack of relatively recent trainer development by US industry. Both single and twin-engine jets and single-engine turboprop-powered airplanes were proposed.

Raytheon: Pilatus PC-9 Mk II, based on the PC-9 that had lost the RAF trainer competition to the Shorts-Embraer Tucano (which was being proposed by Northrop). It was powered by a Pratt & Whitney PT6 turboprop engine and had first flown in May 1984. The first customers for the PC-9 were Saudi Arabia, Myanmar, Switzerland, and Australia.

Cessna: 526 Citation Jet, a two-seat, twin-engine trainer that used the wings, engines (repositioned), and landing gear of its 525 CitationJet business jet. The fuselage, empennage, and cockpit were new. However, Cessna claimed 75% commonality with the 525 because the 526 used the same electrical, hydraulic, and fuel system along with other components. Cessna built and flew two company-funded prototypes, the first on 20 December 1993 and the second on March 2, 1994.

The Raytheon Company proposed a modified Pilatus PC-9. This one was photographed at Andrews AFB in September 1991 while on a US tour. *S.H. Miller Photo via T. Panopalis*

The Cessna Citation Jet was the only twin-engine airplane proposed for JPATS. It was based on Cessna's first executive jet, which was specifically created to be safely flown by a relatively low-time, inexperienced pilot-owner. *Cessna Textron*

Lockheed: Aermacchi MB-339B to be powered by one Rolls-Royce Viper. It had first flown in July 1978 and was now being operated by eight different countries as a trainer including Italy. Lockheed would manufacture the airplane under license in the United States. Marketing included a US tour in July and August 1992 of an ex-Argentinian MB-339 that had been reengined with a Rolls-Royce Viper 680 engine. Lockheed referred to it as the T-Bird II to hopefully link it in the mind of the customer to the highly regarded T-33. It was arguably too big and advanced for use as an initial trainer but probably required the least redesign to meet all the requirements.

Northrop: The single-engine turboprop EMB-312 "Super" Tucano that first flew in Brazil in August 1980. It was selected by the Royal Air Force in 1985 to be license built by Short Brothers. In addition to Brazil and England, several other countries had purchased the Tucano for their air forces.

Grumman: SIAI Marchetti S.211 that first flew in April 1981. It was a single-engine jet. Grumman modified the airplanes that were used for the flight evaluation from two former Haitian Air Force 211s.

The Aermacchi MB-339 civil registered in the US as an experimental aircraft, N339L, was at NAS Patuxent River in May 1993. *Terry Panopalis Collection*

The EMB-312H Super Tucano was developed by Embraer with an eye toward winning the JPATS program. PT-ZTV was the second of three prototypes. It first flew in May 1993. *Tony Chong Collection*

Airplane manufacturers were promoting their JPATS entries well before the US military flight evaluation was finally conducted. This picture of a SIAI Marchetti S.211 demonstrator was taken on September 5, 1990, at the Farnborough Air Show. *Courtesy and Copyright Malcolm Clarke*

The Deutsche Aerospace/Rockwell Ranger 2000 was based on an airplane with a very different propulsion system, a mid-fuselage mounted ducted fan driven by an Allison Engine Company 450 shp turboshaft engine. Instead, a turbofan jet engine was mounted in its place as part of a complete redesign. *Darold Cummings*

As the basis for its JPATS proposal, Vought selected the IA 63 being developed by an Argentine aerospace company, Fabrica Militar de Aviones, and designated it the Pampa 2000. Eighteen had been built at that point and were in service with the Argentine Air Force. *Bill Spidle Collection*

Rockwell: The Deutsche Aerospace/Rockwell Ranger 2000 was originally based on the Rhein-Flugzeugbau GmbH (RFB) Fantrainer but powered by single Pratt & Whitney JT15D-5C turbofan engine rather than a turboshaft or piston engine turning a ducted fan for propulsion. However, specific JPATS requirements like cockpit pressurization dictated a complete redesign that only resembled the Fantrainer. First flight was accomplished on January 15, 1993, at the Deutsch Aerospace (DASA) Manching facility in Germany.

Vought: Pampa 2000, a modified Fabrica Militar de Aviones (FMA) IA 63 that was developed in a partnership with Dornier for the Argentine Air Force. It was powered by a single Garrett TFE731 turbofan engine and had first flown in October 1984.

By the time the RFP was issued, some of the requirements had been reduced to accommodate the trainers likely to be proposed. However, the cockpit was now required to accommodate not less than 80% of female pilots as well as the ninety-fifth percentile of male pilots. The level of bird-strike protection, four lbs. at 270 knots, was challenging but in the Air Force's opinion, justified by fatal T-37 and T-38 crashes resulting from bird strikes. Non-developmental had been deemphasized by the desire for something closer to bespoke from the training commands' standpoint.

JPATS still retained the essence of a fly-before-buy competition, however. When the RFP was finally released on May 18, 1994, one of the proposal requirements was the availability of a "properly certificated" airplane for a flight evaluation. This was intended to demonstrate the non-developmental status of the proposed designs like Cessna's and Rockwell's from a basic performance and handling qualities standpoint. These evaluations began at Wright-Patterson AFB, Ohio in July 1994.

Even before the availability of JPATS, the Air Force and Navy began to explore integration of their respective primary training programs. In September 1993, Navy instructor pilots joined the 35th Flying Training Squadron at Reese AFB, Texas. Navy student pilots were to follow to begin their primary flight instruction in Air Force T-37s.

Similarly Air Force instructor pilots were assigned to the Navy's VT-3 primary training squadron at NAS Whiting Field, Florida, in February 1994 and began checkout in the Navy's T-34Cs. The intention was that this initial exchange of instructors and students would result in a joint syllabus that met the needs of both services.

There were differences to be ironed out. In primary training, the Navy placed more emphasis on instrument training; the Air Force put greater emphasis on operating in formation. Each needed to modify its syllabus to reflect the competency expected of a student in each service's advanced training program. Otherwise, for example, an Air Force student trained at a Navy squadron would be going to advanced training with less formation flying experience than an Air Force student assigned to an Air Force squadron.

In 1994, the respective training commands were to anticipate the arrival of the JPATS in 1999 with the first deliveries to Randolph AFB, Texas. The Navy would receive its first airplanes in 2000. There would eventually be five Air Force and five Navy primary training squadrons.

The two finalists in the evaluation were the turboprop proposals from Raytheon and Northrop. Lower cost of development and ownership had trumped higher performance. Raytheon's proposal based on the Pilatus PC-9 with Flight Safety Services Corporation providing the ground-based training system as a subcontractor was judged to be the better of the two.[21] The selection was announced on June 22, 1995. However, the contract award was delayed until February 1996 because of formal protests by both Cessna and Rockwell this time. (Lockheed Martin also filed a complaint with the Department of Defense but did not formally protest.) Cessna claimed that the selection rules had been changed from "best value" to lowest cost/price, which meant its candidate was not evaluated fairly. Rockwell, on the other hand, believed that Ranger 2000 had a lower life cycle cost than Raytheon turboprop. Neither protest was successful.

The new T-6, Texan II, was far from non-developmental. Cockpit pressurization and more capable (zero-zero) ejection seats had to be added along with a new canopy and other structure changes that provided the required level of bird-strike protection. A more powerful engine was installed along with a new, four-bladed propeller to accommodate the increased gross weight.

The Air Force's acceptance of a turboprop-powered trainer was a significant compromise because the addition of the propeller introduced handling qualities that the student would have to unlearn when he or she transitioned to jets. To minimize this, the engine's electronic engine control system was tailored to provide more jet-like thrust response to throttle movement in addition to providing

Randolph AFB, Texas, was the first to receive the T-6A Texan II. The aircraft were painted in a white/dark blue scheme similar to the one on the T-37s that they were replacing. *US Air Force photo by Master Sgt. David Richards*

over torque and rpm protection. A rudder-trim compensator was also incorporated to automatically trim out propeller and torque effects and provide more jet-like handling qualities.

Most of the avionics and cockpit instrumentation was new as well. As a result, the development and qualification program took longer than intended. The first production airplane flew on July 15, 1998.

A seven-month Multi-Service Operational Test and Evaluation began in June 2000 at Randolph AFB. The 12th Flying Training Wing, Randolph AFB, received its first T-6A in May 23, 2000, a year behind schedule. It was used to train the first Air Force and Navy T-6A instructor pilots who would form the initial cadre of instructors. The first student pilots were to be trained by the 479th Flying Training Group at Moody AFB, Georgia. Its first T-6A arrived on May 1, 2001. Training began on November 20, 2001, with an inaugural class of thirteen Air Force and two Navy students.

The Navy finally began flight training of student Naval Flight Officers with the T-6A in August 2003 but elected to procure an improved version for pilot training with a cockpit that more closely matched those of its front-line fighters. This Texan II variant was designated the T-6B. The changes included heads-up and multifunction displays and HOTAS (Hands-On Throttle and Stick) for display and system management as well as the addition of GPS/INS navigation capability. As a result of the need for development and certification of the changes and improvements, the first T-6Bs weren't delivered to a Navy training squadron until September 2009. The last Navy T-34C training flight occurred at VT-28 from NAS Corpus Christi, Texas in 2015 although it will continue to be flown by other Navy units for a few more years.

However, the joint primary pilot training program didn't even survive until the retirement of the T-34C. The Navy and Air Force elected to go their separate ways in 2013.

Primary training had come full circle in fifty years. The Air Force and the Navy were once again using the same trainer. *Plus déjà-vu*, it had the same designation as one of those joint-service trainers, T-6, and the popular name, Texan, used by the Air Force for the T-6 and the Navy for its counterpart, the SNJ.

The Navy T-6B cockpit featured heads-up and multifunction displays to provide early experience with a state-of-the-art cockpit and a better lead-in to flying the T-45C. *Tommy H. Thomason*

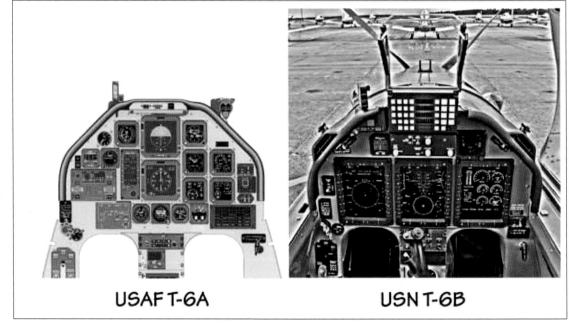

USAF T-6A   USN T-6B

The T-6B had a cockpit as advanced as any Navy fighter in the fleet. Ring binders and a simple cockpit procedures trainer no longer sufficed as training aids. Here, simulator instructor Dave Sloyer is instructing Ensign Jeffrey Lewis, assigned to Training Squadron (VT) 28 at Corpus Christi, the fundamentals of radio instrument flight in the new T-6B Texas II Unit Training Device (UTD). *US Navy photo by Richard Stewart*

At the 2007 Randolph Air Force Base Air Show in Texas, a restored World War II T-6/SNJ flew in formation with its namesake, the new US Air Force T-6A Texan II. *US Air Force photo by Steve White*

267

D. USAF T-X

In 2014, the T-38 was still the USAF's advanced trainer as it had been since 1961, more than fifty years earlier. The last of more than 1,000 was delivered in 1972, which meant that the youngest T-38 was forty-two years old, and counting.[22] Of course, like George Washington's proverbial ax, much of any specific T-38 was younger, in part the result of a modification program begun in 1982 and a subsequent major update in the early aughts that resulted in the T-38C. About half the fleet was modified with structural and avionics upgrades that were intended to extend the service life of those White Rockets to at least 2020.

Another factor in the T-38 replacement requirement is the reality of a future where most of the USAF fighters will be single-seat F-22s and F-35s, the two-seat F-15s and F16s having been retired. While simulation can fill some of the training needs like sensor management and air-to-air intercepts, others cannot be properly experienced in a simulator like sustained-G maneuvering and air-to-air refueling. As it is, pilots selected to fly the F-22 have to, among other things, receive instruction in night refueling and other maneuvers in a two-seat F-16 before they are qualified to do so in the F-22.

The introduction of a new trainer therefore had to be accomplished before the existing two-seat operational trainers began to be retired. Air Force studies of the requirement had been ongoing in parallel with the NGT/PAT programs since the T-37 and T-38 replacements had to complement each other from a syllabus standpoint. By 2010, the Air Force began to increase its attention on the T-X, which resulted in marketing efforts by contractor and contractor teams to influence the specifications in favor of their prospective offer. These included BAE Systems—teamed this time with Northrop Grumman—for a Hawk derivative powered by an uprated Rolls Royce engine; Korea Aerospace Industries teamed with Lockheed Martin for the KAI T-50 Golden Eagle; and Alenia Aermacchi teamed with a General Dynamics division to propose its T-100 (aka M-346 and Yak-130).

Keith Barnes, 571st Aircraft Maintenance Squadron contractor, performs final checks to the T-38 Talon prior to Lt. Col. Ripley Woodard, 415th Flight Test Flight commander, taking off from Joint Base San Antonio-Randolph, Texas on May 17, 2012. The T-38 was being returned to the training squadron at Sheppard Air Force Base, Texas. *US Air Force photo by Rich McFadden*

	T-38	BAE HAWK T.2	T-100	KAI T-50
FIRST FLIGHT	1959	1974 (HAWK T1)	1996 (YAK-130)	2002
MAX TO WEIGHT (LBS.)	12,000	20,000	21,000	30,000
NUMBER ENGINES	TWO	ONE	TWO	ONE
VMAX (KNOTS)	746	550	590	850
FLIGHT CONTROL	MECHANICAL	MECHANICAL	FBW[1]	FBW[1]
SALES[2]		UNITED KINGDOM	ITALY	KOREA
		US (T-45)	RUSSIA	INDONESIA
		FINLAND	SINGAPORE	IRAQ
		INDONESIA	ISRAEL	PHILIPPINES
		OTHERS		

Notes
[1] Fly By Wire.
[2] Partial List.
Note that only the T-50 of the existing trainer candidates is capable of supersonic speed in level flight like the T-38.

In October 2012, the US Air Force released a lengthy list of draft T-X Key Performance Parameters (KPP), Key System Attributes (KSA), and Additional Performance Attributes (APA). One KPP was Operational availability, with a minimum of precisely 64.7%. KSAs included fighter-type instantaneous and sustained turn rates and maneuvering at an angle of attack of more than twenty degrees. A minimum top speed was not among the metrics, denying a possible advantage to the T-50. The trainer had to at least simulate the mission equipment of the F-22 and F-35 from a pilot's perspective in a similar cockpit. While actual aerial refueling would not be a requirement, so-called dry contact with a boom-equipped tanker would be required for training.

As was now customary, T-X would also require a training system comprised of weapon system trainers, operational flight trainers, unit training devices, self-teaching software, course management, etc. all of which would have to be tailored to the Air Force's preferences and specifications.

The BAe Hawk T2 was to be the basis for the Northrop Grumman T-X proposal. This Royal Air Force T2 is flying low level along the Machynlleth Loop, a series of valleys in Wales, UK on May 11, 2011. Northrop Grumman subsequently decided on a clean sheet of paper approach for the air vehicle. *Ron Kellenaers Photo*

General Dynamics had chosen to partner with Alenia Aermacchi to propose a derivative of the M-346, branded T100, for the USAF T-X program. GD subsequently dropped out; Alenia then teamed with Raytheon. *Alenia Aermacchi*

Two other candidates emerged in December 2013, Boeing/Saab's and Textron AirLand. Boeing announced that it was teaming with Saab in December to propose a new design for the requirement, whatever it turned out to finally be. While it has yet to release any details, Boeing did display a T-X artists concept in its booth at the September 2011 Air Force Association's annual convention. It appeared to be in the T-38 size class and definitely was powered by a single engine. The configuration featured a very T-38-like forward fuselage; legacy F-18 LERX (Leading Edge Root Extension), inlet, and wings; and a V-tail somewhat reminiscent of the X-32A, its losing demonstrator for the JSF program that was won by Lockheed.

Also in December, Textron Airland flew its twin-engine two-seat Scorpion for the first time. A joint venture of Textron and AirLand Enterprises LLC, it self funded the demonstrator. Textron AirLand initially promoted its Scorpion as a low-cost airplane for intelligence, surveillance, reconnaissance (ISR) missions as well as light attack but in August 2014 announced that it would be proposed for

the T-X program. It would have a gross weight of a little over 20,000 lbs, the same size class as the GD/Alenia Aermacchi T-100.

In February 2015, Northrop Grumman announced that it had decided to proceed with an all-new design rather than proposing an upgrade of the Hawk, which had constituted the lower end of the competitive options. Moreover, it stated that it was in the process of designing a demonstrator to be built at its Scaled Composites division. It was to fly in late 2015. While no details were available as this was written, what Northrop has revealed suggests that it will be powered by a single General Electric F414 engine.

The Air Force's increasingly detailed statement of the T-X requirement and usage dictated Northrop Grumman's change of heart. It had become clear that the Hawk would be at a competitive disadvantage from a performance standpoint—probably not even responsive without major modification—particularly if the T-X was also to be used as an "aggressor," the adversary in combat training such as the Air Force's Red Flag exercises, replacing the F-15C and F-16. However, unlike Boeing, it was committing to invest in a demonstrator with no certainty that it would be what the Air Force would want in a T-X. While the Air Force had finally included a line item for the program in its 2016 budget request, its T-X Capability Development Document was in the process of being completed and had yet to be approved. Some requirements were still to be determined. For one thing, there was not yet a specific and approved requirement for maximum speed, although that conceivably will be a fallout from other requirements like acceleration, maximum sustained g, time to climb, etc. rather than being a requirement *per se*.

In January 2015, Air Force Secretary Deborah Lee James announced that the T-X would be subjected to her Bending the Cost Curve initiative, "When it comes to T-X, we are about two years away from a request for proposals stage, and this new process should allow us to directly engage industry as we develop an understanding of how to best evaluate our objective and our threshold requirements."[23] For example, General Robin Rand, commander of the Air Education and Training Command, had announced at the September 2014 Air Force Association conference that there was no pre-RFP preference for an off-the-shelf versus all-new or single versus twin-engine airplane. Many of the announced requirements were focused on low operating cost.

In light of the fact that four of the five announced competitor teams already had an airplane in being or work, that suggested that the Air Force might create a requirement based on the airplane that it liked the most but with enough wiggle-room to attract at least one or two other bids to insure price and terms competition as in the NGT competition. Note that this doesn't necessarily work to the Boeing/Saab team's advantage. If Northrop Grumman guessed right or one of the trainers in production was what the Air Force decided was needed, then Boeing would be at a disadvantage from a schedule-risk standpoint.

Following the release of an updated set of requirements in March 2015, General Dynamics, which had teamed with Alenia Aermacchi, announced that it was dropping out of the competition. No specific reason was given for the decision but there was informed speculation that the addition of a requirement for a sustained 6.5 G with an objective of 7.5 G was a concern. In July 2015, the requirement was modified to allow a loss of altitude and only require the G be sustained throughout 140 degrees of turn, possibly in order to keep the T-100 viable as is from an engine standpoint. This improved Alenia's chances of finding another US partner, if not winning the competition. In February 2016, Alenia teamed with Raytheon, whose management had been in T-X discussions with the Air Force—although it no longer has a division that designs and builds airplane. (Raytheon sold its Beechcraft Division, which produced the T-6 Texan

II, in 2006; it was acquired by Textron in 2014.) The Textron AirLand Scorpion is likely to be withdrawn even after the reduction in the sustained G requirement unless thrust is added to it at a minimum and probably significant airframe redesign accomplished as well.

One aspect of the budget request had already become controversial. It included a plan to procure a modification kit for conversion of the trainer into an "aggressor." This was a non-trivial consideration in judging the benefit of a proposed airplane versus its cost, since the most aggressor-capable airplane would require advanced-fighter speed, acceleration, sustained g, etc. in addition to providing weight, space, and stores provisions for avionics and other mission equipment needed to fully simulate a fighter adversary. For example, the T-38's supersonic capability was rarely used in Air Force

The Textron AirLand Scorpion is a private venture conceived to address the need for a low-cost reconnaissance and light attack jet. A T-X proposal based on the Scorpion was considered but would now not meet the requirements without major changes. *Textron AirLand*

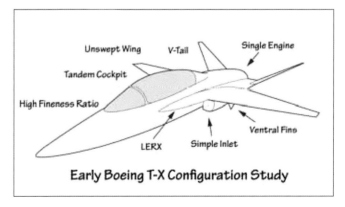

While the eventual Boeing/Saab T-X proposal is unlikely to closely resemble the artist's concept that Boeing displayed in 2011, some of the features, particularly the choice of a single-engine, may be retained. *Tommy H. Thomason*

Korea Aerospace Industries and Lockheed Martin unveiled a T-X demonstrator based on the KAI T-50 in December 2015. It is likely to be the fastest and most expensive of the T-X candidates. *Lockheed-Martin/Todd McQueen*

flight training—reportedly on only one flight in the entire syllabus—and a maximum speed requirement continues to be unstated for the T-X. In fact, afterburning is explicitly *not* a requirement, only the need to move the throttle through a detent to reach maximum thrust, simulating selection of afterburner. Moreover, General Rand subsequently stated that an aggressor capability was not yet an approved option and, "At this time, there have been no decisions to use the T-X in any other capacity (than as a trainer). This could take us off track of what the airplane was originally intended."[24]

If recent US military procurement difficulties are any indication, this will be another hotly contested and contentious competition, with the specification and performance details of the forthcoming request for proposals being a key factor. Each T-X candidate has strengths and weaknesses. They vary in size, number of engines, avionics (while those can be upgraded, that increases the program cost and schedule risk), and development/qualification/production status.

Of the two existing trainers, the Lockheed/KAI T-50 is essentially a modernized two-seat F-16 with supersonic performance that would double effectively as an aggressor; however, it has a price to match. The Alenia Aermacchi T-100 is a newish, high thrust-to-weight-ratio trainer design. It is also being procured by a discerning buyer and US ally, Israel, and has an "embedded virtual simulation system" that allows the student pilot to become familiar with war-fighting systems it does not actually carry, like radar and electronic warfare. However, it would have limitations as an aggressor from a performance standpoint.

Although the two demonstrators, the Textron/AirLand Scorpion and Northrop's T-X candidate, will not be ready for rate production, at least some of the development and qualification of modifications required to complete them as the T-X will also be required to fully configure the existing airplanes in accordance with the Air Force's detailed equipment list and functionality requirements, leveling the playing field.

The Boeing/Saab team can tailor their proposal to the Air Force's requirements since they have a clean sheet of paper; on the other hand, the Air Force may not have the near-term funds required for the development of an all-new airplane and not much stomach for the schedule risk of one, given the need to replace the T-38 as soon as possible.

The Air Force also has to consider the proposer as well as the proposed design. The Pentagon is already concerned about the prospect of Lockheed being its only supplier of fighters, which might affect the T-50's prospects. The Textron AirLand entity does not involve a foreign partner but is also not a "real" aerospace company. Congress has yet to heard from on the acquisition program and will undoubtedly weigh in on the source decision, with a foreign team member possibly being a handicap; it has demonstrated a proclivity in the past to redirect programs based on the desires of the constituents of its most powerful members. Given those considerations, Northrop Grumman might well have an advantage, particularly now that it has opted for a strategy of combining a bespoke trainer design with the perceived schedule-risk reduction of a demonstrator. Another factor is maintaining the industrial base for military airplane design and production, with Northrop Grumman and Boeing having a definite advantage in that regard.

Hopefully, the Air Force will be able to avoid the delays and false starts that have plagued many of its recent procurements. Among them are the cancellation of the Boeing HH-47 combat search and rescue helicopter; the successful Boeing protest of the original KC-X program award to a team including a non-US airframe manufacturer (that resulted in a new competition, which was won by Boeing); the recompetition of the Air Force Light Air Support program after a protest by the losing competitor (it lost the second time as well, however); and the cancellation of the Expeditionary Combat Support System for logistics management.

As of early 2016, the T-X RFP was to be released in late 2016 with a contract award a year later. The Air Force was planning to begin training students in the T-X in 2023.[25] It has extended its contract with Boeing for support of the T-38 fleet through 2026.

A US Air Force Northrop T-38A-65-NO *Talon* aircraft from the 560th Flying Training Squadron, Randolph AFB, Texas (USA), flying over the Texas countryside on November 13, 2001. *SSGT Jeffrey Allen, USAF*

The development of the T-X may be rocky whether it is all new or somewhat "non-developmental" like the T-6. The Air Force T-46, an all-new design, disappointed at first although it was reportedly on track to overcome its unexpected shortcomings when the Air Force decided to forgo a new trainer in favor of the advanced fighter and bomber then in development. (*Déjà vu*: the T-X program will have to compete with F-35 production and the development of a new bomber for budget.) The Navy elected to buy an existing jet trainer modified in accordance with its carrier landing requirements for its VTXTS program as the T-45; its development turned out to be much more difficult than expected although it was eventually successful. The JPATS program was a success by comparison: it necked down to the two least costly and somewhat off-the-shelf proposals; nevertheless, the planned schedule for certification and delivery was not met in part due to the extensive redesign to meet the Air Force and Navy requirements.

History therefore suggests that the venerable White Rocket, augmented by F-16Ds, may still be used to train the great grandchildren of the first neophyte fighter pilots to get their wings in the T-38.

Chapter Ten Endnotes

1. VTX-TS: The V stood for heavier than air (the convention dates back to 1920; no one is certain why "V"), T for trainer, and X for experimental. TS stood for Training System. The differentiation by a dash (sometimes a backslash) appears to have disappeared early on, probably to help signify that it was to be a single integrated program.

2. A head-up display was similar in appearance to a gun sight. It consisted of a clear glass screen on which flight data was displayed. A glass cockpit utilized computer screens. In the simplest form, the computer screens were simply substitutes for mechanical analogue instruments like the artificial horizon. In the more elegant version, the information previously displayed by various analogue instruments was provided on one or more large screens, which could be reconfigured by the pilot to depict the information desired.

3. Fairchild Republic had previously blundered by prematurely rolling out its Air Force T-46 trainer and hiding the fact that it was incomplete. Actually taxiing the T-45 during its rollout ceremony demonstrated its near readiness for first flight, which is typically what a rollout is supposed to represent.

4. The approach speed exceeded the specification by only two knots. The Douglas program manager thought that the Navy should have accepted the existing speed rather than insisted on a program that included reducing it, increasing cost and delaying the program. However, the other low-speed problems were serious and required resolution in any event.

5. The investigation of the crash found nothing wrong with the airplane or the carrier. The weather was good. The student had successfully completed the required Field Carrier Landing Practice training the day before the accident. Over 200 landings or touch and goes had already been made on the carrier the day of the accident; two students had already used that particular T-2C to qualify that day. It appears that the student simply made a mess of his first—and sadly only—look at the boat.

6. The Air Force Vice Chief of Staff, General William V. McBride, had actually kicked off what was to become the Next Generation Trainer program in July 1976 when he asked ATC for two studies, one addressing the replacement of the T-37 and the other, recommendations for producing a better, more economically trained pilot.

7. *Flight International*, April 13, 1985, "T-46: A Class Apart," Graham Warwick, pp.24-27.

8. There were other side-by-side jet trainers in service, e.g. the Saab 105 and the Canadair CT-114 but these had been out of production for at least a decade.

9. Burt Rutan subsequently founded Scale Composites at Mohave in April 1982 to build research aircraft.

10. Proposals were considered within the competitive range if they at least addressed the RFP's minimum requirements, did not have major deficiencies, and had a reasonable chance of being chosen for award.

11. The New York senators at the time were Alfonse M. D'Amato and Daniel Patrick Moynihan. Spoiler alert: five years later, they would go to considerable lengths in an effort to save the program.

12. United States General Accounting Office letter B-206430 dated November 8, 1983, Evaluation of Contract Award for the Air Force's Next Generation Trainer (NGT) Aircraft (GAO/NSIAD-84-16).

13. More unusual than not exceeding the specification weight was the fact that the contract reportedly did not have one; the performance specifications were intended to suffice.

14. Flight International, October 26, 1985, pg 8 "T-46A is flown"

15. http://www.aero-web.org/specs/fairchil/t-46a.htm

16. GAO Briefing Report to the Honorable Robert Dole, United States Senate, Aircraft Procurement: Development and Production Issues Concerning the T-46A Aircraft, May 1986, GAO/NSIAD-86-126BR.

17. GAO/NSIAD-86-126BR, *op.cit.*

18. *Goldwater* by Barry Goldwater and Jack Casserly, Doubleday, published 1988.

19. *New York Times*, "D'amato's Marathon: Give-And-Take For T-46." By Esther B. Fein, October 18, 1986.

20. National Defense Authorization Act for FY 1989, Report 100-989.

21. Between the start of the program and the final selection, Northrop acquired both Grumman and Vought (later sold to the Carlyle group). It therefore had three proposals in the competition, none of which were successful. As it turned out, JPATS was also the last Rockwell competition.

22. There was a suggestion in the late 1980s that the Air Force replace its T-38s with Navy T-45As. The Air Force rejected it as uneconomical and inappropriate.

23. *Aviation Week*, February 6, 2015, "Northrop Pivots to Clean-Sheet T-X Trainer."

24. *Aviation Week*, February 13, 2015, "The Tale of the Unclaimed T-X Aggressor."

25. *Aviation Week*, April 13-26, 2015, "New Training Track."

Chapter Eleven
CIVILIAN-OWNED TRAINERS

Civilian ownership of military aircraft dates back to the end of WWI when surplus government airplanes were sold on the civilian market. Curtiss Jennies, deHavilland DH-4s, and other types were sold in large numbers for barnstorming, airshow exhibitions, and civilian flight training. In fact, ex-military aircraft sales volume after WWI was so large that the health of the emerging commercial aviation industry was impacted. History repeated itself after WWII when the disposal of surplus military aircraft to civilians was encouraged at astoundingly low prices. Some aircraft were purchased for salvage while others were returned to flight status as crop dusters, firefighters, cargo haulers, business transports, and recreational aircraft. By the 1960s, the collection and restoration of former military aircraft had grown in popularity. Large regional airshows became the perfect venue to display and fly these aircraft. The Warbird Movement was an organized response to the

growing interest in preserving airworthy examples of military aircraft. Trainers, because of their relative simplicity and affordability, became the most numerous types to be preserved. Hundreds of PT-17s, T-34s and T-28s were restored and operated by individuals (albeit wealthy ones). According to historian Nick Veronico, sales of military aircraft to civilians were curtailed about the time Litchfield Park, the Navy's surplus storage facility, was closed in 1964. A few propeller types like C-47s, C-54s, P-2s, T-28s and T-34s were sold to civilian operators on a limited basis, but turbine aircraft were precluded. Nevertheless some jet trainers entered the civil fleet through foreign sales or rebuilt airframes cobbled together from salvage components.

The following is a survey of notable civilian owned trainers that are flying, for the most part, with their original equipment and authentic color schemes. They provide a living display of post-WWII trainer development.

Many former military training aircraft have been acquired, maintained and flown by civilian pilots but jets are rare. Only two T-37s are on the civil register, this one is owned by Jim Allen. *Henning Henningsen*

This restored Stearman N2S-3 owned by Nick Ziroli Jr. is typical of the vast number of primary trainers that survived the war. The Navy continued to use this type for the early stages of flight training for several years after the war. *Sal Calvagna*

A. Stearman N2S-3

The Allied victory in WWII can be attributed, in part, to the success of flight training. The Stearman Model 70 was a key contributor to that success. Developed in 1934 with private funds, Stearman won an Army primary trainer competition. Because of limited Army funds, the first production order came from the Navy who took delivery of sixty-one examples between 1935 and 1936 under the designation NS-1. These were powered by surplus Wright J-5 engines that the Navy specified. In 1936, the Navy expanded their order substituting a Continental R-670-14 engine for the Wright J-5. This model became known as the N2S-1. The Army also ordered this version of as their PT-17 that was virtually interchangeable with the Navy's N2S-1. Because engine production lagged behind airframe production in the late 1930s and early 1940s, the services looked to alternative suppliers. Thus, a Lycoming R-680-8 version was designated N2S-2 by the Navy and PT-13 by the Army. A further engine change to the Continental R-670-4 was called the N2S-3 that became the most common Navy primary trainer. In aggregate the Stearman series became the most prominent US primary trainer. Its ease of manufacture and durability allowed it to survive the war in huge numbers. Both services continued using the Stearman as their standard Post-War primary trainer, while excess inventory was sold at surplus auctions throughout the country. As a result, numerous Army Air Corps and Navy Stearmans entered the civil register after WWII just as the Curtiss Jenny had after WWI.

Stearman 41-8844 was originally delivered to the Army in 1941 and served through the early part of the War as a trainer at Lakeland Aux. Field, Florida. It suffered unspecified damage on June 24, 1943 and was declared surplus in 1944. It was sold by the Reconstruction Finance Corp. to John Kipp for $282 after the War and served as a crop duster until 1979. A new owner, James Gaynier, restored the Stearman to Navy N2S-3 standards by removing the spray equipment and installing a Continental R-670 engine in place of the Pratt & Whitney R985 that had been used for crop dusting. In 2006, after passing through 3 more owners, it was restored to better than new condition by Big Sky Aviation. In 2011 it was acquired by Nick Ziroli Jr. of Ronkonkoma New York who flies it for recreation and airshow displays.

B. North American SNJ-5

In 1935, North American Aviation, using corporate funds, built the prototype of a new trainer that would evolve into one of the most important training aircraft of all time. North American assigned the designation NA-16 to the project and built more than 16,000 examples for the Army, Navy and numerous Allied governments during WWII. The Army version was designated AT-6 while the Navy's were designated SNJ. The AT-6 and SNJ survived the War in great numbers and continued to serve actively in the training commands of both services until the middle 1950s. In fact, the AT-6/SNJ training role was expanded after the war providing everything from primary to instrument training and even carrier landing training.

North American SNJ-5, Bureau Number 43779 was manufactured for the Navy on February 1, 1944. It was assigned to training Squadron 15 at Kingsville, Texas, where it provided advanced and instrument instruction throughout the war. At the conclusion of the war it became part of a pool of aircraft assigned to reserve pilots who used it to maintain flight proficiency. In 1947, it was placed in storage at the Naval Facility, Litchfield Park AZ. In 1950, the Navy decided to begin using SNJs for primary training and SNJ 43779 was selected for that program. On February 13, 1952, it was sent to the Overhaul & Repair Facility at NAS Pensacola, Florida. where it was given a thorough inspection. It was released from Overhaul & Repair and transferred to BTU-2 (Basic Training Unit) at Corry Field on April 14, 1952, where it was assigned to primary training duties. About that time the Pensacola training complex experienced a series of mid-air crashes and near misses due to the volume of air traffic around the training fields. CNATRA (Chief of Naval Air Training) issued a letter directing that twelve SNJ aircraft be painted in a high visibility scheme of either white or silver with a Glossy Sea Blue contrasting color on the cowling, elevators, rudder and the trailing half of the wing. CNATRA also specified that three aircraft would be painted glossy yellow overall to compare to the blue and white or silver scheme. Ultimately the yellow scheme was selected by CNATRA and it became standardized throughout the entire training fleet. SNJ 43779 was retired on April 28, 1958. In later years it was acquired by Clyde Zellers of Warbird Aviation Rendezvous Inc., Springfield Illinois who restored this historically significant SNJ to its exact 1952 Corry Field appearance during the color scheme evaluation. He uses the SNJ to perform authentic Navy training aerobatics at large regional airshows. He also offers aerobatic and formation instruction to private students who want to learn how it was done in the 1940s and 1950s.

A huge inventory of North American Texans was available after WWII. Although it was used as an advanced trainer during the war, the Air Force and Navy used it for all phases of flight training by the late 1940s. This SNJ-5 was restored by Clyde Zellers and re-painted in the experimental blue and white scheme that it wore when it served in the Training Command at Pensacola Florida in the 1950s. *Mark Houpt*

C. Fairchild T-31 (XNQ-1)

Two XNQ-1s were built by Fairchild Aircraft Division in response to a Navy primary trainer specification of April 26, 1945. After prolonged testing and two competitive evaluations Fairchild failed to win a contract and withdrew from the trainer business (see chapters two and three). The first example, 72525, was demolished during a gear up landing at Patuxent River Naval Air Station. The second, 72526, was also damaged in a similar mishap, but was repaired, stricken from the Navy's inventory, and in 1953 transferred to the Civil Air Patrol. It was last flown in 1955—a lack of funds caused it to deteriorate into a derelict condition. In 1978 the disassembled Fairchild was shipped to Waco, Texas where it was to be restored for the Antique Airplane Association Museum. But before restoration work was begun the airframe was purchased by Don Pellegreno in 1982. After ten years Pellegreno returned the airplane to airworthy status and flew it on June 1, 1992. As the only XNQ-1 (later designated the T-31) in existence, it generated great acclaim at the EAA Convention, Oshkosh, Wisconsin and the Antique Airplane Association Fly-In, Blakesburg, Iowa that summer.

The sole surviving Fairchild XNQ-1 from the late 1940s was acquired and restored by Don and Ann Pellegreno. It is seen here flying at one of the many antique airplane fly-ins where it has won awards. *G.R. Dennis Price*

D. North American T-28A

The newly formed Air Force issued a trainer development contract to North American Aviation for two XT-28s in 1948. This 800 hp, tricycle landing gear trainer was intended to replace the aging T-6 and combine both primary and basic training characteristics in one airplane. The XT-28 made its maiden flight on September 26, 1949 and the Air Force ordered 266 production T-28As in 1950. The order was later increased to 1,194 before production was halted in 1953. In Training Command service the T-28A proved too heavy and powerful for primary training and the Air Force was forced to retreat to the lighter, less complex T-34A. By the late 1950s, as the Air Force experimented with All-Jet training, T-28As were stricken from inventory. Some were sold to foreign militaries, while some were placed in long-term storage at Davis-Monthan AFB. Serial number 49-1592 was sold to the Mexican government in July 1958 where it served until 1988. It was acquired as surplus by noted T-28 restorers Rudy Blakey and Linc Dexter. It received a complete rewiring, an avionics update, a zero time engine, a new canopy, and was repainted in the Training Command scheme that it wore in the 1950s. In 2006, it was acquired by Scott McClain who continued to enhance the restoration while flying it actively. McClain changed the scheme to the colorful red and yellow markings of the T-28As assigned to the Air Force Test Pilot School in the early 1950s. To preserve authenticity Scott painstakingly applied all of the airframe markings including complete stenciled service instructions. The rebuilt Wright R-1300 engine still provides 800 hp and a maximum speed of 283 mph. It weighs 5,107 pounds empty and 7,462 fully loaded.

A North American T-28A owned by Scott McLain is painted in the 1950s color scheme of the Test Pilot's School at Edwards Air Force Base. *Scott McLain Collection*

E. North American T-28C

The T-28A had been in service with the Air Force since 1950 while the Navy continued to use the late 1930s designed, tailwheel equipped SNJ. In 1952, after evaluating the new Air Force trainer the Navy agreed to order a more powerful version designated the T-28B Trojan. Originally intended to serve as an advanced instrument trainer, the T-28B's role grew as it was assigned to eleven training squadrons. It was used for the entire basic training curriculum with the exception of carrier qualification because it was not carrier capable. The Navy continued to use antiquated tailhook equipped SNJ-5Cs for carrier instruction but it was apparent that their days were numbered. In 1955, North American added a tailhook and reinforced the structure of a T-28B to evaluate it for carrier training. After successfully demonstrating its carrier compatibility 299 examples were ordered under the new designation T-28C. They were delivered between 1955 and 1957.

On May 30, 1986 retired airline and now corporate pilot, Tom Passalacqua, acquired T-28C BuNo 146242 in an unusual transaction. This T-28C, one of the last built, was delivered to the Naval Air Training Command on July 9, 1957. It was assigned to VT-5 at Whiting Field where it served until June 2, 1977. At the end of its service it was placed in long-term storage at Davis-Monthan. At that time Passalacqua and his partners owned a non-airworthy F-80C that had served as a training tool at a technical school. The Air Force was interested in reacquiring the F-80C for static display, so Passalacqua and his partners agreed to trade the Shooting Star for a flyable T-28C. They were permitted to inspect and remove 146242 from storage and undertook an arduous nine-year restoration project to return the aircraft to assembly line condition. In 1996, he began flying the Trojan to numerous regional airshows where he repeatedly won awards for the quality of his restoration. It is one of the few T-28s flying with an original serial number engine and correct propeller—it represents one of the most authentic "C" model Trojans in the air.

One of the last T-28Cs delivered to the Navy was acquired by corporate pilot Tom Passalacqua and his partners. It was immaculately restored to airworthiness over a nine-year period and flies frequently to airshows throughout the country. *Mark Frankel, Trish Passalacqua*

G. Beechcraft T-34A Mentor

After a prolonged evaluation the Air Force awarded a contract to Beechcraft for 450 T-34As on March 5, 1953. This perfectly restored example, serial 53-3393 was delivered to the Air Force in March 1955. It accumulated only 1485.4 hours in training service before it was transferred to the 325th Fighter Interceptor Squadron at Truax Field, Madison, WI, in June 1958, then it was assigned to utility duties at Ellington AFB until it stricken from the Air Force inventory on August 13, 1964, with only 1654.4 hours of flight time. It was operated by the Civil Air Patrol until August 1972. It had passed through a series of private owners when it was acquired by Leroy Lakey on November 2, 1987. Lakey painstakingly restored it to its original condition and won the Judges' Choice award at the EAA AirVenture Convention, Oshkosh, WI, in 2002. Currently owned by Brett Austin, it is seen at airshows and fly-ins throughout southern California, and is considered one of the best-preserved and most authentic T-34As in existence.

F. Temco T-35 Buckaroo

The T-35 Buckaroo evolved from the GC-1B Swift, a side by side two-place civilian light plane produced by Temco which acquired the production rights from Globe Aircraft Corporation. Seeking a military application for the Swift, Temco modified a standard GC-1B (N77634) by revising the cockpit and controls to tandem, adding a new canopy, and squaring off the rudder. This modified Swift was hastily cobbled together—no engineering drawings were prepared—so that it could be included in the Air Force primary trainer competition of 1949. This modified Swift received the factory designation of TE-1A, but failed to receive any government orders. In late 1949, Temco was invited to participate in a second evaluation as the government continued to search for a new primary trainer. Using this as an opportunity to improve their earlier TE-1A, Temco engineered a substantially improved TE-1B that they nicknamed "Buckaroo." The fuselage and wing center section were totally redesigned, and the power was increased from 145 hp to 165 hp. The outer wing panels were strengthened to withstand 9 Gs, the horizontal stabilizer was raised, and the cowling was revised to reduce drag and provide more efficient cooling. The Air Force conferred the designation YT-35 on the three Buckaroos that participated in the Randolph Field evaluation, but Temco failed to win any orders from the Air Force yet again. The Saudi government, however, gave Temco an order for ten Buckaroos in 1953. The three Air Force YT-35s were sold as surplus to Hardwick aircraft on May 5, 1954. The last of the three, 50-740, was restored to airworthy condition and re-engined with a fuel-injected Continental IO-360-D. It was acquired by the founder and president of the Swift Museum Foundation in Athens Tennessee, Charlie Nelson, who maintained it in pristine condition.

A frequent award winning Beechcraft T-34A is owned by Brett Austin. It was originally restored by Leroy Lakey and won the Judge's Choice Award at the EAA Convention. Here Brett is flying at the T-34 Association Fly-In at Palm Springs CA. *Eric Van Gilder*

Joe Pardi's T-34B was restored to its exact appearance from 1956 when it served with in the Naval Air Training Command with primary training squadron VT-1. Even the instrument panel is original in the remarkable restoration. *Greg Moorehead*

H. Beechcraft T-34B Mentor

The Navy awarded a contract to Beechcraft on June 17, 1954, to build a modified version of the T-34A that was already in production for the Air Force. The Navy specified a castering nose wheel (non-steerable), an additional degree of dihedral, a 28-volt electrical system with a larger battery, removal of the fairing at the base of the rudder, and several other minor changes. The Navy assigned the designation T-34B and ordered 423 of them, the first being delivered on 17 December 1954, and the last on December 12, 1957. The T-34B proved highly successful in the Naval Air Training Command and remained in active training service until it was replaced by a turbine-powered derivative, the T-34C, in the late 1970s.

T-34B BuNo 140778 was manufactured in December 1955. It was accepted by the Navy at NAS Pensacola in January 1956 where it became one of the first Mentors assigned to the newly formed primary training squadron, VT-1, in December 1956. It served in that capacity until December 1957 when it was sent to long-term storage then stricken from Naval inventory on November 29, 1972. It was surplused to a quasi-government agency, and then sold to a private owner. In September 2003, it was purchased by Joe Pardi, the operator of a flight school at Willow Run Airport, Detroit Michigan. Because of its low airframe time (1,400 hours), Pardi decided to do a complete restoration of 140778 to its original VT-1 condition. The result is a virtual time capsule glimpse of the Naval Air Training Command at Saufley Field in mid-1950s. Not only is the airframe, powerplant, and paint authentic in every detail, but the instruments are original. This is possibly the most perfect stock restoration in the T-34 fleet and Pardi's diligence was rewarded with the coveted Best T-34 and Silver Wrench awards at the 2005 EAA AirVenture.

I. Lockheed T-33 T-Bird

When the Army Air Corps first introduced the P-80 Shooting Star into front line service at the end of WWII there was no jet trainer. New P-80 pilots were given 180 hours in the T-6, 50 hours in the P-51, and twenty-five hours in a static P-80 that was secured to the ground known as the "Captivair." This proved to be a very ineffective method of training new jet pilots—the P-80 accident rate was appalling. Recognizing the need for a two-place jet trainer, Lockheed used corporate funds to add a second seat and dual controls to a P-80C. Designated the TP-80C, Lockheed test pilot Tony LeVier flew the modified Shooting Star from Van Nuys airport, California on March 22, 1948. The newly formed Air Force was very impressed with the trainer and ordered an initial batch of twenty aircraft. These first TF-80Cs (the "P" designation was changed to "F" on June 11, 1948) were demonstrated at Air Force Bases and Naval Air Stations around the United States and generated enormous enthusiasm. Air Force and Navy orders grew rapidly as it became the US military's standard jet trainer. By the end of production in August 1959 Lockheed had built 5,691 T-33s (the designation changed from TF-80C to T-33 on May 5, 1949) and it received the affectionate nickname "T-Bird." The T-33 proved so successful that it was acquired by numerous allied nations and license produced in substantial numbers by Canadair in Canada and Kawasaki in Japan.

Noted warbird collector, Dr. John Swartz, acquired a former USAF T-33 as a restoration project in 2010. This T-Bird was built by Lockheed in 1951 with the serial number 51-17445. When it was declared surplus by the Air Force in the 1960s it transferred to Belgium to serve as a trainer for NATO forces. It survived its overseas service and was returned to the United States in the late 1970s when it was acquired by the Valiant Air Command, a foundation formed to perpetuate the history and culture of military aviation. Unrestored, it passed through a series of private owners until Dr. Swartz purchased it and started an aggressive program with Heritage Aero to restore the T-Bird to its USAF glory. The restored aircraft was flown at EAA AirVenture 2014. It is finished in the scheme of a T-33 attached to Lowry AFB in the late 1950s.

This Lockheed built T-33 is owned by Dr. John Swartz who acquired it from the Valiant Air Command. It has been flown by Dr. Swartz at EAA Airventure in 2014 and 2015. *Henning Henningsen*

J. Temco TT-1 Pinto

On June 29, 1956, the Navy issued a contract to the Temco Aircraft Corporation for 14 TT-1 Pintos to be evaluated as a jet primary trainer. The Pinto was selected over the Beechcraft Jet Mentor, a turbojet powered derivative of the T-34B. Both the Pinto and the Jet Mentor were powered by a single Continental J69-T-2 engine, and both had similar performance, but Temco was willing to spread its development costs over an anticipated production run of 500 aircraft while Beechcraft insisted on a more rapid payback. As low bidder Temco delivered the first Pinto on September 3, 1957, and the last on July 14, 1958. The TT-1 Pinto displayed pleasant flying qualities and was easy to master by student pilots with no prior flying experience, but it was extremely fuel limited, it had very poor wave-off characteristics, and it proved expensive to operate. In the spring of 1960 the Navy abandoned their jet primary trainer experiment and ferried the nine surviving Pintos (five had been lost during the evaluation) to the Naval Air Facility, Litchfield Park, Arizona for storage and disposal.

Since 1960, seven Pintos have been restored to airworthy condition. Most have been reengined with General Electric J85 or CJ-610 turbojets which provide more than three times the thrust of the original J69, but this engine upgrade requires enlarged inlets and tailpipe as well as wingtip tanks to carry additional fuel which changes the original appearance of the airplane. However, one Pinto restoration was very faithful to the original configuration. Warbird collector Ed Couches of American Aircraft Sales, Hayward California acquired BuNo, 144227 which had only 413 hours of flight time when it was stricken from inventory. Couches installed a J69-T-25 engine, an improved version of the Pinto's original J69-T-2. The new engine was lighter and provided 105 pounds of additional thrust giving Couches' delightful performance. Couches flew his authentic Pinto at numerous airshows in northern California but a fuel starvation mishap resulted in a forced landing damaging the airplane beyond repair. Nevertheless Couches restored a second Pinto, BuNo 144236 (the last Pinto built), but this time he installed the more modern J85 engine and added tip tanks.

The only civilian-owned Temco TT-1 Pinto to retain its original J69 engine is this example that was owned by Ed Couches. Unfortunately this Pinto was lost in a landing accident, but Couches restored a second example this time installing a more modern J85 engine. *Chris Hall Collection*

K. Beechcraft T-34C Turbo Mentor

In 1973, the Navy issued a development contract to Beechcraft Aircraft for the modification of three T-34B airframes (two flying articles and one static test article) to turboprop power. Beechcraft considered several powerplants but settled on the Pratt & Whitney PT6 and beefed up the airframe structure with Baron wings, Duke landing gear, and a Travel Air tail. The modified T-34Bs were designated YT-34C Turbo Mentors and underwent five years of development. The first production T-34Cs were placed in Training Command service in January 1978 and remain in limited service thirty-seven years later. Current plans are to use the T-34C in a number of utility roles through the fourth quarter of 2017. The Navy purchased 352 T-34Cs during its production run.

Civilian ownership of T-34Cs is extremely rare, but in 2013 Kevin Clark, who operates out of Paine Field in Everett, Washington, learned of an exported T-34C-1 that was available. The aircraft had been used as an escort for the presidential aircraft of Gabon in west equatorial Africa. It was corrosion free, undamaged, and very low time. Unlike a domestic Navy T-34C, the export T-34C-1 version has four hard points to carry NATO ordnance and an uprated PT6 engine to handle the higher gross weight. Clark started a complete inspection and reassembly in February 2014. By November the airplane was essentially in one piece and the systems are slowly being powered up. Clark considers this the most critical stage of the project but doesn't anticipate any insurmountable issues. He hopes to have the reconditioned T-34C-1 flying by mid-2015, and then he plans to repaint the Turbo Mentor in a Navy scheme.

Currently in the final stages of restoration, this T-34C-1 is one of a few Turbo Mentors in civilian hands. This example served with the African nation of Gabon and was acquired by Kevin Clark when that government retired it. *Kevin Clark*

Only 2 Cessna T-37s are on the civilian register, this example is owned by Jim Allen. It is a T-37C that was built for export and was restored by Lud Corraro and Wayne Brooks when it was retired by the Peruvian government. It has been flown at numerous airshows around the Midwest including the EAA Convention. *Henning Henningsen*

L. Cessna T-37C Tweet

In 1952, the Air Force launched the TX trainer program to "teach students all maneuvers and techniques which are required of the military jet pilot with the exception of ordnances." A development contact for three XT-37s was awarded to the Cessna Aircraft Company of Wichita KS, a company with very limited military experience. The first prototype was completed in eighteen months and flown four months later. The XT-37 went through a long gestation process in which numerous shortcomings were addressed, not the least of which was unpredictable spin behavior. The T-37 trained its first class of students in July 1957 and proved so effective as a primary trainer that the Air Force decided to eliminate all propeller training. Early models of the small Cessna jet were designated T-37A but an uprated engine and improved avionics resulted in the T-37B model. The T-37, affectionately nicknamed Tweet, served as the Air Force's only primary trainer for more than fifty years when it was finally retired in 2009.

Cessna also manufactured an export variant, the T-37C that had provisions for wingtip tanks and four under-wing hard points. In the early 1990s warbird collectors Lud Corrao and Wayne Brooks from Carson City, Nevada acquired four T-37C airframes from the Peruvian air Force. The four airframes provided enough parts to assemble two airworthy T-37s. The restoration was completed in the late 1990s, the two Tweets were test flown by Reno race pilot Skip Holm, painted in matching camouflage color schemes of the 524th Fighter Squadron, and offered for sale by Corrao and Brooks. In 2008, Jim Allen, a former T-33 owner was informed of the T-37s availability and jumped at the chance to own a jet that had never been available on the civilian market. Allen and his partner, Paul Walter ferried the jet to their hangar in Waukesha Wisconsin where it has been carefully maintained and flown at airshows throughout the Midwest including EAA Air Venture. Allen's T-37C, serial 13618, is a very rare airplane. Of the thousands of examples that Cessna built, only two are privately owned.

M. North American T-2B Buckeye

In December 1956, the Navy issued a Request For Proposal for an all-purpose jet trainer to be used for student pilots who had been selected for the fighter pipeline during primary training. The new trainer was to provide basic and advanced training through carrier qualification and fighter tactics. The Request specified the use of either Allison J33 or Westinghouse J34 engine. The winning proposal was submitted by North American with a conservative design that borrowed many proven features from the T-28. The aircraft was designated T2J-1 Buckeye (T-2A after 1962) and 217 were built. The T2J-1 had excellent flight characteristics (new pilots were able to transition into it after only thirty-five hours in the T-34B) but it was considered to be underpowered with its single J34 engine. In August 1962, North American flew a new version powered by twin Pratt & Whitney J60 engines that provided nearly twice the thrust at a lower installed weight. Designated the T-2B this version provided the performance that the Navy was looking for. Only 97 "B" models were manufactured before another twin-engine version, the T-2C powered by two General Electric J85s, was placed in production.

T-2B BuNo.155226 was retired from training service in 1972 as the T-2C was being introduced. The surplus Buckeye was acquired by an aviation trade school in Detroit Michigan where it was used for maintenance instruction. The school went out of business in 1990 and the T-2B was purchased by a warbird collector in Seattle Washington who started to restore it but soon put the project up for sale. Dr. Rich Sugden, a former Navy flight surgeon and experienced jet pilot, purchased the Buckeye and shipped it to Victoria Air Maintenance in Victoria, British Columbia in 1994. It was carefully returned to its original airworthy standard and was repainted in an authentic VT-23 scheme. The post restoration test flying was performed by a North American Aviation celebrity, Ed Gillespie, test pilot for the first T2J-1, BuNo.144217, in 1958. Gillespie (recently deceased) took special pride in the Sugden Buckeye: " … I was very pleased when my friend, Dr. Rich Sugden, set a new lap record at the Reno races, in his personal T-2B (J60s) by exceeding 500 mph throughout. As far as I know, he won the first and ONLY closed course race in which a T-2 had ever officially been entered."

This North American T-2B Buckeye is owned by Dr. Rich Sugden, a former Navy flight surgeon. It was restored by Victoria Air Maintenance in Canada in 1994. Its post-restoration test flights were performed by former North American Chief test Pilot, Ed Gillespie. *EAA Warbirds of America*

Probably the most complex civilian trainer is this Northrop T-38 Talon owned by Chuck Thornton. It was assembled from salvaged components and returned to airworthy condition by Thornton Aviation. It has recently been sold to the Civilian Test Pilot School in Mojave CA. *Robert B. McGregor*

N. Northrop T-38A Talon

Designed by a team headed by the legendary Edgar Schmued (designer of the P-51 Mustang and F-100 Super Sabre) the T-38 Talon was developed in response to a 1955 General Operating Requirement for a supersonic trainer. The first YT-38 was flown on April 10, 1959, powered by twin General Electric J85 turbojets. Both the airframe and the engines were remarkable achievements employing numerous innovations that resulted in the world's first purpose built supersonic trainer. After an intense but generally trouble free test program the Talon entered training service at Randolph AFB in 1961. Dubbed "The White Rocket," it was flown by every Air Force student pilot regardless of career path until the early 1990s when a more specialized syllabus was adopted. The T-38 is expected to remain in training service until 2020 when it is expected to be replaced by a new trainer that will be developed under the T-X program.

In the late 1970s, warbird owner Chuck Thornton undertook a restoration project that many considered impossible. He envisioned building an airworthy T-38 Talon from damaged airframes that the Air Force had released as economically unrepairable. By combing aircraft salvage yards and keeping a close eye on Department of Defense disposal sales Thornton was able to amass enough T-38 assemblies and components to build a complete airframe. He organized a crew of skilled T-38 technicians and assembled a new Talon from the ground up—a stunning achievement. It was test flown in 1984 then licensed by the FAA. During the restoration Thornton was able to acquire a large inventory of spares to keep the Talon flying. In addition to flying the supersonic jet for personal pleasure Thornton also makes it pay its way by using it for movie, television, and flight test work. Thornton's Talon was featured in *Dragnet* starring Tom Hanks, and Dan Akyroyd, and several television commercials.

O. Douglas TA-4J

In 1964, Douglas completed a design study for a two-place version the A-4E Skyhawk. The Navy was impressed and ordered two prototypes as the TA-4E as a replacement for the aging TF-9J Cougar. With the exception of fuel capacity, the TA-4E retained all of the operational characteristics of the single seat A-4E. The first production example of the TA-4E was delivered within a year of the prototype's maiden flight suggesting that development went smoothly. The designation of the production articles was changed to TA-4F and ultimately 352 examples were ordered. While the TA-4F could be used for either training or tactical roles, a similar lighter, lower thrust TA-4J was used only as a trainer.

The Collings Foundation Skyhawk, BuNo 153524, was accepted by the Navy as a TA-4F in 1968 (although it was built as an F, some of the operational equipment has been removed therefore the Collings Foundation refers to it as a J). It operated with Marine Air Group 43 before it was transferred to NATC (Naval Air Test Center), Patuxent River, Maryland where it served in the weapons test division and the Test Pilot School. Declared excess to the Navy's requirements in August 1994 it was flown to AMARC (Aircraft Maintenance and Regeneration Center), Tucson, AZ. The Collings Foundation, noted for its collection of immaculately restored, flyable, historic aircraft, convinced the Department of Defense that it had the competence to operate and maintain a complex jet. It required Congressional legislation and extensive negotiations with Navy attorneys, but after 4½ years a deed of gift was completed. A thorough inspection restoration and program was begun in October 2004 at the facilities of AvCraft, Myrtle Beach, SC. Technical experts from New Zealand's Safe Air Ltd were retained to help with the airframe reassembly and engine runs. The first post-restoration test flight was conducted by Capt. Bert Zeller (USNR) on December 15, 2004. The Collings Foundation operates the TA-4J at airshows throughout the country. It is also used for specialized flight instruction.

The Collings Foundation operates this Douglas TA-4J as an airshow display and training aircraft. It served as an advanced trainer with the Navy until 1994 when it was retired. It acquired by the Collingings Foundation through an Act of Congress and was restored to airworthy condition by AvCraft of Myrtle Beach SC and Safe Air Ltd. of New Zealand. *Ryan Harris*

Appendix I
LEARNING TO FLY

Learning to fly, certainly in the military, begins with a lengthy period of ground school. Instructors cover the theory of flight, the function of the flight controls, the information provided by the instruments, how to preflight the airplane, the use of checklists, the maneuvers to be flown, etc.

Regardless of how well all this material was covered, the first flight itself is usually a revelation. The instructor taxis the airplane out, takes off, climbs out, and flies to the training area. The student is generally required to follow through on the controls to begin his familiarization with their function. However, given the noise and vibration (if a propeller-driven airplane), the low-fidelity radio communications between the instructor and the controllers, increase in g-loading in turns, erratic and sometimes jarring movements of the airplane in vertical and horizontal gusts, the wholly different view of the world from altitude, etc., the student will usually be in sensory overload.

The airplane's response from the movement of the controls is intuitive, particularly in a jet airplane. Pushing the right pedal yaws the nose to the right. Moving the stick to the left causes the airplane to roll to the left. Pulling the stick back causes the nose to move higher above the horizon.

Things get complicated quickly, however, because the aircraft's initial response to control movement is almost immediately accompanied by a secondary, non-intuitive response. Left stick by itself rolls the airplane but the lift added to raise the wing creates drag that causes the nose to swing to the right, opposite the intended direction of turn. If this adverse aileron yaw is not minimized by the control system design, the pilot has to add a touch of rudder in the direction of the roll. Pushing the left rudder pedal yaws the nose to the left but also results in a roll to the left, which is what left stick is supposed to be for, because the wing moving forward generates more lift and the wing moving aft, less.

The actual result from movement of the controls in a propeller-driven airplane is even more complex. Pulling the stick back causes the nose to move above the horizon but as a result of propeller factor (the down-going propeller blade on the right side of the propeller disc providing more thrust than its counterpart going up on the left side), the nose also yaws to the left if right rudder is not used in conjunction with the stick. Depending on the airplane

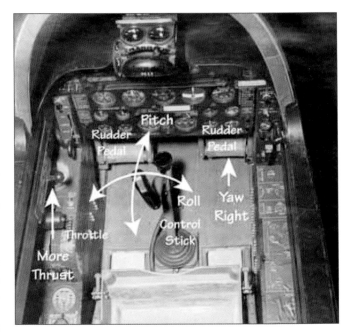

Cockpit Flight Controls. *US Navy photo annotated by T.H.Thomason*

and its attitude, adding power with the throttle might result in the nose going up or down as well as yawing and or rolling to the left.

Sorting all this out begins with the student simply trying to fly straight and maintain a constant pitch attitude: keeping the wings level, the line of the horizon at the same height in the windscreen, and the ball of the turn indicator centered. (Sometimes the instructor "gives" the student one control at a time, e.g. only the rudder pedals, so he can experience its function in isolation.) The degree of difficulty is increased as the training progresses: the student not only has to keep the wings level, but maintain a heading; he not only has to keep the pitch constant but hold altitude.

Turns are next. Airplanes are best turned by banking but unlike a sled or a boat or a car, the turn control is not held for the duration of the turn. Instead, the airplane is rolled into a bank with the ailerons, which are then neutralized until the time comes to roll back to level flight. If the control system does not automatically take care of the adverse aileron yaw, rudder is required to offset it while the ailerons are used to roll into and out of the bank. Some backpressure on the stick has to be used while in the turn

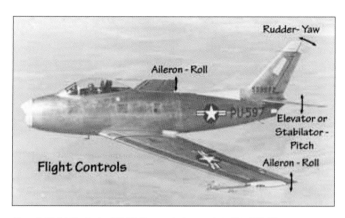

Aircraft Flight Controls. *US Air Force photo annotated by T.H.Thomason*

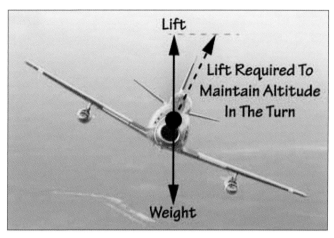

Lift Required in Turns. *US Air Force photo annotated by T.H.Thomason*

to increase lift since the lift vector of the wings is now tilted to one side and its vertical component no longer equals the airplane's weight. The objective is a coordinated turn, neither slipping (too much "top" rudder) nor skidding (too much "bottom" rudder), with the ball centered in the turn and bank indicator. "Top" and "bottom" refer to the rudder pedal locations relative to the horizon when the airplane is banked.

Once the basics of the turn are understood, precision is introduced. The student is required to roll the airplane to a specific bank, say 30 degrees, not 25 or 35. He is required to roll out on a heading, which requires some anticipation since the airplane will continue to turn while it is rolling out. Then the turns have to be made while holding a specific altitude, all increasing the degree of difficulty.

Climbs are generally next. To begin the climb, the nose is raised above the horizon with backpressure on the stick. As the airplane slows, the student needs to add power for the climb. In addition, some rudder movement will also be required a propeller-driven airplane. The concept of trimming out the aft-stick pressure required at the slower speed used for climb is now introduced. Once all that is sorted out, climbing turns are next. Finally, the process of leveling out at a desired altitude, resuming cruising speed, setting cruise power and retrimming is demonstrated and practiced.

Descents are relatively easy, initiated by a power reduction that might very well require other control changes to achieve the desired position of the nose below the horizon in order to lose altitude at cruising speed. By this time, turning and retrimming will have become somewhat second nature as well. Next, the student is generally introduced to slow flight and gliding, which are maintaining altitude or descending respectively at a relatively low airspeed, roughly the same as the speed used to climb; the primary difference among the three flight conditions is the amount of power used.

Being introduced to and achieving a modicum of competency at all these basic maneuvers usually requires several flights over the space of some days and a gradually increasing degree of precision in maintaining airspeed, bank angle, heading, altitude, etc. Nevertheless, at some point even earlier, the instructor might coach the student through his first takeoff. As increasing mastery of the controls is attained, the instructor will talk the student through an approach to landing or even all the way to touchdown and rollout.

Before serious landing practice begins, however, the student needs to be introduced to and practice stalling the airplane. Stalling involves increasing the angle of attack (the angle between the horizontal axis of the airplane and the relative wind) until the lift that the wing provides is no longer increasing with the increasing angle of attack. At that point, the airplane begins to fall and one wing might drop more quickly than the other. In accordance with the airplane's inherent stability, the nose also drops in spite of the stick being held aft or even moved farther aft. Avoidance of unintended stalls is so important that stall warning is mandatory, either inherent (increasing airframe/control buffet) or artificial (warning horns or stick shakers/pushers).

Recovery from a stall is straightforward but counterintuitive. The backpressure on the stick needs to be released even though nose is going down. The recovery is expedited if power is added but too much power too soon might result in a response in pitch and yaw with which the student can't cope the first time or two.

Once the basic stall and recovery is learned, other types of stalls are introduced, beginning with stalls while climbing, descending, or gliding. Next are stalls in the landing configuration with the wheels and flaps down. The response is frequently different in detail from those with the wheels and flaps up. Recognition of an impending stall in the landing configuration is particularly important because the airplane when so configured is likely to be close to the ground, minimizing the altitude available for recovery. Accelerated stalls, e.g. at airspeeds higher than in level flight at 1 G, can be experienced either in a turn or with a quick pull up at speed; depending on the airplane type, its change in attitude following an accelerated stall might again be very different from the 1 G version.

Cross-control stalls come in two variations, the slip and the skid, both generally associated with the approach to a landing. In a slip, "top" rudder is used to keep the airplane from turning the way it is banked; when the airplane stalls, it tends to roll back toward the wings being level rather than doing anything untoward. (Slips are useful in crosswind landings and for losing altitude quickly on approach.) In a skid, on the other hand, the rudder is being used to turn the airplane faster than it should for its angle of bank; this is all too often the case when the pilot is turning from base leg to final on the landing approach. Slowing to stall speed in a skid will eventually result in a sudden increase in angle of bank and loss of altitude as the wing on the inside of the turn stalls first, the beginning of a tailspin. Doing so at low altitude is very likely to be fatal. (For more on spins, see Chapter 1.)

Landings are the most difficult phase of flight to master initially. A good landing for a low-time pilot begins with a well-executed approach that results in the proper airspeed on final approach. (Military approaches generally start with airplane flying over or to one side of the landing runway in the direction of landing, with the pilot then executing a racetrack-type pattern while losing altitude and lining up for the final approach.) The result should be that the airplane is lined up with the runway at the correct approach speed and height for the distance from the threshold. All the student has to do then is maintain the airspeed and that angle of descent until the time comes to flare (raising the nose to slow the speed and more importantly, slow the rate of descent) for the touchdown.

The proper timing of the flare is all-important. Begun too high and/or too quickly, it will result in a high rate of sink on touchdown at best; worse case is a stall well above the runway with a wing dropping enough to hit the ground first. Begun too low and/or not quickly enough will result in the nose wheel touching first. That might cause it to collapse or at best, result in a bounce that can be recovered from. If the bounce is bad enough and the student (or instructor) doesn't response quickly enough, the airplane will nose back down to an even harder touchdown.

Wind gusts or a crosswind add a degree of difficulty to landings, with a gusting crosswind being the worst. Constant correction in power is required if the wind speed

is changing in order to stay on the glide path and pitch corrections might very well be required to maintain airspeed. Crosswinds require compensation by either angling into the wing or side slipping on approach so that the airplane is tracking along an extension of the runway centerline. Many students, so overloaded with maintaining track and glide path, forget to flare on their first crosswind landing.

However, if the student doesn't give up and the instructor is adequate to the task, the time eventually comes when the student has demonstrated adequate mastery of the landing in addition to all the other basics of flight. His or her reward is a first solo flight, which sometimes comes as a surprise to the student, particularly when he or she is not as confident as the instructor must be when the time arrives.

A major milestone in the student pilot's training, the first solo is nevertheless a baby step, with the student confined to the pattern for a few takeoff and landings under the watchful eye of the instructor. He or she won't be released to the practice area until the instructor is sure that the student can cope with an engine failure by selecting an appropriate emergency landing site and making a successful approach to it with the engine throttled back.

Still to come are control of the airplane solely with respect to instruments and planning and execution of cross-country trips. At some point, the short-field and soft-field takeoff and landing variations have to be mastered along with flight maneuvers like turns around a point, which is an excellent illustration of the effect of wind on the flight path of the airplane (long ago it was helpful in identifying the name of a town on a water tower for navigation purposes). In the case of the military aviator, the student pilot has to learn aerobatics as well as the eccentricities involved in joining up with and flying in formation close to other airplanes. If successful in avoiding elimination from the program at each phase, he or she then progresses to other military-specific training like the precise task of air-to-air refueling, where the airplanes are not only flying in formation but physically connected. Even more challenging is the three-dimensional chess involved in the employment of weapons, both air-to-ground and particularly air-to-air, where all the pieces are moving. US Navy pilots also have to become proficient in the art of taking off from and landing back on an aircraft carrier, probably the most difficult skill that a military aviator has to master.

Earning your wings is an apt phrase for the process of learning to fly.

Appendix II
TRAINER MARKINGS AND PAINT SCHEMES

In general, aircraft markings perform five basic functions: national identity, branch of service identity, organizational assignment, individual aircraft identification, and servicing or safety advisory. In general, the markings applied to trainers conformed to the directives for those in other US military service applications. The star-and-bar national insignia was almost always present in full color in four positions: upper left wing, lower right wing, and both sides of the fuselage in sizes dictated by specification.

Paint schemes vary as a result of the trade offs between production cost, e.g. natural metal versus corrosion protection and the desire for conspicuity or camouflage. Trainers, except for the bright yellow used in Primary, initially followed the standard practice in each service. However, both services subsequently evaluated and implemented high visibility schemes for aircraft assigned to their training commands.

A. Air Force Markings

All non-camouflaged Air Force trainers since 1947 carried "USAF" on their upper right and lower left wings to identify the branch of service. Further, "U.S. Air Force" was initially placed on the vertical tail surfaces in small letters over the radio call sign. In the mid-1950s this was moved to the fuselage sides in large letters, and even (in the case of the T-34A) displaced the fuselage national insignia. Insignia Blue paint was specified for the "U.S. Air Force," but Insignia White was generally used when placed on dark backgrounds.

The Air Training Command placed its insignia initially on the noses of its trainers but moved it to the vertical tails after 1955, where it was retained after becoming the Air Education and Training Command in 1991. In the early 1950s, the Air Force Base of the training wing was painted over the ATC emblem, but when ATC changed from its circular command emblem to the current shield design, the base name was dropped from use and it was virtually impossible to identify the home base of any ATC aircraft until unique two-letter tail codes were gradually introduced in the mid-1980s. The style and location of the ATC/AETC tail codes was standardized to conform to the style used throughout the USAF and remains in use as this is written. The use of tail codes also led to the gradual introduction of squadron emblems or nicknames displayed on colored bands placed in the aircraft vertical tails.

Individual aircraft designation and serial number for all USAF aircraft including trainers is placed in small letters in a data block located below the windscreen on the left side of the aircraft. All aircraft had its radio call sign, consisting of the last digit of the fiscal year in the aircraft serial number plus the aircraft sequence number of that fiscal year, applied to the vertical tail surfaces in Black letters. The radio call sign initially had a minimum of four digits, but this was changed around 1955 to have a minimum of five digits. In practice, when the sequence number had more than five digits (i.e. 10,000 or more aircraft procured in a given fiscal year) the last digit of the fiscal year was dropped from the radio call sign. The adoption of tail codes led to a change in the presentation of the aircraft radio call sign with the last three digits of the sequence number applied in large size and the letters "AF" and the first two digits of the radio call sign applied 40% of the height of the "last three" and placed to its right.

At the end of World War II, the Army Air Forces developed a series of codes to identify low-flying aircraft performing unauthorized maneuvers over bases and civilian communities. These "Buzz Numbers" were designed to provide a way for individuals on the ground unfamiliar with aircraft recognition to identify the type and serial number of the offending aircraft. These markings were continued after the Air Force became a separate service in 1947 and remained in use until the mid-1960s. The Buzz Numbers consisted of a two-letter code, the first letter of which indicated the aircraft class (T- for trainer) and the second letter the type of aircraft (TA- for T-6 Texan, TD- for T-34 Mentor, etc). The letters were followed by the last three digits of the aircraft serial number for positive identification of the airplane and therefore its pilot. When there were two, three, or four of the same type of aircraft with the same last three digits, a suffix (A, B, or C) was sometimes added to the Buzz Number.

B. Air Force Paint Schemes

Air Force trainers, like most of its postwar non-tactical types, flew in natural metal finish, a practice started late in World War II. With the exception of T-6Gs used as primary trainers in the early 1950s, natural metal was continued through the T-37 in the late 1950s. Anti-glare panels were applied in matte Medium Green and Flat Black, as were the inboard surfaces of wingtip mounted fuel tanks. The Northrop T38 Talon, however, was finished overall in Insignia White due to non-uniform colors of the various skin panels.

Due to a series of fatal airliner in-flight collisions in the late 1950s, many US military aircraft had high visibility fluorescent ("Day-Glo") paint applied to nose, wingtip and tail surfaces. These bright panels were carried until around 1963, when they were dropped due to high maintenance cost and man-hours, increased aircraft weights and, in the case of tactical types, military responses to the Berlin Wall and Cuban Missile crises as well as the escalation of combat activity in Southeast Asia.

By the late 1960s, the need for improved corrosion control came to the forefront with aircraft service lives measured in decades rather than years while operating in such hostile climates as the jungles of Southeast Asia and the polluted skies at home. Tactical units camouflaged their combat jets, but camouflaged trainers were deemed not in keeping with the mission. In the early 1970s, Air Training Command tested a number of potential schemes for its T-37 fleet at Laughlin AFB, TX. The "Candy Cane Air Force" looked at both highly visible schemes as well as some relatively bland ones, ultimately settling on the scheme used for over ten years on the T-38 fleet—overall Glossy Insignia White. The all-White ATC trainer fleet remained until the mid-1980s when a split scheme of Insignia White over Medium Blue was introduced. This scheme still exists as of this writing, but is only applied to primary trainers—the T-6A Texan IIs.

Advanced and combat lead-in/conversion trainer schemes were identical to those in use in the combat commands, with the exception of the T-38 which was Insignia White overall until the mid-1980s. By then, the AT-38B lead-in fighter trainers (LIFT) had adopted a variety of camouflage schemes similar to those used by T-38s flown by the tactical Aggressor Squadrons. After AETC regained the LIFT mission in the early 1990s, a three-tone blue camouflage scheme was adopted for their AT-38s. As the twenty-first century approached, AETC reversed its decision on camouflaging its flight trainers and soon a two-tone scheme of Glossy Aircraft Gray and Glossy Engine Gray was adopted for the T-38A and T-38C trainers.

C. Navy Markings

Each Navy aircraft has been assigned a serial number when it is delivered from the manufacturer. It is commonly referred to as the Bureau Number, after the Bureau of Aeronautics, which was an early name for the Navy organization that procured aircraft for Navy and Marine Corps use. The numbers are sequential and usually assigned to procurement contracts in blocks. For example, the fourteen production Temco TT-1s were assigned BuNos 144223-144236. (The serial numbers reached six digits in 1945; not all assigned Bureau Numbers are actually used because of production cancellations.)

The full Bureau Number is usually placed on the aircraft on the sides of the aft fuselage and only a few inches high. Often the last four digits of the number are repeated on the vertical fin, several inches high.

When assigned to an aviation unit, the Bureau Numbers are used mainly for maintenance records. However, in cases where the unit is only assigned one or two aircraft of a particular type, the last three digits of the Bureau Number are usually used as the side number.

Squadrons that operate more than one or two of the same type of aircraft typically assign each one a side number for identification by ground crew, dispatch, pilots, air traffic control, etc. These can range from one to three digits depending on the quantity being operated and might be segmented into 1XX, 2YY, 3ZZ ranges for convenience of identification by squadron within a wing or subunit within a unit or squadron. These side numbers are marked on the nose of the airplane and sometimes repeated on the wings and elsewhere to readily identify a specific airplane from any aspect.

The units themselves are identified by a tail code, which is also frequently marked on a wing as well. These first became assigned as letters toward the end of World War II. The usage has ranged from a single letter to a letter plus a number to two letters. The training command initially used one or two letters. A single letter or the first of two letters identified the base or station while the second letter identified the squadron or other differentiation. For example, in 1951 WC was the tail code for Basic Training Unit One North (BTG-1N) at North Whiting Field and WB was the tail code for Basic Training Unit One South (BTG-1S) at South Whiting Field.

There were subsequent changes and refinements to the tail codes with a major change in September 1956. The tail code was now to consist of a number and a letter: the number 2 was assigned to Basic Training Command aircraft, 3 to Advanced Training Command Aircraft, and 4 to Technical Training Command Aircraft. The letter to be used varied by Command.

The unit designation was also frequently marked on an aircraft's aft fuselage. Up until 1960, the Basic and Advanced Training Commands used different systems for unit numbers. The Basic Training Command units were identified by single digits, e.g. BTG-2. The Advanced Training Command units were assigned a three-digit number: the first digit was 1 or 2 for non-ASW intermediate (none after 1958) and advanced respectively; the second digit (0/1/2) differentiated units that had the same syllabus at the same base; and the third digit indicated the base, e.g. 2 was assigned to NAS Kingsville, Texas. ATU-222 was the squadron providing advanced training in F11Fs there.

The major change in unit designations occurred in 1960, when Basic Training Groups/Units and Advanced Training Unit were redesignated as training squadrons. Basic Training Group 3 at Whiting became VT-3; Advanced Training Unit 203 at NAAS Chase Field became VT-24.

The last major reorganization occurred in 1971 with the change to Training Air Wings. In mid- to late 1975, the training command tail codes were changed to single letters assigned to each training wing, with units within the wing differentiated by three-digit side numbers, the first digit denoting the specific unit.

D. Navy Paint Schemes

Roughly speaking, at the end of World War II the Navy's primary trainers were overall glossy Orange Yellow, basic/intermediate trainers were natural metal and advanced/operational trainers were the same overall blue that they had been in fleet squadrons. Yellow basically signified that a student pilot might be flying the airplane and appropriate caution and deference were to be accorded. Green bands were added to the fuselage and wings of airplanes in the instrument-training units to suggest an extra degree of caution to pilots encountering one of them.

In early 1952, Training Command requested that the natural-metal SNJs also be painted overall Orange-Yellow to make them more conspicuous in the crowded skies over the training bases and in the practice areas. This also provided some benefit from a corrosion-control standpoint.

In May 1952, in response to those concerns, BuAer directed the Training Command to conduct an evaluation of high-visibility color schemes. Various ones, some incorporating "Day-Glo" (a commercial brand of fluorescent paint) were evaluated on SNJs in BTU-1 and -2 at Whiting and Corry Fields as well as helicopters and twin-engine Beech SNBs being used for training. The result was an instruction in November 1953 to paint the SNJs, the new T-28Bs, and helicopters overall Orange Yellow. The SNBs were to be painted in a split International Orange and Insignia White Scheme with the top half of the fuselage and forward half of the wings and empennage painted white and the remainder and nose of the airplane painted International Orange.

In late 1954, International Orange and Insignia White began to be used on the previously natural metal jet trainers as well to make them more conspicuous, beginning with the TV-2, although the areas of White versus International Orange varied considerably. For example, the front half of the wing was painted International Orange and the aft half White, probably to increase the head-on visibility.

In late 1958, Red-Orange fluorescent paint was dictated for the high-visibility areas of the paint scheme. However, this paint proved to lack durability and quickly faded, not only losing the visibility enhancement but also becoming unsightly. As a result, the use of fluorescent paint was discontinued in 1964 and the use of International Orange resumed.

International Orange, which is more red than orange, was subsequently deemed to provide more visibility than Orange Yellow, which is more yellow than orange. The T-28B/Cs and T-34Bs began to be painted in White and International Orange schemes in 1962. There was an evaluation of chrome yellow versus International Orange areas on a few T-34Cs in 1989. However, the International Orange color prevailed, albeit in greater proportion of the overall surface area than it had been.

POSTWAR NAVY TRAINERS

Drawings on this page to the same scale

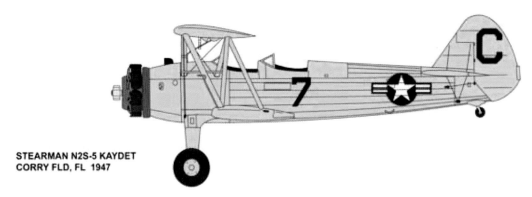

STEARMAN N2S-5 KAYDET
CORRY FLD, FL 1947

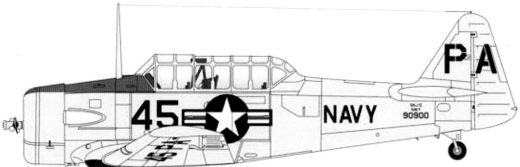

NORTH AMERICAN SNJ-5 TEXAN BuNo. 90900
IBTU
NAS PENSACOLA, FL 1952

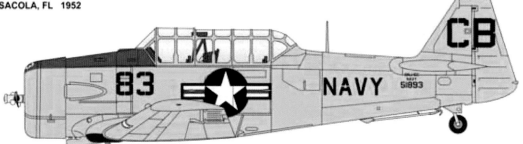

NORTH AMERICAN SNJ-5C TEXAN BuNo. 51893
CQTU-4
CORRY FIELD, FL 1950

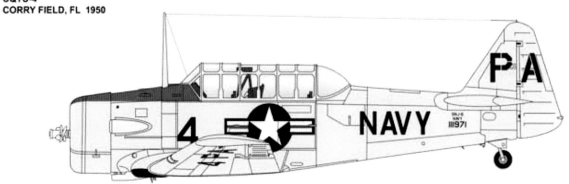

NORTH AMERICAN SNJ-6 TEXAN BuNo. 111971
IBTU
NAS PENSACOLA, FL 1951

© 2015

NORTH AMERICAN T-6 TEXAN

T-6C-10-NT 42-43993
HAMILTON AAB, CA 1947

T-6F-NT 44-82017
1947

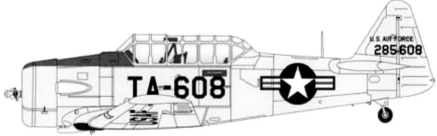

T-6D-10-NT 42-85608
3555th PTG
PERRIN AFB, TX 1951

T-6G-NF 49-3477
3560th PTG
COLUMBUS AFB, MS 1952

T-6G-NF 49-3190
3306th PTG (Contract)
BAINBRIDGE AB, GA 1954

USAF BASIC TRAINER COMPETITION
1947-1948

Drawings on this page to the same scale

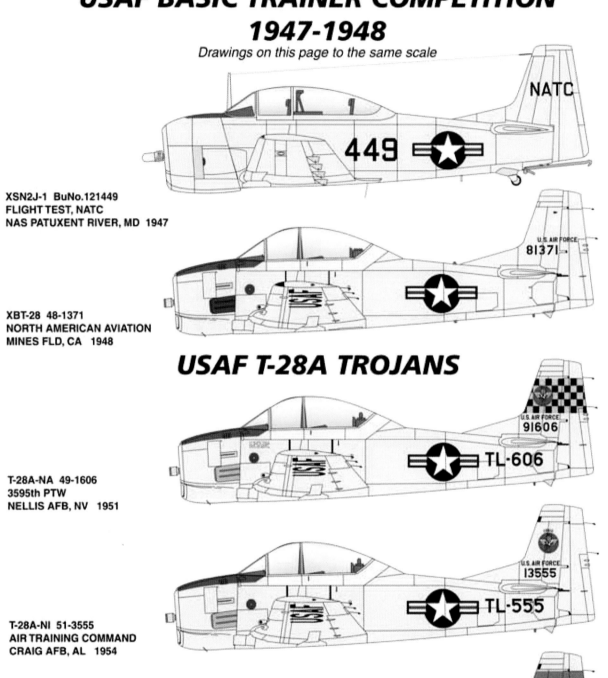

XSN2J-1 BuNo.121449
FLIGHT TEST, NATC
NAS PATUXENT RIVER, MD 1947

XBT-28 48-1371
NORTH AMERICAN AVIATION
MINES FLD, CA   1948

USAF T-28A TROJANS

T-28A-NA 49-1606
3595th PTW
NELLIS AFB, NV 1951

T-28A-NI 51-3555
AIR TRAINING COMMAND
CRAIG AFB, AL 1954

T-28A-NT 52-1186
AIR TRAINING COMMAND,   1959

© 2014

NORTH AMERICAN T-28B/C TROJANS

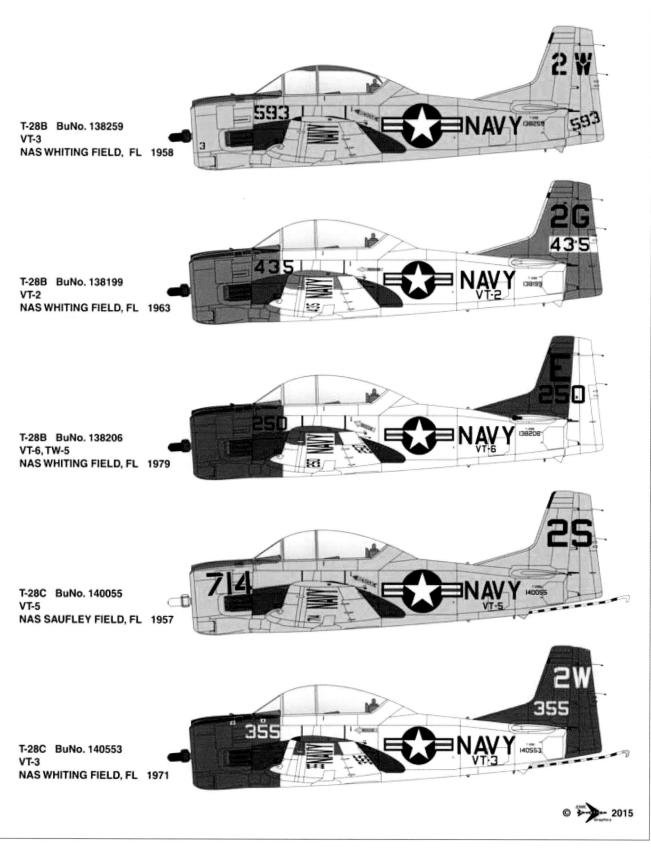

T-28B BuNo. 138259
VT-3
NAS WHITING FIELD, FL 1958

T-28B BuNo. 138199
VT-2
NAS WHITING FIELD, FL 1963

T-28B BuNo. 138206
VT-6, TW-5
NAS WHITING FIELD, FL 1979

T-28C BuNo. 140055
VT-5
NAS SAUFLEY FIELD, FL 1957

T-28C BuNo. 140553
VT-3
NAS WHITING FIELD, FL 1971

© IONK Graphics 2015

NORTH AMERICAN T-28B FOUR-VIEW

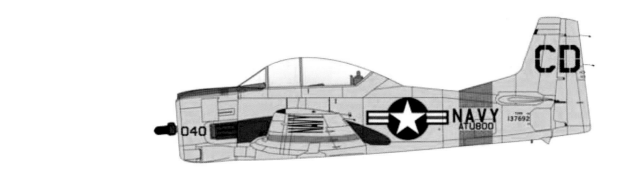

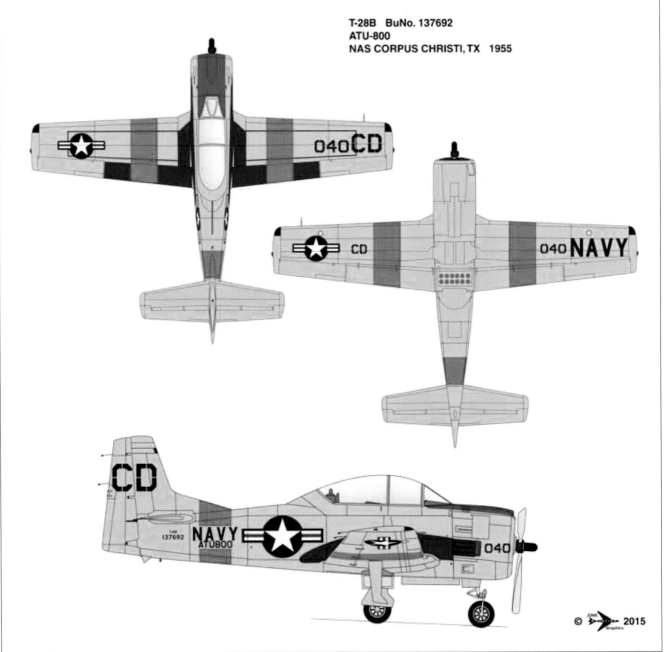

T-28B   BuNo. 137692
ATU-800
NAS CORPUS CHRISTI, TX   1955

USAF PRIMARY TRAINER COMPETITION
1949-1950

Drawings on this page to the same scale

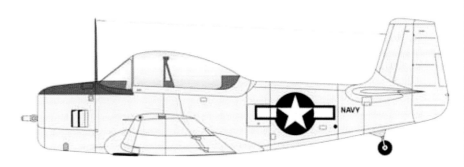

XNQ-1 BuNo. 75725
FAIRCHILD AIRCRAFT CORP
HAGERSTOWN, MD 1946

XT-31 BuNo. 75726
FAIRCHILD AIRCRAFT CORP
HAGERSTOWN, MD 19496

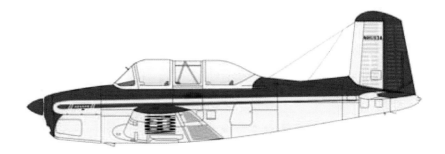

BEECHCRAFT 45 N8593A
BEECH AIRCRAFT CORP
WICHITA, KS 1950

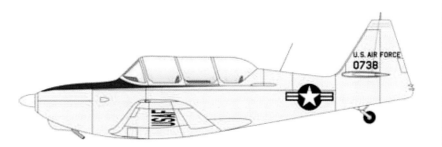

YT-35-TP BUCKAROO 50-738
TEMCO AIRCRAFT CORP
DALLAS, TX 1952

© 2015

BEECH T-34A MENTORS

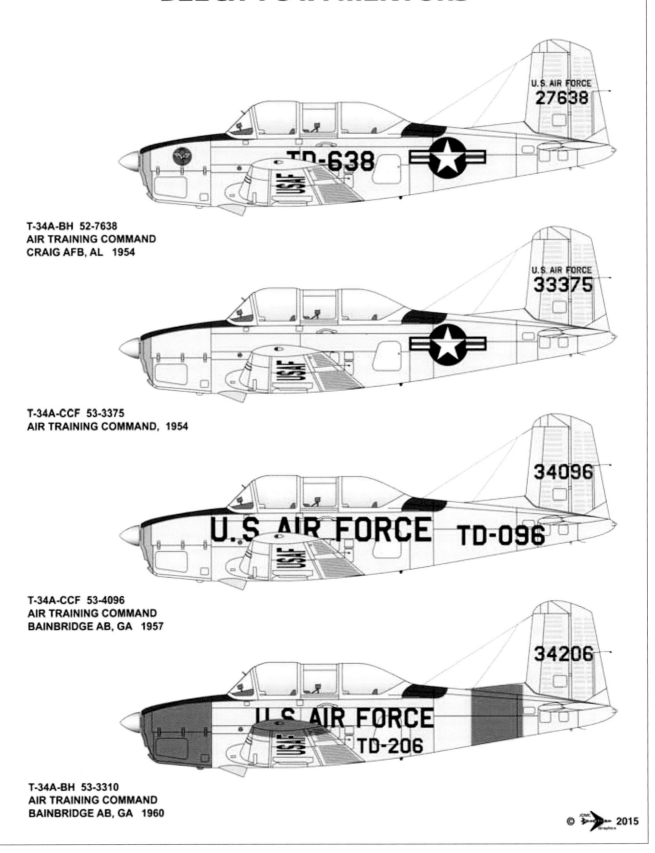

U.S. AIR FORCE
27638

TD-638

USAF

T-34A-BH 52-7638
AIR TRAINING COMMAND
CRAIG AFB, AL 1954

U.S. AIR FORCE
33375

USAF

T-34A-CCF 53-3375
AIR TRAINING COMMAND, 1954

34096

U.S AIR FORCE TD-096

USAF

T-34A-CCF 53-4096
AIR TRAINING COMMAND
BAINBRIDGE AB, GA 1957

34206

U.S AIR FORCE
TD-206

USAF

T-34A-BH 53-3310
AIR TRAINING COMMAND
BAINBRIDGE AB, GA 1960

© 2015

BEECH T-34B MENTORS

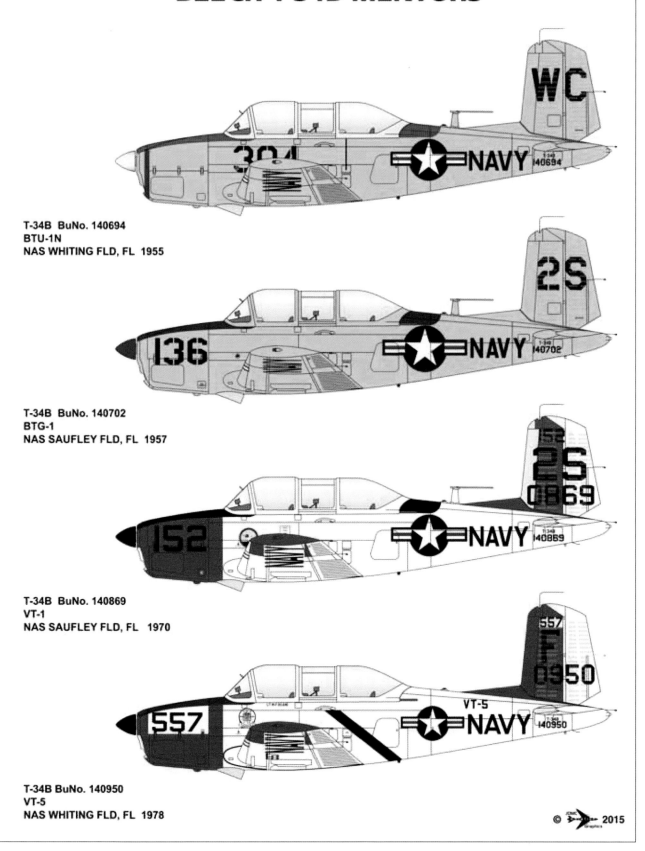

T-34B BuNo. 140694
BTU-1N
NAS WHITING FLD, FL 1955

T-34B BuNo. 140702
BTG-1
NAS SAUFLEY FLD, FL 1957

T-34B BuNo. 140869
VT-1
NAS SAUFLEY FLD, FL   1970

T-34B BuNo. 140950
VT-5
NAS WHITING FLD, FL 1978

© 2015

BEECH T-34B FOUR-VIEW

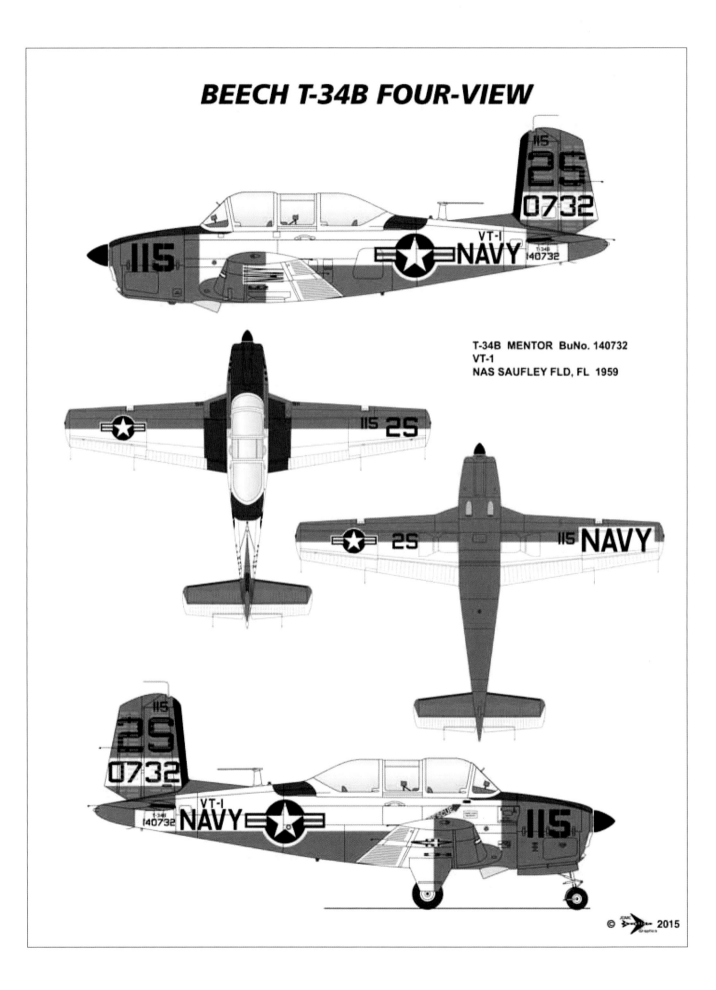

T-34B MENTOR BuNo. 140732
VT-1
NAS SAUFLEY FLD, FL 1959

© 2015

304

NAVY LOCKHEED JET TRAINERS

TO-1 SHOOTING STAR BuNo. 33860
ATU-200
NAS KINGSVILLE, TX 1951

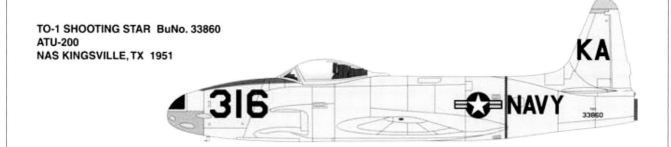

TO-2 SHOOTING STAR BuNo. 131816
ATU-200
NAS KINGSVILLE, TX   1955

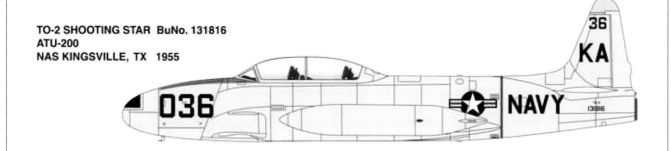

TV-2 SHOOTING STAR BuNo. 137981
ATU-205
NAS PENSACOLA, FL 1958

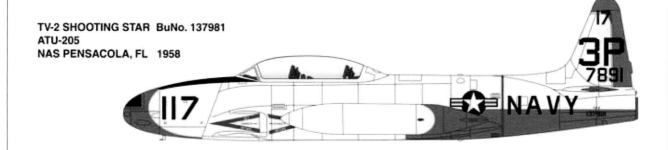

T2V-1 SEASTAR BuNo. 144176
BTG-7
NAS MEMPHIS, TN 1960

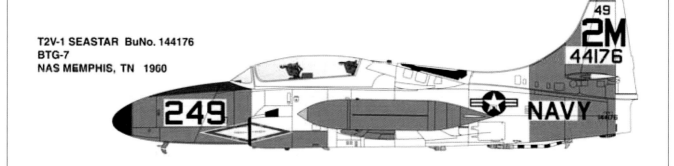

 © 2015

Appendix II

LOCKHEED T-33A "T-BIRDS"

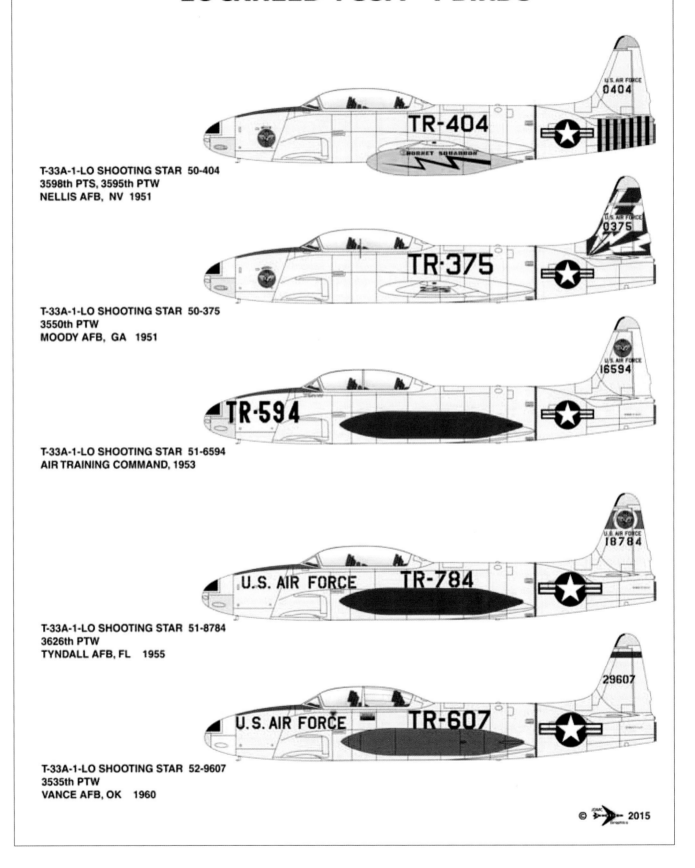

T-33A-1-LO SHOOTING STAR 50-404
3598th PTS, 3595th PTW
NELLIS AFB, NV 1951

T-33A-1-LO SHOOTING STAR 50-375
3550th PTW
MOODY AFB, GA 1951

T-33A-1-LO SHOOTING STAR 51-6594
AIR TRAINING COMMAND, 1953

T-33A-1-LO SHOOTING STAR 51-8784
3626th PTW
TYNDALL AFB, FL   1955

T-33A-1-LO SHOOTING STAR 52-9607
3535th PTW
VANCE AFB, OK   1960

© 2015

NAVY ATU GRUMMAN FIGHTERS I

Drawings on this page to the same scale

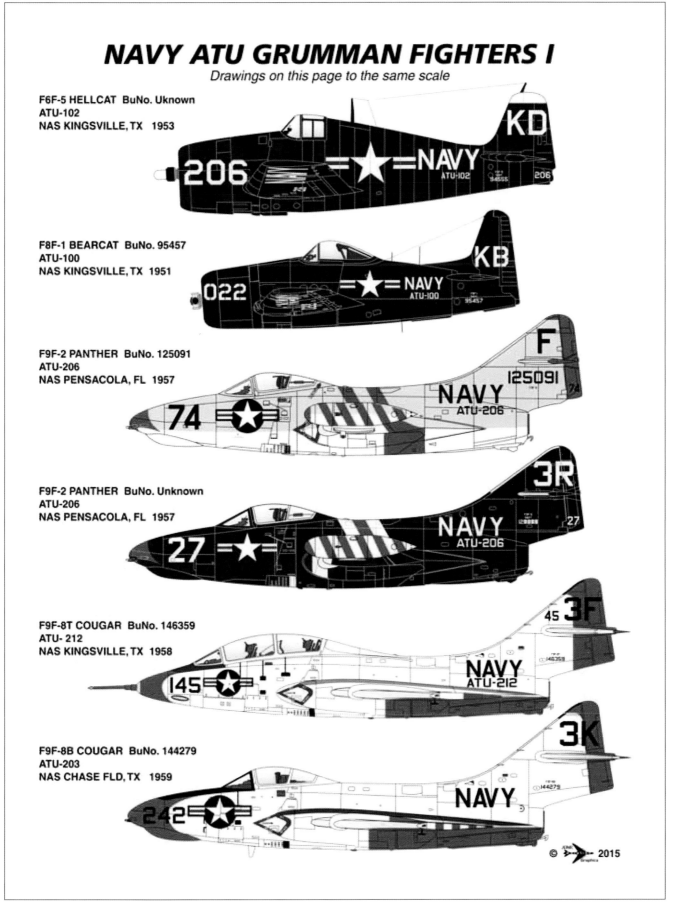

F6F-5 HELLCAT BuNo. Uknown
ATU-102
NAS KINGSVILLE, TX 1953

F8F-1 BEARCAT BuNo. 95457
ATU-100
NAS KINGSVILLE, TX 1951

F9F-2 PANTHER BuNo. 125091
ATU-206
NAS PENSACOLA, FL 1957

F9F-2 PANTHER BuNo. Unknown
ATU-206
NAS PENSACOLA, FL 1957

F9F-8T COUGAR BuNo. 146359
ATU- 212
NAS KINGSVILLE, TX 1958

F9F-8B COUGAR BuNo. 144279
ATU-203
NAS CHASE FLD, TX 1959

© 2015

GRUMMAN F9F-2P PANTHER FOUR-VIEW

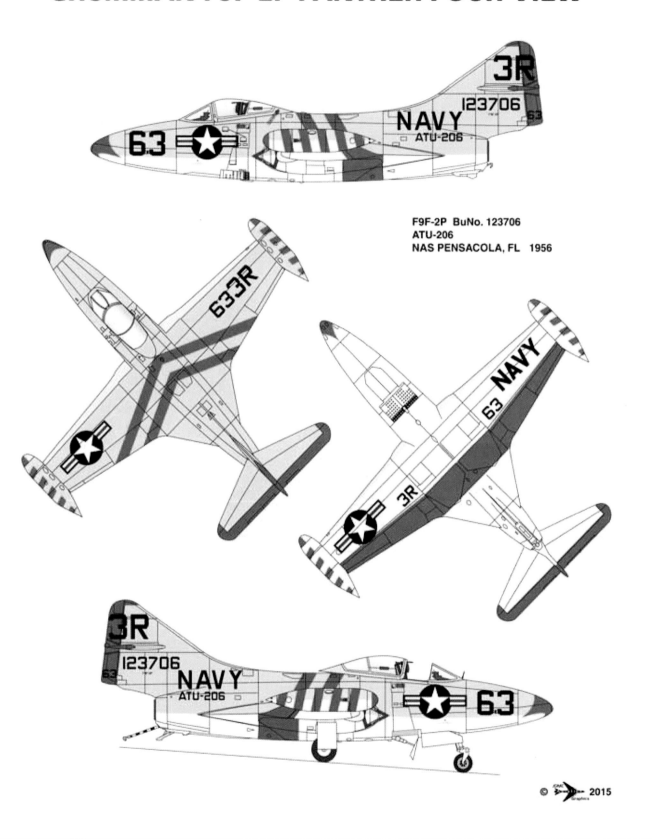

F9F-2P BuNo. 123706
ATU-206
NAS PENSACOLA, FL   1956

NAVY ATU GRUMMAN FIGHTERS II

Drawings on this page to the same scale

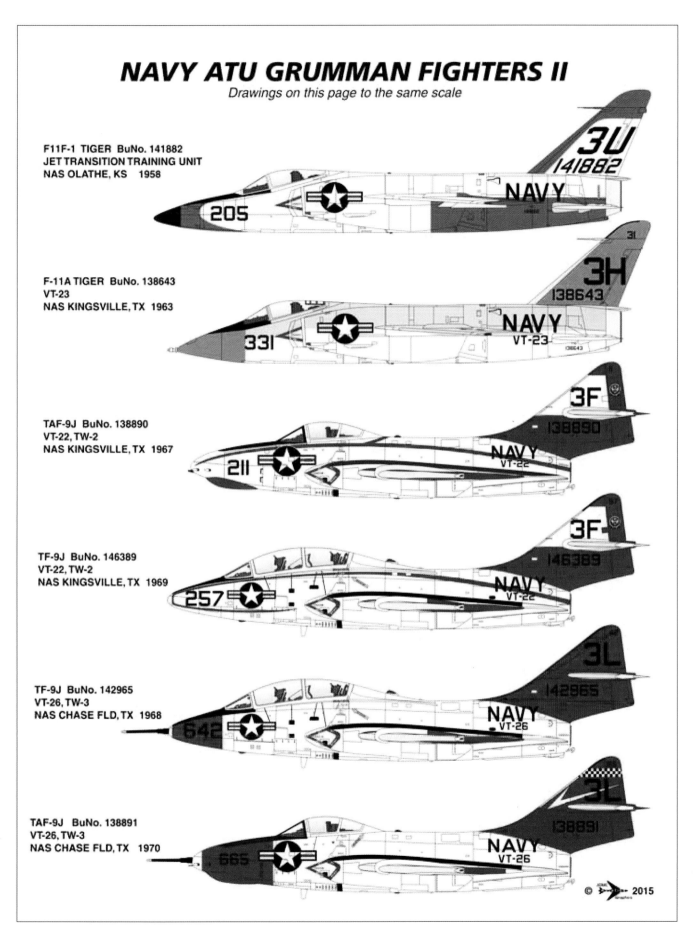

F11F-1 TIGER BuNo. 141882
JET TRANSITION TRAINING UNIT
NAS OLATHE, KS   1958

F-11A TIGER BuNo. 138643
VT-23
NAS KINGSVILLE, TX 1963

TAF-9J BuNo. 138890
VT-22, TW-2
NAS KINGSVILLE, TX 1967

TF-9J BuNo. 146389
VT-22, TW-2
NAS KINGSVILLE, TX 1969

TF-9J BuNo. 142965
VT-26, TW-3
NAS CHASE FLD, TX 1968

TAF-9J BuNo. 138891
VT-26, TW-3
NAS CHASE FLD, TX 1970

© 2015

CESSNA T-37A/B "TWEETS"

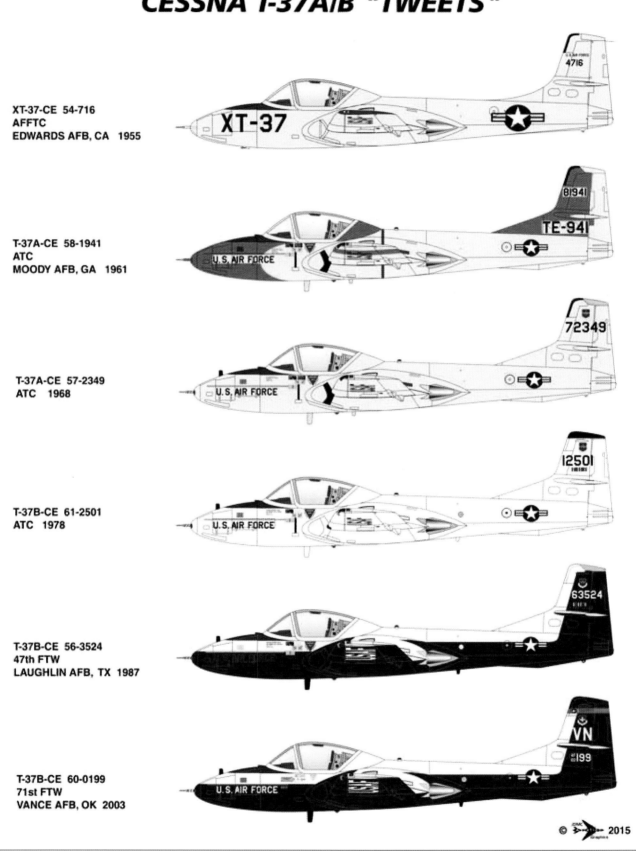

XT-37-CE 54-716
AFFTC
EDWARDS AFB, CA 1955

T-37A-CE 58-1941
ATC
MOODY AFB, GA 1961

T-37A-CE 57-2349
ATC 1968

T-37B-CE 61-2501
ATC 1978

T-37B-CE 56-3524
47th FTW
LAUGHLIN AFB, TX 1987

T-37B-CE 60-0199
71st FTW
VANCE AFB, OK 2003

© 2015

"CANDY CANE AIR FORCE"
ATC Color Scheme Evaluation. Laredo AFB, TX, 1971

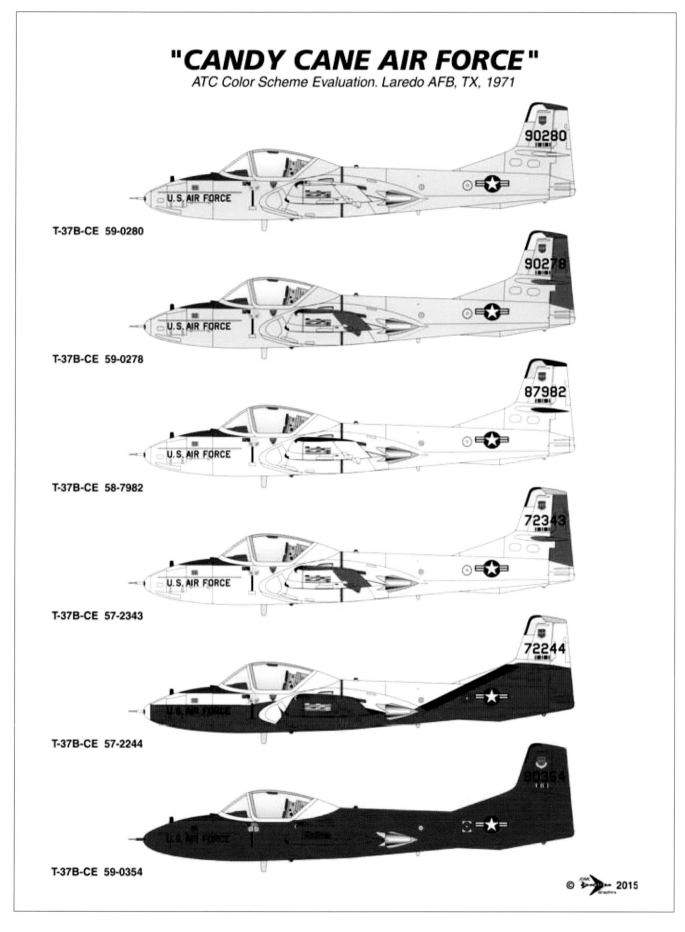

T-37B-CE 59-0280

T-37B-CE 59-0278

T-37B-CE 58-7982

T-37B-CE 57-2343

T-37B-CE 57-2244

T-37B-CE 59-0354

CESSNA T-37B FOUR-VIEW

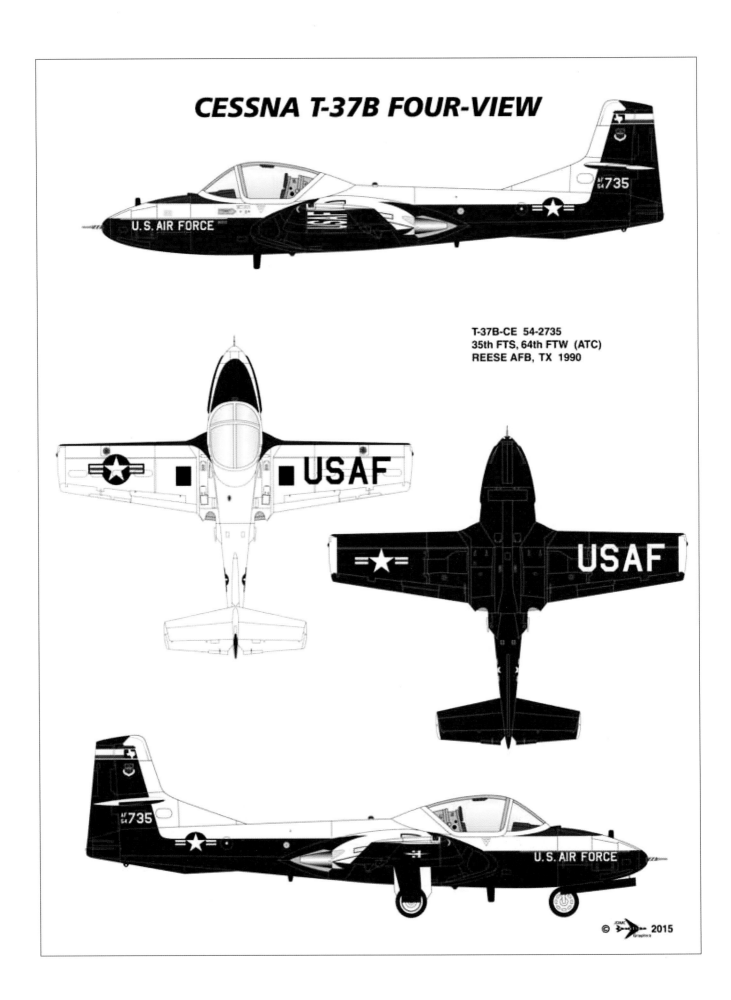

T-37B-CE 54-2735
35th FTS, 64th FTW (ATC)
REESE AFB, TX 1990

© 2015

NAVY TURBINE PRIMARY TRAINERS

Drawings on this page to the same scale

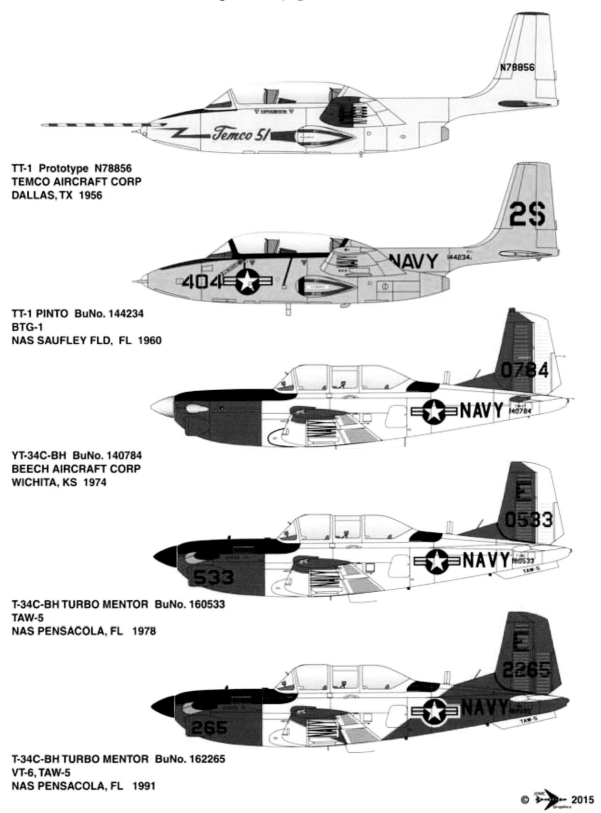

TT-1 Prototype N78856
TEMCO AIRCRAFT CORP
DALLAS, TX 1956

TT-1 PINTO BuNo. 144234
BTG-1
NAS SAUFLEY FLD, FL 1960

YT-34C-BH BuNo. 140784
BEECH AIRCRAFT CORP
WICHITA, KS 1974

T-34C-BH TURBO MENTOR BuNo. 160533
TAW-5
NAS PENSACOLA, FL 1978

T-34C-BH TURBO MENTOR BuNo. 162265
VT-6, TAW-5
NAS PENSACOLA, FL 1991

© 2015

Appendix II

NAVY T-34C EXPERIMENTAL SCHEME

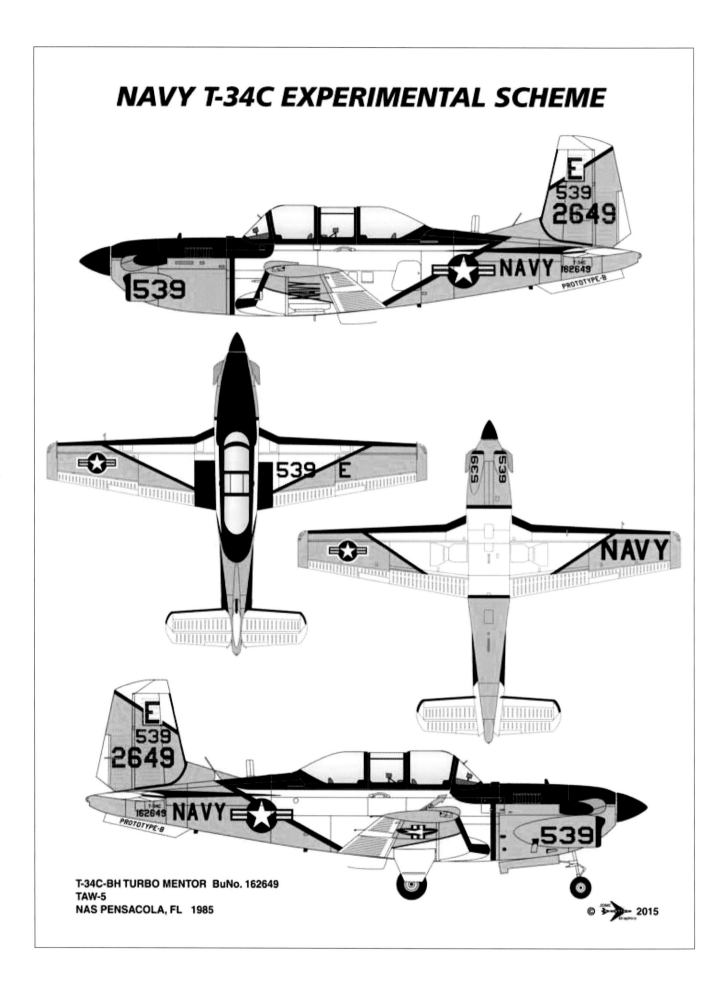

T-34C-BH TURBO MENTOR BuNo. 162649
TAW-5
NAS PENSACOLA, FL 1985

© 2015

NORTH AMERICAN T2J/T-2 BUCKEYES

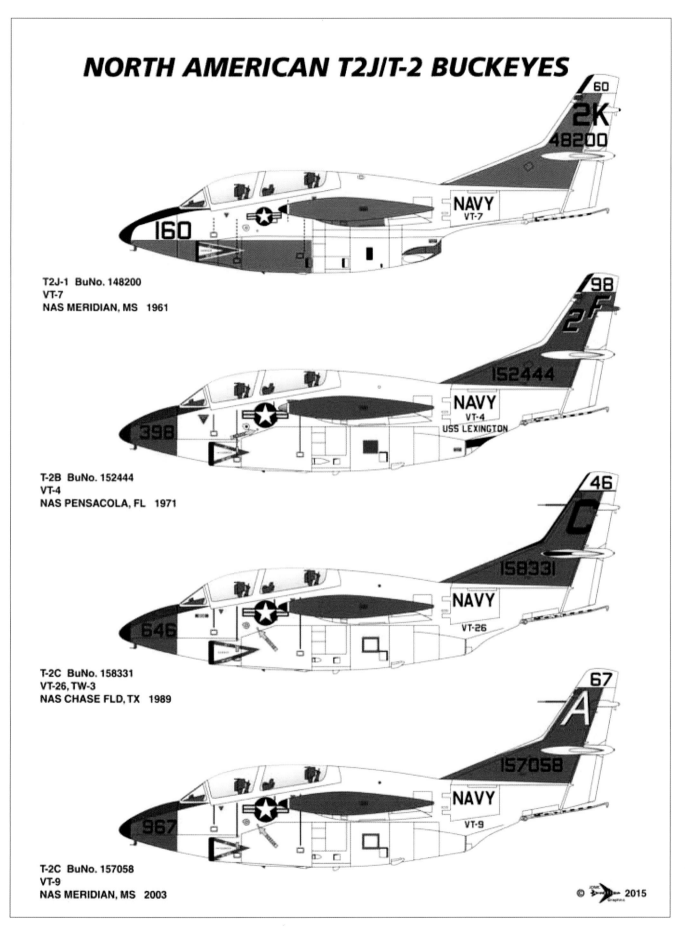

T2J-1 BuNo. 148200
VT-7
NAS MERIDIAN, MS   1961

T-2B BuNo. 152444
VT-4
NAS PENSACOLA, FL   1971

T-2C BuNo. 158331
VT-26, TW-3
NAS CHASE FLD, TX   1989

T-2C BuNo. 157058
VT-9
NAS MERIDIAN, MS   2003

© 2015

McDONNELL-DOUGLAS SKYHAWK TRAINERS

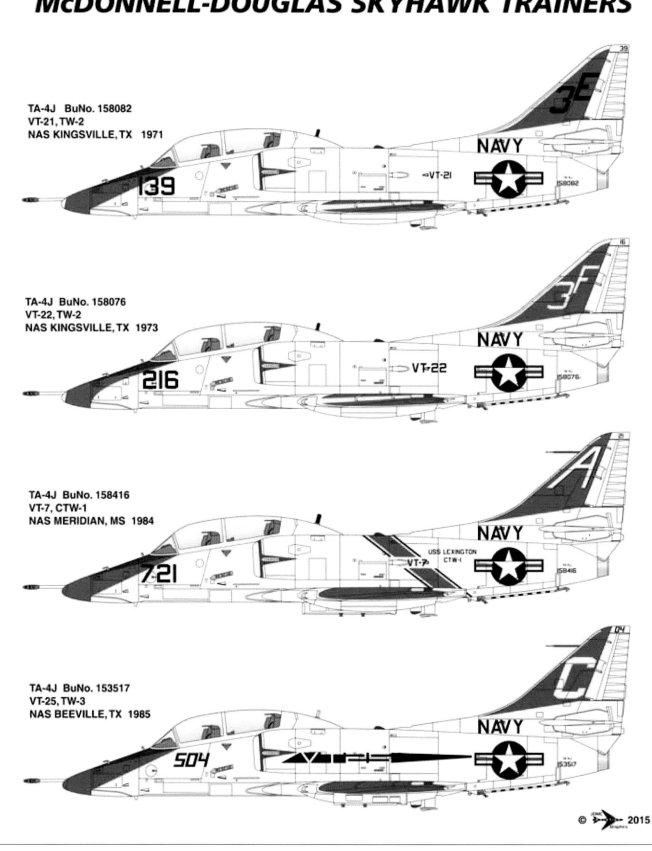

TA-4J BuNo. 158082
VT-21, TW-2
NAS KINGSVILLE, TX 1971

TA-4J BuNo. 158076
VT-22, TW-2
NAS KINGSVILLE, TX 1973

TA-4J BuNo. 158416
VT-7, CTW-1
NAS MERIDIAN, MS 1984

TA-4J BuNo. 153517
VT-25, TW-3
NAS BEEVILLE, TX 1985

© 2015

BOEING/BAE T-45 G0SHAWKS

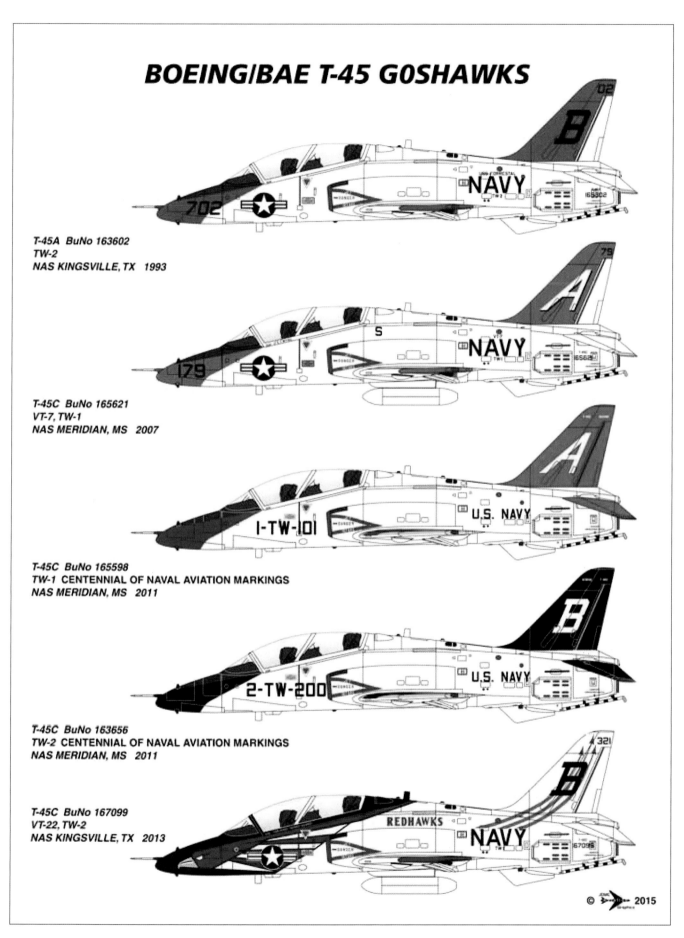

T-45A BuNo 163602
TW-2
NAS KINGSVILLE, TX   1993

T-45C BuNo 165621
VT-7, TW-1
NAS MERIDIAN, MS   2007

T-45C BuNo 165598
TW-1 CENTENNIAL OF NAVAL AVIATION MARKINGS
NAS MERIDIAN, MS   2011

T-45C BuNo 163656
TW-2 CENTENNIAL OF NAVAL AVIATION MARKINGS
NAS MERIDIAN, MS   2011

T-45C BuNo 167099
VT-22, TW-2
NAS KINGSVILLE, TX   2013

© 2015

EARLY TACTICAL TRAINER PROTOTYPES
Drawings on this page to the same scale

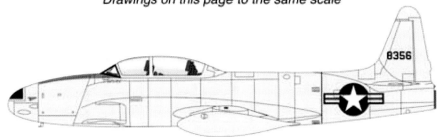

TF-80C-LO "T-BIRD" 48-356
LOCKHEED AIRCRAFT
VAN NUYS, CA 1948

TF-86F-NA SABRE TRAINER 52-5016
NORTH AMERICAN AVIATION
EDWARDS AFB, CA 1954

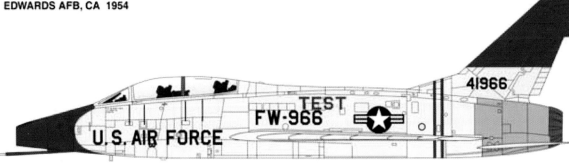

TF-100C-NA SUPER SABRE 54-1966
NORTH AMERICAN AVIATION
INGLEWOOD, CA 1956

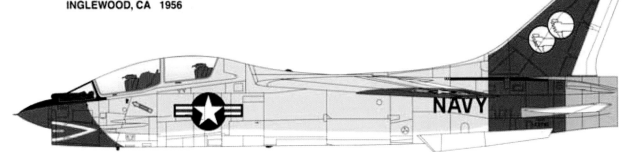

F8U-1T "TWOSADER" BuNo. 143710
VOUGHT AIRCRAFT
NAS DALLAS, TX 1962

© 2015

318

AIR TRAINING COMMAND TACTICAL TRAINERS
Drawings on this page to the same scale

TF-80C-LO SHOOTING STAR 48-370
3525th PTW (ATC)
WILLIAMS AFB, AZ 1949

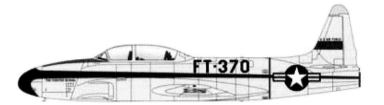

F-86A-5-NA SABRE 49-1092
3595th CCTW (ATC)
NELLIS AFB, NV 1952

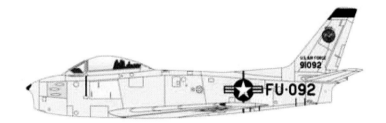

F-100A-5-NA SUPER SABRE 52-5775
3595th CCTW (ATC)
NELLIS AFB, NV 1956

F-102A-65-CO DELTA DAGGER 56-1203
3555th FTS (ATC)
PERRIN AFB, TX 1962

© JDMC 2015

CENTURY SERIES TWO-SEAT TRAINERS

Drawings on this page to the same scale

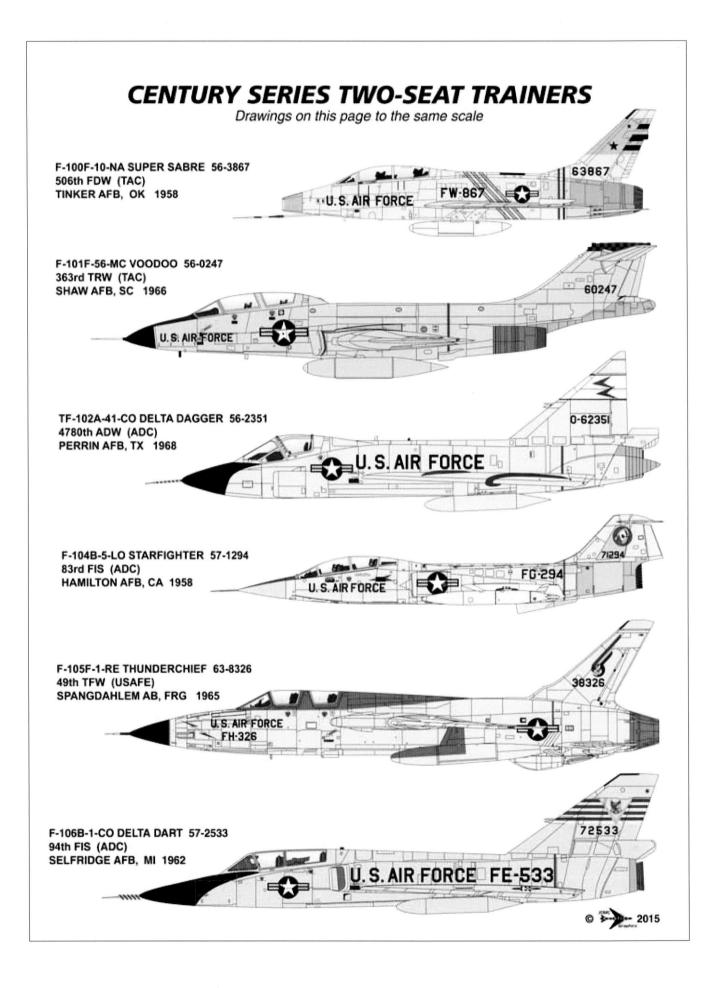

F-100F-10-NA SUPER SABRE 56-3867
506th FDW (TAC)
TINKER AFB, OK 1958

F-101F-56-MC VOODOO 56-0247
363rd TRW (TAC)
SHAW AFB, SC 1966

TF-102A-41-CO DELTA DAGGER 56-2351
4780th ADW (ADC)
PERRIN AFB, TX 1968

F-104B-5-LO STARFIGHTER 57-1294
83rd FIS (ADC)
HAMILTON AFB, CA 1958

F-105F-1-RE THUNDERCHIEF 63-8326
49th TFW (USAFE)
SPANGDAHLEM AB, FRG 1965

F-106B-1-CO DELTA DART 57-2533
94th FIS (ADC)
SELFRIDGE AFB, MI 1962

© 2015

NEW TAC TRAINERS AFTER 1962

Drawings on this page to the same scale

F-4B-15-MC PHANTOM II 62-12187
4453rd CCTS (TAC)
MacDILL AFB, FL 1963

F-4C-15-MC PHANTOM II 63-7418
4454th CCTS, (TAC)
DAVIS-MONTHAN AFB, AZ 1971

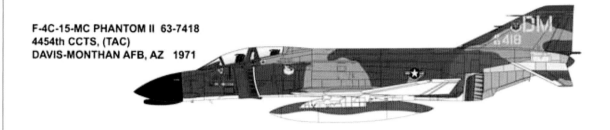

F-111A-CF 66-0026
442nd TFTS, 474th TFW (TAC)
NELLIS AFB, NV 1969

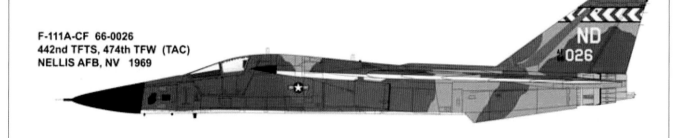

TF-15A-17-MC EAGLE 73-0108
555th TFTS, 58th TFTW (TAC)
LUKE AB, AZ 1975

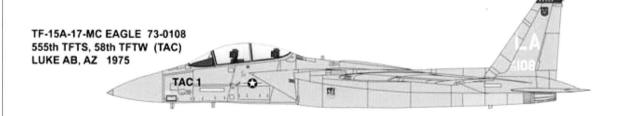

F-16B-5-CF FIGHTING FALCON 78-0088
16th TFTS, 388th TFW (TAC)
HILL AFB, UT 1979

© 2015

NORTHROP T-38 TALONS

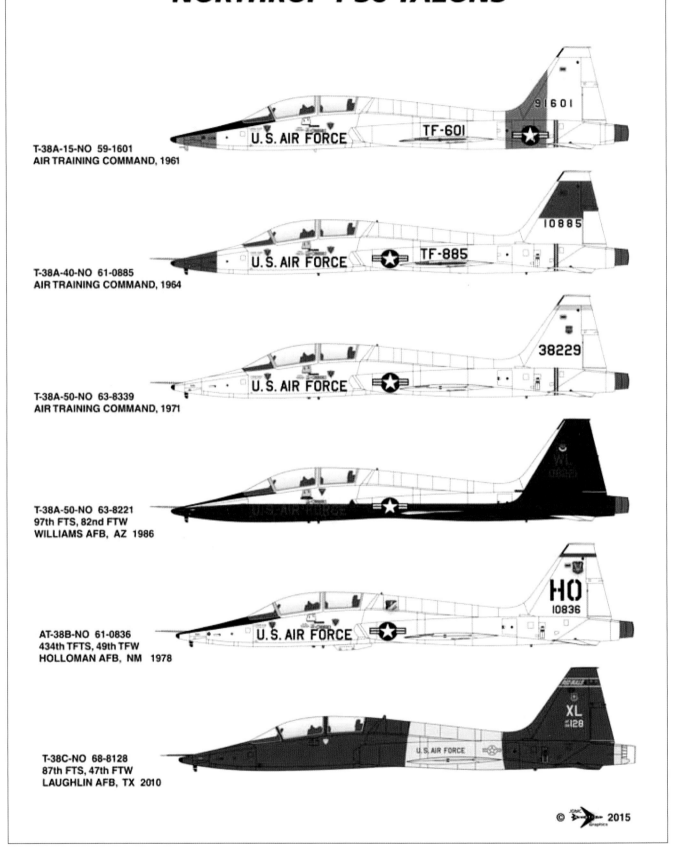

T-38A-15-NO 59-1601
AIR TRAINING COMMAND, 1961

T-38A-40-NO 61-0885
AIR TRAINING COMMAND, 1964

T-38A-50-NO 63-8339
AIR TRAINING COMMAND, 1971

T-38A-50-NO 63-8221
97th FTS, 82nd FTW
WILLIAMS AFB, AZ 1986

AT-38B-NO 61-0836
434th TFTS, 49th TFW
HOLLOMAN AFB, NM 1978

T-38C-NO 68-8128
87th FTS, 47th FTW
LAUGHLIN AFB, TX 2010

© 2015

NORTHROP AT-38B FOUR-VIEW

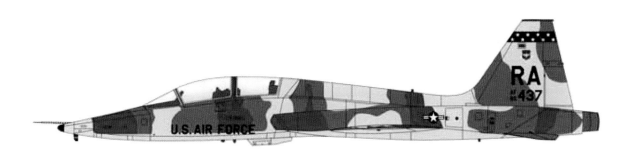

AT-38B-NO 65-10437
560th FTS, 12th FTW
RANDOLPH AFB, TX   1995

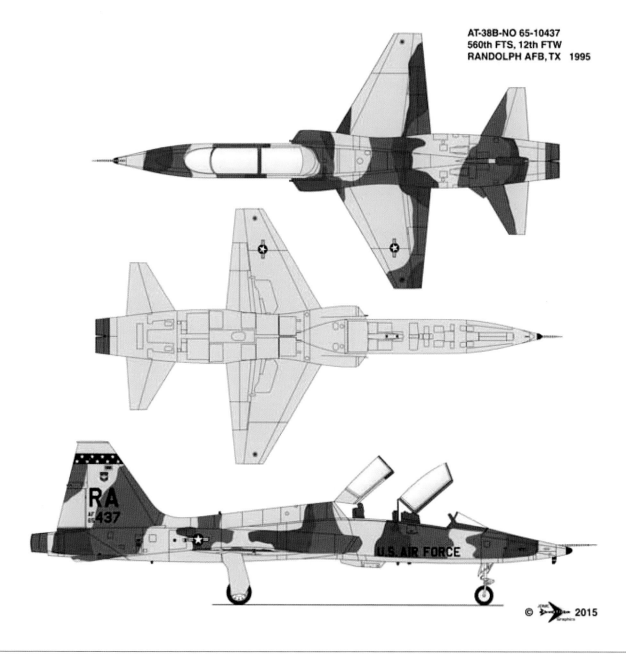

© 2015

JPATS PROGRAM

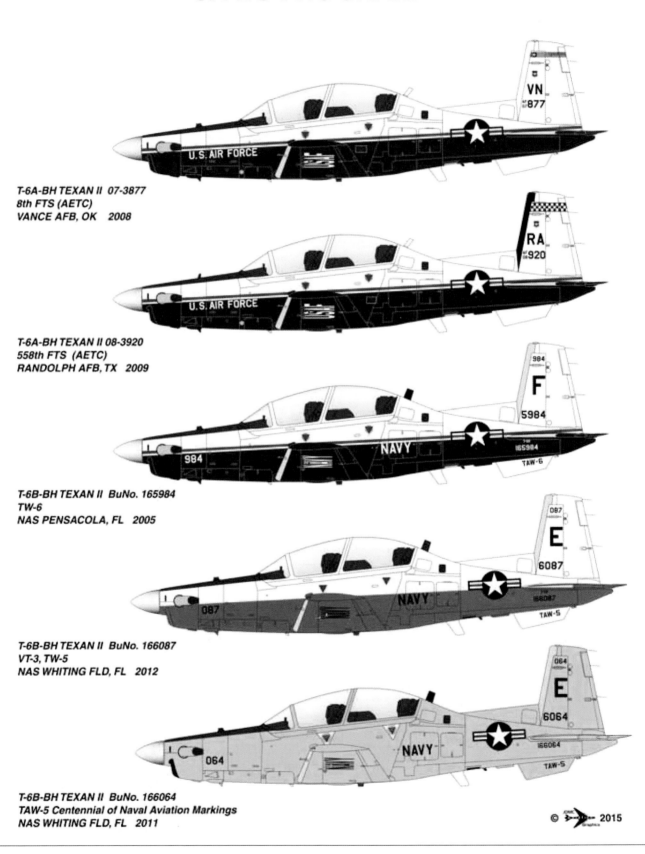

T-6A-BH TEXAN II 07-3877
8th FTS (AETC)
VANCE AFB, OK   2008

T-6A-BH TEXAN II 08-3920
558th FTS (AETC)
RANDOLPH AFB, TX   2009

T-6B-BH TEXAN II BuNo. 165984
TW-6
NAS PENSACOLA, FL   2005

T-6B-BH TEXAN II BuNo. 166087
VT-3, TW-5
NAS WHITING FLD, FL   2012

T-6B-BH TEXAN II BuNo. 166064
TAW-5 Centennial of Naval Aviation Markings
NAS WHITING FLD, FL   2011

© 2015

Selected Bibliography

A. Books

Abel, Alan. *Fairchild's Golden Age.* Brawley, CA: Wind Canyon Books. 2008.

Adcock, Al. *T-28 Trojan in Action.* Carrollton, TX: Squadron/Signal Publications, Inc. 1989.

Anderson, Fred, *Northrop an Aeronautical History.* Los Angeles, CA: Northrop Corporation. 1976.

Arnold,Rhodes Lt. Col. USAF Ret. *Shooting Star T-Bird & Starfire: A Famous Lockheed Family.* Tucson, AZ: Aztex Corporation, 1981.

Avis, Jim, Martin Bowman. *Stearman a Pictorial History.* Osceola, WI: Motorbooks International. 1997.

Bissonette, Bruce. *The Wichita 4: Cessna, Moellendick, Beech & Stearman.* Destin, FL: Aviation Heritage Inc. 1999.

Boyce, J. Ward, Robert O'Hara. *Training Aircraft of the US Air Force, 1925–1965.* North Hollywood, CA: Challenge Publications, 1965.

Bowers, Peter M. *Curtiss Aircraft 1907-1947.* Annapolis, MD: Naval Institute Press. 1979.

Bowman, Martin W., Matthias Vogelsang. *Lockheed F-104 Starfighter.* Wiltshire, England: The Crowood Press Ltd. 2000.

Cameron, Rebecca Hancock. *Training to Fly Military Flight Training 1907–1945.* Air Force History and Museums Program. 1999.

Carpenter, David. *Flame Powered, The Bell XP-59A and the General Electric I-A Engine.* Jet Pioneers of America, 1992.

Chinnery, Philip D. *50 Years of the Desert Boneyard.* Osceola, WI: MBI Publishing Company. 1995.

Converse, Elliot V. III, *Rearming for the Cold War 1945-1960.* Washington, DC: Historical Office, Office of the Secretary of Defense. 2012.

Davies, Peter E., David W. Menard. *North American F-100 Super Sabre.* Wiltshire, England: The Crowood Press Ltd. 2003

Davis, Larry. *P-80 Shooting Star/T-33/F-94 in Action.* Carrolton, TX: Squadron/Signal Publications, Inc, 1980.

Davis, Larry. *T-6 Texan in Action.* Carrollton, TX. Squadron/Signal Publications, Inc. 1989

Donald, David. *Century Jets USAF Frontline Fighters of the Cold War.* Norwalk, CT: AIRtime Publishing Inc. 1995, 1996,1998, 1999, 2002, 2003.

Drendel, Lou. *F-5 in Action.* Carrollton, TX: Squadron/Signal Publications. 1980.

Drendel, Lou, *T-34 Mentor in Action.* Carrollton, TX: Squadron/Signal Publications, 1990.

Eltscher, Louis R., Edward M. Young. *Curtiss-Wright Greatness and Decline.* New York, NY: Twayne Publishers. 1998.

Elward, Brad. *The Boeing F/A-18 E/F Super Hornet & EA-18G Growler A Developmental and Operational History.* Atglen, PA: Schiffer Publishing Ltd., 2012.

Farney, Dennis, *The Barnstormer and the Lady Aviation Legends Walter and Olive Ann Beech.* Kansas City, MO: Rockhill Books. 2010.

Francillon, Rene J. *Grumman Aircraft since 1929.* Annapolis, MD: Naval Institute Press. 1989.

Francillon, Rene J. *Lockheed Aircraft since 1913.* Annapolis, MD: Naval Institute Press. 1987.

Francillon, Rene J. *McDonnel Douglas Aircraft since 1920.* London, England: Putnam & Company, Ltd. 1979.

Frankel, Mark. *Temco TT-1 Pinto.* Simi Valley, CA: Steve Ginter. 2006.

Goldwater, Barry, Jack Casserly. *Goldwater.* New York, NY: Doubleday, 1988.

Ginter, Steve. *Grumman F9F-8T/TF-9J Two-Seat Cougar.* Simi Valley, CA: Steve Ginter, 2007.

Ginter, Steve. *Lockheed T2V-1/T-1A Seastar.* Simi Valley, CA: Steve Ginter, 1999.

Ginter, Steve. *North American Rockwell T-2 Buckeye.* Simi Valley, CA: Steve Ginter, 1987.

Ginter Steve. *North American T-28 Trojan.* Simi Valley CA: Steve Ginter, 1981.

Ginter, Steve. *USN/USMC Two-Seat Skyhawks.* Simi Valley, CA: Steve Ginter, 2008.

Ginter, Steve. *Vought TA-7C/EA-7L/AF A-7K "Twosair."* Simi Valley, CA: Steve Ginter, 2007.

Hagedorn, Dan. *North American's T-6 a Definitive History of the World's Most Famous Trainer.* North Branch, MN. Specialty Press. 2009.

Hurt, Hugh. *Aerodynamics for Naval Aviators.* Government Printing Office, Revised 1965

Jackson, A.J. *De Havilland Aircraft since 1909.* Annapolis, MD: Naval Institute Press. 1962, 1978, and 1987.

Johnsen, Frederick A. *Northrop F-5/ F-20/ T-38.* North Branch, MN: Specialty Press. 2006.

Kelly, Lloyd L., Robert B. Parke. *The Pilot Maker.* New York, NY: Grosset & Dunlap, Inc. 1970.

Lake, Jon. *McDonnell F-4 phantom Spirit in the Skies.* Westport, CT. Airtime Publishing Inc. 1992.

Leyes II, Richard A., William A. Fleming. *The History of North American Small Gas Turbine Aircraft Engines.* Reston, VA: AIAA. 1999.

Logan, Don, *Northrop's T-38 Talon A Pictorial History.* Atglen, PA: Schiffer Publishing Ltd. 1995.

Love, Terry. *A-37/T-37 Dragonfly in Action.* Carrollton,TX: Squadron/Signal Publications. 1991.

Meyer, Corwin "Corky." *Grumman F11F Tiger.* Simi Valley, CA: Steve Ginter. 1997.

Miller, Jay. *Lockheed's Skunk Works: The First Fifty Years.* Arlington, TX; Aerofax, Inc. 1993.

Moran, Gerald P. *The Corsair, and other Aeroplanes Vought 1917–1977.* Terre Haute, IN: Aviation Heritage Books. 1991.

Mutza, Wayne. *Convair F-102 Delta Dagger.* Atglen, PA: Schiffer Publishing Ltd. 1999.

Ohlrich, Walter, Jeff Ethell. *The Incredible T-6 Pilot Maker.* Osceola, WI: Specialty Press Publishers and Wholesalers, Inc. 1983.

O'Leary, Michael. *Jet Warbirds.* Osceola, WI: Motorbooks International Publishers & Wholesalers. 1990

Pace, Steve. *P-59 Airacomet.* Simi Valley, CA: Steve Ginter, 2000.

Pape, Gary R., John M. Campbell. *Northrop Flying wings A History of Jack Northrop's Visionary Aircraft.* Atglen, PA: Schiffer Publishing Ltd. 1995.

Parmerter, Robert K., *Beech 18 A Civil & Military History.* Tullahoma, TN: The Staggerwing Museum Foundation, Inc. 2004.

Peeters, Willy. *Uncovering the Northrop T-38A/ AT-38/ T-38C.* Antwerp, Belgium: DACO Publications. 2004.

Pelletier, A.J. *Beech Aircraft and their Predecessors.* Annapolis, MD: Naval Institute Press.1995.

Phillips, Edward H. *Stearman Aircraft a Detailed History.* North Branch, MN: Specialty Press. 2006.

Phillips, Edward H., *Beechcraft Staggerwing to Starship an Illustrated History.* Eagan, MN: Flying Books, 1987.

Phillips, Edward H., *Travel Air Wings over The Prairie.* Eagan, MN: Flying Books. 1982.

Phillips, Edward H., *Wings of Cessna Model 120 to the Citation X.* Eagan, MN: Flying Books. 1994.

Richardson, Doug, Mike Spick. *Modern Fighting aircraft F-4.* New York, NY. Arco Publishing Inc. 1984.

Rolfe, J.M., K.J. Staples. *Flight Simulation.* Cambridge, England: Cambridge University Press. 1986.

Scutts, Jerry. *Northrop F-5/F-20.* Surrey England: Ian Allan Ltd. 1986.

Shiel, Walt, Jan Forsgren, Mike Little. *T-41 Mescalero the Military Cessna 172.* Lake Linden, MI: Slipdown Mountain Publications LLC. 2006.

Shiel, Walt. *Cessna Warbirds a Detailed & Personal History of Cessna's Involvement in the Armed Forces.* Iola, WI: Jones Publishing Inc. 1995.

Smith, Robert T., Thomas A. Lempicke. *Staggerwing Story of the Classic Beechcraft Biplane.* Kissimmee, FL: Cody Publications Inc. 1979.

Spitzmiller, Ted. *The Century Series the USAF Quest for Air Supremacy 1950–1990.* Atglen, PA: Schiffer Publishing Ltd. 2011.

Swanborough, F.G. Peter Bowers. *United States Military Aircraft since 1909.* New York, NY: Putnam. 1963.

Swanborough, Gordon. Peter M. Bowers. *United States Navy Aircraft since 1911.* New York, NY: Funk& Wagnalls. 1968.

Thomas, Stanley G. *The Globe/Temco Swift Story.* Destin FL: Aviation Heritage Inc, and Aviation Publishing Inc. 1996.

Thomason Tommy. *Grumman Navy F-111B Swing Wing.* Simi Valley, CA: Steve Ginter. 1998.

Thomason, Tommy H. US *Naval Air Superiority: Development of Shipborne Jet Fighters 1943–1962.* North Branch, MN: Specialty Press, 2007.

Thompson, Kevin. *North American Aircraft 1934–1999, Volume 2.* Santa Ana, CA: Narkiewicz/Thompson. 1999.

Thompson, *William D. Cessna Wings For The World II Development of the 300 Series Twins and Miscellaneous Prototypes.* Bend, OR: Maverick Publications. 1995.

Veronico, Nicholas A., Ron Strong. *AMARG America's Military Aircraft Boneyard.* North Branch, MN: Specialty Press. 2010.

Veronico, Nicholas A., Kevin Grantham, Scott Thompson. *Military Aircraft Boneyards.* Osceola, WI: MBI Publishing Company.2000

Wagner, Ray. *Mustang Designer Edgar Schmued and the P-51.* Washington, DC: Smithsonian Institution Press. 1990.

Wegg, John. *General Dynamics Aircraft and their Predecessors.* Annapolis, MD: Naval Institute Press, 1990.

Wooldridge, E.T. Jr. *The P-80 Shooting Star: Evolution of a Jet Fighter.* Washington, DC: Smithsonian Institution Press, 1979.

B. Publications

Air Classics
Air Force Magazine
Air Forces Monthly
Air International
Air Progress
Airpower
Aviation Week & Space Technology
Combat Aircraft Monthly
Flight International
Flying Safety
Foundation, National Naval Aviation Museum
Journal, American Aviation Historical Society
Naval Aviation News
New York Times
Sport Aviation, EAA's Monthly Membership Magazine
The Hook, Journal of Carrier Aviation
Warbird Digest
Warbirds, EAA Warbirds of America
Wings

C. Reports, Unpublished Papers, and Studies

AMC Memorandum Report No. MCREOA-5-8 dated 13 October 1948, Mock-up Inspection of the XT-30 Airplane.

Anderson, R.C. Major, USAF. AF Technical Report No. 6161 dated September 1950, Final Douglas XT-30 Trainer Aircraft Phase I Report.

Ashcroft, Bruce. *We Wanted Wings: A History of the Aviation Cadet Program.* Headquarters AETC Office of History and Research. 2005.

Begin, Lee F., *The N-156F Weapon System—How and Why.* Norair Division, Northrop Corporation, 1961.

Bowman, James S., Frederick M. Healy. Free-spinning-tunnel investigation of a 1/20th scale model of the North American T2J-1 airplane by, Jr. and, Langley Research Center NAS TM SX-245, undated.

Crawford, Charles C. Jr., Swart H Nelson, Captain USAF. *YT-38 Category I Flight Test.* Air Force Flight Test Center, Edwards Air Force Base, CA. January 1960.

Crupper, R.J. *Model T-37A Phase I, Part I, Handling Characteristics.* Cessna Aircraft Company, Wichita, KS. February 1957.

Daniel, Walter F., Maj., USAF, William J. Knight, Captain, USAF. *T-37B Qualitative Spin Evaluation.* Air Force Flight Test Center, Edwards Air Force Base, CA. November 1961.

Gannett, James R., Captain, USAF. *Phase II and IV Flight Tests on the T-34A Aircraft No.27626.* Air Force Flight Test Center, Edwards Air Force base, CA. February 1954.

Grumman Engineering Corporation. Super Cougar marketing brochure, October 1961.

Hays, Michael D. *The Training of Military Pilots, Men, Machines, and Methods.* Air University Maxwell Air Force Base, AL. June 2002.

Hobbs, Thomas H., Captain USAF, Swart H. Nelson, Major, USAF. *Category II YJ and J85-GE-5 Engine Follow-On Evaluations.* Air Force Test Center, Edwards Air Force Base, CA. October 1961.

Hussey, Ann Krueger. *Air Force Flight Screening: Evolutionary Changes, 1917–2003.* Office of History and Research, Headquarters AETC, Randolph Air Force Base, TX. December 2004.

Johansen, William A. Colonel USAF. Contract Versus Military Pilot Training in Today's Air Force. Air University, Maxwell air Force Base, AL. May, 1987.

Lusby, William A., Captain USAF, Swart H. Nelson, Major USAF, Norris J. Hanks, Captain USAF. *T-38 Spin Evaluation.* Air Force Flight Test Center, Edwards Air Force Base, CA. August 1961.

McNamar, Lawrence F., Henry C. Gordon. *T-38A Category II Performance Test.* Technical Documentary Report No. 63-27. Air Force Flight Test Center, Edwards Air Force Base, CA. November 1963.

NATC report AC-67101.3, T2J-1 Fleet Introduction Program, Report No.1, Final Report of 12 July 1959

National Defense Authorization Act for FY 1989, Report 100-989

Nickle, Barry H., *Contract Flying Training In Air Training Command 1939–1980.* History and Research Division headquarters air Training Command. September, 1981.

Siegfried, Doug, CDR (USN Ret.). *Cleared to Solo.* Unpublished manuscript on Naval Aviation flight training.

Stuart, William G., *Northrop F-5 Case Study in Aircraft Design.* Northrop Corp. Aircraft Group. September 1978.

Trimble, Harry W. Lt. Colonel, USAF, Dean E. Smith, 1/LT. USAF, Reese S. Martin, Captain, USAF. *T-37A Phase IV Functional Development.* Air Force Flight Test Center, Edwards Air Force Base, CA. January 1957.

Van Pelt, Larry G., Colonel USAF. *The Evolution of Flight Test Concepts.* Air Force Flight Test Center, History Office Edwards Air Force Base, CA. June 1982.

Worthington, Forrest W. 1/Lieutenant, USAF, Emil Sturmthal, Captain USAF. *T-37B Category II Performance Test.* Air Force Test Flight Center, Edwards air Force Base, CA. April 1961.

Glossary

AAF—Army Air Forces. The aviation arm of the US Army formed on June 20, 1941. It was replaced by the United States Air Force (USAF), a separate military service, on September 18, 1947.

Ab Initio—The initial stage (literally: from the beginning).

AFB—Air Force Base.

Aileron—A control surface typically hinged to the outboard-wing trailing edge used to provide roll control.

Airfoil—The shape of a cross-section of a flying surface, propeller blade, or jet engine compressor or turbine blade.

AIRLANT—Abbreviation referring to Commander, Naval Air Force US Atlantic Fleet.

AIRPAC—Abbreviation referring to Commander, Naval Air Force US Pacific Fleet.

ALF—Auxiliary Landing Field.

Angle of Attack—The angle between the oncoming air or relative wind and a reference line on an airplane or wing.

Area Rule—A design technique to reduce drag at transonic and supersonic speeds by insuring that the total cross-sectional area of an airplane, including the wing and empennage, smoothly increases to its maximum and then smoothly decreases.

Aspect Ratio—The ratio of length to height (strake) or span to chord (wing).

Axial-flow Compressor—A jet engine compressor in which the air flows parallel to the axis of rotation.

Biplane—A fixed-wing aircraft with two wings, one located approximately above the other.

BIS—Board of Inspection and Survey, a formal Navy practice to insure the suitability of ships and aircraft for the intended use.

BLC—Boundary Layer Control, a system using bleed air from a jet engine to add high-energy air over the upper surface of the wing and/or flaps. This results in a delay in wing stall to a higher angle of attack, which results in a slower approach speed.

Buffet—Low-frequency vibration of the airframe generally caused by unsteady flow off the airframe or from the extension of landing gear, flaps or speed brakes.

BuAer—Bureau of Aeronautics, the US Navy organization that manages the procurement and development of Navy and Marine Corps aircraft.

BuNo—Bureau Number, the serial number of a Navy, Marine Corps or Coast Guard aircraft, usually displayed on the aft fuselage.

Center of Gravity—The longitudinal point at which the airplane would balance on a knife edge. The range of permissible center of gravity locations was limited by stability-and-control considerations. The center of gravity vertically and horizontally was also a design consideration.

Century Series Fighters—A series of high-performance Air Force fighters beginning with the North American F-100 Super Sabre and ending with the Convair F-106 Delta Dart. (The F-103 program was cancelled before detail design was complete.)

CNATRA—Chief of Naval Air Training

CNAVANTRA—Chief, Naval Air Advanced Training

Conventional Landing Gear—A landing gear configuration that consisting of two main wheels and a tail wheel. Familiarly referred to as a tail dragger.

Critical Mach Number—The lowest Mach number at which the airflow over some point of the aircraft reaches the speed of sound but does not exceed it.

Davis Barrier—A modification to the standard barrier on an axial-deck aircraft carrier that protected the personnel and planes forward of the landing area required by the introduction of airplanes with tricycle landing gear. Instead of being suspended about four feet above the deck, the steel barrier cables were laid flat on the deck and pulled up by a canvas strap by the nose landing gear so as to catch on the main landing gear struts.

Dihedral—The upward angle of a wing or tail surface from the root to the tip measured from horizontal.

DoD—Department of Defense.

Dorsal Fin—a fixed surface ahead of and integral with the vertical fin that provides increased directional stability.

Elevator—A control surface typically hinged to the trailing edge of the horizontal stabilizer used to provide pitch control.

Empennage—The tail group consisting of a horizontal surface (stabilizer) and vertical surface (fin) and their control surfaces.

Fineness Ratio—The ratio of fuselage length to the maximum cross section.

Flat Opposed Engine—A reciprocating engine with the cylinders arranged in a flat line to the left and right of the crankcase.

G-Force—A measurement of the acceleration experienced in flight perpendicular to the pilot and airframe. At constant speed and pitch angle, the g-force is one, equal to the pull of gravity on a stationary object; it increases or decreases when the aircraft is maneuvered as in pulling into a turn or pitching up or down. A 60-degree banked turn in level flight results in a g-force of two.

GOR—General Operating Requirement. A specification promulgated by the Secretary of the Air Force.

Horizontally Opposed Engine—See flat opposed engine.

IFR—Instrument flight rules.

Immelmann—An aerobatic maneuver that begins with the first half of a loop but instead of completing it, the pilot rolls the airplane upright at the top of the loop.

Inline Engine—A reciprocating engine with all cylinders arranged in one or more lines either above or below the crankshaft.

IP—Instructor pilot.

Knots—A measure of speed in nautical miles per hour. One knot is equal to 1.15 statute miles per hour or 6,076 feet per minute.

LIFT—Lead In Fighter Training: An advanced syllabus usually administered to winged pilots before joining an operational squadron.

LSO—Landing Signal Officer: The LSO was stationed on the left rear side of an aircraft carrier to provide guidance and direction to the pilot of a landing aircraft.

Mach Number—The ratio of aircraft calibrated airspeed (indicated airspeed corrected for static-source error) to the speed of sound at that altitude and temperature.

MAW—Marine Air Wing

MCAS- Marine Corps Air Station

Mockup—A large-scale or full-size model of a proposed design. The level of detail and functionality incorporated depends on its planned use, which can range from simple for marketing purposes to complex for engineering and customer evaluation.

Monoplane—An aircraft with one set of wings as opposed to two (biplane) or three (triplane).

Multi-function Display—A small video screen surrounded by push buttons used to change the information on the display as desired.

NACA—National Advisory Committee for Aeronautics. A US government agency established in 1915 for aeronautical research.

NAS—Naval Air Station

NASA—National Aeronautic and Space Agency. A US government agency established in 1958 replacing the National Advisory Committee for Aeronautics (NACA).

NATC—Naval Air Test Center located at Patuxent River, Maryland,

NPE—Navy Preliminary Evaluation. An early stage in the flight-test program of Navy aircraft where Navy pilots evaluate its performance and handling qualities within a contractor-approved flight envelope.

Glossary

OPEVAL—Operational Evaluation. The final phase of a US Navy test and evaluation program before a new aircraft is fully accepted.

Pitch—The nose up or down movement of an aircraft about its lateral axis. Also the angle of a propeller blade in relation to the thrust line.

Pitot—A small tube that provides the air pressure produced by forward flight to the airspeed instrument in the cockpit or to the air data computer that calculates airspeed.

Podded Engine—Engine mounted in a structure that is suspended from the wing or fuselage.

Pusher Engine—An engine mounted in the rear of the fuselage or trailing edge of the wing with a propeller aft of the engine.

Radial Engine—a reciprocating engine with the cylinders arranged in one or more circles around the crankcase.

Radial-flow Compressor—A turbine-engine air compressor with an airflow path perpendicular to the axis of rotation. Usually found on early jet engines.

RAG—Replacement Air Group (currently referred to as Fleet Replacement Squadron): provides naval aviator training in a specific aircraft type.

RCVG—Reserve Carrier Air Group

Reciprocating Engine—An internal combustion engine that produces power from pistons that transmit energy from the combustion to a crankshaft-mounted propeller.

RFP—Request for Proposal.

Roll—The rotational motion of an aircraft around its longitudinal axis.

Rudder—A vertically mounted control surface that provides yaw control (nose right or left).

Slats—A wing leading-edge device that provides increased lift when deployed.

SLEP—Service Life Extension Program.

Speed brakes—pilot-controlled surfaces that could be extended to increase drag when desired.

Spin—The rotational loss of altitude that can develop after a stall usually due to uncoordinated control inputs. In a spin, the airspeed is constant and the wing remains stalled; in a spiral dive, the airspeed increases rapidly and the wing is not stalled.

Spool-up—Following a throttle increase, the increase in rotational speed of a turbine engine that produces a corresponding increase in thrust. Early turbine engines suffered from prolonged spool-up times.

Stall—The point at which wing lift begins to decrease rather than increase with increasing angle of attack.

Steam Gages—A derogatory nickname for analog instruments used before the introduction of modern digital multi-function displays.

Strake—a low-aspect ratio aerodynamic surface used to influence airflow or increase stability.

TACAN—TACtical Air Navigation: A military navigation system that provides the bearing and distance (slant range) to a ground station.

Tandem Seating—an in-line seating configuration.

Tractor Engine—An engine mounted at the nose of a fuselage or leading edge of a wing with a propeller forward of the engine.

Tricycle Landing Gear—A landing gear configuration consisting of nose gear and two main gears.

Trim Tab—A small control surface mounted on a primary control to eliminate control loads at a given airspeed and weight distribution.

Turbine Engine—An internal combustion engine which produces thrust from the combustion by the expulsion of exhaust gases (turbojet or turbofan), or uses the exhaust gases to drive a propeller (turboprop).

USAAS—United States Army Air Service. The aviation branch of the US Army from 1918 until 1926.

Ventral Fin—an aerodynamic surface located on the underside of the fuselage to reduce lateral stability and/or increase directional stability.

VFR—Visual flight rules.

Yaw—Rotation about the vertical axis in a right or left direction.

Index